Virtual Trading

How Any Trader with a PC Can Use the Power of Neural Nets and Expert Systems to Boost Trading Profits

**Jess Lederman &
Robert A. Klein, Editors**

PROBUS
PUBLISHING

Chicago, Illinois
Cambridge, England

© 1995, Jess Lederman and Robert A. Klein

This publication is designed to provide accurate and authoritative information in regard to the subject matter covered. It is sold with the understanding that the author and the publisher are not engaged in rendering legal, accounting, or other professional service.

ISBN 1-55738-812-1

Printed in the United States of America

BB

1 2 3 4 5 6 7 8 9 0

JB

To Don, Kristi, Jay and Lorene,
The "Midnight Express" from the Shady Lanes

TABLE OF CONTENTS

PREFACE

Over the past decade, artificial intelligence (AI) has transformed the investment landscape. AI products are not a magic wand; the title of this book is not *How to Make a Million in Thirty Days or Less!* Lots of hard work and creativity and market savvy are still required for success. The important point is this: Although AI was at one time available only to the largest and most sophisticated market participants, it has evolved into an affordable technology that can be accessed by any trader with a personal computer and a modest software budget.

In this breakthrough book, top traders and AI systems development experts—including some of the "founding fathers" of AI financial applications—explain how neural networks, fuzzy logic, genetic algorithms, expert systems, and other AI techniques can be used to create powerful trading strategies. Unlike other books, which emphasize theory, *Virtual Trading* is eminently practical. It shows how to proceed from data collection and system development to actual trading, and includes a wealth of information on specific AI trading software.

Many thanks must be given to each of the contributing authors for the time and energy they took from their hectic schedules to produce this important book. And thanks is also owed to the superb staff at Probus Publishing, who once again produced an outstanding product in record time.

Jess Lederman
Robert A. Klein

CONTRIBUTING AUTHORS

Gerald A. Becker

Mr. Becker is publisher of Knight Ridder Financial Publishing, and vice president, marketing, for Knight Ridder Financial/Americas. Previously, he served as vice president and publisher of *Futures* magazine, and earlier served with CRC Press and Penton Publishing. He has lectured worldwide on futures and options markets, focusing on trading systems and money management. He also serves as president of the Futures Industry Association-Marketing Division, FIA Chicago Division Board of Directors, FIA member of the Expo Steering Committee, and representative of the FIA Board of Directors.

Mr. Becker earned a B.S. in journalism at Scripps-Howard School of Journalism at Ohio University.

Casimir C. ("Casey") Klimasauskas

Mr. Klimasauskas is a cofounder of NeuralWare, Inc., and serves as its director of financial services. He has over 25 years of experience in using advanced technologies to develop solutions in business and industry. Mr. Klimasauskas is a well-known author and speaker on the application of neural networks and genetic algorithms in finance. He also serves as an adjunct professor at Carnegie Mellon University.

Mr. Klimasauskas holds a degree in mathematics from the California Institute of Technology.

Peter C. Davies

Mr. Davies is the founder of Expert Solutions, a Toronto-based consulting and development firm specializing in neural network and expert system applications. He has over 20 years of work experience in computer science as a consultant, software engineer, research scientist, and teacher. For the past 11 years, Mr. Davies has concentrated on applications of artificial intelligence. His firm's current focus is on applications in banking and the stock market. The company has completed many AI development projects and studies for financial organizations and others in the private and public sectors, and also provides training in advanced technology.

Mr. Davies holds a Ph.D. in mathematics from the University of Toronto.

Mark G. Jurik

Mr. Jurik is the founder of Jurik Research and Consulting (JRC), which designs systems using neural networks, fuzzy logic, and genetic algorithms, and produces software tools for financial traders. His first accomplishment was to redesign a radar emitter identification paradigm that earned him a Special Letter of Appreciation from the U.S. Air Force. Other military projects included voice identification and intruder detection, as well as an expert system aid for satellite image analysis. Mr. Jurik invented the successful Backpercolation algorithm for neural networks, which is currently used in commercial software products. He has also taught university-level classes in neural network theory and produced an internationally popular video course called NeuroTapes.

Mr. Jurik holds degrees in electrical engineering, chemistry, and psychology, and has 15 years of experience in computerized pattern recognition.

Jeffrey Owen Katz

Mr. Katz is president and founder of Scientific Consultant Services, Inc., a company dedicated to providing high-tech solutions to a diverse range of problems. He has provided innovative contributions to many of his fields of expertise, from developing a new approach to solving the "simple structure rotation problem" in factor analysis, to designing and developing a noninvasive alternative to angiography. His interest in applying AI technology to the problems of trading the financial markets began in the mid-1980s, which stimulated his design of unique AI tools for professional traders. Mr. Katz has published articles in professional and trade publications, taught at universities in both the U.S. and the U.K., consulted for major institutions (both private and governmental), and been a guest speaker for a wide range of organizations.

Mr. Katz received a B.A. in mathematics from the State University of New York at Stony Brook, where he continued on the doctoral level in pure mathematics but, prior to the completion of his dissertation, changed his major to population biology and genetics. In 1983, he received a doctorate in psychophysiology from the University of Lancaster, England.

John Kean

Mr. Kean is a private investor and trader and principal of Kean Analytics, a provider of financial market analytical software. He has authored a number of articles on financial market analysis, including the application of artificial intelligence methods, and the determination of optimum leverage in trading.

Ronald V. Ogren

Mr. Ogren is the founder of Future Wave Software. He has 30 years of experience in aerospace engineering, where he specialized in control systems, data analysis, and system engineering. Combined with his appreciation of the major advance in computer learning due to neural network algorithms, this provided a natural opportunity for application of neural networks to market prediction. It required a year of effort to develop his first useful neural network indicator, which led to the view that a data preprocessing tool could be very useful for investors, and led to the development of Stock Prophet over a seven-year period.

Mr. Ogren holds a master's degree in electrical engineering. He is a member of the Los Angeles Society of Financial Analysts, the Association for Investment Management and Research, and the American Association for Individual Investors.

Lou Mendelsohn

Mr. Mendelsohn, founder of Mendelsohn Enterprises, Inc., is a world-renowned technical analyst and investment software pioneer. In the early 1980s he invented the concept of historical simulation and system back-testing for microcomputers, and by the mid-1980s his concept of system testing had become the backbone of computerized technical analysis. In the early 1990s, he announced the creation of *synergistic market analysis*, and began licensing *VantagePoint*, a revolutionary intermarket analysis software program. With clients in 30 nations, Mendelsohn Enterprises, Inc., licenses trading software to institutional clients as well as individual traders, provides consultation, and develops proprietary models dealing with price forecasting, trend analysis, and global asset allocation. Mr. Mendelsohn has authored articles for numerous national business periodicals. He has been a speaker at many international investment conferences, and appeared as a guest on the Financial News Network and CNBC national television.

Mr. Mendelsohn holds a B.S. degree in administration and management science from Carnegie Mellon University, a master's degree from the State University of New York, and an M.B.A. degree with honors from Boston University.

Donna L. McCormick

Ms. McCormick is vice president of Scientific Consultant Services, Inc., where she is responsible for administrative and marketing operations. She was previously affiliated with the oldest psychophysical research institute in the United States, where she served as administrative director, and also researched the psychophysiological concommitants of anomalous cognitive and perceptual phenomena, often in cooperation with various universities and government and law enforcement agencies. Ms. McCormick has published in a number of professional and financial publications, lectured to a variety of academic and institutional audiences, and held memberships in professional organizations, including the American Association for the Advancement of Science. She was editor-in-chief of the *ASPR Newsletter* for over six years, and has worked as a freelance editor of professional and technical publications.

Ms. McCormick graduated cum laude from Brooklyn College of the City University of New York with a B.S. in experimental psychology.

Joe Shepard

Mr. Shepard has been developing neural network software for the past eight years for RaceCom, Inc. His professional experience in electrical engineering ranges from the development of the Polaris missile computer to computerized optical recognition.

Mr. Shepard attended the Rochester Institute of Technology, where his undergraduate work involved electrical engineering and business administration, and his graduate work concentrated on statistics.

Yin Shih

Mr. Shih is a member of the technical staff of Cheshire Engineering Corporation, which develops, supports, and markets a variety of neural network products. He is the developer of Neuralyst for Excel. Mr. Shih has written numerous articles for journals, as well as books on high-performance computing and neural networks.

Mr. Shih holds B.S. and M.S. degrees from the California Institute of Technology.

J.D. Smith

Dr. Smith is the founder of AIQ, publisher of artificial intelligence-based expert systems for stock market trading. He is responsible for all knowledge engineering of the AIQ expert systems. Dr. Smith began to work in the field of artificial intelligence on mainframes and minicomputers in the 1960s. When microcomputers evolved in the 1970s, he was among the first to apply AI to software systems for personal computers.

Dr. Smith received his Ph.D. from the University of California at Los Angeles.

Sara Unrue

Ms. Sara Unrue is a developer of Braincel, the original neural net embedded in a spreadsheet. Currently, she is marketing director for Promised Land Technology. She is a cum laude graduate of Yale University.

PART ONE

MASTERING THE BASICS

Chapter 1

INTRODUCTION TO ARTIFICIAL INTELLIGENCE: Basics of Expert Systems, Fuzzy Logic, Neural Networks, and Genetic Algorithms

Jeffrey Owen Katz, President
Donna L. McCormick, Vice President
SCIENTIFIC CONSULTANT SERVICES, INC.

INTRODUCTION

In an effort to find new, more profitable ways to cope with today's fast-changing markets, financial analysts and traders have become attracted to technologies based on the science of artificial intelligence (AI). In this chapter we will briefly discuss the history of AI in the world of trading and how interest in such technology has grown in recent years. We will also attempt to provide you with a basic understanding of the various forms of AI and show how they individually and collectively address the problems of traders. Before we proceed, however, let us first cover some of the fundamentals.

WHAT IS ARTIFICIAL INTELLIGENCE?

In a nutshell, "artificial intelligence," or AI, is a field that grew out of attempts to get computers to emulate the intelligent behavior of living systems in order to solve larger, more complex problems. In its infancy, the problem-solving capacity of computer technology was restricted largely to simple "algorithmic" tasks, that is, tasks that can be accomplished with an exact and highly logical set of instructions that allow the computer to derive a correct solution to a problem. An example might be provid-

ing the computer with an enormous amount of numerical data upon which to perform specified calculations, like analyzing U.S. Census data to determine the average
educational level of the population. But the vision of science and the needs of modern
humankind were grander. The goal was not simply to have at everyone's disposal the
convenience and efficiency of a high-powered calculator, but to extend the problem-
solving capabilities of computers to include the symbolic reasoning skills of their creators. In other words, the goal became to get computers to process and manipulate
information in some of the same ways that we do, e.g., to reason using rules, logic,
and even heuristics (rules of thumb), to observe and recognize patterns in noisy environments (like scanning a crowd and recognizing one face in it), to make intelligent
judgments (including those that may involve a degree of truth, expectation, or uncertainty), to understand and use languages, and even to trade the financial markets
profitably.

There are three main divisions of AI technology. The following are brief descrip-
tions, but elaborations can be found in subsequent sections of this chapter:

Knowledge-Based Systems: Also called expert systems, this form of AI technology attempts to model such logical, hard-edged, rule-based reasoning as is
involved in solving syllogisms, proving theorems, diagnosing faults, choosing
antibiotics or playing chess. Such rule-based systems try to emulate the kind of
"IF . . . THEN . . ." logical thinking often used by experts when attempting to
solve problems in their own particular domain of expertise. In these systems,
the rules involve what is referred to as "crisp" logic, that is, things are either
true or false, yes or no, etc. An example of a rule in a knowledge-based
system for trading stocks might be "IF the slope of the 50-day moving average
is greater than 0, THEN the market is trending up."

Fuzzy Logic: This division of the technology is an outgrowth of Lotfi Zadeh's
"theory of fuzzy sets," which has been around for a long time but is new in
the world of AI. Fuzzy logic replaces the hard-edged aspect of rule-based reasoning with a *softer* logic that allows for matters of degree, quantity, and
uncertainty. This technology attempts to model the kind of logical reasoning
that a person engages in when dealing with issues or elements that are not
precisely defined and/or that involve aspects of degree or quantity. An example of a fuzzy logic rule that might be found in a fuzzy-knowledge-based
system for traders: "IF the price is now *slightly* above the moving average,
AND was previously *much* above the moving average, THEN consider the
price *near* moving average support."

Neural Networks: This technology, also known as the "connectionist" approach, attempts to capture the more intuitive, wholistic kind of thinking involved in, for example, picking out a face in a crowd or recognizing a
handwritten character as an *A* rather than a *V.* In the realm of trading, the
trader looks at a chart and says, "I've seen that pattern before and almost
every time it was present the market crashed!" Neural networks attempt to
do the same. Basically, this technology can be equated to the subjective processes used by traders: They learn in a *Gestalt*-like manner from past experi-

ence and, hopefully, generalize such learning to future events. Neural networks are especially useful for tasks involving pattern recognition.

Although it is not properly a form of AI, but rather of AL (artificial life), we shall also be including a discussion of "genetic algorithms" in this chapter. We do so because this technology is becoming increasingly popular, and it can be *very* effective when used in combination with the AI paradigms described above.

Genetic Algorithms: These are step-by-step procedures that attempt to model the processes of natural, biological evolution (mating, mutation, recombination, etc.) in order to optimize programs, parameters, rules, or virtually anything else that can be properly formalized. For example, genetic algorithms can be used to "breed" (and thus evolve) rule-based trading systems. Sets of rules, which may be considered as individuals, are mated with other sets of rules to obtain new, or offspring, rule sets. Through recombination, mutation, and occasionally other genetic operations, rules are altered and recombined. Selection is applied to the whole breeding population, weeding out the less fit rule sets and leaving behind the more fit rule sets to continue breeding. The hope is that the process will eventually lead to individuals (rule sets) that exhibit the desired behavior, which is defined by the user through a fitness function. Genetic algorithms are not limited to any one of the AI technologies but may be used to evolve neural networks, rule bases, fuzzy systems, or hybrid entities composed of one or more of these components. To put this in the terms of AI, genetic algorithms implement a kind of systematic, and efficient, trial-and-error learning process that involves creation, recombination, and the weeding out of ideas or problem-solving fragments.

While AI technology is still some time away from the sophistication of the androids and other computerized systems depicted in sci-fi novels and films, it has passed its infancy in terms of its usefulness in today's world. In the next section, we will discuss why traders have taken an intense interest in these fledglings and how they are currently being put to work.

THE HISTORY OF AI IN FINANCE

While the term "artificial intelligence" was coined in 1956 by John McCarthy at a Dartmouth College workshop attended by the pioneers of AI (John McCarthy, Marvin Minsky, Allan Newell, and Herbert Simon), such research was already being done in the 1940s. However, it was not until the late 1970s that AI technology caught the eye of the trading community. The full engagement did not begin in earnest until the late 1980s but, once it was started, an inseparable union soon followed. By the 1990s, it was easy to see the effects of this team.

The financial community took so long to fully embrace the technologies of AI for a variety of reasons. Aside from the tendency of institutional traders to be somewhat circumspect in their adoption of new approaches to the markets, two very practical considerations kept them apart: the absence of readily available software that would allow traders to easily try out the technology, and the absence of hardware adequate to run such software.

In the days of main-frame computers and languages such as Basic, FORTRAN, Pascal, and COBOL, adventurous technical analysts (some of whom worked for large institutions) would attempt to write and test trading systems involving numeric computations and simple rule-based logic. Later, with the advent of personal computers, or PCs, the individual trader began using similar programming languages to develop and test their own trading systems using the new, more powerful hardware. The subject matter covered by the articles in the early days (1982-1983) of the magazine *Technical Analysis of Stocks and Commodities* exemplifies this phase in the development of computer-intelligence-assisted trading.

The trend in the direction of computerized technical analysis continued with the appearance of software tools that facilitated the construction of trading systems. These tools (such as Omega Research's "System Writer Plus") were basically shells that contained programming languages, graphics capabilities, data handling, etc. In short, they had everything necessary to easily and efficiently write and test trading systems using mathematical computation together with simple IF . . . THEN . . . rules, as well as the means to back-test such systems on historical data. With such a tool, one could, for example, compute an indicator (e.g., a moving average) and write a rule (e.g., "IF yesterday's close is less than yesterday's moving average AND today's close is greater than today's moving average, THEN buy at open . . ."). This was the beginning of an attempt to facilitate the computerization of some of the processes that traders use when trading the markets. This was not strictly AI, but it was a few steps farther on the road that borders the realm of knowledge-based systems.

As the capacity and power of PCs and workstations grew, and they became more readily available, various forms of full-blown AI began to be applied to the financial markets. A leap was taken from the simple systems described above to the much more sophisticated knowledge-based systems that use rule-based and logic-based reasoning together with AI software tools (e.g., OPS-5, CLIPS, and Neuron Data's NEXPERT) and programming languages (e.g., Prolog, LISP) derived from academic research.

Around this time, the financial community also became interested in neural networks and their supposed ability to recognize very subtle, yet potentially profitable, patterns in noisy market data in a way similar to that of a talented intuitive trader. Neural network shells became commercially available (e.g., BrainMaker from California Scientific Software, NeuroShell® from Ward Systems Group, NeuralWorks™ from NeuralWare, N-TRAIN® from Scientific Consultant Services) and the technology captivated the hearts and imaginations of traders. After the shells came out, pretrained neural trading tools for specific markets also began to appear (e.g., Scientific Consultant Services' THE PREDICTOR® for the S&P, and Mendelsohn Enterprises' Vantage-Point for bonds). The ready availability of such software only served to further fan the flames of interest in this new, sci-fi-like technology, since both technically sophisticated and nonsophisticated traders could all be accommodated. As neural network shells proliferated, software vendors began to seek niche markets by providing alternative pattern recognition approaches, such as "abductive logic" (or, more correctly, polynomial network modeling found in AIM™ from ABTECH), to "nearest neighbor modeling" (as implemented in ModelWare™ from TeraNet).

AI technology, in the form of neural networks and knowledge-based systems, now had a foothold in the financial community; more and more traders were giving it a try. It was, therefore, only natural that other technologies even tangentially related to AI should become of interest. Fuzzy logic was next to appear. Like traditional knowledge-based systems, fuzzy logic works with rules and logic in various ways. However, since it allows rules that involve *quantity* and *degrees* of truth and even, in some sense, *vagueness* to be expressed, the user can build expert systems that are much more flexible and robust than the traditional ones based on "crisp" logic. Fuzzy logic has more potential for financial applications, such as trading, that involve matters of judgment and uncertainty.

WHY DO TRADERS FIND AI SO APPEALING?

Earlier we discussed the practical considerations that influenced the timing of the financial community's attraction to AI. In this section, we will attempt to analyze the reasons for that attraction.

The initial attraction to AI technology grew out of the desire of technical analysts to computerize (and, therefore, improve the efficiency of) what they were already doing, that is, developing and testing trading systems. The technology not only held the promise of speeding up development time, but it also had the lure of powerful potential (both real and imagined) to create immensely profitable trading systems, and to do so without a great many of the human stumbling blocks that usually occur along the way.

When knowledge-based systems first appeared, trading systems could be developed that contained rules, written in the formal structure of a computer language, that expressed the knowledge of a successful expert trader. In that way, others could have access to the trader's expertise long after he or she was gone. Moreover, with the new technology, a system could be efficiently "back-tested" by the computer, i.e., it could be paper-traded on extremely large quantities of historical data, and an efficient and objective assessment of the system's performance could be obtained. In that way, too, subjective human elements, such as hindsight in system evaluation, could be avoided. With the proper tools, many trading ideas could be tested much more quickly and objectively than was ever before possible.

As interest in this kind of technology grew, it extended to cover and utilize a greater proportion of the findings of AI research; it may also have stimulated such exploration. Tools became available that permitted the technology to be used more easily, and that allowed greater flexibility. Those advances helped system developers further actualize the goal of replicating the abilities of successful traders. For example, one of the characteristics that can be found among successful traders is their ability to recognize patterns that recur in various charts. The brain and eye can recognize these patterns but it would be difficult, if not impossible, to formalize or specify in a simple knowledge-based system the precise rules that define these patterns. Since it appeared to answer the need for this kind of pattern recognition, consideration was then given to neural network technology. Neural networks were also attractive because they could be trained to detect patterns that the trader himself could not recognize as present or significant because they were too subtle. Also, unlike a knowledge-based system, where someone has to elicit knowledge from an expert and express it in a formalized computer language, neural networks promised adaptivity—they could *learn* from experience, even adapt to markets as conditions changed. Fuzzy logic is catching on for the simple reason that it allows the trader to express and formalize knowledge that has an element of judgment, imprecision, or quantity and therefore permits the trader to express his or her trading principles more naturally.

AI TECHNOLOGY: MYTH VERSUS REALITY

The powerful capabilities inherent in AI technology have not only revolutionized the world of trading but have also contributed to the formation of what seems to be a new mythology. This phenomenon has, we believe, occurred mainly because of the relatively abrupt appearance of the applied form of this technology in the financial community, and because of the concurrent paucity of easy-to-understand literature explaining these paradigms and their implementation. It is also apparent that certain forms of AI are more subject to this phenomenon than others.

The primary focus of this new mythology is neural network technology. A kind of mystique has formed around neural networks—a mystique fostered largely by their ability to "learn." Some traders seem to construe their computers as magical lamps that just need to be rubbed to get the neural genie to appear and produce systems that are profitable beyond their wildest imaginations. Unfortunately, in the interest of marketing their products, this image of neural nets has been encouraged by some vendors of neural development tools; this strategy has, to some degree, backfired, resulting in a great deal of disillusionment among traders who attempted to use neural networks but who later abandoned the technology because it was not as easy to achieve successful results as they were led to believe. Fortunately, the myth is now being tempered with reality.

Knowledge-based systems, whether in traditional (crisp) form or involving fuzzy logic, never had a mythical or "black box" quality because the production rules, or knowledge formalizations, are accessible: The developer writes them; they do not come out of nowhere. Price, or other kinds of data, cannot be thrown at such systems in the expectation that they will magically discover or learn the real relationships in the data.

An air of hopeful fantasy, not dissimilar to the mystique surrounding neural networks, is forming around "genetic algorithms." Genetic algorithms have a mystical quality because, through an amazing process of randomness and selection, they promise to yield something useful and potentially very profitable without the trader having to specify the structure, components, or parameters of the resultant system. In other words, the trader can turn on his or her computer and let it *evolve* a trading system; the process of evolution can adapt the system to changing market conditions, etc. But, like neural networks, the process of system development also requires a good deal of work on the part of the trader. That aside, the fact alone that genetic algorithms are modeled after humankind's own evolutionary path makes it likely that the technology will inspire a sense of awe and wonderment.

Since myths very often develop as a response to the unknown, let us now turn our attention to seeking further understanding about the various divisions of AI. In the sections that follow, we will attempt to pull back the curtains and take a better look at the technologies that will be increasingly visible through the window of to-morrow.

KNOWLEDGE-BASED SYSTEMS

Knowledge-based systems (also known as expert systems) attempt to model logical, symbolic, rule-based reasoning. Such rule-based systems attempt to emulate IF . . . THEN . . . logical thinking. In traditional systems, the rules involve what is referred to as "crisp" logic, that is, things are either true or false, yes or no, etc.

Among nonfinancial applications, knowledge-based systems have been developed to play chess, determine which antibiotic might be effective against a given disease organism, and prove simple mathematical theorems. While knowledge-based systems have also been used in the financial domain (primarily on the institutional level), very little has been published about them: Not only is there a paucity of articles about knowledge-based systems in, for example, *Technical Analysis of Stocks and Commodities* or *Futures,* there are few, if any, advertisements for products related to this technology in traders' magazines. However, articles and ads for expert system shells can be found in such publications as *AI Expert* and *PC AI.* Therefore, although institutions have developed knowledge-based systems for a variety of financial uses, including the rating of bonds, the assessing of mortgage risk, asset allocation and, of course, trading, this form of AI technology has apparently not been widely used among private or individual traders.

The Components of Knowledge-Based Systems

There are three main elements in every knowledge-based system:

> *Inference Engine:* This is core of the system, the function of which is to reason. The inference engine manipulates the rules contained in the knowledge base in order to find a solution to the problem at hand: It applies the knowledge in the "knowledge base" (perhaps in the form of production rules) to the facts in the "fact base" in order to generate more facts; eventually it reaches some goal or solution to a problem. The solution may be in the form of a specific fact, which constitutes a conclusion that results from the use of the rules in the knowledge base. In some implementations, the knowledge base and the fact base may be one and the same, with facts taking the same form as rules. For example:

Rule or fact #1:	All men are mortal.
Rule or fact #2:	All programmers are men.
Conclusion (also of the same logical form):	All programmers are mortal.

Inference engines are available in many forms, e.g., as components of knowledge-based system shells, intrinsic in such programming languages as Prolog and LISP, or in libraries that can be used with such programming languages as C or C++.

Knowledge Base (or Rule Base): This is the set of logical statements or propositions that the system uses when reasoning. This portion of the system contains the general knowledge that is available to the system about the problem domain currently being addressed. In systems used in the financial world, these statements usually take the form of IF . . . THEN . . . rules that represent the heuristics, or rules of thumb, used by an expert trader, bond rater, credit risk assessor, insurance adjuster, etc.

Database or Factbase: This element of the knowledge-based system contains data *specific* to the problem at hand, data that are going to be analyzed by the reasoning function of the inference engine which, in turn, employs the rules stored in the knowledge base to solve the problem. In other words, the information contained in the database is the particular problem to which the expert is going to apply his expertise.

The rules or logical elements in a knowledge base, and the facts in a factbase, may be accompanied by strength, belief, or certainty values. For example:

IF	Price > Moving Average
THEN	Trend Up
Confidence	0.75

Fuzzy logic greatly extends this type of thinking in terms of degrees of truth or shades of gray, rather than in black and white.

Factors Involved in Constructing the Knowledge Base

Knowledge-based systems are generally built by a "knowledge engineer," who may be the domain expert or the user of the system. Unlike neural network systems, which learn from experience, the knowledge in a knowledge-based system is almost always placed there by an outside agency; these days, one exception is when the knowledge is generated or modified by an evolutionary process using genetic algorithms.

While the inference engine is usually available in an expert system shell or as part of a programming language (e.g., PROLOG), the user must construct the knowledge base. To construct a knowledge base, the knowledge engineer must first find an "expert" in the domain of interest and work with that expert in order to elicit the rules that he or she applies when reasoning about problems in his or her area of expertise. As they are elicited, these rules must be cast into the formal language of the expert system development tool or language being used. The expert would also be consulted about what would constitute good test problems in his or her domain. He or she would be queried as to which problems could be solved using the knowledge, and which could provide a test for how well the knowledge-based system is mimicking his or her reasoning. Once one or more experts have participated, and a set of rules and test problems have been elicited, a knowledge base can be assembled and the shell can be used to "run" the rules on a set of test problems to see how well the knowledge-based system performs. The expert would then be consulted to help determine how successful the system is at reaching the right conclusions.

There is a lot of work involved in the development of a knowledge-based system. The standard expert system does not learn on its own from past experience; rules must be formulated and entered into the knowledge base, or selected from the knowledge base and edited by a human knowledge engineer or user. However, a well-constructed knowledge-based system can perform remarkably well and it can effectively simulate much of the expert's reasoning, especially when this reasoning involves explicit, well-defined rules and straightforward logic.

Some of the foremost difficulties in developing a knowledge-based system are (1) finding, in the case of the financial markets, an expert trader; and (2) finding an expert who is conscious enough of the processes he or she employs so that, with proper questioning, the rules that expert uses can be elicited. The preference would, of course, be a trader who does have some kind of clear-cut mental rule-set or approach to reasoning about the markets. Conversely, the knowledge engineer should try to avoid experts who trade on gut instinct, tacit knowledge, or pattern recognition—kinds of thinking less appropriately modeled by knowledge-based systems.

How do you elicit rules? One way is by direct questioning. However, as mentioned above, not many experts are fully conscious of the rules and types of reasoning they employ. A somewhat more effective way is to present the expert with a variety of problems, and have that person work through the problems out loud, while being questioned about the various aspects of the problem he or she is noting and the general decision processes being applied.

Example of Knowledge-Based System Development

If you wanted to construct a knowledge-based system to determine the best times to buy OEX index options, you would first find a successful trader in that domain. You would then ask that trader what information he or she would look for when making such a determination. The trader might say something like, "Look for the market to make a pull-back in the context of a strong trend." You then might ask the trader how he or she determines whether the market is in a strong trend. If you are lucky, the expert might be able to tell you, e.g., "The price is above its 50- and 200-day moving averages and has not broken a long-term trend line."

You would then ask how to determine where a trend line is and again, hopefully, you would get an answer. You might then formulate a rule, such as: "IF the price is above the 50-day moving average, AND the price is above the 200-day moving average, AND the price is above the trend line, THEN the market is trending up."

The next step would be to find out how the trader recognizes a pull-back in the context of a trend. He or she might say that if the S&P drops about three or more points but does not break the trend line, then a pull-back has occurred. You now have another rule: "IF the price is less than the previous price minus three, AND the price is above the trend line, THEN buy five calls at market." (Note that in this rule, since we were not using fuzzy logic, we had to code the expert's "about three or more points" as a crisp three.)

You might then ask the expert under what conditions he or she would avoid purchasing calls on a pull-back in the context of a trend. You might be able to elicit some more rules, and modify the existing rules. With such modifications, the last rule above might now read: "IF the price is less than the previous price minus three, AND the price is above the trend line, THEN assert precondition number one." You would use "precondition number one" as part of another "IF . . ." clause; that clause would consider the exceptions and would be followed by another clause—e.g., "THEN purchase calls"—in which (because of the consideration of the exceptions) "purchase calls" is true only if the exceptions have not been fired, which would render the decision void.

There is a chance that you might not be able to easily elicit the rules the expert uses to go long or short by purchasing or shorting puts or calls. If the expert is unable to state his or her rules directly, another approach would be to present that person with historical charts or data, and to ask that he or she make a decision each day as to whether he or she would go long, go short, exit, or do nothing. You could then attempt to query the expert about each decision in order to elicit the rules used in making the decision.

If you are successful at eliciting rules and casting them into the appropriate form for the tools you are using, you may have an expert system that produces decisions that match the expert's own decisions with a fair degree of closeness. Testing will determine whether this is the case, and further work with the expert may be able to improve the match.

Another approach to developing knowledge-based systems is to construct the knowledge base on likely hypotheses and then run the system to see how well it performs, that is, test its decisions on historical data, and attempt to successively modify and add to the rules in order to improve the system's performance. If you do this, however, beware of the dangers of "curve fitting."

Disadvantages of Knowledge-Based Systems

There are several main reasons why knowledge-based systems have not had the popularity of, e.g., neural networks. These reasons range from the difficulties involved in formulating rules based on expert knowledge, to the relative lack of access to truly successful expert traders, to the "brittleness" of such systems and their lack of adaptability to changing market conditions.

One practical consideration in the development of knowledge-based systems is the problems one encounters when attempting to explicitly and usefully define the various elements that may be referenced in the knowledge base. For instance, one rule used by an expert trader might be:

IF   There is a "head-and-shoulders"
                pattern
THEN   Short X contracts at market

The problem arises when it comes to defining a "head-and-shoulders" pattern using IF . . . THEN. . . logic. A rule or set of rules (perhaps even a computational subroutine) is needed in the system that will allow it to evaluate whether a head-and-shoulders pattern is present. Creating a set of rules to define such a pattern may be almost impossible because of the fuzzy, *Gestalt*-like, mostly visual recognition involved in deciding whether prices have formed a head-and-shoulders pattern on a chart. You know one when you see one, but how do you *precisely* define one in a programmable algorithm or set of rules? To deal with such problems, we might choose to use a "hybrid system" (which we will discuss later), where some of the "rules" are implemented as neural networks that have been trained to recognize various patterns on a price chart.

Another problem one might encounter in knowledge-based system development relates to the expert: The expert's "explicit" knowledge might not be very useful! The expert trader may tell you that he or she looks for a head-and-shoulders pattern and then waits for the stochastics to roll over. So the knowledge engineer develops a head-and-shoulders pattern detector, a few rules to test for the presence of a stochastics rollover, and a rule that combines these to say "Go short X contracts." The system is then tested: It trades terribly, losing money by the truck-load. Yet the expert on whom the system is based has an incredibly successful track record! What's going on here? It may be that the expert normally applies additional "tacit" or context-dependent knowledge in making decisions. Maybe he or she recognizes some broader market configuration in the context of which the head-and-shoulders/stochastic pattern leads to profitable trades, but of which he or she is not fully aware and, therefore, which is not recognized and implemented in the rule base. Maybe the expert is not even looking for a head-and-shoulders pattern at all, but only thinks he or she is! Good luck! It's back to the drawing board for the knowledge engineer.

One of the other drawbacks of knowledge-based systems is their lack of adaptability. An expert trader can "adapt" his or her own decision-making knowledge base, modifying internal rules, as markets change. However, unlike neural network systems, traditional knowledge-based systems lack the ability to adapt on their own to changing market conditions. Therefore, when used for trading, the knowledge-based system, which you have gone through so much trouble to construct, will have to be maintained by the system developer to keep up-to-date with the expert's rules and/or changing market conditions.

FUZZY LOGIC

Fuzzy logic is very much like traditional or "crisp" logic in that it can be used to define rules, draw inferences, and come to conclusions. The difference between the two is in the fact that fuzzy logic allows for the expression of matters of degree, quantity, and even vagueness. In crisp logic, statements contain such expressions as "greater than," "lesser than," "equal to," and "is," and these statements are either *true* or *false.* In fuzzy logic, there are shades of gray: The expressions used by this form of logic include such elements as "slightly above," "very much below," "about the same as," and, rather than being simply true or false, statements may be true to a greater or lesser degree. For example, a rule formulated in crisp logic might read as follows:

> *IF the closing price for a given bar is* greater than *the moving average for that bar, AND the closing price for the same bar is* less than *the moving average plus 2 percent for that bar, THEN price is at moving average support.*

A similar rule formulated in terms of fuzzy logic might read like this:

> *To the extent that it is true that the closing price for a given bar is* just above
> *the moving average for that bar, that is* the extent to which *it is true that the*
> *price is at moving average support.*

Note the use of such terms as "just above," "slightly below," and "the extent to
which" in the fuzzy logic version of the rule. It is common for people to reason using
such constructions; however, it is difficult to implement such reasoning efficiently in
traditional knowledge-based systems. Fuzzy logic (and knowledge-based systems that
use fuzzy logic) are attractive to traders because it allows them to formalize the kinds
of thinking they themselves use in a more natural way.

History of Fuzzy Logic

Fuzzy logic arose from the theory of "fuzzy sets" proposed in 1965 by Lotfi Zadeh, a
professor at the University of California at Berkeley. In its early days, it received less
than a favorable reception from the proponents of traditional logic and related systems. However, the merits of fuzzy logic were most heartily embraced by the Japanese, who use it heavily in process control and engineering. It seems that only in
1987, when the subway system in Sendai, Japan, proved successful with its use of
fuzzy logic, did the United States begin to take notice (Viot, 1993).
    Speculation has it that American companies were (and still are) reluctant to use
fuzzy logic because of the term "fuzzy," which was apparently interpreted as the
quality of the results, rather than the type of problems the technology excels at handling. More venturesome companies have applied the technology, but they are
guarded about revealing the fact, or they give it another name. But this trend does
seem to be changing. Whether tauted or not, fuzzy logic has had wide applications in
the United States: from use in the transmission systems of General Motors' Saturn, to
analyzing failure modes and effects at GE Airplane Engines; to a project cost estimating system at Vista Polymers; to a risk underwriting system developed for Aetna; to a
fraud detection system in managed health care developed by Metus Systems Group;
to a military force resolution system developed for the U.S. Army by Fuzzy Logic Inc.
(Walsh, 1993). In short, fuzzy logic can be found in everything from air conditioners
and washing machines to elevators, VCRs, and military support systems. However,
while fuzzy logic is construed as most appropriate for decision-making tasks and information processing that involves matters of degree and certainty (both of which are
present in trading), the financial community did not start catching on until the 1990s.
    The first commercially available fuzzy logic shell was introduced in 1990 by
HyperLogic Corp. (Packert, 1994); since that time, others appeared (FIDE from Ap-
tronix; fuzzyTECH from Inform Software Corp.; TILSHELL from Togai InfraLogic).
However, interest was not evidenced among individual traders until 1993, when articles started appearing in the trade magazines. The reason for that delay might be
similar to the one for the slow growth of interest in knowledge-based systems: The
developer of such systems has to enter rules and, prior to the availability of shells
specifically developed for the financial community, it was difficult to implement the
technology without programming knowledge. When domain-specific shells were intro-

duced, interest started growing. However, in our opinion, the interest in fuzzy logic will not grow as rapidly or as dramatically as it did for neural networks, although we do expect that a greater number of traders who work with neural network systems will use fuzzy logic for preprocessing their data.

The Components of Fuzzy Logic Systems

The various parts of a fuzzy logic system are quite similar to those of a knowledge-based system: There is the "inference engine," which may be a component in a fuzzy logic shell or supplied as a library for use with a programming language, and which manipulates the rules in order to find a solution; the "knowledge base" (or fuzzy rule base), which basically contains the rules the system will use in its reasoning; and the "database" (or factbase), which contains the domain-specific data that are going to be analyzed by the system. The main difference between the two types of systems is that the rules contained in traditional knowledge-based systems are formulated using crisp logic; in fuzzy logic, the rules contain the expressions of degree, quantity, or uncertainty that we described above. Because of the novelty of this difference to systems developers, it is worth spending some time taking the "fuzziness" out of this form of logic in order to better understand how it operates.

How the Expression of "Fuzziness" Is Achieved

While it is easy to say that, in fuzzy logic systems, traditional crisp logic phrases such as "greater than" may be replaced with such expressions as "slightly above," how does a fuzzy logic system *know* what we are talking about when we use such terminology in our rules?

In traditional systems, whether something is "greater than" something else is a simple matter: It is either *true* (given a value of 1) or it is *not true* (given a value of 0). If the traditional system contains the antecedent of a rule: "IF the closing price for a given bar is *greater than* the moving average for that bar . . . ," and if the data you present the system contain a closing price of 0.6 for the bar and a moving average of 0.5, then the system merely has to decide whether 0.6 is or is not "greater than" 0.5; its conclusion would be that it is *true* that 0.6 is "greater than" 0.5 (and the antecedent of the rule would be given the value of 1; the rule would "fire"). How does it reach that conclusion? The system compares the numbers against one another: It contains the knowledge that 0, 0.1, 0.2, 0.3, and 0.4 are all numbers less than 0.5, and that 0.6, .07, 0.8, etc., are all numbers greater than 0.5. But what criteria does a fuzzy logic system use to decide whether something is "slightly above" something else? How does it interpret the term "slightly"?

In order to cope with this interpretation problem, fuzzy logic systems contain something known as "membership functions." The raw inputs that are fed to the system are categorized by the developer into "fuzzy sets." If we rewrote the antecedent to the rule in the paragraph above for a fuzzy logic system, it might read: "IF the closing price for a given bar is *slightly above* the moving average for that bar . . . ." Given this rule, the system developer would have to define a fuzzy set for the term "slightly above" as used in this context. The developer would have to specify the *degree* to which each number is a member of that set or, put another way, the *degree of truth* of the statement "X is slightly above the moving average" for all X. No longer do we have a black or white, true or untrue interpretation; we now have the shades of gray, the expression of vagueness. The actual value (between 0 and 1) that the developer assigns to the statement for each X, and which determines its degree of membership in that set, is called a "membership function." The process of assigning that value is called "fuzzification." And the variables or values that result from this process are called "fuzzy inputs."

This is the way in which fuzzy logic formalizes the *shades of gray* and terms that refer to approximations of quantity. Fuzzy logic and fuzzy sets are inextricably interwoven. Consider again the antecedent of the rule, "IF the closing price of a given bar is slightly above the moving average for that bar . . . ." This fragment might be represented by a membership function that looks like Figure 1.

In Figure 1, the *y*-axis (vertical) represents the degree of membership (or truth) for the fuzzy clause "X is slightly above the moving average"; it represents what is meant by "slightly above" in the context of the moving average. The *x*-axis (horizontal) represents the ratio of the closing price to the moving average. Figure 1, in its entirety, represents the membership function that expresses the relationship between the degree of membership in the set, or truth of the statement "the closing price of a given bar is slightly above the moving average," and the ratio of price to moving average. Note that the degree of membership is 1.0 when the price is 2 percent (1.02 on the *x*-axis) above the moving average. This means that the expert who provided the fuzzy membership set described above believed that this price-to-moving-average ratio best exemplified what is meant by "slightly above" in the statement "closing price of a given bar is slightly above the moving average." According to the way this membership function is defined, a price that was 10 percent above the moving aver-

Figure 1.   Illustration of a simple fuzzy logic memberhip function.

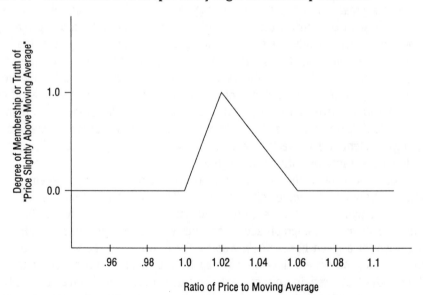

age could in no way be considered "slightly above," nor could a price that was 2 percent below the moving average (membership = 0.0). However, a price of 4 percent above the moving average could, to a certain degree, be considered "slightly above the moving average," as could a price that was 1 percent above the moving average (membership = 0.5, making the statement "X is slightly above the moving average" half true).

We should, perhaps, point out that if we restrict our membership functions to having values of 0 = False and 1 = True—that is, to rectangular shapes—then the "fuzzy" aspect of fuzzy logic disappears; the model is reduced to "crisp" logic. The logic becomes, or "reduces to," the more traditional crisp logic (as a sort of special case).

Given such a representation of truth as degree of membership in a fuzzy set, one can easily define the standard logical operations such as the "conjunctive" (e.g., AND) and "disjunctive" (e.g., OR). Such operations help form the basis of "propositional logic," which is considered to be the oldest form of logic and which is based on simple statements about the world that can be assigned values of truth or falsity, e.g., "There are 24 hours in a day" or "The world is square."

One common way to define the two operations described above is:

A AND B is defined by MINIMUM (A,B)

A OR B is defined by MAXIMUM (A,B)

where A and B are fuzzy membership values

So the truth of the statement

Price is just above the moving average

AND

Moving average is sloping up

would be the *minimum of the truth,* or "membership value," of each of the clauses conjoined by the AND operation.

Similarly, the truth value of

Neural forecast is Strong Up

OR

Seasonal forecast is Strong UP

would be the *maximum of the truth,* or "membership value," of each of the clauses conjoined by the OR operation.

This is an incomplete exposition. We have covered AND and OR, but have left out implication. However, by properly formalizing these various logical operations, one can build a fuzzy logic shell or engine, just as is possible with more traditional forms of logic. For each of the operations, or components of traditional logic, there are corresponding forms for the fuzzy variety.

Example of Fuzzy Logic System Development

Let us, for a moment, take a breather from the world of trading and look at fuzzy logic systems from a different perspective. In this example, we will pretend to be the developers of a diagnostic tool for health care professionals.

In the development of a real medical diagnostic system, we would want to specify a variety of different symptoms and delineate their possible relationships to various illnesses. For this example, however, we will just look at one of the symptoms that would be present in such a system—temperature.

To start, we might want to define five different classifications, or "fuzzy sets," of temperature: Very high, slightly high, normal, slightly low, and very low. We define these sets to the system by assigning "membership functions" to them, that is, for each set we specify the relationship between a specific temperature and the extent to which it is a member of the set: For example, given the temperature 98°, to what extent is it a member of the "very high" temperature set? Of the "slightly high" temperature set? Of the "normal" temperature set? Of the "slightly low" temperature set? Of the "very low" temperature set? We do the same for 97.5°, 97°, and for 99°, 100.5°, etc. This "fuzzification process" can be accomplished in a variety of ways. For example, the individual systems developer may be enough of an expert to make such determinations; or he or she might wish to get a group of doctors to fill out a questionnaire and have them assign a truth value (between 0 and 100 percent or 0 and 1) for every temperature, when compared against each of the temperature set classifications, then take the average of the truth values for each temperature in each set and use them as the membership functions.

The system developer would also have to write a series of rules that utilize these fuzzy sets. (Note: The rules can also be written prior to the fuzzification process, depending on the developer's preference or needs.) The following might be included in the list of rules:

> IF temperature is very high, THEN acute bacterial infection is probably present.
>
> IF temperature is slightly high, THEN attenuated viral infection might be present.
>
> IF temperature is normal AND patient is itchy, THEN allergy is present.
>
> IF temperature is slightly low, THEN thyroid function may be impaired.
>
> IF temperature is very low, THEN patient is dead.

From this point on, the procedure would be the same as for any knowledge-based system: The system would be tested on a set of examples specific to the system's domain of expertise, and it would be assessed on the basis of its performance, i.e., how successfully its conclusions match those of the expert(s). If it performs well, it can be used as a diagnostic tool. If it fails in its performance, then the developer would have to go back and determine what went wrong, e.g., the rules might not be representative or the membership functions might need to be adjusted.

The Advantages of Fuzzy Logic

One of the main advantages of fuzzy logic is that it more closely models the kind of reasoning that a person engages in when dealing with issues or elements that are not precisely defined and/or that involve aspects of degree or "judgment." For traders, this technology allows them to express their thinking about the market more accurately. Traders do not always think in terms of sharp boundaries; they often employ reasoning that involves matters of degree or probability and ranges of values. Because fuzzy systems are good at modeling such reasoning, the development and use of such systems is often a lot easier than those that depend on crisp logic. The knowledge provided by the expert does not have to be quite as precisely formalized as in traditional systems; with fuzzy logic, one can have approximate inputs and obtain precise outputs. Moreover, fuzzy systems usually contain fewer rules than traditional systems and therefore are easier to maintain.

Lastly, fuzzy systems are very often more robust than traditional systems. In a traditional system you might have a rule that says: "IF the opening price is 0.5 greater than the closing price for the previous day, THEN buy tomorrow at market." The problem is that if the opening price is only 0.49999 greater, then the system would not say "buy" (it might even say "sell") and the trader would miss what might have been a profitable opportunity (or actually take a loss). In a fuzzy system, the rule would have read: "IF the opening price is *moderately* greater than the closing price for the previous day, THEN buy tomorrow at market." Because of the gracefulness of fuzzy systems, if the price had been only 0.49999 greater, it would have still said "buy," but with somewhat less force of belief. That is, fuzzy systems avoid the sharp discontinuities of crisp logic. This property is responsible for the smoothness of, e.g., the Sendai train or an elevator controlled by fuzzy logic.

Disadvantages of Fuzzy Logic

The disadvantages of fuzzy logic systems are the same as those found in traditional knowledge-based systems: Someone has to write rules, which means that expert knowledge, in one form or another, has to be available and formalized. These systems, generally, cannot learn on their own, nor can they adapt to changing market conditions, except by manually rewriting the rules, adjusting the membership functions, and/or using genetic algorithms or other specific rule-finding methodologies.

NEURAL NETWORKS

Neural network technology arose from an attempt to model the behavior of neural tissue in living systems by implementing, on the computer, structures composed of simulated neurons and neuronal interconnections (synapses). Neural network technology endeavors to emulate the kind of information processing and decision making that occurs in living organisms.

Neural networks come in a variety of flavors, depending on their "architecture," that is, the particular ways in which the simulated neurons are interconnected and the internal behavior of the simulated neurons, i.e., their signal processing behavior or "transfer functions." The most popular kinds of neural networks, and the most useful for traders, are the "feed-forward, back-propagation" variety, the Kohonen, and LVQ (learning vector quantization) networks, the various adaptive reasonance networks, and recurrent networks.

Neural architectures differ in the ways they learn: Some networks employ "supervised learning" and others "unsupervised learning." *Supervised learning* occurs when the network is shown something and "guided" to produce a correct solution by being shown the correct solution. In other words, a kind of "paired-associate learning" is in operation: There are inputs that the network sees and a desired output for every set of inputs; for every set of inputs, the task of the network is to learn to produce the desired outputs. In contrast, *unsupervised learning* involves networks that simply take presentations of inputs and learn to organize the patterns as the networks themselves see fit. If an analogy is made to statistics, unsupervised networks would be more akin to clustering models, whereas the supervised networks would be closer to various forms of regression and discriminant analysis.

Among other things, neural networks make excellent pattern recognizers. They have been applied to solve a wide range of problems, such as assessing credit risk, recognizing spoken and written words, processing sonar signals, filtering out noise in electronic communications systems, and more. Recently, they have become the rage of traders.

The Explosive Growth of Interest in Neural Networks

Research on neural networks began, on a theoretical level, in the 1940s. At that time, however, computer technology to implement the theory adequately was not available. Around the time when computer technology had become sophisticated enough to accommodate neural network research, Minsky and Papert, in their book *Perceptrons* (1969), brought such research to a standstill: They "proved" that a special kind of two-layer neural network could not, in any way, solve "the exclusive 'or' problem"; this was enough to discourage further study of the subject for years. The field did not recover from that blow until gradient descent optimization ("back-propagation") was applied to finding the connection weights in neural networks containing more than two layers and employing sigmoid transfer functions. Since three-layer nets *can* solve "the exclusive 'or' problem," the objections Minsky and Papert expressed were rendered irrelevant and research began again, in earnest.

In recent years, neural network technology has attracted a great deal of interest from traders. There has actually been an explosive growth of interest in this domain: Before 1988, there were no articles on neural networks in *Technical Analysis of Stocks and Commodities,* but by 1993 there were seven articles comprising more than 60 percent of the articles in that publication for the year! New periodicals that deal specifically with the use of AI technology in trading (with particular emphasis on neural networks), such as *NeuroVe$t Journal* and *AI in Finance,* also appeared around this time. While the trade publications of this industry have increased their coverage of neural technology, the information explosion seems like a "pop" when compared with the "boom" produced by the proliferation of software vendors who offer neural shells and related products. In 1989, there were only a few vendors of neural network development tools; when we (Scientific Consultant Services, Inc.) came on the scene with N-TRAIN® in 1992, there were a few more vendors, but still not very many. Now, in 1994, the count of neural network vendors has burgeoned to over 50!

Perhaps it is the imbalance that occurred between the availability of educational materials, which provide understanding about the nature and use of neural networks, and the vastly greater availability of self-serving promotional materials from some vendors of neural technology that accounts for the fact that, for many traders, neural networks are still a puzzling and mysterious matter. Traders have become enticed by the technology because of the great promise it holds for recognizing subtle, but profitable, patterns in the markets—that is, its potential capacity to identify hard-to-detect patterns in very noisy (or chaotic) data, a task that is otherwise difficult to accomplish. However, when they get the tools in their hands, many would-be system developers become overwhelmed. This is the Janus-like attitude toward neural networks currently experienced by the trading community. One face has formed from the technology's very own potential and has resulted in the belief that a neural network is like a magical genie that can quickly and easily yield profitable trades at a keystroke; this is the face that usually represents one's *beginnings* with neural technology. The other face is the one seen on newcomers when the myth is confronted by the realities of developing a successful neural trading system; unfortunately, this face is all too often (and needlessly so) representative of the beginner's *endings* with neural networks (Katz and McCormick, 1994a). In short, understanding about the nature and use of neural networks has not accompanied the proliferation of tools to implement the technology, and the realities have not quite caught up with the myths. However, it is hoped that this book will provide a greater balance and increase the probability of success for the reader contemplating neural system development.

What's the Attraction?

As we mentioned above, one of the reasons that neural networks have caught the interest of traders is because they appear to possess the potential to fulfill trading fantasies. Traders hear success stories and get carried away. For example, one neural network we developed signaled four out of five tradeable bottoms in the S&P 500, almost as if it were a "perfect" oversold/not-oversold oscillator; this is especially impressive considering that the data were collected almost a year after the network had last been trained! However, that system was not developed with one quick and easy keystroke.

Another reason for the allure is that neural networks can cope with "fuzzy" patterns (those easily recognized by eye but difficult to define using precise rules—for example, the head-and-shoulders formation) and deal with probability estimates in uncertain situations. Neural networks are also able to integrate large amounts of information without becoming stifled by detail. The ability of neural networks to "learn" from experience is another reason that they have captivated the hearts and minds of traders: The design of such systems is not dependent on having an already-expert trader on whose expertise one formulates the rules of a knowledge-based system. Another reason for the interest in neural networks is that they may be retrained and, therefore, adapt to changing market behavior. Finally, under the correct circumstances and with proper training, neural networks have the potential to recognize almost any pattern that exists in any market. By examining the capabilities of this technology, it is easy to see why neural networks have caught the fancy of traders. What is not visible, however, is the great amount of trial-and-error experimentation and user-sophistication that is involved in the development of a successful neural network trading system. Therefore, let us start balancing our perspective by turning our discussion toward the matter of neural network systems development.

Components of Neural Network Systems

There are four basic components needed by developers of neural network systems:

Neural Network Shell: A neural network shell (sometimes referred to as a "neural network development system") provides an environment in which the user can configure, train, test, and otherwise manipulate neural networks. The most important component of the shell is the neural "engine." Like the inference engine of knowledge-based and fuzzy logic systems, a neural network engine implements the simulated neural structure together with the process by which it learns. A good neural development shell will provide access to a stable, efficient, and reliable engine.

A good shell should also provide the user with the ability to customize network behavior, to determine the relative contribution or importance of each of the inputs to the model being developed, and to "script" or automate such protocols as "walk-forward testing" (which is an especially important feature for traders). In addition, a good shell should provide components or "hooks" that allow the user to utilize the networks he or she develops from within other kinds of software, e.g., system profitability testing and real-time trading and charting tools. We have discovered, through personal experience and in discussion with our clients, that popular neural network shells vary a great deal in their capabilities, quality, and numerical as well as statistical robustness. Therefore, before purchasing a shell, we recommend that neural developers do a bit of study, e.g., read *independent* reviews and objective tests of relative performance (e.g., Jurik, 1993). Beware of shells with dazzling front-ends because, in order to obtain such interfaces, the performance of the engines might have been sacrificed. Since neural network trading systems are difficult and time-consuming to develop, it is important to be sure that the engine is the fastest and most reliable one available—it will be a major determinant of success in development. Go for speed, power, and especially stability over glitz (Katz and McCormick, 1993; 1994a).

Instead of a shell, some neural systems developers might prefer using a programmer's library (such as Scientific Consultant Services' LOGIVOLVE™), or a computer language, e.g., C, Visual Basic, FORTRAN, PASCAL (or even perhaps LISP and PROLOG), for facilitating the development of hybrid systems.

Data Preprocessing Tool: One of the tasks that faces every neural systems developer is the need to "preprocess" data before presenting it to the network. Preprocessing data refers to "massaging" or manipulating it in various ways, a matter that we will discuss further in Chapter 2, "Neural Networks in Trading." Some neural network development shells come with their own preprocessing and data-handling modules; most successful developers, however, use other preprocessing tools. The preference may be because the systems developers are already familiar with the other tools, or their data are already formatted for use with them, or simply because tools that were specifically designed as data managers (e.g., spreadsheets, systems such as Omega Research's TradeStation™, etc.) are almost always more sophisticated and more powerful than those provided by neural network vendors—a reason to look for compatibility with other software in a neural shell!

When preprocessing the data, it must be cast into "examples" or "facts" from which the network can learn. A "fact" consists of a complete set of inputs together with the desired output(s). Many such examples need to be assembled before training and testing begins. In a spreadsheet, each row may be set up to contain an example: The first so many cells in the row being the inputs, and the last cell (or cells) being the desired output(s) or target(s).

Training Set: This is a set of examples, often in the form of a datafile assembled during the preprocessing stage that will be used to train the network; this is the raw material from which the network will attempt to learn.

Testing Set: This is another set of examples, also prepared during the preprocessing phase and also in the form of a datafile. These examples are ones the network has never before seen, or been trained on. They are used to test the capability of the network to do the job for which it was trained. This would be analogous to a set of test problems used to test the behavior of a knowledge-based system.

The Structure of a Feed-Forward Neural Network

We will now discuss the structure or "architecture" of one of the most commonly used neural networks among traders. A typical "feed-forward" network is composed of neurons arranged in layers. The "input layer" is the first layer found in such a network: It receives data from the outside world, or "inputs," which consist of "independent variables" (e.g., market or indicator variables upon which the system is to be based) from which some inference is to be drawn or a prediction is to be made. This layer is massively connected to the next layer, which is usually called a "hidden layer" since it has no connections to the outside world. The hidden layer's outputs are, in turn, fed to the next layer, which may be another hidden layer (in which case the process repeats), or it may be the "output layer." Each neuron in the output layer produces an "output" from the network. The outputs form the predictions, classifications, or decisions made by the network.

Networks can be of varying sizes, from only a few input variables to hundreds or thousands of them, and from only three layers to dozens. The size usually depends on the complexity of the problem at hand. In almost all cases, a three- or four-layer network (that is, a network with one or two hidden layers) will perform well; exceeding four layers is rarely a benefit and will add to the training time. In general, the layer that immediately follows the input layer will have anywhere from two to three neurons to perhaps twice the number of input neurons, depending on the problem. In a four-layer network, the layer that immediately precedes the output neuron may have anywhere from one to two neurons to perhaps three or four times the number of output neurons. These numbers may vary, depending on the forecasting problem and several other considerations that will be discussed in our Chapter 2, "Neural Networks in Trading."

Figure 2 (Katz, 1992) depicts the structure of a typical three-layer, feed-forward neural network that contains three input or first-layer neurons, four neurons in the second (middle) layer, and one output neuron. In each neuron, "summation" takes

Figure 2.   Depiction of a 3-layer neural network. Neurons are described as N_{ij}, where i = the layer and j = the placement of the neuron in the layer. Weights are described as W_{ijk}, where i = the pair of layers, j = the source neuron, and k = the destination neuron.

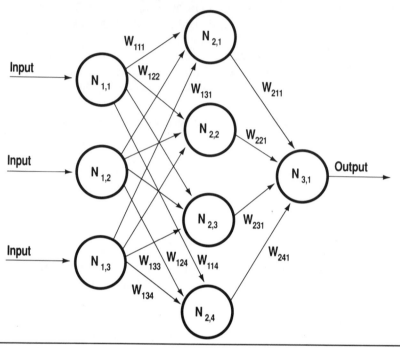

place, that is, all stimuli targeted at that neuron are summed. The "transfer function" (which defines how a neuron responds to varying levels of stimulation at its inputs) is then applied, and the neural output(s) is then "fed" via interconnections that vary in strength (as specified by interconnection "weights") to neurons in the second ("hidden" or "middle") layer. The neurons in the hidden layer respond accordingly, summing their inputs and passing them through their transfer functions, and the resultant neural outputs are again passed through interconnections to the third or output layer. Summation again takes place and the transfer function(s) is again applied to obtain the output(s) from the neural network. Neural networks involving more than three layers follow the same basic design.[1]

How Does a Neural Network Learn?

While neural network technology is available in the shell or programming language, there are a lot of tasks to make successful use of it. Unlike expert systems, which require the knowledge engineer to enter rules, neural networks learn from past experience. The system developer must therefore take the role of a teacher and provide

---

[1] From "Developing Neural Networks for Trading" by Jeffrey Owen Katz, *Technical Analysis of Stocks and Commodities,* Vol. 10, No. 4 (April 1992) © 1992, Technical Analysis, Inc. Used with permission.

the network with adequate training examples, i.e., provide an adequate past from which the system can learn. The difficulties in developing a neural network are in finding and effectively "massaging" historical data into training examples or "facts" that highlight patterns so that neural networks can learn efficiently and not be put astray or confused. As previously mentioned, training a neural network involves repeatedly presenting pairs of inputs and desired outputs (facts) to the network. This is done so that the network can "learn," based on examples of past occurrences, how to make accurate predictions or classifications.

During the training process, the strengths of the "weights," which form the connections between the layers of the network, are continuously adjusted in order to maximize the correspondence between the network's actual outputs and the "targets" (desired outputs). Within the trading community, the "back-propagation learning algorithm" is the most frequently used "model" for determining how the network is to adjust the weights (connection strengths) in response to a training fact. It is through such adjustments to the connection strengths that learning occurs.

A new neural network is usually initialized with a random set of weights; training then begins. The network engages in a kind of "hypothesis testing" in which it makes "guesses" about the targets or desired outputs. It does this on the basis of the data just received and the theories, or "constructs," about the market that it has thus far formed. If the forecast is wrong, the learning algorithm adjusts the weights in such a way as to make the network's output better agree with the target. Training then moves on to the next "fact," which consists of input data for the network and a target against which the network's output can be compared. Training continues as additional facts are fed to the network and corrections made to the weights, that is, to the internal construction of its world. This process is repeated as long as the network trains. As training proceeds, the correspondence between the network's outputs and the targets usually improves, and so the quality of the forecasts increases. Finally, there comes a point when additional training yields little improvement in the results. Training is then terminated and the network is examined to evaluate its performance on the data on which it was trained, as well as on data it has never seen before (the latter to determine whether the network can "generalize" or successfully apply what it has learned to new situations). If the training is judged to have been successful and the network is producing accurate forecasts, then it can be used for trading.

Example of Neural Network Systems Development

Instead of obtaining knowledge from an expert trader, the neural systems developer needs to collect a variety of data series that are considered to be relevant to the matter he or she is trying to predict, e.g., to buy or sell an option on the S&P 500. Since there is no expert to guide the developer, this can be a difficult task. It is absolutely critical to massage that data in a way that will highlight the aspects that are relevant so that the network will effectively learn, rather than go astray or develop a learning disability. There is bound to be some difficulty in this for the beginner. When files of examples are assembled through the process of massaging the raw data, it is important to make sure that there are a sufficient number of examples so that two sets of examples can be composed: one for training and one for testing. *The training set hopefully will be fairly large so that the network will be forced to form generali-zations instead of memorizing the few examples presented to it.* Next comes the process of training the network, then testing it. The usual shell will have some form of routine to assess the importance of the various inputs to the model. It is most likely that the developer will then need to go back, modify the preprocessing, possibly even find new raw data to improve the model, alter the method of data massaging, return to the training/testing, go back to the data and then to the training, in an iterative process of refinement.

The first commercially available pretrained neural network forecasting system (Scientific Consultant Services' The Predictor™, later known as NexTurn™) was for the S&P 500. It employed a simple feed-forward/back-propagation neural network to predict, at each day's close, whether that close would become a low, a high, or neither, in the context of the prices for the next several days; that is, would the next three or four closes be greater than today's close in a currently down-trending market, or would they be less than today's close in a currently up-trending market? The neu-ral network attempted to mark turning points *as they happened,* so that the trader could enter the market at the best possible times. The input to the neural network was the last 25 days of price changes, properly normalized. This simple model worked rather well for about one year, real-time, before its performance deteriorated. In fact, there were many signals that were nothing short of uncanny! Figure 3 (Katz, 1992)

Figure 3. **The output values of a neural network trained to detect bottoms in the S&P 500. Values above 40.00 indicate a rally is due.**

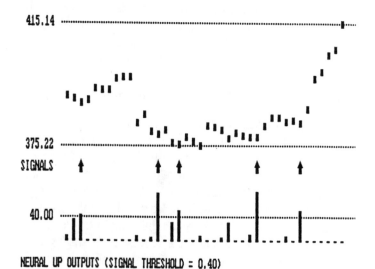

CLOSING PRICES AND NEURAL OUTPUTS FOR THE S&P 500 CASH INDEX
11/1/91 to 12/30/91

shows the closing prices for the S&P index and the output of the network designed to detect bottoms from which the S&P would rise.

Developing a profitable neural network trading system is not easy: Expect a lot of hard work. Of course, the same could be said to the prospective developer of any kind of trading system. This is because the "efficient market hypothesis," while not *entirely* true, is *close* to true: In the market, there are very weak signals buried in a sea of noise. One must search for tiny islands of inefficiency upon which one can capitalize. And, since markets are close to zero-sum games, other intelligent and re-sourceful players have to be outwitted—you are not the only one searching for those islands of inefficiency!

We do not mean to imply that it is impossible to develop successful trading systems, whether neural or otherwise. In fact, several of our clients have produced incredibly profitable systems. But enter the game knowing that there will be a lot of hard work along the way and that, most of the time, effort will be expended in the search for good data (variables) and the optimal "massaging" or preprocessing thereof.

In Chapter 2, "Neural Networks in Trading," we will discuss in greater detail the practical development of trading systems using neural networks. Other authors in this anthology shall also be contributing their knowledge of neurals in finance. There-fore, rather than risk redundancy, in this section we have simply attempted to convey an understanding of neural network technology and its history, and have saved the discussion of considerations in and illustrations of trading system development for later.

GENETIC ALGORITHMS

Genetic algorithms are not strictly a class of AI technology, but instead belong to the field of artificial life (AL). They represent step-by-step procedures ("algorithms") that attempt to implement, on the computer, parts of nature's own "optimization" proc-esses. Nature optimizes, or evolves, its organisms through an adaptive process involv-ing a combination of randomizing, recombining, and selecting forces. Similarly, genetic algorithms use randomization, recombination, and selection to "breed" a solu-tion to an optimization problem. They can be used to find the best set of model parameters, rules, neural network architectures, and connection strengths—even to evolve hybrid systems—through a process of breeding better and better solutions. Genetic algorithms have a *very* wide range of potential applications.

History

Genetic algorithms came on the scene about 20 years ago with the appearance of a book by mathematician/psychologist John Holland (1975). Extrapolating from models in biology and economics, Holland developed a genetic optimization algorithm. Ge-netic algorithms, however, became popular in the computer sciences only about five years ago (Yuret and de la Maza, 1994). It is only in the past year or so that genetic algorithms have really caught the attention of traders and financial analysts. In that time, a number of commercial software products have appeared: EOS VBX by Man Machine Interfaces, Inc.; Evolver by Axcelis, Inc.; and our own LOGIVOLVE™ for C and for Visual Basic. LOGIVOLVE™ was the first publicly available tool kit for implementing "neurogenetics" (a term that we coined and a technology that is now patent pending), i.e., it combines genetic algorithms with neural networks (Katz and McCormick, 1994b). Later, a number of vendors added a genetic training option to their neural development shells as an alternative training method to back-propagation.

To our knowledge, articles on genetic algorithms began to appear in major financial periodicals only during the past few years. The May 1993 issue of *Futures* contained an article that described the nature of genetic algorithms and discussed a project being undertaken at the Santa Fe Institute in New Mexico: "Richard Palmer, Brian Arthur, Blake LeBaron and John Holland have created a virtual stock market with 100 traders/agents that are actually computer programs. These programs trade a mythical stock issue among themselves. The researchers hope to learn why markets behave the way they do and how traders learn to trade profitably" (Burke, 1993, p. 26).

Among the other articles was one that appeared in the March 1994 issue of *AI Expert*. The author described how "classifier systems," another rule-based pattern-matching technique, are being evolved to model consumer choice behavior (Oliver, 1994). Another article, published in the June 1994 issue of *Technical Analysis of Stocks and Commodities,* was on the use of genetic algorithms to "breed" trading systems (Yuret and de la Maza, 1994): The authors used simple LISP rules as the basis for this system, which used genetic algorithms to evolve the rule sets.

The presence of such publications seems to indicate the growing interest in using genetic algorithms to solve practical problems. In the financial world, genetic algorithms seem to be today where neural networks were in the late 1980s: The first volley of papers and software has just occurred.

Part of what has kept more people from using genetic algorithms is the absence of easy-to-use shells or "canned" systems. Genetic algorithms are *very* general algorithms and are not yet easily amenable to slick graphic-user interface (GUI) presentations, that is, not without great loss of generality or power. Tool vendors have, therefore, emphasized erector sets that may be used to build a variety of solutions. General purpose programming languages provide the greatest flexibility and are the first step in developing a visual shell; perhaps that is why most tools currently take the form of libraries for programmers. Ways to package the power and generality of genetic algorithms in forms that are more suitable to less sophisticated users are, in all likelihood, down the road a little. Application-specific genetic algorithms will probably appear first in "friendlier" GUI dress, as they do not require the complete flexibility that might be needed for general problem solving across a variety of domains.

How Do Genetic Algorithms Work?

To evolve solutions to problems, it is first necessary to define "entities" or individuals (i.e., potential solutions) with behaviors that are specified by chains of codes (analogous to genes on chromosomes or strands of DNA). The codes in the chains must "map to," or specify, rules or rule fragments (either fuzzy or crisp), connection weights or neural architectures, parameters (numbers), or other such elements that comprise the parts of solutions to a problem, i.e., the determinants of an individual solution's behavior. In addition, a means of rating or ranking potential solutions, in terms of how well they solve the specified problem (i.e., an evaluation or "fitness" function) is needed. Also required is an algorithm for mating pairs of potential solutions (i.e., the chains of code referred to earlier) in order to obtain offspring or "child" solutions. Finally, a regime is needed for selecting pairs of solutions to mate, the number of children to produce, and for weeding the population in order to remove the "less fit" solutions from the population while encouraging the proliferation of "more fit" entities; this is comparable to "natural selection" in biology. The problem is then solved using the following steps:

1. Create a population of random, distinct individuals. These potential solutions will, of course, be mostly terrible. But there is no need to worry at this point about the quality of these solutions, as you will soon see.

2. "Breed" additional population members by mating pairs of existing individuals. A combination of "mutation" and "crossover," and perhaps other genetic operations, will probably be used in the mating process. "Mutation" introduces new elements or variation into the population, while "crossover" allows for recombination of existing elements, elements being regarded as codes or series of codes that represent fragments of potential solutions. It might be desirable to make the number of children, for any set of parents, dependent on the "fitness" of the parents so that better fragments accumulate in the population and have more chances to recombine.

3. Weed out the poorer solutions from the population, that is, perform "selection."

4. Check the fitness of the solutions in the current population. If these are inadequate, go back to step 2 and repeat the breeding and selection process until either a satisfactory solution is "evolved" or the developer gets fed up.

The basic idea is that good solution fragments accumulate and recombine in the population, while bad fragments decline in frequency and are weeded out, as generation after generation of solutions goes through mating and selection.

Mutation prevents the population from reaching a quick dead end because it constantly introduces new problem-solving fragments (new genes or codes) into the evolving population of solutions.

This is the essence of how problems may be solved, how "optimization" may be performed, using a simulation of the evolutionary process described by Charles Darwin.

Example of How Genetic Algorithms Are Applied

To illustrate the use of genetic algorithms, let us apply this methodology to the fairly simple problem of optimizing the parameters of a simple trading system that consists of four moving averages. The first three moving averages will be used to compute an MACD (or moving average convergence/divergence oscillator) and a signal line; the fourth moving average will simply be compared to the current price. The system will be "long" if the MACD is above the signal line and the price is above the fourth moving average. We envision a system in which the MACD is slow and smooth and is used as a trend filter, and in which the fourth moving average is "short" and is used to trigger trades in the direction of the longer trend. The system will be short if the MACD is below the signal line and the price is below the moving average. It will be out of the market for all other configurations of the MACD, signal line, moving average, and price.

To apply genetic optimization, we must first define a "chain of objects" that maps to the four parameters. In this case, we can simply let the first object on the chain be an integer that specifies the period of the first moving average of the MACD; the second object can be an integer that specifies the period of the second moving average; and so on. We then have to create a population of such chains, with each chain being a unique, random sequence of four integers in the specified range.

Each of these chains specifies an individual system, each with different trading behaviors. Using our "fitness function," we evaluate the trading behavior of each individual and save these evaluations in memory. During the course of our evaluations, we will find that some individuals will trade better (profit more or lose less) than others; most will produce losing trades. We then mate pairs of individuals in order to generate offspring. We might also choose to generate more offspring (mate more often) from those parents that evidence greater "fitness" (i.e., better trading behavior). We further apply selection and remove a number of the worse traders from the growing population. We repeat this process of evaluation, breeding, and selection again and again. After several generations, we will probably have a number of individuals that represent the best sets of parameters for a system of the kind we have specified. How does this happen?

In the mating process, we combined the two parent chains of objects by snipping each chain in one or more places and "recombining" the snippets to form a new chain. For instance, Parents A and B might be represented by the following chains:

$$\text{Parent A:} \quad A_1 - A_2 - A_3 - A_4$$
$$\text{Parent B:} \quad B_1 - B_2 - B_3 - B_4$$

We then recombine these parent chains to produce the following offspring chain:

$$\text{Offspring:} \quad A_1 - B_2 - B_3 - B_4$$

The particular snippets we take from each parent are determined by a random number generator and will vary each time mating occurs.

We may also "mutate" one or more of the objects on the chain (in this case, integers) to obtain altered or new objects (different integers). We might have one individual system defined by the following series:

$$12 \quad\quad 26 \quad\quad 9 \quad\quad 5$$

This string of integers means that the system has an MACD computed from the difference between a 12 and 26 bar moving average, a signal line generated by a 9 bar moving average of the MACD, and a 5 bar moving average against which to compare the price.

Another individual in the population might be defined by the following series:

5   10   3   10

If we mate these two series, we obtain an offspring that is comprised of characteristics from each parent. As a result of crossover, the new string may be:

12   26   9   10

Mutation might occur and result in the following as the actual "child" system-controlling chromosome gene string:

12   20   9   10

Note: This child has a very similar MACD and signal line to that of the first parent (except for mutuation of the longer moving average of the MACD) and the moving average from the second parent.

If both parents were good traders, it probably means that there is something especially good about the particular MACD and moving average used—perhaps the parameters jibe with cycles in the market. The recombining of these "good" components from different parent systems may result in an even better child; it could also result in a combination that does not work. But, eventually, good fragments of good systems will be recombined in good ways and yield a great system. This becomes more likely as good fragments accumulate in the population, fragments that are contributors to the parents' good performance. Bad fragments are, of course, weeded out by selection.

Why is mutation important? It introduces new elements (variation) into the population and so prevents stagnation (helps avoid the kinds of problems that might result from inbreeding). Over time, mutation leads to the appearance and accumulation of *new,* good fragments in the population. Therefore, even if the original population did not have the necessary fragments that, when optimally recombined, would result in the desired performance, such fragments will slowly be introduced and proliferate. In this way, the process *uses* randomness—in the form of random recombination of existing strings or chain fragments, and of random perturbations in such fragments, causing the introduction of new fragments—together with selection to steer the random process in the right direction.

The elements on the chain, in the example, were simple parameters. They might be weights in a neural network, or rules from an expert system, or, in the case of "hybrid entities," (which we will discuss below) some combination of both.

How is a genetic algorithm implemented for rules? Yuret and de la Maza (1994) illustrated the use of a genetic algorithm to evolve rules in LISP to trade the OEX! Consider a string of rules such as the following:

((> (C 1) (C 2)) (> (C 2) (C 3)) (> (C 3) (C 4)))

This string of rules may be regarded as the "genome" of one individual entity or trading system. This string is a LISP language statement that is TRUE (meaning, in this case, "be long the market") if the close one day ago is greater than the close two days ago, *and* the close two days ago is greater than the close three days ago, *and* the close three days ago is greater than the close four days ago.

Another member of the population might be:

$$((< (C\ 1)\ (C\ 2))\ (< (C\ 2)\ (C\ 3))\ (< (C\ 3)\ (C\ 4)))$$

This string is a LISP language statement that is TRUE (meaning, in this case, "be long the market") if the close one day ago is less than the close two days ago, *and* the close two days ago is less than the close three days ago, *and* the close three days ago is less than the close four days ago.

Mating the two might, through crossover at the places marked by the arrows, yield a child such as:

$$((> (C\ 1)\ (C\ 2))\ (< (C\ 2)\ (C\ 3))\ (< (C\ 3)\ (C\ 4)))$$

In other words, the child was formed by taking the following condition from the first parent:

$$(> (C\ 1)\ (C\ 2))$$

and combining it with the following conditions from the second parent:

$$(< (C\ 2)\ (C\ 3))\ (< (C\ 3)\ (C\ 4))$$

Yuret and de la Maza were able to evolve sets of rules "that are accurate more than 90 percent of the time and predict moves that are, on average, more than two OEX points" on in-sample data (1994, p. 62). On out-of-sample data, the accuracy was about 70 percent and the OEX move was about 0.88 point.

Crossover could occur at several places (randomly chosen) in a large string, if one wishes. In LOGIVOLVE™, we use multiple random crossovers when mating neural networks. In the case of rules like the ones above, crossover can create longer or shorter series; strings of conditions or rules need not be of fixed length. And mutation could include the deletion of a condition from the chain. Finally, crossover can be treated as yielding two children, not just one.

Currently, there is no such thing in the field of genetic algorithms as the "best" scheme to use; we suspect that no one scheme will always be optimal but that different ones will be required for different problems. As long as there is a process of recombination (crossover) and another (mutation) involving random introduction of new elements, together with, of course, selection, the algorithm will, to one degree or another, be able to solve a wide range of problems with reasonable efficiency.

Hybrid Entities

Because of the generality and power of genetic algorithms, they may be used to develop "hybrid entities," which are systems composed of more than one kind of building block. For example, genetic algorithms can be used to evolve a trading system composed of several parameter-determined indicators, one or more neural networks, and a bunch of rules, so as to possess the user-specified behavior or performance, e.g., highest total profitability with a minimum drawdown. The genetic algorithm will find the set of parameters and neural network connection weights and rules that, *as a whole,* create a system that will yield the desired overall results. The trick is to find an appropriate coding method that will map objects on chains (the alleles on the chromosomes) to the actual elements that determine the hybrid entity's behavior. In the above case, the "objects" on the chain may be the parameters, connection weights (real numbers), and rules that make up the system, arranged in a specified order.

A tool kit for evolving hybrid entities or systems that contain neural networks, feedback loops, simple rules, and parameter-controlled elements is commercially available (i.e., Scientific Consultant Services' LOGIVOLVE™). One user I have spoken to has been very successful in evolving a highly profitable S&P trading system that is always in the market and has better than 90 percent winning trades!

CONCLUSION

Trading the markets is becoming more and more difficult and competitive as the technology advances and is used by a greater number of traders. Since playing the markets is close to, though not quite, a zero-sum game (at any given instant, for every trader who wins, there must be someone on the opposite side of the trade who loses), every edge is critical. Those trading without the assistance of AI are in a weak position and, in all probability, will wind up on the losing side. This is even indicated in the title of a recent article in *AI in Finance:* "Traders Using Nets Beat Those Who Don't" (Loofbourrow, John and Tod, 1994). It is, therefore, imperative to become familiar with the use of AI in trading if one wishes to stay competitive as a trader in the future.

Because the number of traders—institutional as well as individual—using this technology is increasing each day, you not only have to keep up, you have to keep one step ahead. You must arm yourself against the competition by diligent study (whether you picked up this book to satisfy your curiosity about AI or to further your understanding of the technology, be assured that, by the last page, you will be better prepared to face the competition and play the game). You must also further your knowledge through hands-on experience. Therefore, follow up on the suggested reading sections at the end of the chapters and try out some of the AI tools that are available. Every page you read and every program you experiment with will add to your edge and help you come out a winner!

REFERENCES

Burke, Gibbons. "Good Trading a Matter of Breeding?" *Futures* (May 1993): 26–29.

Holland, John. *Adaptation in Natural and Artificial Systems.* Ann Arbor, MI: University of Michigan Press, 1975.

Jurik, Mark. "Consumer's Guide to Neural Network Software." *Futures* (July 1993): 36–42.

Katz, Jeffrey Owen. "Developing Neural Network Forecasters for Trading." *Technical Analysis of Stocks and Commodities* (April 1992): 58–68.

Katz, Jeffrey Owen, and Donna L. McCormick. "Vendor's Forum: The Evolution of N-TRAIN. *PCAI* (March/April 1993): 44–46.

Katz, Jeffrey Owen, and Donna L. McCormick. "Neural Networks: Some Advice to Beginners." *Trader's Catalog and Resource Guide*, in press. (1994a)

Katz, Jeffrey Owen, and Donna L. McCormick. "Neurogenetics and Its Use in Trading System Development." *NeuroVe$t Journal* (July/August, 1994b).

Loofbourrow, John and Tod. "Traders Using Nets Beat Those Who Don't." *AI in Finance*, (premier issue, 1994): 51–59.

Minsky, M., and S. Papert. *Perceptrons.* Cambridge, MA: MIT Press, 1969.

Oliver, Jim. "Finding Decision Rules With Genetic Algorithms." *AI Expert* (March 1994): 32–39.

Packert, Bonnie. "Vendor's Forum: Fuzzy Decisions. Designing CubiCalc." *PCAI* (May/June 1994): 28–30.

Viot, Greg. "Fuzzy Logic: Concepts to Constructs." *AI Expert* (November 1993): 26–33.

Walsh, Birrell. "Fuzzy Logic: The American Market." *AI Expert* (November 1993): 35–39.

Yuret, Deniz, and Michael de la Maza. "A Genetic Algorithm System for Predicting the OEX." *Technical Analysis of Stocks and Commodities* (June 1994): 58–64.

SUGGESTED READING

Davis, Lawrence, ed. *Handbook of Genetic Algorithms.* New York: Van Nostrand Reinhold, 1991.

Fishman, Mark B., Dean S. Barr, and Walter J. Loick. "Artificial Intelligence and Market Analysis." *Technical Analysis of Stocks and Commodities* (bonus issue, 1993): 18–27.

Gonzalez, Avelino J., and Douglas D. Dankel. *The Engineering of Knowledge-Based Systems: Theory and Practice.* Englewood Cliffs, NJ: Prentice Hall, 1993.

Parsaye, Kamran, and Marc Chignell. *Expert Systems for Experts.* New York: John Wiley and Sons, 1988.

Trippi, Robert R., and Efraim Turban, eds. *Neural Networks in Finance and Investing.* Chicago: Probus Publishing Co., 1993.

Yager, Ronald, and Lotfi Zadeh, eds. *Fuzzy Sets, Neural Networks, and Soft Computing.* New York: Van Nostrand Reinhold, 1994.

Chapter 2

NEURAL NETWORKS
IN TRADING

Jeffrey Owen Katz, President
Donna L. McCormick, Vice President
SCIENTIFIC CONSULTANT SERVICES, INC.

In Chapter 1, we briefly covered some of the basics needed to understand neural network technology and its use in the trading community. In this chapter, we hope to provide you with some practical information that you can use in the development of your own successful neural network systems. As one of the leading providers of neural network technology to the financial markets, we constantly receive calls from people who either are curious about neural technology or are actually in the process of developing their own neural trading systems. This chapter is based on the most frequently asked questions we receive, so you should find that the following pages directly address many of your own questions regarding the use and development of neural trading systems. We have tried to categorize the questions and answers and to present them in the order in which they might arise. We are sure that you will come up with questions of your own as you proceed further along this road; when you do, don't hesitate to contact us and we will be happy to provide whatever answers we can.

THE NATURE OF NEURAL NETWORKS

Q: What does a neural network do?

A: A neural network is a form of multiple regression. Like regression, it takes a number of input variables and uses them to predict a target. Imagine you want to predict crop yield (the "dependent variable," or "target") on the basis of temperature and rainfall (the "independent variables," or "inputs"). In a *linear* multiple regression, you would model your data as: predicted crop yield = $a + b*$ rainfall $+ c*$ temperature; where a, b, and c are "parameters" that would be determined by a statistical procedure. Basically, you are fitting, in a least-squares sense, a line, plane, or hyperplane (depending on the number of independent variables) to the points in your data space. In the example above, you are fitting a plane: the x and y axes represent rainfall and temperature (respectively), and the height of the plane at each x,y coordinate pair represents predicted crop yield.

A feed-forward, back-propagation neural network implements a particular form of multiple *nonlinear* regression: the plane or hyperplane of multiple linear regression is replaced by an n-dimensional *curved* surface with peaks and valleys. You have a number of input variables and you are trying to find a nonlinear mapping that will give you an output from the network that is in some way a best fit to the target. In the network, this is accomplished through the nonlinear elements called neurons, which are connected; the weights of these connections are adjusted to fit the surface to the data. The training algorithm is used to adjust the weights so as to get that particular curved surface that best fits the data points. As in a standard multiple regression model, where you have to find the coefficients of the regression to define the slope of the plane or hyperplane, with a curved surface you have to find the parameters (weights) that will give you the particular curves with valleys and hills in just the rights places so that they optimally fit the data. In this respect, neural networks, like multiple linear regression, may be considered a data modeling technique.

Q: Can you think of a nonmathematical, nonstatistical analogy to neural networks?

A: Paired-associate learning, or pattern recognition. For example, you are presented with a number of items on the left side of a sheet (input variables) and then you see an item on the right side of the sheet (target); you have to form some kind of association between the pattern you see on the left and the item on the right, so that when you are shown another pattern, you can make a guess as to what the item on the right side of the sheet will be before it is seen. You are basically learning to recognize recurrent patterns. This is a simplified description of what neural networks do: They make excellent pattern recognizers, which is one reason neural networks are of interest to traders.

Q: What does feed-forward mean? What about back-propagation?

A: "Feed-forward" refers to network architecture. "Back-propagation" is a training method.

A feed-forward network is one in which inputs feed into a layer of neurons; the outputs from that layer of neurons are then fed into another layer of neurons, the outputs of which, in turn, connect into another layer of neurons, and so on until there are connections to the output neurons, which become the outputs of the network. *The signals propagate in only one direction: from input to layer to layer to layer to output, always moving forward, hence the term "feed-forward."* The layers are usually fully connected with one another, although they do not have to be (we have a version of N-TRAIN® that allows partially connected feed-forward networks).

Back-propagation is a learning algorithm, that is, a way of adjusting the parameters—or, in the case of a feed-forward network, the connection weights—in order to effect learning of the training data by the network. Back-propagation is actually a form of "steepest-descent gradient optimization," meaning that the weights are moved in small steps in those directions that make the network's performance improve most rapidly. Back-propagation is not the only way to "train" a network: You may, for example, "train" a network by using genetic algorithms: Instead of modifying the weights using gradient descent, you breed sets of weights until you achieve a good network. The final result looks much the same as a feed-forward network trained using back-propagation; the only difference is that the weights are obtained through mutation and recombination, i.e., "breeding," rather than through gradient descent.

Back-propagation is a fairly standard algorithm, but there are small variations on it which people have used to try to speed up convergence. For example, many tools will implement back-propagation with "momentum," that is, with a small modification to back-propagation where you are not letting the ball roll in the direction of steepest descent on each step, but where you are asking, "What is the previous direction in which the ball rolled?" and you add a proportion of that direction to the direction the ball now wants to roll in, and then move it in that direction. That methodology is actually not very stable: It can produce "chaotic" oscillations in certain data sets and, since you do not know which data sets this will occur in, it adds uncertainty to the training process. If you have a data set on which it really works, however, it may speed the training 20 percent, but is it worth the finickiness? It also takes extra computation time, which may use up that 20 percent advantage. There are other approaches to gradient descent that yield greater benefits, e.g., "conjugate gradient" methods; however, a discussion of these is beyond the scope of this chapter.

Q: What paradigms should I use?

A: There are many different paradigms. The dominant paradigms most useful for traders and financial analysts are the Kohonen networks (which are good for clustering, preclassification, and preprocessing); Kohonen LVQ, or Learning Vector Quantization (which is a supervised Kohonen network useful for classification); and the standard feed-forward back-propagation networks (useful for a wide variety of problems). Of the other paradigms, some are only of academic interest, others may be of practical interest in the future, and some are currently being researched. In most instances, the novice would be well advised to begin with feed-forward, back-propagation models, and to branch out from there as his or her understanding grows.

Q: What is the advantage of genetic algorithms over neural networks?

A: Genetic algorithms (GAs) provide an optimization technique, so in that respect, you cannot really speak of the "advantage" of genetics over neural networks. Genetics can, in fact, be applied to neural networks (i.e., "neurogenetics," a term coined by Katz). For example, instead of back-propagation, you can use genetic optimization to determine the optimal weights in a feed-forward or recurrent network. You may also use genetic algorithms to find the best parameters for trading systems that have no neural networks in them at all. Genetic algorithms provide a very efficient search strategy, which is effective in finding the global minima or maxima. Also, GAs are not subject to some of the restrictions of back-propagation.

If you are trying to solve a problem that involves a multiplicity of rules, various parameters, various indicators, and one or more neural networks, and you want to solve the problem as a whole, genetics may be the way to go. You can breed trading systems to have the properties and behavior that you want—e.g., to not overtrade or undertrade, to keep the drawdown within constraints, etc. It would be time-consuming to breed such a system, but it might result in large profits down the line!

DATA FILES

Q: What is a fact file?

A: Fact files contain examples (cases, records) that may be used to either train or test a neural network. Each "fact," or example, in a fact file consists of a number of input or independent variables, and one or more targets or dependent variables. For example, one fact in an S&P prediction model might contain the last 10 price changes of the S&P as the inputs, together with the next price change in the S&P as the target. Each fact would be a different set of 10 inputs or 10 price changes, followed by the next price change. If you had a data series of 100 days of S&P data, your first fact might consist of the price changes for bars 1 through 10, with the target being the price change for bar 11. The next fact might be the price changes for bars 2 through 11, with the target being the price change for bar 12, etc., throughout your series. With 100 days of data, you would end up with about 90 facts. Usually you want to provide the network with as many facts or examples to learn from as possible.

Q: What is a "training set"?

A: A training sample is a fact file that contains the facts or examples that are going to be used to construct ("train") the model. It is the sample of data on which you are going to fit your parameters, train your network, estimate your statistics.

Q: What is the "testing set"?

A: The testing set is a fact file that contains a set of examples that the network has never seen, and that will be used to test the network. Testing sets are used to help determine whether the model holds up on out-of-sample data. When you start trading, it will be on data that the network has never seen before and has never trained on. Testing the trained network on such data is a way to get some sense of security or confidence that the model is going to hold up on data it has never previously seen before you begin trading.

PREPARING DATA FOR THE NETWORK

Q: What is meant by "preprocessing"?

A: "Preprocessing" refers to massaging the data and assembling it into fact files for training, testing, or running. *Preprocessing is the most critical aspect of neural network development;* one that can make or break your system.

Q: What are some forms of preprocessing that you have found useful?

A: There are many useful preprocessing techniques. The primary goal is to highlight for the neural network any relevant features in the data and to downplay irrelevant ones so that the network will easily learn the relevant relationships in the data and not be put astray or confused by the irrelevant ones.

For example, if you are not too experienced, you might take the last 10 prices to predict the next price; this is very bad preprocessing because it is the *absence* of preprocessing: you are just feeding the network the raw prices. By doing this, you will get a correlation in the high .90s, but it will not necessarily be useful for trading. Why? If you look at the S&P over the past 10 years, it has ranged from 100 to 400; in any one day, however, it does not move very much. So yesterday's price, over that time span, correlates very highly with today's price; in fact, the best predictor of today's price is yesterday's price! If we know the S&P is 395 today, we know that tomorrow it is, most likely, going to be between 390 and 400, not 100. The network will immediately lock onto this kind of relationship and give you a model with a .98 correlation and will estimate tomorrow's price as, basically, today's price. Will this be useful for trading? No, not at all.

When trading, you are not concerned with absolute price as much as you are with change in price. You may be concerned with absolute price in the sense of wanting to know where to set a limit order, but then it should be expressed as price relative to some set-point. If you want to train a network to look at market direction, you might use simple preprocessing on the inputs: Calculate price *differences* rather than the price itself. This will remove the absolute price, which is probably irrelevant. Another approach would be to subtract the mean of the past prices from each individual price.

The creation of special kinds of indicators would be another way to preprocess data. For example, has a new high been made by this stock within the past month? Yes (1) or No (0). This can serve as one of your input variables for the neural network. Perhaps you have noticed that, when trading the S&P, the opening price acts as support or resistance throughout the day. You might, therefore, want to create a variable that represents "support at opening price," and that takes on the value of 1 if the price is within a few ticks above the open and takes on a value of zero for every other price. We have found, as another example of a derived variable indicator (in this case, one for certain kinds of stocks), the correlation of a simple linear regression of price on time for the past 18 months tends to be a good predictor for price change over the next week and makes a good neural input variable. Fuzzy logic is a useful tool for doing this type of preprocessing. You can easily create variables that represent "price near support," "open interest rapidly dropping," or "market very overbought" that may serve as inputs to a neural network. If you are concerned with cycles, you might preprocess your data to deemphasize noncyclic activity, e.g., trending behavior and noise.

Another suggestion: Instead of using data from each bar to the previous bar, use data from the previous bar, the bar before it, the bar before that, and then jump two bars back, then four bars back, then eight bars back. The exact rate of increase in span, of course, is up to you. In this way, you can span a longer period of time with fewer input variables and without much loss of important information.

Preprocessing so that the most salient aspects are emphasized, and selecting appropriate variables that contain a lot of relevant information, are probably the two most important factors in determining success with neural networks. These two factors, if optimal, may even help compensate for weaknesses in the other vital aspects of development work, e.g., the selection of proper network parameters.

Q: Are there any circumstances under which raw data is acceptable?

A: There are certain financial modeling problems in which "raw" data is appropriate for direct input to a neural network. If you are training a neural network to price options (an alternative to the Black Schoals model), you may use variables like time to expiration, interest rate, volatility, and so on, in their raw form. You might improve the results a little by minor transformations, e.g., instead of option price, you might use option premium as the target. But, basically, you would be using input variables that are fairly close to the raw data.

Fundamental data, such as M1 and M2—the money flow indicators—and long-term interest rates might, for example, be used "raw" to predict the theoretical "fair value" of the S&P.

Q: Do targets also need to be preprocessed?

A: Yes. It is generally worthwhile to "massage" the network's target as well. A trader starting out in neural network development might be tempted to take the last 10 days of price data and try to predict the next price bar; after learning a little more about neural networks, he or she would be more inclined to give the network the task of predicting the next price change.

A more sophisticated kind of target processing for a network might be to take the slope of a "reverse moving average" (one that works its way back from the future) as the target. In this way, you smooth the data to reduce the amount of noise in what you are predicting and, therefore, provide the network with a variable that may be easier to predict.

Q: What is "noisy" data?

A: All data has noise in it to one degree or another. When we discuss "noise," we are referring to characteristics that make the data hard to model, that make it close to random, or that hide obvious patterns. To give a concrete example, let us take data that relates how far the accelerator in a car is pushed down to the speed the car is traveling; that is very "unnoisy" data: If you plot the points of how far the accelerator is down on your x-axis and how fast the car is going on the y-axis, the points will all fall along a nice curved line—the farther down the peddle, the faster you are going. There will be some "topping out" (at some point, the line will plateau after rising steeply), but the points will all fit very closely to the line. If you try to model data like that with a neural network, you will get correlations in the .90s in both training and testing samples. There are nice, strong, clear relationships with very little noise.

On the other hand, you might be trying to receive a signal, to pick up a certain tone, from a distant low-power transmitter. This is very likely to be noisy data, more noisy to the extent that the transmitter is far from the receiver. The greater the amount of noise, the weaker the tone you want to detect. If you try to get a network to predict whether a tone is present as the transmitter gets farther away or lower in power—i.e., as the noise increases—the degree to which the network is able to accurately identify the presence of the tone at the receiving end will be less and less.

Data in the financial markets are particularly noisy. There are relationships in such data, but the relationships are fairly weak and buried under a sea of noise; the correlations will be fairly small even if they are sufficient to give you a trading edge. It also means you will need to "dig" for variables, and discover a massaging (preprocessing) that will give you an advantage—not an easy task.

Q: What is "difficult" data?

A: Data may be difficult for one of several reasons. A lot of noise makes data difficult. Data may also be difficult because of special characteristics: For example, if you have a process described by a surface with "poles" in it (poles are places on the surface that go to infinity and exhibit other strange kinds of behavior), a neural network may not yield a good model. Because of that, the data can be considered "difficult" but, if you knew what the underlying structure was and you had the equation, you could get an almost perfect correlation, and so the data could not be considered noisy.

Most of the relationships in market data are not going to be that difficult to model in this sense. However, difficult data can be found in the hard sciences and engineering, and can often be handled by using the right kind of transfer functions and giving sufficient attention to numerical stability. N-TRAIN®, for example, has been demonstrated to be able to solve certain equations and provide a good model in cases where other popular neural shells fail.

Q: How many facts do I need to train on? One vendor said that I needed to reduce the number of facts after I encountered problems training a network on his software. Could that explain my poor results in training and testing?

A: The answer here is fairly simple. Generally, assuming you can find *representative* facts or examples on which to train the network, the more facts the better. The more facts you have, the more likely that the results you get on the training set will be the same as those you get on the testing set, and the more likely you will have similar results in the future when actually trading.

The software that you were working with obviously had limitations and/or the vendor was misguided in terms of his knowledge of statistics. There are certain cases where you might not need many facts, where you can use a small sample and get good results. There are some cases where you cannot obtain a large sample that is representative. But as long as you can get representative examples (i.e., ones that represent the same universe and type of behavior in the market), the more facts the better.

We have routinely trained networks on problems with 100,000 facts and up! On small time frames—e.g., 3-minute bars on the S&P—there are 181 bars per day, which means that in six months you will have lots and lots of facts, and the sample will probably be representative. The network will take longer to train on such a large number of facts, and the correlations in the training sample will be lower because you cannot curve-fit as much, but the results will be much more likely to hold up in the future when you begin trading the system.

Sometimes training on a small sample will give you better results, usually because the sample is more representative or certain characteristics are more highlighted. For example, for one of our systems that uses weekly S&P data, models involving a number of indicators and fundamental data were trained on between 200 to 300 examples and did fairly well. It is a matter of experimentation.

Q: **How large a sample do I need, and what if there are lots of bars but only a few trades?**

A: Again, we suggest the largest *representative* sample you can get. If there are only a few trades out of lots and lots of bars, and some event you are looking for is a fairly rare one, you might want an even larger sample. Why? Because you want the number of good trades, or instances of the particular pattern you are looking for, to be represented often enough to give you good modeling. If some event is fairly rare, you would want at least 100 or so instances of the event, and it might take tens of thousands of bars of data to get that 100 cases. If you have too few instances of the event, you *will* run into problems.

Q: **What if you are trying to predict a major crash, such as the one that occurred in 1987?**

A: Think of it this way: From seeing one crash, can you predict other crashes? Probably not on a statistical basis. You would need at least several crashes and some minicrashes to get anywhere, otherwise you will be running the risk of gross curve-fitting. If you are trying to look for extremes in the market, you are better off looking for the largest moves that have occurred over some time span. Or you can try going back over a very long period of time. For example, if you go back 100 years on the S&P, you will find a few huge crashes and lots of smaller ones, and a lot of them will look the same, so you might find a useful pattern.

Q: **But if the S&P changed a few times over that period, e.g., in 1954 and 1983, would that still be a representative sample for this kind of analysis?**

A: You would have to try it and see. With regard to the major crashes, the essential market may not have changed all that much. We have plotted the 1929 crash and the few months preceding it, and we did the same for the 1987 crash and, laying one chart over the other, we were amazed at the similarity of the two curves.

Q: **What is meant by "scaling" the data?**

A: Scaling is a matter of adjusting the range of the data to fit the numerical range preferred by the neurons. This is normally accomplished within the neural network shell, rather than during data preprocessing. For example, price changes on the S&P may vary from 0 (no price change) up to perhaps +/−100 points, but networks do not like numbers with such a broad range; the network wants to see inputs that range between −1 or −2 to +1 or +2. Therefore, you will need to rescale the data by dividing all of your price changes by the absolute value of the largest price change; if the largest price change is 1, all the other price changes will be expressed relative to that, from 0 to +/−1, which will better fit the input range of the neural network. Scaling, in this respect, is almost always accomplished by the simple equation: $y = a + bx$, where y = the scaled variable, a = a constant peculiar to that variable, b = another constant, x = the unscaled variable. The stochastic oscillator, which varies between 0 and 100, could not be predicted with a network in which the output range is between 0 and 1, so you would rescale by, for example, taking $a = 0$, $b =$

0.01, and x = stochastic oscillator value, and use the above equation to obtain a value that ranges between 0 and 1.

Usually for inputs, if you are using linear followed by sigmoid or all sigmoid transfer functions, you would want a "standard deviation" type of scaling: Take the mean and the standard deviation of each input variable and express the input variable as a z-score, i.e., subtract the mean from the input variable and then divide that number by the standard deviation, so you are representing that variable in regard to the number of standard deviations it is above or below the mean; that becomes your input. For the output, you would want to scale so that you will span the whole range of the data: so that a network output of 1 maps to the highest target, and 0 to the lowest target.

SELECTING VARIABLES

Q: How do you find good variables to use as inputs to a neural network?

A: The prime consideration when trying to find good variables is whether they contain predictively useful information, i.e., information that will help the network generate predictions about the matter you are trying to forecast (the target). We usually recommend that neural network developers "prescreen" the variables they are considering. This is a step that would come after preprocessing the data, but before actually feeding the data to the network during training. One way that prescreening may be done is by taking thousands of variables, and evaluating their correlations with the target or desired outcome in order to determine which variables have the strongest correlations. You will find that most of the variables do not have any value according to this measure, but if you prescreen enough of them, you will definitely find some useful ones. Do this on a number of different subsamples. For example, break your stock data into 20 different months, which will give you 20 correlations for each variable. If you have a bunch of correlations on the same thing from different samples, you can get a good estimate of the stability of the relationship. You want variables that are going to highlight for the neural network those features or characteristics that are important (and that they will not necessarily learn on their own). You should note that correlation will detect only linear relationships, and so some "good" variables might slip through, but at least you can get a rough first-cut screening of your data.

The ultimate determinant of whether a variable is good is whether it contributes to a model. The RELCON utility in N-TRAIN®, for example, allows you to determine the importance of each variable to the neural model. In essence, RELCON extracts a variable from the model and reassesses the correlation of the network's output with the target: If the correlation declines substantially from the previous correlation (when the variable was still included in the model), then that variable was probably very important to the model, and the information it contributes cannot be reconstructed from the other variables; if the correlation does not decline substantially, then that variable probably was not very important. For example, if you pulled out a given variable and the correlation dropped from .5 to .2, you would know that it was an important variable that was contributing a lot to the model; if, on the other hand, the correlation only went from .5 to .48, then the variable probably is not contributing very much. REL-CON does this automatically for every variable in the model. Such information is valuable because it helps you design the simplest model possible so that you avoid curve-fitting. If your prescreening efforts provided you with 50 or 100 good variables, a utility such as RELCON will allow you to further reduce the model by discarding the variables that are least relevant to the overall performance of the model.

Q: How can I narrow down my initial search for good variables?

A: Begin your search by thinking of all those variables that might be fundamentally or intrinsically related to what you are trying to predict or detect. Also, try to find variables that are not being used by everyone: The market is more likely to be inefficient with respect to such less popular variables, i.e., they may have sustainable relationships that have not been eliminated from the market due to their use in everyone's systems.

If you are trying to predict the S&P, instead of just using prices alone, try, for instance, the future premium compared to its fair value: If the premium is way above the fair value, you can probably guess that program trading might kick in and that it will return to fair value very swiftly, so you might expect the futures to drop in price. Among previous price changes, you are probably likely to find price changes that correlate if you look at unusual time frames. For example, if you look for price changes back roughly 63 trading days, you might find some more substantial correlations than you would, e.g., five trading days ago. Why? Because earnings reports repeat and will contribute to a 63-trading day (one calendar quarter) rhythm in the market. If your time frames are right, you may pick up seasonality. On small cap stocks, if you look at the slope of the best fitting line to prices over the past year, or the past six months, you may get a better correlation. The same holds true for volume: Look at the best-fitting line, in the least-squares sense, and the correlation coefficient of that line, to volume. In other words, do not just do obvious things such as taking the last two or three volumes or the last four or five price changes; you will find that such an approach will generally yield poor results.

Q: I have a lot of variables that have low (and, on their own, relatively useless) correlations. Could these be collectively useful?

A: If you have enough cases (facts), you could try putting all those variables into a model and then running a utility like N-TRAIN®'s RELCON, which determines how much each variable contributes to the model. This would allow you to toss out the weaker variables. The danger you risk in doing that is making the model more complex, and the more complex the model, the more likely you are going to get curve-fitting, and the less likely you are going to get generalization to out-of-sample data. *Generally, there should be at least 10 to 50 times as many examples (or facts or cases) as there are variables.* Therefore, if you are trying to predict the price change of the S&P from today to tomorrow, and you only have 3,000 examples, do not exceed 50 to 100 variables. Why? If you are using a neural network that has three middle-layer neurons, and you have 100 input variables and one output, the network will have 300 connections; your 3,000 examples provides only 10 times as many examples as connections, which will increase the likelihood of curve-fitting. Therefore, it is important to get the total number of variables down, which means to prescreen them in some manner in order to find ones that have better relationships with the target. If the number of variables you are starting out with is very small, then you can probably rely on a utility like RELCON to do your screening.

Q: Can I or should I use fundamental data with neural networks? If so, are there any special preprocessing needs?

A: If there are fundamental data that bears on the problem, by all means use it! One principle to keep in mind in any trading system development effort is that, to the extent that there are relevant variables that are *heterogeneous* or different and that all contribute to the model, the better the results. In other words, if you have included price, you probably do not want to include five different measures of price, like five moving averages and the stochastics, because they will all be providing somewhat similar information. Therefore, adding more and more variables of that kind will not necessarily improve the model because they will not be contributing information that the other variables of that type have not already contributed. However, if you then add fundamental variables, which are not very highly correlated with these price variables, they will add new and different information to a model. If that information is also useful and predictive, you will get a better model.

Q: Can I use neural networks to recognize Elliott Waves?

A: Yes, if you understand Elliott Waves, and have sufficient programming skills to construct a specialized preprocessor and rule base that will allow certain features that characterize Elliott Wave movements to be extracted and fed to a neural network. It is a difficult problem, but one that can be done: Neural networks are good pattern recognizers, if the patterns are presented properly. The set-up and construction of targets, etc., will take a lot of careful work. It is not simply a matter of tossing some data at a network and hoping for great results. The same thing applies for those trying to incorporate Gann's work into a neural model.

Q: Basically, then, I cannot just throw a lot of raw data at a neural network and hope that it will come up with its own answers. It is not a magical black box.

A: It may be able to come up with some kind of result if you just toss in data and keep your fingers crossed. But the chances of success are very, very small. This is partly due to the competitive nature of the markets. Everyone tried doing just that when neural networks first came out and it may have worked for a while, but when everyone is doing it, there is no longer an edge. So you have to go beyond the crowd! The saying among computer hacks, "Garbage in, garbage out," applies here too. When it comes to the markets, 99.9 percent of the data is "noise," i.e., garbage, and there is a very small amount of "signal" or inefficiency that one can grab. What is present is buried under the garbage and you have to go digging for it.

NEURAL NETWORK ARCHITECTURE

Q: How do I determine the best size for my network?

A: Usually you will use three layers; sometimes four; more rarely, two. What you really want to do is to find the simplest model (the one with the fewest connections or "free parameters") that gives good performance in the training sample and adequate generalization in the testing sample. The number of layers and neurons is ultimately determined by one critical factor: how well the system performs. The model should be kept as simple as possible while still achieving a reasonable degree of performance. In a neural network, the complexity of the model is specifically a function of the total number of connections in the network. It boils down to a statistical issue concerning "degrees of freedom."

Q: What is meant by "degrees of freedom"?

A: Degrees of freedom is a statistical concept that has to do with things like curve-fitting, and the number of parameters being estimated, in relationship to sample size, etc. Suppose you were fitting a line to two points on a plane. For any two points, you could easily find a line. If you had two data points and one line, there would be no degrees of freedom. Any line can be specified by two parameters and can be defined as: $y = a + bx$, where a and b are two parameters. Each parameter "uses up" a degree of freedom. If you have two points, you have two cases, two parameters, and you have no degrees of freedom, meaning you can always get a tautological, or perfect, fit. If you have three points but two unknowns to the equation for a line, you cannot fit a line perfectly unless your data permits you to do so. In other words, if you took three random points on a plane, you could not draw one line that goes through all of them; under such circumstances, you would have one degree of freedom, namely, there is one more data point than there are parameters. As you can see, the more degrees of freedom, the less the degree of "curve-fitting."

In general, you want the maximum number of degrees of freedom that can be achieved, and this is obtained by having as large a sample as possible relative to the number of parameters (e.g., connection weights) being estimated. The larger the sample, and the more degrees of freedom, the less the error of estimates for any of the parameters, and the more likely it is that any measures based on those parameters (e.g., model correlation coefficient) will be close in the testing sample to what they were in the training sample. *The number of degrees of freedom is roughly equal to the number of cases in a sample minus the number of free parameters being estimated.* Therefore, as the number of parameters being estimated approaches the number of cases, you run out of degrees of freedom and run into total curve-fitting. If you had as many parameters as there were cases, you could always get a perfect fit, even if the data were perfectly random, but it would not mean anything—it would not generalize to any other sample. So the basic idea with a neural network is to use the smallest neural network, in terms of total numbers of connections, that achieves a reasonable result in your training sample because that is the network that is most likely to generalize to out-of-sample data, all else being equal.

Q: What is "curve-fitting"?

A: You are curve-fitting when you have so many parameters that you are optimizing in a model or trading system that you are basically just fitting to historical data; when this happens, the system will work well on historical data but will not work on anything else. Basically, you are tuning a model so well to the past data that it is not going to mean anything. It is like memorization in a neural network. For example, if you have two trading models, one with two parameters that you are fitting, and one with 50 parameters, the model with two parameters is much more likely to hold up in the real world than the one with 50. Why? Because the model with 50 parameters can too easily be tuned to the historical data, that is, unless you are using very, very large samples, which make curve-fitting difficult.

Any kind of fitting of a model to data is a kind of curve-fitting. Most traders think that curve-fitting is bad. However, curve-fitting is neither bad nor good. It is only when it becomes what we call "tautological curve-fitting" that it becomes bad, i.e., it begins to take advantage of purely chance idiosyncrasies that occur in historical data but will not necessarily hold up in future data. The secret to avoiding that particular kind of curve-fitting is to keep the number of parameters, the model complexity, fairly low relative to the number of cases or data points or samples or facts that are being used to construct the model.

By "fitting the model" we mean adjusting the characteristics or elements of a system, e.g., a trading system, in order to maximize its performance on a given set of historical data. The term "model" is used to refer to the trading system itself and its parameters, or the neural network and its connection weights. In other words, a model is something that expresses relationships in the data.

Q: How can I find the smallest or simplest network that still does the job?

A: Start with a very simple network, then gradually increase its complexity. As the complexity of the network increases, you will find the training results get better and better but, at some point, the testing results, although initially improving, will start to become worse. The point at which you get the best testing results, before the testing results start falling apart, determines the appropriate complexity of the model.

Q: How can I determine the number of connections in a network?

A: The number of connections can be derived from the number of neurons in each layer: Multiply the number of neurons in the first layer by the number of neurons in the next layer, then add to that the number of neurons in that second layer multiplied by the number of neurons in the third layer, then add to that the number of neurons in the third layer multiplied by the number of neurons in the fourth layer, and so on for however many layers are in the network.

Q: How do I determine the number of layers I should use?

A: Generally, you will want to use a three- or four-layer network. The question is really whether you can get better results, better generalization, with fewer connections in a four-layer network than you could in a three-layer network; if so, you should probably use the four-layer network. In other words, if you can find a model that uses fewer connections in a four-layer network than you could in a three-layer network, then the four-layer network is better because it is simpler, even though it has four layers. Sometimes, with certain kinds of data, you can find a model with a four-layer neural network that requires fewer connections in the middle layers than a model with a three-layer network. For example, to get the same kind of performance in a training sample, a three-layer network might require 20 inputs, 40 middle-layer neurons, and 1 output; the four-layer network might still require 20 inputs, but only

15 second-layer neurons, 3 third-layer neurons and 1 output, thus making the total number of connections less and providing a simpler and better network. Generally you never have to go to five layers because anything can be done with a three or four-layer network; five-layer networks rarely add advantage. Two-layer networks basically reduce to a form of multiple regression, either logistic or linear, depending on the transfer function (if you use a sigmoid transfer function, it is logistic; if you use a linear input and linear output, it is linear); it certainly provides you with the simplest model, but it may not give you enough, so you will probably end up going to three layers.

Q: Any suggestions about how many neurons to use in each layer?

A: Generally, it is a matter of experimentation: Start with a three-layer network and maybe two middle-layer neurons (the number of first-layer neurons or inputs is determined by the number of variables), then gradually increase the number of neurons. Another advantage to smaller models is that they train more quickly, which makes it easy to start with the simpler models and work your way up in complexity. You would stop increasing the number of neurons (or middle layers and neurons) when generalization gets worse, because that is an indication that too many parameters are being estimated, i.e., there are too many connections in your network; at that point, pull back.

Q: Where does learning take place in the network?

A: Learning takes place in the connections, which are basically parameters (i.e., the connection weights) being estimated. It is in the estimating of those parameters that learning takes place. In fact, learning is the adjustment of those parameters with successive presentations of examples. No matter how many layers or how many neurons, learning takes place when weights are adjusted.

Q: So if there are fewer neurons, does that mean that less learning is going on?

A: Not less learning, but the network cannot learn as many different patterns or nuances in the data. That means that it has to learn the more general characteristics or patterns present in the data, which, in turn, means that the network is more likely to generalize from what it has learned to new data. With lots and lots of neurons, the network begins to get the capability of learning all the little specific variations, which may only apply to the training data and nothing else; that is, it can start memorizing chance events, i.e., curve-fitting.

Q: What about a second middle layer? Does it help to refine what the network has learned?

A: A four-layer network becomes better than a three-layer network when you have data in which there are some unusual kinds of interactions, or from which abstractions can be made, and then some combinations of inferences (based on those abstractions) can be made as a further set of abstractions. If there are some simple features that can be detected in the data, and then you, knowing those features, have some very simple kinds of rules to tell you what the target is going to be, a four-layer network will do the job. Why? Because the second layer (the one after the input layer) will develop neurons that represent or detect the features, and the third layer will represent the inferences (from the combinations of features) regarding the nature of the target. If you are looking at volume and price, a four-layer network may do better because there are patterns in volume and patterns in price that can be abstracted, and the second layer will indeed abstract; the third layer will then look for relationships between the patterns of both volume and price to generate the targets in the fourth layer.

Q: Would adding a fifth layer refine the learning even further?

A: Generally not. When you start getting into a fifth layer, you are starting to add more complexity, e.g., the number of connections will rise. In fact, it can be mathematically proven that, if you have enough middle-layer neurons, a three-layer network can map almost any smooth nonlinear function. A three-layer network, given a sigmoid transfer function, can map any function that could be mapped by a four or five-layer network with the same kind of transfer function, except you may need a lot more middle-layer neurons, resulting in more connections than you would have with the larger networks. And, of course, if you have more connections, you will have a model that will more likely tend to curve-fit; it will not generalize as well because you are using up more degrees of freedom. Basically, three or four-layer networks, and sometimes a two-layer one, are all you will need.

Q: Is there any preferred ratio between the number of neurons in each layer?

A: People used to think there was, but we really have not found that to be the case. Again, it seems best to start with the simplest model possible, one or two middle-layer neurons in a three-layer network, then see how it performs during training and testing. Then jump up to four or five middle-layer neurons, train and test; then go up to eight middle-layer neurons, and then maybe to 16, each time taking bigger and bigger jumps. You will probably find that, up to a point, the training and testing results get better, the model fits the data better (but it is not yet curve-fitting), and the better fit continues to show up in the testing sample as well as the training sample. But, as the complexity gets greater (and more time-consuming), you will see the model fall apart: Training will get much better, but the testing will get worse. That is telling you that you have reached the point where curve-fitting is occurring, rather than generalization; you will then want to step back to a simpler model.

TRAINING CONSIDERATIONS

Q: What is the "seed" or "starting point," and how important is it when you are training neural networks?

A: Starting points are the initial weight vectors and the corresponding places on the error surface from which training begins. They can either be specified (in the form of a random number generator seed) by the network developer (if the shell permits) or determined automatically. *This is one of the most critical factors in training a network.* Imagine having a surface, the "error surface," with lots of hills and valleys. You want to get down into the lowest valley—the one with the best solution, the least amount of error or discrepancy between the network's output and the target. If you drop a ball somewhere on the surface, it will land on the side of a hill and roll down into the nearest valley. However, the nearest valley might not necessarily be the valley you want. There may be another valley somewhere else that is much deeper; but if the ball does not land on the correct side of that hill, it will not roll down into that valley. How would you find the deepest valleys? One way would be to drop a bunch of different balls over the error surface. They will fall on different hills and roll down into different valleys; hopefully, some of those valleys will be the deeper ones. If you transpose this analogy to neural networks, the places where you drop the balls can be considered the different starting points. This is done by starting a number of different networks training at different locations, each network being randomized with a differ-ent initial randomization of its weights. In N-TRAIN® you can specify the random number seed for the random number generator that controls the generation of the weights. In this way, you can create, e.g., 20 different networks, each with a different starting point, then train them and see which ones do best. Some will do better than others. Some will generalize better than others because they are in better valleys.

Q: **What is a good value for the initial randomization seed that determines the starting point of training?**

A: There is no one good value, because different networks, with different data, will have different error surfaces. A starting point that is good for one network may not be good for another. The only value that may be considered "good" is one that tests out well for your particular problem. The secret is to start training a number of networks, each with a different, distinct random starting point or seed. It does not matter what the numbers are because you are, essentially, tossing a number of balls up in the air and they are landing at random places on a surface; your hope is that one of those balls (numbers) will fall into the deepest valley on the error surface, i.e., find the global minima. In other words, you are trying to find the randomization that will produce the best result in the training and testing sample, and that then holds up on another testing sample.

Q: **Will my development shell allow me to specify the starting point? How do I keep track of the starting point?**

A: A well-designed shell will allow you to specify a starting point. Some shells, however, do not let you specify the seed or alter the system's randomization method, which may or may not be a true randomization technique. The better shells will allow you to alter the starting point and, of course, you can just record the value. If the tool allows you to set it, you can always just experiment with the values and then return to any starting point you want.

Q: **What is the point of keeping a record of the starting point if I cannot use it for different networks?**

A: If you want to go back and construct the same network using the same data, you can start training from the same initial point. In other words, if you know you arrived at a good solution one way, and then you need to backtrack on the same data with the same size network, you can start out with the same randomization seed and retrace your steps to reproduce it or return to an earlier phase in training.

Q: **Why would I want to return to an earlier phase in the training or restart the network? Would one instance be when I am trying to screen variables for their contribution to the solution, as when using RELCON, e.g., after substituting new variables for insignificant ones?**

A: No. In that case, you would be dealing with another model, with different inputs, different weights, and different relationships between the data; so you are, in effect, training a new network. The architecture of the network might be the same but, since you are dealing with new inputs, you should construe it as a new network. But let us say that you overtrained the network and you want to go back to an earlier stage in training to when the network was not as overtrained. A way to do that is to rerandomize with the *same* seed (starting point) that gave you the overtrained network, start training again, and then stop it at an appropriate place before it becomes overtraining.

Q: **What is "overtraining"?**

A: You will usually find that, as you train a network, the correlation or performance of the network on the data on which it is being trained will rise and rise and rise because the network is learning patterns in the data. The more the network is trained, the better it gets. In a good, reliable tool that does not have numerical instability, you will see the training curve rising, then plateauing, rising, then plateauing; it will never fall, it will just keep rising until it finally hits a plateau and stays there. You will find that, as the training gets better, initially the correlation in the *testing* or out-of-sample data will also improve; however, there comes a point where additional training leads to a worsening of the correlation in the testing phase, despite the improved correlation in the training set. This is evidence that overtraining has set in. What has happened is that the network has already modeled, or curve-fit, to some of the characteristics that are fairly recurrent in the data and that will hold up in future data sets (i.e., has found the general patterns in the data), but now it is starting to curve-fit, or "memorize," the idiosyncratic patterns in the training data that will not necessarily hold up on out-of-sample data. So overtraining is basically a form of excessive curve-fitting. You usually want to stop a network before it gets too overtrained. We recommend using a train-test protocol to help avoid this: When you see the correlations start to drop in the testing data, you want to stop training the network any further and save the network (possibly you have set up a script that automatically saves the best network, as based on the testing sample).

Also, the larger the training set, or the smaller the model (i.e., the more degrees of freedom), the later the stage at which overtraining occurs. So if you had a huge sample on which you were training, you might never see overtraining: You might train and train and train, and the correlations keep getting better on both the training and testing sets. However, if the training set is small, you are more likely to see overtraining set in fairly quickly as the network starts to memorize patterns.

Q: How does a network recover from overtraining?

A: If you have recorded the seed or random starting point that you used to begin training, you can restart the training process from square one and get back to wherever you want. Usually, however, with a good development tool, you can set the system to save the network every tenth run (or however often you like) to a file; you would then look through the statistics and pick whichever network you liked the best from the ones you saved and then delete the rest.

Q: What are "transfer functions"?

A: Transfer functions describe the behavior of neurons in a neural network. A neuron receives input from a number of other neurons, the total input stimulations being referred to as "activation." The activation is passed through a function—a "transfer" or "squashing" function—to get the output from the neuron. The transfer function defines the relationship between neural output and total input activation. The most commonly used transfer functions are the sigmoid, the hyperbolic tangent, the Gaussian, and the linear. There are others, such as the various hard-edged transfer functions, which are of less concern to us here.

The *sigmoid transfer function* is the most popular. This function varies between 0 (for very large negative inputs) and 1 (for very large positive values). The sigmoid transfer function is a good "general purpose" transfer function.

The *hyperbolic tangent transfer function* is basically the same thing as the sigmoid; it is just scaled differently so that the output ranges from -1 to +1, instead of 0 to 1. Theoretically, the networks you can get with this transfer function are identical to those you can get with sigmoids because, for every network that has sigmoids, if all the weights and thresholds are changed appropriately, you can get the exact same model using hyperbolic tangents.

The *Gaussian transfer function* peaks at some level of activation and falls off as the activation of the neuron moves away from that value. If you are dealing with variables that have the kind of relationship in which, if the variable is too high it is no good, and if it is too low it is no good, but if it is somewhere in between it is very good, then you might get the best results from a network that has one or more middle layers that are Gaussian.

For the *linear transfer function,* you take the total activation of the neuron (the sum of the stimulations coming into it) and simply pass that on (perhaps with some scaling) as the output of the neuron. A linear transfer function is often used for input neurons that serve as "pass-through" nodes into a network. You would also use a linear transfer function when, e.g., you want to compute a straight multiple linear regression: Specify a neural network with two layers, each with linear transfer functions, and you have set up a multiple linear regression—you are finding a weighted set of the inputs that will best predict the target in a least-squares sense. This is often a baseline model.

Q: What would be the normal pattern of transfer functions across layers?

A: The pattern of transfer functions that you would normally use (that N-TRAIN® defaults to) would be a linear input, and sigmoids for all the rest of the layers. This would be a standard network for most purposes.

If your data have a lot of "outliers" (when variables occasionally take on very extreme values, e.g., when the S&P makes a 50-point move in a day), and you want to minimize the impact of those extreme values, then you can change the linear input to a sigmoid input, which will dull the effects of the outliers. If you have glitches in the data, e.g., every so often they take on crazy values, the sigmoid will squash the range of the inputs.

You might want to try the Gaussian transfer functions for a middle layer if you think there are certain variables that have optimal values—e.g., if they go above or below the optimal values, the target you are trying to predict will decline. or if the variables have the optimal values, the target would be at its maximum. This is a matter of experimentation.

Most other transfer functions are for experimental purposes. In many cases, back-propagation *cannot* be legitimately used to train a network with them because these transfer functions may have points where a derivative (slope) cannot be computed.

Q: What are "error functions"?

A: Error functions are used to measure how good the network is—how great the discrepancy is between the network's output and its target. Most common are the sum-of-squares, the absolute differences, the sum-of-the-fourth-power, and the asymmetric error functions.

In the *sum-of-squares error function,* the training algorithm minimizes the sums of the squared errors, over all facts, between the output from the network and the targets. That is, you take the difference between the output of the network and the target, square this difference, then add the squared values for all of your examples to obtain a total sum-of-squares error.

In the *absolute differences error function,* you take the sum of the absolute values of the errors: Take the absolute value of the difference between the output of the network and the target, then sum those numbers. This error function would be used when you want to give less emphasis in the training process to extreme data points and more emphasis to data points that are in the common or modal range. If, for example, you had data that contained a crash, that isolated event will not have as much relative impact on the results as it would with least-squares error.

If you are more concerned about extreme or more unique cases and you want to develop a good model for that, and are not concerned with small variations in data, then you might go to the *sum-of-the-fourth-power error function.*

When using an *asymmetric error function* (e.g, asymmetric least-squares), errors in one direction (the network says "low" when it is actually "high") are given more weight than errors in the other direction. Instead of simply summing the squares of the errors, you take a look at the direction of the error and, if the direction is one way, you would take the square of the error and add it to the running sum; if the direction is the other way, you would take some multiple of the squared error and add it to the sum. This becomes useful when, for example, the loss in not taking a trade would be less than the loss in taking a bad trade; it takes into account the direction in which the risk is worst.

Q: What are "learning rates"?

A: The learning rate is the rate at which the network adapts its knowledge to the facts (examples) being presented to it. Learning rates are found in all back-propagation networks. In back-propagation, you are basically taking a starting point in weight space on some hilly error surface and trying to move in steps in the direction of steepest descent, the most abrupt slope down toward the solution. The size of the step you take is the learning rate. If you take bigger steps, you will get down the hill of the error surface more quickly, but you may end up jumping back and forth over a low spot on the surface—evidenced by instability and lack of convergence. Therefore, the smaller the learning rate, the greater the stability and the better the convergence. However, as the learning rate gets smaller, it will take more and more steps to get to the solution. So the goal is to use the highest learning rate that does not produce instability, because you want the greatest speed of solution without running into trouble. Generally, we are conservative, and err toward a smaller learning rate; we then get stable and reliable training (convergence).

In some products (like N-TRAIN®) learning rates can be adjusted for each of the different layers of the network. In other products, there is only one global learning rate. The advantage of having the ability to adjust the learning rates on a per-layer basis is that sometimes the input layer weights will not change very much as the network is training, but the output layer weights change a great deal (or vice versa). Under such circumstances, you want the input layer weights also to show modification; if the neural tool permits, you can increase the learning rate for the earlier layers and decrease it for the later layers to balance things out and to allow the earlier layers to show as much change and adaptation as do the later layers.

Q: What is meant by "polishing" a network?

A: That is a term coined by Jeffrey Katz. If you train a network and are using a fairly large learning rate, you may end up with a network that has an output containing a consistent bias in it, i.e., the target may have a mean that is somewhat different from the mean output from the network. A somewhat exaggerated example would be targets of 101, 103, 105, etc., and network outputs of 1, 3, and 5, respectively; that kind of consistent bias (which is usually a lot smaller) can be "polished away" by turning the learning rate way down to some small value, e.g., 0.1 or 0.01, and then training the network for a few additional runs, e.g., 10 runs through the fact set. The threshold value going to the last neuron will adjust itself so that the mean output of the network will equal the mean of the target. By the way, if you try this technique with some neural development shells, especially those that use 16-bit arithmetic, expect poor results, or none at all.

GENERALIZATION AND CORRELATIONAL MEASURES

Q: What do correlations measure?

A: Correlations can tell you whether a real relationship exists between variables and whether that relationship is predictively useful. With neural networks, correlation is a measure of the relationship between the output of the network and the target that it is trying to predict. We find that they are a good starting point when developing a trading system, that is, correlational measures help you select or evaluate variables. Warning: Correlation only shows *linear* relationships.

Q: Why do I get good correlations on the training sample, but poor ones on the testing sample?

A: This question bears on the matter of the network's ability to "generalize." Generalization refers to the degree to which a network's performance holds up on "out-of-sample" data (e.g., test data withheld from the net during training). The situation described in the question indicates that the network does not generalize well. This can be due to a number of factors.

Training a neural network can be seen as a problem in parameter estimation. When dealing with neural networks, the parameters being estimated are the connection weights. In this way, training a neural network is very much like fitting a multiple regression model, except that the net is nonlinear and the regression is linear. As with regression, you are more likely to get something that holds up if you conserve degrees of freedom and use a large sample for estimating your parameters. By "conserving degrees of freedom" we mean keeping the model complexity (numbers of parameters being estimated) as low as possible relative to the sample size: *Generally, there should be at least 10 times as many cases or "facts" as there are connections in the network!* And you want as many facts as possible while still maintaining representativeness. The larger the training sample and the simpler the model (numbers of connections in your net), the better the generalization. Generalization is also influenced by the clarity and strength of the patterns in your data; this is another reason to pay attention to the optimal preprocessing of your data: The better the preprocessing, the clearer the patterns and the greater the chance of obtaining good out-of-sample performance.

Q: Someone told me that convergence is irrelevant and that any tool vendor who claims fast convergence doesn't understand generalization. Is this true?

A: It is true that convergence alone will not guarantee good generalization. However, *the absence of convergence will guarantee that you will not get good generalization,* because generalization means that something that has been learned from the training set holds up in the testing set. If you have no convergence, it would mean that no learning occurred in the training set, so what would there be to generalize? Therefore, *convergence is a necessary prerequisite for generalization, but not a sufficient one.* Anyone who says that convergence is irrelevant, or that fast convergence is meaningless, does not really know what he or she is talking about. The person is right in that fast convergence alone will not ensure generalization, but it is a 100 percent certainty that the absence of convergence will guarantee the absence of generalization.

Q: I get a correlation of .95 in training after just a few runs, and 0.95 in the test data. Is it possible to get such good results, or am I doing something wrong?

A: Neural networks can achieve 95 percent accuracy or better for a lot of problems in the hard sciences, but rarely in the financial markets. If you get a .95 correlation, it is probably spurious and/or will not provide information that is useful for trading. For example, if you use raw prices and train a network on the S&P over the past 15 years, you will get a correlation in the high .90s because today's price actually correlates that highly with tomorrow's price. However, all this correlation is telling you is that the S&P does not move very much from day to day, but has moved tremendously over the past 15 years!

Q: So a high correlation might be real, but it's not going to be very useful?

A: A correlation of anywhere near .95 is very suspect in terms of usefulness for trading. Chances are you got that correlation by doing something like using raw prices to predict raw price, or by trying to predict an indicator that itself is computed on past values. The correlations may be very high, but they will not necessarily be very useful because they are, to some degree, tautological, i.e., the correlation is there because the thing you are predicting is, to some extent, based on measurements from data that the network has already seen. A correlation of .95 is very, very suspicious. There are certain exceptions; for example, if you are trying to predict the price of an option based on things like interest rate, time to expiration, volatility of the underlying of the option, etc. In such instances, you can expect legitimate .95 correlations.

Q: So what is considered, under ordinary circumstances, a good range for the correlations?

A: There is no one good range. If you try to predict price changes or events of change in the future—such as the market moving up at least 5 percent in the next two weeks, or tomorrow forming a bottom in the sense that the next five days are all going to close higher than tomorrow, etc.—do not expect correlations anywhere near .95 or .8 or even .7; be very suspicious if you get very high correlations. More likely, you will see correlations that are in the .05 to .3 range. A correlation of .2 that holds up in a large enough sample or in several samples can be *very* useful for trading.

Q: How can I tell whether my correlations are useful ones?

A: Basically, you have to get your correlations and then evaluate them within context to determine whether or not they are useful. Examine the outputs from the network and the actual values the network is trying to predict: How do they look on an actual plot or histogram? You might also chart the signals; for example, plot the neural network on one line and the prices on another. How does it look? You should also try to verify whether a correlation is stable by doing several independent out-of-sample tests and then examining the mean and standard deviation of the correlations over those several different samples. If in one sample it is .1, and in another sample it is .15, in another it is .08, the standard deviation is very small and you know you have a stable correlation, even if it is a small one (even a small edge is better than no edge).

Q: What kind of correlation would you expect if the network is just memorizing the data?

A: You would see a high correlation in the training set, but a zero or very small correlation in the testing set. "Memorization" occurs when the network is learning during training but is not generalizing its learning to out-of-sample data. If the training sample correlation is a lot larger than the one in the testing sample and, in testing, the correlation declines while in training it improves, it implies the occurrence of memorization. In general, if the samples are large enough, the training and testing correlations should be relatively in line with each other; the training might be slightly higher and the testing might be slightly lower, but both will be in the same range.

Q: What is going on if you get a low correlation in the training sample but a high correlation in the testing sample?

A: It may be just statistical variation. You can get a 0 correlation in training before the network starts learning and yet have a testing correlation of .2; it's just random error. Again, see whether the correlation holds up across a number of testing samples and whether it is useful for trading. When screening variables, we routinely use straight correlations and, when testing neural networks, we use up to 20 independent out-of-sample, data sets. In this way, statistical estimations can be made without making assumptions about the distributions of the underlying variables. By knowing the standard deviation, and the mean of a given correlation over 20 samples, we can get an estimate of what the range should be in the future.

Q: If a network performs poorly on out-of-sample data, how can generalization be improved?

A: Increase sample size, simplify the model, and find variables with stronger relationships to the target. The larger the sample of data on which you train a network, the more likely you will get behavior on the out-of-sample data that is the same as on the in-sample data. It is basically just a statistical consideration: The larger the sample (as long as it is a representative sample), the more accurate and stable the network.

Another consideration in generalization is the size of the model, i.e, the number of variables, or the number of connections in the network. For a given sample size, the more complex the model, the more curve-fitting you can get, and the less likely it becomes that you will get generalization.

Another rule of thumb is that, for any given model size, *you want at least 10 times more cases than there are total number of connections and variables.*

You can also try improving generalization by using at least two testing sets. Different networks predicting the same thing will generalize to different degrees, and the most important determinant of that is often the starting point. Some valleys on the error surface are more representative of reality, in the sense that they are in different samples and are more characteristic of the universe of the data; other valleys that are local minima may represent the peculiarities of the particular data on which the training was done. What you will often find is that when you look at training and testing samples, certain seeds or initial randomizations will yield a network that generalizes better than networks generated with other seeds. If you are doing this, you are, in a sense, using the testing sample to select which of the different trained networks to use. Since the testing set was contributing a little to the model, to be statistically safe, you want a second testing sample that has never been seen by the network. This will help determine whether the network that was selected on the basis of its performance on the first sample really holds up when it is evaluated with a sample that had not previously been used to make any decisions regarding it. That is something that any neural network developer should set up: A train-test protocol for generating a bunch of different random seeds, training networks, testing their ability to generalize on one out-of-sample set, and then, after the best few networks are selected, testing those networks on a second set of out-of-sample data.

Q: What is a "train-test" protocol?

A: We recommend that you break the training up into a series of train-test sequences when developing a neural network. This allows you to monitor and assess more closely how well the network is training. It also helps avoid such things as overtraining.

You would typically do maybe 10 or 20 training runs, then a testing run, then another 10 or 20 training runs, then another testing run, and see what happens. You could also watch the correlation in the training set and, after the correlation in the training set rises from, e.g., .1 to .2, you stop training and do a test; then you train again and let the correlation rise to .25 or .3, then do another test.

Another popular train-test sequence is "walk forward testing." For example, you would specify one time period as the training sample, then specify the next time period as the testing sample; you would then create a new training sample that would be a time window moved over a little bit in the future (from the original), with the next testing sample as the time period that follows that, etc. You are walking it forward, as if in a simulation. It is another legitimate way of creating training and testing samples that are independent and that keep moving forward in time, as will happen when you are actually trading.

DECIDING WHETHER TO USE NEURAL NETWORKS

Q: I already have a trading system. Will a neural network improve it?

A: A neural network may improve an existing nonneural trading system; the determination is dependent on how the network will be used within that system. You can use neural networks to improve almost any kind of system. You just have to think the problem through with respect to exactly how the network will be implemented.

Let us take an example of a breakout system, i.e., a system that looks for a move that goes beyond a certain range and, therefore, signals that the market has started trending in some direction so that the trader can jump on the trend. In a breakout system, there are a lot of whipsaws, so the trader may only win on 40 percent or 50 percent of the trades. Hopefully, the moves in the winning direction will be bigger than the moves in the losing direction so that, overall, the system will be profitable. One way to use a neural network to improve such a system would be to try to find variables and a neural network that can predict whether a breakout taken on the next bar would be a good breakout or a whipsaw breakout. In this way, the network could be used to vet or approve whether or not to act on a given breakout. To implement this, you would feed the network examples of all the breakouts that occurred in the past; the amount of profit or loss that occurred on the breakout is the target, and the network will try to predict, based on data from the previous bars, whether the breakout is going to be a success or not, or how much of a success. You may get improved results by adding neural networks in this way; with good variables, you can probably improve the system quite dramatically.

You might have a system that requires some kind of subjective judgment, for example, the behavior you see on a chart indicates to you that something significant is going to happen. You might train a network to perform that subjective judgment so that you can implement it in the computer. That is a complicated use of a neural network because it will probably require some programming to accomplish. You will have to create examples, possibly in a spreadsheet, in which you mark whether the pattern was present or not by putting a 1 or a 0 in a cell, and you have all of your input variables and try to train the network to imitate you. The problem here might also be coming up with an adequate number of examples of the phenomenon.

Yet another example: You might be using an indicator that, if filtered in some way, or predicted a bar ahead, would improve the results of the system. You could train a network to predict the indicator a bar ahead, or reduce the noise level (networks make good filters when used in certain ways and there are some tricks to doing this), all of which might improve the trading system.

Q: Has anyone developed a profitable trading system using neural networks? How long did it take? How did they do it?

A: There are a number of people who have developed successful neural-network-based trading systems. Some are so amazingly profitable that it boggles the mind. However, the ones who succeed are usually those who study incessantly and spend a lot of time and hard work developing the system. It doesn't come easy. One small group of individuals we know of constructed a highly successful S&P trading system that was profitable beyond their wildest dreams: This took a full year of several developers' time working on advanced computers to achieve. In other words, yes, it can be done, but expect to be spending six months to a year studying, testing, thinking, and generally immersing yourself in the task. Remember, the markets are a competitive game: If you want to spend the time, and you have some intelligence, you can gain an edge, but it will take some serious effort.

Q: Do you know of any successful systems that are not proprietary that you can describe?

A: All the systems we know of that have been successful are definitely proprietary. The developers of such systems trade them rather than sell them. From our experience, the systems that are sold may have been profitable at one time but, when they lost their profitability (and, given time, most systems do start to fail), the trader decided to sell the system and squeeze the last few dollars out of it that way. In a few rare instances, there have been systems that were sold simply because the trader developed a better one for himself or herself. And, on still rarer occasions, you will find people marketing their system because, while they are still trading it in certain ways themselves, they hope to benefit by influencing the market in a certain direction through others trading the system. More often, traders will market tools or system components they develop in order to generate more revenue; there is no risk here because there are so many ways the components can be combined that the developer will not lose the edge he or she has worked so hard to gain. Again, the best advice we can give is to put your time and money into developing your own system and, if you do contemplate buying someone else's, be on your toes as a consumer.

CHOOSING YOUR TOOLS

Q: Neural network development work sounds very complex. Would working with a Windows tool make it any easier?

A: Not really. It is not the training of the neural network (which is accomplished using the tool) itself that is difficult; the hard part is selecting the right variables, preprocessing and massaging them, and assembling them into examples—in short, preparing the data on which the neural network will be trained. Going from a command line to a Windows shell or the reverse may, to some small degree, affect the ease of actually training the network. But training the network is the simplest, easiest, and smallest part of the whole project. Most of your time will be focused on the data; that is where 80 percent to 90 percent of your effort will go. Relative to that, you are spending very little time doing the actual training. For example, training a network in the command line version may be as simple as telling the system the number of layers and a few other bits of information and then typing "TRAIN." In a Windows version, rather than typing in one or two words, you would click on a few buttons, type in the input files, type other data into a dialog box, and then click on a "TRAIN" button. So the command line versus Window issue is not relevant in this context.

Q: What are the advantages to each kind of tool, i.e., command line and Windows?

A: Each has its own particular advantages. The command line shell has the advantage that the user can easily set up a script or batch file that can automate the entire training and testing process. Such a file would automate such procedures as selecting the different starting points, executing the train-test sequences, etc. With a little bit of experience, you could write a batch file that would contain the whole script of events that, after setup, could reduce the entire training process to a matter of typing a couple of words, then going off and having a swim rather than attending to every step of the process. When working with a Windows tool, you cannot do this kind of scripting; instead, you have to stay with the program every step of the way. On the other hand, the Windows tools generally have more elaborate graphics that allow you to see how training is progressing on a chart. The best of both worlds would be to have some kind of graphics utility that has windowing capabilities to allow you to monitor the training process in graphic detail, together with a tool that has scripting capability so you can automate frequently used sequences of events down to a keystroke or two. For example, N-TRAIN® could be used in a DOS box under Windows and in conjunction with, for example, a spreadsheet, which would enable you to jump between the two systems and have all the advantages.

Q: Aren't there also limitations in Windows development tools in terms of the size of networks?

A: Windows has traditionally been a 16-bit operating system and, because of that, there were a lot of limitations in terms of the ability of Windows systems to handle large data sets. It could be done using segment manipulations, but that meant large, slow, buggy software. As a result, developers of neural shells running in Windows would simply opt for limited memory capability, which meant limiting the tool user to small networks and fact sets.

DOS is also a 16-bit operating system but, several years ago, DOS extenders became available, which made it simple and even practical to write full-blown 32-bit memory model programs. We took that opportunity to write N-TRAIN® as a full 32-bit system, so there is basically no limit to the size of the problems it can handle; moreover, its speed and performance are often two-to-four times greater than for 16-bit products. People who are trying to develop such things as trading models where there is a lot of noisy data, and who therefore need large data sets on which to train, should probably look for a 32-bit system so that they can get reasonable speed and performance out of it on their large data sets.

Windows tools for 32-bit programming are soon to become available. When that happens, 32-bit neural network development tools for Windows will start to appear, that is, if the publishers are willing to rewrite their neural shells from scratch. Traders who are waiting for such an upgrade should query the tool publishers to make sure that they actually did rewrite their programs to take advantage of the new Windows capabilities. The best way to tell is to ask what size problems the system handles. If it can handle a half-gigabyte of facts, it is either 32 bits or it is efficiently handling segment manipulation. A way to tell for sure is to ask whether the product requires Windows 4.0 ("CHICAGO"), Windows NT, or Win32S extender to run; if it does, then it probably is a 32-bit system.

Q: What is meant by "stability" when applied to a neural network development tool?

A: There is variation in the way different tool publishers have implemented back-propagation with respect to how much attention they paid to the underlying mathematics when the tool was being developed. Lack of proper attention and finesse can result in training problems that are caused by such things as "numerical instability." For example, using inadequate precision can cause round-off errors to accumulate so rapidly that the whole system is thrown into chaos. There are tricks to writing a really good back-propagation algorithm, and they would not necessarily be known by someone who can program, gets a book on neural network algorithms, and then tries to design a tool just to make money selling it.

Q: What are "round-off errors"?

A: When computations are done, there is usually only a certain amount of accuracy. If you are doing lots and lots of computations, such as the number of computations going on when training a neural network fact after fact, those small roundoffs, or small absences of precision, can accumulate to very big quantities. That can completely throw off the training process and cause unusual phenomena, e.g., the network starts learning then collapses, oscillates wildly, or just does not learn at all.

Q: What is the difference between 16-bit, 32-bit and 64-bit arithmetic?

A: The kind of arithmetic used in a neural network shell is one thing that affects the system's numerical stability because it bears directly upon the system's mathematical precision when performing its computations, e.g., the issue of round-off errors mentioned above. One product (written about eight years ago and not fundamentally updated since) uses 16-bit integer arithmetic, which means only three to four digits of accuracy (i.e., the computations begin rounding off after three or four significant digits), that causes numerical instability. 32-bit arithmetic is standard, single-precision arithmetic with about seven to eight digits of accuracy; it is better than 16-bit arithmetic and may be adequate for smaller problems, but it can still cause problems. 64-bit arithmetic has about 15 to 17 digits of accuracy, and if you have a back-propagation system written with that much precision for all internal computations, it will usually converge with a lot more stability (if everything was correctly implemented) than a system with less precision; it will converge faster and do so without oscillations or finicky behavior.

Q: What is the best hardware setup for developing neural networks?

A: If you are planning to pursue the training of large neural networks seriously, go for the fastest, most powerful hardware you can find. That would be either a very fast 486, or a Pentium, or possibly an 860. These days, we would choose the Pentium because it is also fast and useful for all the other software that is now becoming available, like Windows NT and CHICAGO. In other words, it is *not* specialized hardware like the accelerator cards sold by neural tool vendors, which are useful only for the specific software package sold by the tool vendor.

ADVICE TO BEGINNERS

Q: I am a novice, approaching neural network trading system development cold. What is your best advice as to where to start, how to learn about the subject?

A: My best advice would be to start reading the trade magazines that deal with neural networks (e.g., *Technical Analysis of Stocks and Commodities, AI in Finance, NeuroVe$t Journal*), get a good spreadsheet or some other general-purpose data-manipulation tool, learn it—and the programming language behind it—fluently (e.g., if you get a spreadsheet such as Excel, learn the Visual Basic Applications macro-language) so that you can easily and conveniently manipulate data, and then start studying statistics, specifically multivariate and univariate regression. If you understand multiple regression, you will have a very good basis for understanding a feed-forward back-propagation neural network, which is basically a form of nonlinear regression. Get books on neural networks (there are lots of them out there, including this one), and read, read, read.

Once you have mastered some of the manipulations with the spreadsheet and have some data you can play with, get a neural network development shell and proceed with your learning by doing. Start with some really simple made-up problem in which you know the relationships between the variables. Create a simple example: Compose three columns of random numbers in your spreadsheet, and then make the fourth column some simple equation involving those random numbers; you might take the first column minus the number in the second column and divided by the third column. You would then put the results in the fourth column, then try to train a network to generate the fourth column or give you an estimate of the fourth column based on the first three columns. By playing with examples, you can see how the network operates. Then you can jump in by taking some data—whether from a stock, a commodity, or the S&P—and start playing with that with historical testing, playing with it in a spreadsheet, train and retrain. At this stage, neural network development is largely a learn-by-doing issue.

Q: I am not used to statistics, don't want to learn programming, and just want to buy a neural development tool, turn on the computer, and hit a few keys. Will I ever be a successful?

A: You are almost certainly going to fail. First of all, the markets are *hard*. They are zero-sum games, i.e., they are competitive and for every winner there is a loser. That means that there are a lot of experts out there—very knowledgeable people who study all the time—and those are the people who will gain the edge over someone who does not want to be bothered learning about the technology, the trading systems, or the markets.

You are going to have to understand a lot of the technology in order to use it properly and effectively. You may not have to know how to write a neural network shell, but you will have to understand in principle (if not in detail) what a neural network does, what data look like, how to preprocess variables, how to work with a spreadsheet or other kind of data manager, etc. In short, if you do not understand these things, you will not have an edge. If you do not have the understanding and you are competing against someone who does, who do you think will win? That also applies to a lot of so-called "super-easy-to-use" development systems that claim they will let you make a lot of money in the market without your doing anything but pushing a few buttons and making a few choices; chances are these systems will not work or, if they work now, they will not work for long because, again, if everyone is using them, who has the advantage, who will take money from whom? The one who will be able to take money from all of them is the person who develops his or her own system that can outsmart the one that is on the market.

Let us close this chapter with an admonition: Be suspicious of any vendor who claims that he or she has the easy solution, that anyone can make a fortune in the market, that anyone can train networks without needing to learn. They are the ones who have the edge—selling products to the gullible who will lose to those who really know what they are doing. In short, the catchword for traders who really want to win in the market is STUDY, STUDY, STUDY. No one we know of or have heard of has ever been truly successful without taking the necessary time to learn the market, the technology, and the trading and money management game. That said, we hope we have provided some useful information to start you on your way and we wish you the best of luck on your journey!

SUGGESTED READING

Brown, Connie. "Neural Networks With Learning Disabilities." *Technical Analysis of Stocks and Commodities* (May 1993): 50–56.

Cassetti, Marlowe D. "A Neural Network System for Reliable Trading Signals." *Technical Analysis of Stocks and Commodities* (June 1993): 78–84.

Eliot, Lance B. "Prefilter Your Neurons." *AI Expert* (July 1993): 9–11.

Fishman, Mark B., Dean S. Barr, and Walter Loick. "Using Neural Nets in Market Analysis." *Technical Analysis of Stocks and Commodities* (April 1991): 18–22.

Jurik, Mark. "Consumer's Guide to Neural Network Software." *Futures* (July 1993): 36–42.

Jurik, Mark. "A Primer on Market Forecasting With Neural Networks, Part 2." *NeuroVe$t Journal* (November/December 1993): 7–11.

Kempka, Anthony A. "Activating Neural Networks: Part I." *AI Expert* (June 1994): 33–37.

Katz, Jeffrey Owen. "Developing Neural Network Forecasters for Trading." *Technical Analysis of Stocks and Commodities* (April 1992): 58–68.

Katz, Jeffrey Owen, and Donna L. McCormick. "Vendor's Forum: The Evolution of N-TRAIN." *PCAI* (March/April 1993): 44–46.

Katz, Jeffrey Owen, and Donna L. McCormick. "Neural Networks: Some Advice to Beginners." *Trader's Catalog and Resource Guide*, Vol. II, No. 4 (1994), p. 36.

Katz, Jeffrey Owen, and Donna L. McCormick. "Neurogenetics and Its Use in Trading System Development." *NeuroVe$t Journal* (July/August 1994).

Loofbourrow, John and Tod. "Traders Using Neural Nets Beat Those Who Don't." *AI in Finance*, premier issue, 1994): 51–59.

Murray, Dan. "Tuning Neural Networks With Genetic Algorithms." *AI Expert* (July 1994): 27–31.

Ruggiero, Murray A., Jr. "Getting the Lag Out." *Futures,* (April 1994): 46–48.

Shih, Yin Lung. "Neural Nets in Technical Analysis." *Technical Analysis of Stocks and Commodities* (February 1991): 62–68.

Stein, Jon. "Neural Networks: From the Chalkboard to the Trading Room." *Futures* (May 1991): 26–30.

Trippi, Robert R., and Efraim Turban, eds. *Neural Networks in Finance and Investing.* Chicago: Probus Publishing Co., 1993.

Yager, Ronald, and Lotfi Zadeh, eds. *Fuzzy Sets, Neural Networks, and Soft Computing.* New York: Van Nostrand Reinhold, 1994.

Vondrak, Ivo. "Object-Oriented Neural Networks." *AI Expert* (June 1994): 20–25.

Chapter 3

DEVELOPING INDICATORS FOR FINANCIAL TRADING

Mark G. Jurik
JURIK RESEARCH & CONSULTING

INTRODUCTION

Developing a financial trading system is one thing. Letting it bet your wallet on the market is quite another. As anxiety builds, you might be thinking: "Will it perform better than me? Deliver better ROI? Should I intervene on occasion?" Suppose the first four trades with your new system each lost profit. You might now be thinking: "Never mind about the returns *on* my money, what about the return *of* my money?" Yes, this is a big undertaking.

Consider the obstacles. First, system building places great demands on your time. You are forever testing your models on gobs of data. Second, it can be expensive. You will need access to a computer with relevant software and you must be willing to plop down (and lose) money several times in a row. Third, it places great demands on your psyche. Watching your hard-earned money alternately disappear and reappear can be gut-wrenching. Traders with deep pockets can sail through these storms while less fortunate participants end up giving these systems nicknames like "The Bond Trader From Hell." Fourth, it places you against everyone else who not only wants to win from the same money pool as you but wants *your* betting money as well.

Despite all this, in the back of many minds lurk two nagging thoughts. First, if some humans can trade consistently well, then why can't a computer? Second, why can't it be *my* computer? Shades of artificial intelligence, have not we heard these questions once before? Yes, but the problem domain is much simpler. After all, we are not talking about the difficult tasks of computer speech recognition, understanding, storytelling, and outright fibbing. Nor are we trying to teach a robot car how to weave through a mass of intermingling people, cars, and cows on the streets of Katmandu. We are talking about applying the techniques of data preprocessing, adaptive pattern recognition, knowledge rule processing, system parameter optimization, and performance testing for predicting the financial market. This is itself a challenge because market dynamics are not too well understood. They are chaotic and often driven by mob psychology on a rampage. Come to think of it, it *is* comparable to driving through Katmandu.

Artificial intelligence, regardless of its formal definition (if it ever had any), translates to hard, and often fruitless, work. Persistence does pay off, however. Structured methodology helps too. There is only one person I know who can actually make progress hopping around ideas like a rabbit, trying out a nibble of this and a nibble of that. For the rest of us, though, systematic experimentation is the recommended modus operandi.

To accomplish this, I designed a flow diagram to help me see the big picture (see Figure 1). It subdivides system development effort into various stages. The first stage involves the boring task of collecting and verifying financial data. It does not help your system's self image by giving it historical prices peppered with zeroes and

Figure 1.   Overview of financial trading system development.

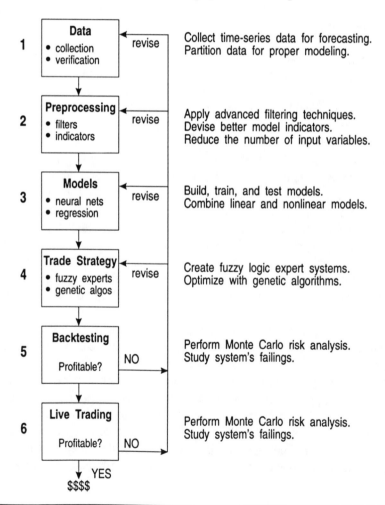

then expecting perfect forecasts. Avoid headaches and lost time: Invest in clean data. So here is the first of my strong recommendations, each of which is enclosed in a box:

Invest in clean data.

The second stage of system development is data preprocessing. Briefly, this is where meaningful indicators are extracted from raw financial data. Good preprocessing makes the next stage run smoothly. Professional modelers realize the importance of this step and focus most of their energy here. However, to the amateur, it has the same appeal as washing laundry.

Stage 3 is where you get to play with and learn about sexy modeling tools such as ARIMA and neural networks. If you created perfect indicators, you can completely skip this stage! However, this is not likely to happen. More likely is that the novice will completely skip stage two and spend months trying to make it all happen in stage three. This typically leads to complaints that the [expletive deleted] neural net is brain-dead.

The fourth stage involves figuring out what to do with your model's output. For example, if your model works well only during trending price activity, then you may need a few rules telling you when to ignore the model's output. Also, if these rules have parameters such as thresholds, they may need adjustment. A good technique here would be to let genetic algorithms evolve the parameter values for you.

The fifth and sixth stages comprise various tests that evaluate system performance. This is where you pore over statistics such as annual return on investment (ROI), expected maximum drawdown (EMD), and if things are real bad, Monte Carlo simulations of expected fiscal half-life (EFHL). This is also where you analyze the system's bad trades and conjure up design modifications. However, as in all aspects of system development, discipline is required. Undisciplined conjuring may lead to overoptimized spaghetti logic, which is a nightmare to maintain.

The Major Issues

Due to inefficiencies in the marketplace, a certain amount of predictability exists. The trick is to exploit it. First, you need relevant information, but exactly what information is relevant is not obvious. Sometimes an economic factor that is useless for making forecasts all by itself is useful when used in conjunction with other factors. For example, the long-term price ratio of gold to oil has been fairly predictable for many years. Thus, if you know the long-term average price of oil, you can estimate the long-term average price of gold. In this case it was the *ratio* of two economic factors that proved to be useful, not either one alone.

A ratio, however, is only one of innumerable ways to capture particular aspects of market behavior. The scope of possibilities is endless. For example, note that market data and a musical score have much in common. Most importantly, they both contain information encoded as measurements changing through time. When we study this information, we usually find that it exists in many forms and on many levels of organization. For example, one might listen to classical music and focus on the melody of a single instrument, the interplay among many instruments, how variations on a theme evolve and return, and the music's overall changing direction, mood, speed, energy, continuity, and so on.

One can view information embedded within a financial time series in similar fashion. You can focus on price patterns and timing in a single market (technical analysis) or on the interplay among many factors affecting supply and demand (fundamental analysis). You may study how economic cycles evolve and how the overall economy changes direction—and let's not forget indicators covering mood (consumer confidence), speed (momentum), energy (volatility), continuity (fractal efficiency), and so on.

There are four mathematical windows through which indicators may view and describe a time series. They are the

+ Space domain

+ Time domain

+ Frequency domain

+ Phase domain

The *space domain* covers relationships among different indicators, regardless of each data record's time stamp. One example is the gold-oil ratio explained earlier. The *time domain* covers relationships among historical values of any one indicator. This is where we would find the saying, "A trend is your friend." The *frequency domain* enables efficient representation of patterns recurring through time. For example, one might discover that a commodity's price takes a dip approximately every 35 days. The *phase domain* enables efficient representation of patterns recurring through space. Most financial chartists probably do not realize that up-down patterns may also exist on price charts that do not contain time along any axis. Within the phase domain one can generate the famous Lorentz attractor and other beautiful patterns that chaos analysts strive to observe.

The rest of this chapter discusses several issues centered on creating a database of indicators for trading system development. These issues are all related to the space domain of a signal.

THE SPACE DOMAIN

Preliminaries

In a typical scenario, information collected for a model can be organized as follows:

$$x_1(t_1), \ x_2(t_1), \ \ldots, \ x_N(t_1) \ \rightarrow \ y(t_1)$$
$$x_1(t_2), \ x_2(t_2), \ \ldots, \ x_N(t_2) \ \rightarrow \ y(t_2)$$
$$x_1(t_K), \ x_2(t_K), \ \ldots, \ x_N(t_K) \ \rightarrow \ y(t_K) \tag{1}$$

where $x_3(t_2)$ is the value of indicator #3 at time bar 2, and $y(t_2)$ is the desired output value of the model at time bar 2. The values of x and y in equation (1) can be arranged on a spreadsheet as follows:

Table 1. Spreadsheet layout of financial data.

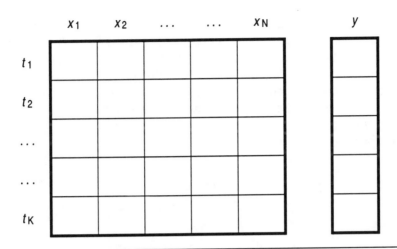

Each row (horizontal grouping) in Table 1 constitutes one data *record* or data *case*. A record can also be thought of as a *point* in N-dimensional space, where the N indicator values in a record are the N coordinate values of the point. For example, Figure 2 shows how a record with three indicator values would correspond to a point in 3-D space.

Figure 2. Geometric view of data record.

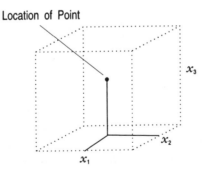

The reader is advised to keep the geometrical view in mind throughout this chapter.

Tossing in the Kitchen Sink

Successful traders have several traits in common, and probably the most important is knowing where to look for good information. They know that even the best model is useless if its input indicators (input variables) are not relevant. Therefore, building a model almost always involves finding the right variables to describe relevant aspects of the financial world.

Where does one begin? First, determine what you want your model to do for you. Then select raw economic data of obvious relevance. For example, if corn prices are trendy and cyclic, the modeler may choose to compare the price of corn to its moving average. The moving average serves to filter out chaotic "noise" in the day-to-day prices, leaving a smooth trend line (see Figure 3). A simple short-term buy/sell policy might be to buy immediately when the price rises above its moving average (and sell later on) or to sell immediately when the price falls below its moving average (and buy later on).

Figure 3.   Example of a moving average.

When aspiring forecasters have no idea which indicators to use, they usually construct models by feeding them lots of data, data that might have any relation to the desired forecast. For example, a model intended to forecast gold prices might be fed historical precious metal prices, oil prices, inflation rate, and GDP as well as estimates of gold's future supply and demand. Since jewelers use a lot of gold, and its demand is a function of the public's perceived ability to buy jewelry, then additional indicators for the model may include estimates of the consumer confidence index and indices related to consumer purchasing.

This collection could swell to a large number of indicators very quickly. Unfortunately, feeding a model more indicators (independent variables) may deliver worse results! Why is this possible? Assuming the input data contains relevant information, the model may still fail as a result of two fundamental issues, commonly referred to as *degrees of freedom* and *multicolinearity.*

Degrees of Freedom

Let's suppose we have some data records arranged as rows, with each record containing a few input variables. For each record, we also have the target output value. As an example, the input variables could be a person's height, weight, and shoe size; the target value could be the person's life expectancy. We would like a simple linear model that provides us with coefficients for calculating target values (life expectancy) from the corresponding input variables (height, weight, and shoe size). Standard regression techniques (like the one readily available in Microsoft Excel for Windows) can produce these coefficients. Unfortunately, the convenience of regression is, in a way, its own drawback. There are many subtleties that often get overlooked. Most importantly, the coefficients may be useless.

For example, consider data points (x, y), each with one independent (input) variable x and one dependent (output) variable y. A formula f that maps input x to output y is generally written as $y = f(x)$. Probably the most often used formula for f is the polynomial

$$c_0 + c_1 x + c_2 x^2 + \ldots + c_D x^D = \sum_{n=0}^{D} c_n x^n$$

Degrees of freedom (DOF) is a measure of the mathematical "flexibility" of a formula. For a polynomial, DOF equals the number of its coefficients. In the formula above, the coefficients to be determined by regression would be $c_0, c_1, c_2, \ldots c_D$, and the polynomial's DOF equals $D + 1$.

Table 2 shows polynomial f with different DOF. Figure 4 shows how well each function f models a set of data points that roughly approximate a parabola. The solid squares to the left of the vertical dotted line are the data points used by regression to find the coefficients for each f. The squares to the right are new data points we will use to test each f.

Table 2. Polynomials with varying degrees of freedom (DOF).

DOF	FUNCTION FORMULA	FUNCTION NAME
1	c_0	constant
2	$c_0 + c_1 x$	straight line
3	$c_0 + c_1 x + c_2 x^2$	parabola
9	$c_0 + c_1 x + c_2 x^2 + c_3 x^3 + \ldots + c_8 x^8$	8th-order polynomial

First, we focus on how well the curves track the training data only. When DOF = 1, f is a constant, shown as a flat horizontal line. This function is useless. When DOF = 2, f is a straight downward sloping line, tracking training data better than the constant. When DOF = 3, f has captured the inherent curvature in the data. When DOF= 9, f not only follows the general curvature, it also bends up and down, getting closer to the training data points. Clearly, this last function has the best performance against the training set.

Regarding performance on test data, the story is quite different. Functions with higher DOF have more coefficients and thus more maneuverability to bend up and down. With this flexibility, the polynomials try to model everything about the data, including random scattering. However, it is unwise to attempt modeling random scattering because random behavior cannot be predicted. Efforts to do so lead to strange

Figure 4.   Forecast performance of polynomials having different DOF.

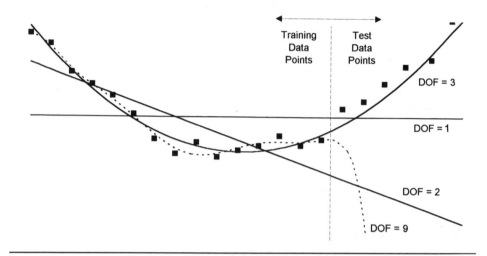

results. For example, right after the last training point in Figure 4, f drops rapidly when DOF = 9. In contrast, a low DOF function cannot afford to bend around each point and is thus forced to ignore random scattering and capture only the data's general trend. Consequently, functions with just enough DOF tend to model test data better than functions with excessive DOF.

This phenomenon has direct impact on how to properly develop a financial model. Models with large numbers of input data have large DOF. They tend to show great promise with the original data (backtesting) but yield disappointing results with new data (forward testing). Models with fewer input variables have lower DOF and experience less drastic performance degradation with new data. Consequently, forecasters strive for the simplest of models, searching for the best combination of only a few choice indicators.

Strive for simple models having only a few choice input variables.

Multicolinearity

Suppose your model's input consists of 100 different indicators. Chances are many of these indicators will be mutually correlated in varying degrees. However, models prefer uncorrelated indicators, and feeding a large number of *mutually correlated* indicators to a model typically degrades its performance.

To see why this is so, consider a database of five records as shown in Table 3. Columns A, B, and C represent three independent variables. Recall from high school algebra that a model with more variables than records is considered "*under*constrained"; that is, there is not enough data to constrain all the degrees of freedom. This results in not one, but an infinite number of sets of coefficients, each of which will map the input data to the target values perfectly. Yet these coefficient sets may produce different answers on new data! This unreliable performance would be unacceptable.

Table 3. Sample data with corresponding target value.

Record	Input			Output
#	A	B	C	Target
1	1.2	3.4	4.6	2.2
2	0.9	2.2	3.1	1.3
3	1.8	1.5	3.3	−0.3
4	2.5	2.7	5.2	0.2
5	2.1	1.9	4	−0.2

Fortunately, the more likely case in the real world is to have more records than variables. Models based on such conditions are typically "*over*constrained," whereby there is so much data that no set of coefficients can deliver a perfect target answer for every record. In such a case, we must simply accept a set of coefficients that offer performance with low overall error, usually least mean square (LMS) error. Standard regression, available in popular spreadsheet application software, is designed to deliver LMS error.

The second sentence in the preceding paragraph is very important. The key word is "typically" because databases with more records than variables are sometimes *under*constrained, or very nearly so. This situation occurs when at least one input variable can be closely approximated by other input variables. For example, suppose regression on the data in Table 3 produced coefficient set (1, 3, −2). We should be able attain the target values by multiplying the three input variables A, B, and C with coefficients (1, 3, −2) respectively. Let's see if this is true. For the first record in Table 3, input data A = 1.2, B = 3.4 and C = 4.6. We then have

Model's Output	=	$1 \times A$	+	$3 \times B$	+	$-2 \times C$
	=	1×1.2	+	3×3.4	+	-2×4.6
	=	1.2	+	10.2	+	−9.2
	=	2.2				

The model's output matches the target value of 2.2. The coefficients (1, 3, −2) work just as flawlessly for the other four records in Table 3. One might believe, then, that this is the best coefficient set for the model. Not so! Amazing as it may seem, there are an infinite number of equally good coefficient sets to this modeling problem. Some other equally good sets are (−1, 1, 0) and (0, 2, −1) and (3, 5, −4) and (7000, 7002, −7001)! This is bad news. To see why, let's compare the performance of a model using coefficients (7000, 7002, −7001) and a model using (−1, 1, 0). Both models are fed a slightly modified version of the first record in Table 2: A = 1.2, B =

3.4, C = 5. Multiplying the new input by coefficients (–1, 1, 0) produces the output value 2.2. However, multiplying the new input by coefficients (7000, 7002, –7001) produces the output –2798.2! Although both coefficient sets produced identical results with the original database, they also produced drastically different results with new, slightly different data. This unreliable performance would be unacceptable.

The reason why this amazing experiment was possible is because column C of the database does not represent a truly "independent" variable. In fact, each value in column C could be calculated by adding the corresponding values in columns A and B. Simply put, C = A + B. As a rule of thumb, interdependence among input variables seriously degrades the ability of regression models (including neural nets) to perform reliably with new data.

What is even more disheartening is that similar damaging effects would occur even if column C were merely *correlated* to the sum of A + B! The greater the correlation, the more pronounced the effects. This is why you should consider giving models decorrelated input variables: The model will not depend on input multi-colinearity.

Unfortunately, financial indicators are highly correlated with each other, causing much frustration among those trying to model market behavior. This phenomenon suggests that the user reduce the number of input variables, hoping it will reduce multicolinearity as well as lower the DOF for improved generalization. To do so, the user may try various combinations of two or more input variables until the best combination is found. Do you know how many possible combinations you can have with 100 indicators? About 10^{30}, equivalent to 100,000 times the number of atoms in a liter of water! Even with just 10 indicators, there are over one thousand combinations to try! Yes, over ONE THOUSAND. Examining the effectiveness of all these combinations could take you a very, very long time!

Some modeling tools try to get around this problem by performing correlation analysis between pairs of input variables. This practice is based on the assumption that if two variables are correlated, you do not need both, and so one of them can be eliminated. This popular practice can easily lead to a dead end. Here's a simple example to illustrate why. Suppose your input consists of three time series:

1. The daily high tide level near San Francisco,

2. The daily high tide level near Los Angeles,

3. The apple production rate in Washington State.

As illustrated in Figure 5, signals A and B are very similar, and therefore highly correlated. One might be tempted to eliminate either one from the set of indicators to a model. But if you do, then the model could never create desired output signal D if its true formula is D = A – B. In other words, a model can only calculate (A – B) when both A and B are present! Therefore removing inputs on the basis of correlation can leave you with insufficient data and a nonworking model.

**Do not remove an input variable simply because it is
correlated to other input variables.**

Figure 5. Example of three signals, A, B, and C.

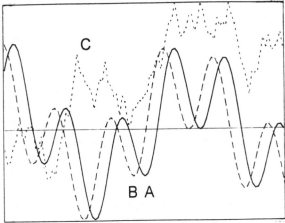

There is a better way to remove multicolinearity. Suppose a long-term medical research study measured blood pressure and cholesterol levels on 1,000 people and later recorded their age at death. Let the points in Figure 6 represent data records, with axis P for pressure and C for cholesterol. The plot reveals three distinct groups, each group having a unique life expectancy.

The plot also shows that you cannot use just blood pressure readings or just cholesterol readings to distinguish which group any point would belong to. This is because some neighboring groups overlap and share similar blood pressure measurements. Other points overlap and share similar cholesterol measurements. Therefore, it

Figure 6. Sample distribution of input data.

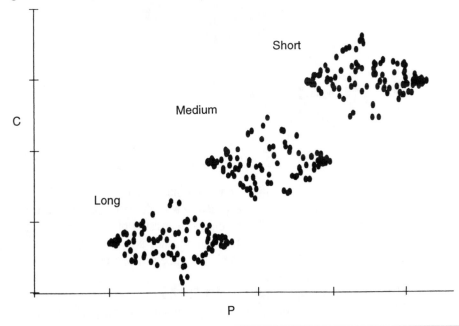

appears that both C and P are required for determining to which group a point belongs.

We might also conclude that if an insurance company built a complex model that needed estimates on life expectancy, the model would also need both measurements. However, in trying to use as few input variables as possible, would it be possible to combine the measurements of blood pressure and cholesterol into one variable that can successfully discriminate among the three life expectancy groups?

Figure 7 shows one way to do this is. We make two new axes: X and Y. Axis X travels through the centers of the three groups and axis Y lies perpendicular to X. We can now represent each point in the graph by giving either its P-C coordinates or its X-Y coordinates. The advantage to using these X-Y coordinates is that only the X axis serves to determine which life expectancy group a point belongs to. The Y axis value serves no purpose. Therefore, concerning the life insurance model, we can represent information on forecasted life expectancy with only one variable, X, instead of both P and C.

Figure 7.   New axes separate the three groups efficiently.

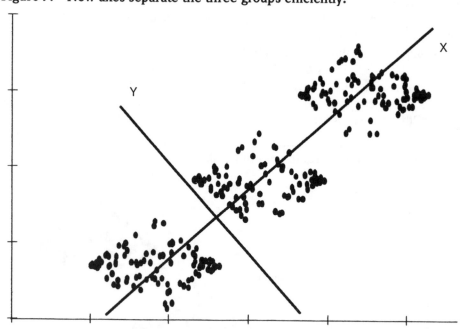

We call this method decorrelation and dimension reduction (DDR). To demonstrate the power of this approach, we prepared three models to forecast future values of a simulated financial time series. This time series consisted of three kinds of market forces: periodic cycles, aperiodic chaos, and random impulses. It was generated using sinusoidal curves, the famous Mackey-Glass chaotic time series, and Brownian noise. A small portion is illustrated in Figure 8.

For all three models, data consisted of 1,500 cases (rows) wherein each case contained 21 independent variables (columns) and a single forecast 10 bars into the

Figure 8. A portion of a noisy chaotic time series.

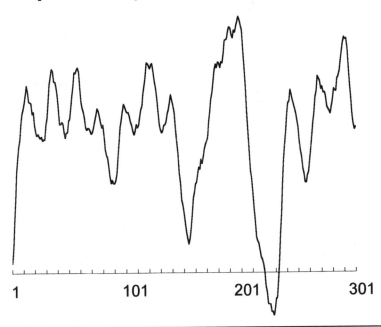

future. The variables included past values of the time series as well as moving average values and other relevant indicators. The first model utilized the popular linear regression method. The second model was a neural network trained on the same data. For the third model, we had DDR decorrelate the data. Only the first *five* columns of DDR's output were used to train a neural network.

The results were astounding. Table 4 shows each model's average forecast error. Standard regression on all 21 variables gave an average percentage error more than twice as large as a neural net using the same data. However, after applying DDR, the neural net needed only the first five columns to produce equivalent performance!

Table 4. Relative error of three models.

Model #	Description	Relative Error
1	Simple regression on 21 columns of original data	15.0%
2	Neural net on 21 columns of original data	6.4%
3	Neural net on 5 columns produced by DDR	6.4%

In summary, try to decorrelate all input variables to your model.

Decorrelate all input variables.

Sensitivity Analysis

Model building is a never-ending process of continual refinement. After a model is developed, sophisticated developers use a process called sensitivity analysis to determine how much impact each variable has on the model's behavior. The intent is to eliminate those variables contributing the least to a model.

With linear models, such as that attained by standard regression, a variable's sensitivity is easily revealed by the magnitude of its coefficient. Large coefficients imply high sensitivity (large impact) and small coefficients imply low sensitivity (small impact). One can extend this technique to nonlinear models, such as neural networks, by slightly changing an input variable's value and noticing how it affects the output. We could then measure sensitivity as a ratio between the two changes:

$$sensitivity = \frac{output\ change}{input\ change} \qquad (2)$$

With regard to building economic models, this is not a reliable approach toward identifying input variables for deletion. It can very easily lead you to draw completely wrong conclusions. Suppose you had a black box with two dials that you can adjust so as to vary a light bulb's brightness. Your task is to determine and then remove that dial having the least effect on bulb brightness. You tweak the first and learn it has no effect. The second dial can vary brightness slowly. Do you remove the first dial? No! To see why, suppose bulb brightness was affected by the two dial readings, as described in the following formula:

Brightness = f_1 (dial #1 reading) + f_2 (dial #2 reading).

Also suppose that functions f_1 and f_2 are as shown in Figure 9. If dial #1 had a reading of any number outside the range of 5.5 to 6.5, then tweaking it would have produced no change in bulb brightness. Tweaking dial #2 at any setting would have affected bulb brightness. Sensitivity analysis would suggest we remove dial #1. Yet we see from the charts that if we had to remove a dial, maximum brightness is attained by keeping dial # 1 and removing #2, since at maximum setting f_1 produces more brightness than f_2.

Figure 9.   Relative brightness contribution of each dial.

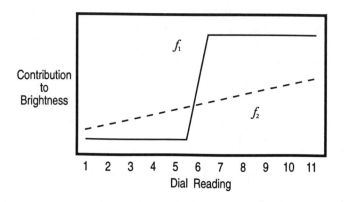

There are many reasons for nonlinear behavior in the economy. First, the financial market is driven partly by mob psychology. Herd mentality is one cause of catastrophic market crashes. Another reason is that the sheer physics of the market contains interactions between market momenta that permit one to control the effect of another. For example, sometimes infusing extra money into the economy by lowering prime rates during major political campaigns achieves the desired effect: the economy picks up just in time and incumbent politicians are re-elected. Sometimes the economy responds much later.

The same argument can be made for neural networks or any other nonlinear modeling paradigm. It is almost impossible for the user to estimate which variables contribute maximally over all predictions. For some models, the answer may be, "None!" The sensitivity of the output to each input variable might not only vary, but also switch signs!

In conclusion, use sensitivity analysis on linear models because an input's importance can be determined right from the formula's coefficients and is not affected by other input factors. In contrast, this technique may deliver unreliable results with nonlinear models. Many users of neural network models, as well as many developers of software products, seem to be unaware of this. The unsophisticated user may notice that for some collection of training data, his model shows low sensitivity to a specific input variable. He may then conclude the variable was not important and decide to remove it. However, that same variable may be very important under other circumstances. Removing variables based on sensitivity analysis is risky business.

> **When trying to remove unimportant input variables, sensitivity analysis of nonstationary or nonlinear models has dubious practical value.**

There are reliable procedures for eliminating input variables under these conditions. However, they may take an enormous amount of computer time to do so. One method uses *genetic algorithms* to iterate through numerous combinations of input variables. The combinations vary in a manner similar to the way chromosomes are hypothesized to have combined and mutated over millions of years to produce various life forms. Details of this procedure are beyond the scope of this chapter.

The second method is more systematic. When presented with the same data, this approach always gives the same answer in the same amount of time. First, build a model using all available input variables. Record its performance as the baseline. Next, remove the first variable from the data set and build a model using the remaining input variables. Record the model's performance on test data and label the results #1. Next, place the first variable back into the data set and remove the second variable. Build a model, record its performance on test data, label the results #2, and place this variable back into the data set. Repeat this procedure for each variable. When finished, select the best one from all the recorded performances. If this performance was attained when you removed variable #N, then permanently eliminate variable #N from the data set.

If you started with, say, 50 variables, then after removal you will have 49. Repeat the entire procedure again, permanently removing another variable. Repeat the procedure over and over until you have only one variable left.

> **To identify weak variables, use the systematic process of elimination and test.**

If you chart the model's performance on training and testing data after each permanent removal of a variable, it may look like Figure 10. This chart was created by systematically removing variables on a model used to estimate the cost of pumping gas through pipelines extending from Texas to New York. There were only about 700 database records, of which I selected 300 for the test set. Note that as the remaining number of input variables decreased, training error increased monotonically. In contrast, testing error decreased as more variables were removed, until only six variables remained, then testing error also increased. The U shape of the test data error curve suggests that removing a few unnecessary variables lowers the model's degrees of freedom, contributing toward improved generalization on the test data. Continually removing more variables cripples the model, causing test error to rise quickly.

Figure 10. Train and test error during systematic removal of variables.

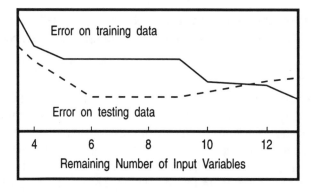

The issues mentioned in this chapter focus on the space domain of a signal. Other issues in this domain, such as clustering and fuzzy dimensional enhancement, were not discussed. A complete discussion on preprocessing in all four domains is being compiled into a forthcoming book by Jurik Research and Consulting.

Chapter 4

NEURAL NETWORK TECHNIQUES FOR FINANCIAL TIME SERIES ANALYSIS

Peter C. Davies, Principal
EXPERT SOLUTIONS

INTRODUCTION

In many applications we attack with neural networks, we are trying to classify data into categories, based on a number of different predetermined variables. Take, for example, a bank wishing to improve the quality of loan decisions. Having first assembled many past loans, the performance of which is known, and having also decided which variables might influence loan quality, the standard multilayer feed-forward architecture can be used. The input nodes would correspond to the variables we are looking at, and the output nodes would correspond to the categories, such as good and poor loan quality. Then we would pick a training algorithm, such as back-propagation, and train the network, experimenting with the number of hidden layers and hidden nodes.

This kind of approach works well with some investment applications. An example given in Yoon & Swales [1991] describes a back-propagation network built to predict stock price performance based on qualitative fundamental data, such as growth, strategic plans, anticipated profits and losses, and economic factors.

Financial applications often require the prediction of future values of a time series. For example, we might want to predict the future value of a stock, or index, based on historical values. Sometimes the standard architecture we have described will suffice but often it will not.

In this chapter we will discuss how to approach this kind of problem. Many different architectures have been tried, but we will concentrate on just a few with promise. We will examine three different approaches and discuss an application developed with these methods in each case.

STATISTICAL APPROACHES VERSUS NEURAL NETWORKS

First we should look at why we would want to use neural networks for analyzing time series. Much work has been done using traditional statistical techniques to develop models for time series analysis. These include autoregressive (AR) models, moving average (MA) models, and combinations such as the Box-Jenkins models ARMA and ARIMA, the autoregressive integrated moving average model.

Although statistical techniques have proved useful, there are some difficulties. First of all, it is not always clear whether a given time series satisfies the assumptions that make the model valid. This is where neural networks are useful, as they do not depend on assumptions but adapt to the training data. Also, neural networks can handle noisy data, which is another feature of most financial time series. Statistical techniques tend to run into trouble when dealing with noisy data.

BACK-PROPAGATION

One approach to time series prediction is to use a standard feed-forward network (see Figure 1), trained using back-propagation. Suppose we are trying to predict m future values based on n previous values. Then we can construct a network with n inputs and m outputs and experiment with the number of hidden units. Thus the temporal information is represented by the order of the inputs.

This straightforward approach has been compared with the standard Box-Jenkins approach on several time series. Sharda & Patil [1990] discuss a test using 75 series, from 111 analyzed previously in the M-competition, a famous study of the ARIMA model (Makridakis et al. [1982]). Sharda & Patil [1992] discuss a second test using all

Figure 1.

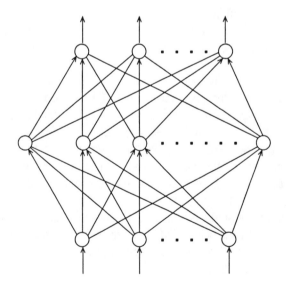

111 series. The conclusion in both studies was that back-propagation networks perform as well as the ARIMA model.

THE CLS+ ALGORITHM

This approach to time series prediction can also be done with other algorithms for multilayer feed-forward networks. One promising algorithm, Constructive Learning by Specialization (CLS+), has been used for currency exchange rate prediction (Refenes [1993]).

The CLS+ architecture is built adaptively during the training process (see Figure 2). We start with a standard three-layer feed-forward network with only one unit in the hidden layer. The network is trained to recognize a single pattern. Then it is tested on the next pattern. If it identifies it correctly, there is nothing to do. Otherwise, another hidden unit is added and the network is retrained until it recognizes the pattern correctly. This process continues until all patterns are recognized.

At each stage, when the network is being retrained, the weights on the connections to and from all hidden units except the new one are frozen. The new unit is connected to the input and output units and also to the previous hidden unit. A gradient descent procedure is used to train the new unit to be active for the new pattern but inactive for all previous patterns. In this way, the new network will eventually recognize the new pattern without disturbing the recognition of all previous patterns.

This method was used to build networks to predict the exchange rate between the U.S. dollar and the deutsche mark. Hourly data was used for a 260-day period, the first 200 days were used for training and the next 60 days for test data.

Figure 2.

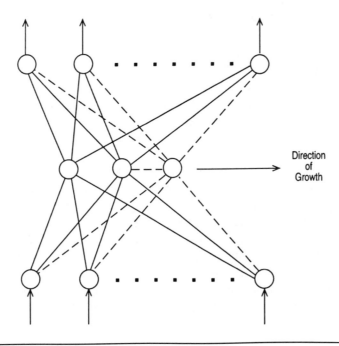

Direction
of
Growth

Refenes discusses the results for single-step prediction, where 12 hours of data are used to predict the exchange rate for the next hour. Then the next rate is predicted again using the actual data. This is not very useful for trading, except as an alarm generator, when the system predicts a large change.

Much more interesting is the discussion on multistep prediction. Here 12 hours of data were used to predict the next hourly rate and then the predicted value was used in the prediction of the rate for the following hour. In this way, the network was used to predict the entire last 60 days. For the first 30 of these days, the network was very accurate in terms of both the general trend and the absolute rate. After this the absolute rate prediction was not very good but trend prediction was still good. This was quite remarkable, given that the general trend in the training data was up, whereas the general trend in the test data was down.

Using a simple strategy of trading at a turning point, paper profits were calculated for the 60-day period. The profit obtained appears good but is somewhat meaningless, as no account was taken for slippage or for transaction and other costs. However, the profit was better than for another network that used standard back-propagation. It was also much superior to a number of statistical techniques applied to the same data.

RECURRENT NETWORKS

One difficulty with the approaches discussed so far is knowing how much of a time series is significant to predict future values. How do the patterns early in a series affect later parts of the series? Can we build networks that can retain this temporal information during training? The most used and successful architecture to date is referred to as *recurrent back-propagation*.

Figure 3 shows a simple example of this network architecture. The nodes A, B, C, D, E, and F form a standard three-layer feed-forward architecture. The input layer (A, B, C) could be three time steps in a time series or three different variables for a single time step. The output (F) could be the predicted time step. We also have a copy of the hidden layer (D^1, E^1) in the input layer and a copy of the output layer (F^1) in the hidden layer. There are also signals fed back from each layer to the previous (i.e., D to D^1, E to E^1, F to F^1). These extra nodes (D^1, E^1, F^1) are the corresponding nodes (D, E, F) for the previous time step.

The training procedure proceeds as with regular back-propagation, each successive input pattern being the variables associated with the next time step(s) in our time series. After presenting the entire series, weight changes are calculated and applied throughout the network and the entire process is repeated until the network can predict subsequent time steps adequately. By using the extra nodes (often referred to as context layers), time-dependent information is absorbed by the network.

This training procedure can be used to recognize several time series, rather than just one. To do this, we pick one of our set of time series, randomly, and present the entire series to the network as above. After applying weight changes, we select another series, again at random, and repeat the process. After we have exhausted our set of time series, we iterate the entire process as in the single series case.

Figure 3.

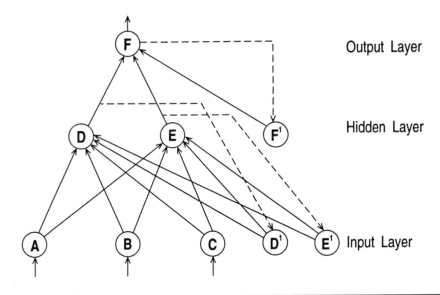

A recurrent network was used to detect triangles in individual stocks (see Kamijo & Tanigawa [1990]). Triangles are patterns in the price history that can signal a significant upward or downward swing in the stock's price (see Figure 4). After examining over 1,152 stocks over a three-year period on the Tokyo Stock Exchange, an expert identified 16 triangles with periods of between 13 and 35 weeks.

Figure 4.

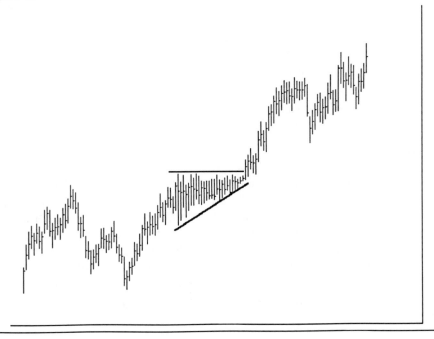

A recurrent network was built with three inputs, which were different variables associated with a single time step, and four outputs—the three outputs for the previous time step and a variable indicating whether, at this point in the series, the stock was in a triangle. The architecture was a modification of the one we have described, in that it contained two hidden layers, of 64 and 24 units. Also, there was a context layer (containing 64 units) in the input layer but none in either hidden layer.

Since the number of triangle samples was small, network training was done using the leave-one-out method. This is a commonly used technique when training data is limited. The network was trained with 15 of the stocks until it could identify each triangle correctly. It was then tested on the remaining stock. This was done 16 times, each time leaving out a different stock. In 15 of the 16 trials it correctly identified the triangle in the stock not used for training.

OTHER ARCHITECTURES

Back-propagation-through-time (BPTT) is an interesting technique, developed originally by Paul Werbos (Werbos [1974]). Suppose we have a back-propagation network that has been trained to simulate some process, so that its inputs describe the state of the process at some time step and its outputs at the next time step. Then we can connect together many copies of the network and then train it through an entire sequence of timesteps.

This technique has been used to solve difficult control problems. For example, a BPTT network was built to simulate a truck backing into a loading bay (Nguyen & Widrow [1989]). A back-propagation network was built to simulate how the truck would change position, based on different movements of the steering wheel. This network was then used as the basic building block for a BPTT network, which was then trained to back the truck into the bay from almost any initial position.

We have included this technique here, since it relates to temporal problems. However, it is difficult to see how this architecture might be employed effectively in stock market applications. Recurrent back-propagation is equivalent to a special case of BPTT. It is not clear that the extra power of BPTT can be used effectively in financial time series analysis to make it worthwhile in this arena.

A good reference that discusses neural network techniques for time series analysis in detail is Williams & Zipser [1990]. Recurrent back-propagation, BPTT, and other techniques, including hybrid approaches, are discussed.

CONCLUSION

In this chapter we have looked at different neural network architectures for time series prediction. We have seen that in some instances straightforward back-propagation can be used effectively, and studies indicate that such networks perform as well as the better statistical techniques. We have also seen how another constructive algorithm, which dynamically builds a network during training, has been used to produce promising results in predicting currency exchange rates. Finally we looked at a general method, recurrent back-propagation, for analyzing time series without having to decide, a priori, how much of the series is required to make accurate predictions of future values.

REFERENCES

Kamijo, K., and T. Tanigawa. "Stock Price Pattern Recognition: A Recurrent Neural Network Approach." *Proc. of the IEEE International Joint Conference on Neural Networks* (1990): 215–221.

Makridakis, S., et al. "The Accuracy of Extrapolation (Time Series) Methods: Results of a Forecasting Competition." *Journal of Forecasting*, Vol. 1 (1982): 111–153.

Nyugen, D., and B. Widrow. "The Truck Backer-Upper: An Example of Self-Learning in Neural Networks." *Proceedings of the International Joint Conference on Neural Networks*, Vol. 2 (1989): 357–363.

Refenes, A.N. "Constructive Learning and Its Application to Currency Exchange Rate Prediction." *Neural Networks in Finance and Investing,* Trippi & Turban, eds. Chicago: Probus Publishing Co., 1993.

Sharda, S., and B.P. Patil. "A Connectionist Approach to Time Series Prediction: An Empirical Test." *Journal of Intelligent Manufacturing.* Chapman & Hall, 1992.

Sharda, S., and B.P. Patil. "Neural Networks as Forecasting Experts: An Empirical Test." *Proceedings of the International Joint Conference on Neural Networks,* Vol. 2 (1990): 491–494.

Tanigawa, T., and K. Kamijo. "Stock Price Pattern Matching System—Dynamic Programming Neural Network Approach." *Proceedings of the IEEE International Joint Conference on Neural Networks* (1992): 465–471.

Werbos, P. "Beyond Regression: New Tools for Prediction and Analysis in the Behavioral Sciences." Ph.D. Thesis, Harvard University, 1974.

Williams, R., D. Zipser. "Gradient-Based Learning Algorithms for Recurrent Connectionist Networks." Tech. Rep. NU-CCS-90-9. Boston: Northeastern University, College of Computer Science, 1990.

Yoon, Y., G. Swales. "Predicting Stock Price Performance: A Neural Network Approach," *Proceedings of the IEEE 24th Annual Hawaii International Conference on Systems Sciences,* 1991.

PART TWO

AI TRADING SYSTEMS

Chapter 5

SYNERGISTIC MARKET ANALYSIS: Combining Technical, Fundamental, and Intermarket Analysis Using Artificial Intelligence

Lou Mendelsohn, President
MENDELSOHN ENTERPRISES, INC.

INTRODUCTION

Recent advancements in telecommunications and computing technologies—often referred to as the "information technology revolution"—coupled with the emergence of derivative instruments, including futures and options, have brought about the globalization of the world's financial markets. Now there is nearly instantaneous worldwide communication and on-line linkages between exchanges along the emerging information, or "electronic," superhighway. The effects of this are best exemplified by the 1987 stock market crash, which can be considered the first instance of a truly global financial market phenomenon.

Now, even a casual reader of a daily newspaper or viewer of the nightly news is aware that the world's markets and economies influence each other on a daily basis in an interconnected web of cause and effect. No longer independent, today's financial markets are now synergistically linked to one another.

Additionally, the proliferation of trading markets in emerging growth regions of the world—including the Pacific Rim, Asia, and Latin America—has contributed to this global interdependence. This trend, which is both unprecedented and irreversible, has serious implications for traders who want to profit from global trading opportunities in the 1990s.

Other Factors Contribute to Market Globalization

The globalization of the financial markets has been further accelerated by other related factors, which include the diminished influence of the G7 western nation central banks in controlling interest and foreign exchange rates, cross-border consolidation of corporations into multinational entities, increased trade by emerging nations, the listing of corporate shares concurrently on multiple exchanges, and the needs of corporate and financial institutions to manage risk on a 24-hour worldwide basis.[1]

The Result: Market Globalization

Global trading is now conducted around the clock by most major financial institutions.[2] By the end of this century the world's financial markets will coalesce into one global market, while each of the individual markets that traders are focusing on today will simply be components or different facets of that one market.

Globalization has altered the character and nature of the world's financial markets, in terms of how they behave and interact. The global markets of the 1990s offer unprecedented trading opportunities.[3,4] Yet, most traders have given little thought to the implications that globalization will have on their trading, particularly during an acute financial crisis in terms of illiquidity and counterparty risk.[5,6] Most traders continue to focus entirely on one market at a time, failing to implement any sort of intermarket analysis or global perspective in their trading. They are content to ignore the intermarket global context through which all financial markets are now linked to one another as component parts of a larger whole.

This is a very serious and potentially costly oversight, since single-market analysis, due to its narrow inward focus, cannot discern the underlying force or *market synergy* in today's globally interrelated markets. Now, new analytic methods are a *sine qua non* for profitable trading. They must be capable of identifying hidden patterns and discovering relationships in disparate data.

Broader Market Analysis Is Needed

Traders need to adapt their trading strategies and methods, in order to survive and profit in this new world order. Today's limited single-market focus must yield to a broader analytic framework that can quantify complex intermarket relationships. What is needed for successful trading is a broader concept of market analysis that recognizes the nonlinear interrelatedness and interdependence of today's financial markets. Trad-

---

[1] Eiteman, D. K., A. I. Stonehill, and M. H. Moffett. *Multinational Business Finance.* Reading, MA: Addison-Wesley Publishing Company, 1992.

[2] Diamond, B. B., and M. P. Kollar. *24-Hour Trading: The Global Network of Futures and Options Markets,* New York: John Wiley & Sons, 1989.

[3] Ibbotson, R. G., and G. P. Brinson. *Global Investing: The Professional's Guide to the World Capital Markets.* New York: McGraw-Hill, Inc., 1993.

[4] Levine, S. N. *Global Investing: A Handbook for Sophisticated Investors.* New York: HarperBusiness, 1992.

[5] Mendelsohn, L. B. "Building a Global Safety Net." *The Journal of Commerce* (Feb. 5, 1990).

[6] Mendelsohn, L. B. "24-Hour Trading: Let's Do It Right," *Futures* (April 1990).

ers can no longer focus solely on individual markets. It is now imperative that they adopt an intermarket trading perspective and utilize analytic tools capable of assessing complex intermarket relationships. To accomplish this, traders must expand their analytic perspective to include external factors in addition to internal factors that affect a given market. It is this broader synergistic context that must become the focus of market analysis for successful trading in the 1990s.[7]

Technical market analysis must encompass the global context of today's financial markets by incorporating the more narrowly defined schools of technical, fundamental, and intermarket analysis as they are presently practiced (see Figure 1). I refer to this more comprehensive method of analysis as Synergistic Market Analysis (SMA). This approach utilizes various mathematical technologies, including neural networks, to quantify relationships and find hidden patterns between related financial markets. By doing so, it allows traders to capture and act upon information reflecting the *market synergy* that drives today's markets.

Figure 1. **Synergistic market analysis. This figure depicts the primary components of SMA.**

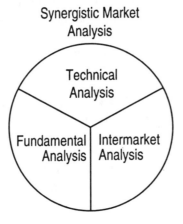

SYNERGISTIC ANALYSIS

Background

In 1983, when I introduced single-market historical simulation and back-testing in microcomputer software[8,9] and developed ProfitTaker, the first commercial PC trading software with this capability, most technical analysis was performed manually or with

---

[7] Mendelsohn, L. B. "It's Time to Combine Fundamental and Technical Analysis for a Total Game Plan." *Barron's* (March 13, 1989).

[8] Mendelsohn, L. B. "Picking Software Programs: Know Their Limitations." *Commodities* (Futures) (May 1983).

[9] Mendelsohn, L. B. "History Tester Important Factor in Software Selection." *Commodities* (Futures) (July 1983).

primitive software programs. By the mid-1980s historical testing had become the backbone of computerized technical analysis, with the emergence of a software industry catering to individual computerized traders.

Yet, as I surmised the likely effect that market globalization would have on technical analysis and trading, it was apparent that single-market analysis alone would no longer be adequate. With formerly isolated markets now interconnected, new analytic approaches would be required for profitable trading.

In 1987, I developed trading software that used a spreadsheet format to correlate the effects of intermarket and fundamental data on price directions of related financial markets. At the same time, other technical analysts began exploring intermarket relationships too, most notably John Murphy, who has since authored an excellent book on the subject, entitled *Intermarket Technical Analysis*.[10] However, these efforts, which identify whether this data is directly or inversely related to a specific market, still do not offer a way to quantify these relationships or assess the simultaneous impact of multiple relationships on a given market.

Implementation

The appropriate tools needed to integrate data from related markets and quantify their influence on one another remained elusive until I began research into various artificial intelligence (AI) technologies. As it turns out, one of them, neural networks, is very well suited to implementing synergistic analysis. Neural networks can be used to synthesize technical, fundamental, and intermarket analysis into one analytic framework, capable of finding hidden patterns and complex relationships in data. The application of this technology to financial market analysis has quickly become a hot subject in the financial industry, with dozens of articles and several books written on the subject in the past few years.[11,12,13,14] Amid all this hoopla, traders must keep this technology in perspective. Neural networks are simply a mathematical tool. It is their ability to quantify intermarket relationships and find patterns in data from related markets that allows neural networks to play an important role in implementing synergistic market analysis in today's global markets.

SYNERGISTIC MARKET ANALYSIS WITH NEURAL NETWORKS

The remainder of this chapter will examine the application of neural networks to synergistic analysis. Traders who prefer to leave the research and development phase of neural networks to the experts, but who are interested in understanding how

---

[10] Murphy, J. J. *Intermarket Technical Analysis.* New York: John Wiley & Sons, Inc., 1991.

[11] Mendelsohn, L. B. "The Basics of Developing A Neural Trading System." *Technical Analysis of Stocks & Commodities* (June 1991).

[12] Chinetti, D., F. Gardin, and C. Rossignoli. "A Neural Network Model for Stock Market Prediction." The Second International Conference on Artificial Intelligence Applications on Wall Street, 1993.

[13] Jang, G., and F. Lai. "Intelligent Stock Market Prediction System Using Dual Adaptive-Structure Neural Networks." The Second International Conference on Artificial Intelligence Applications on Wall Street, 1993.

[14] Trippi, R. R., and T. Efraim. *Neural Networks in Finance and Investing: Using Artificial Intelligence to Improve Real-World Performance,* Chicago, IL: Probus Publishing Company, 1992.

neural networks can be applied in their own trading right away, may want to skip to the section entitled "Implementation," where I describe my firm's neural network software program, called VantagePoint. This "turnkey" system, which requires no expertise in neural network development by the user, performs synergistic analysis to predict prices and trends for various financial futures markets.

For traders interested in what goes on "under the hood" of neural networks, the following sections will detail issues that must be addressed and potential pitfalls to be avoided when researching and developing financial applications with this technology. Emphasis will be on price and trend forecasting utilizing market data from a target market, related intermarkets, and fundamental inputs (see Figure 2). Attention will be focused on how to choose appropriate neural network paradigms, architectures, and training regimens for this type of application. Where appropriate, other artificial intelligence technologies will be discussed in terms of how they can be used in conjunction with neural networks to create hybrid information and trading systems.

Figure 2.   SMA with Neural Networks. Overview of the basic model.

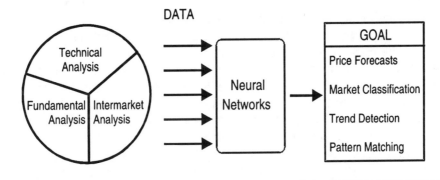

ARTIFICIAL NEURAL NETWORKS

Artificial neural networks[15,16,17] are loosely based on models of how the human brain processes information. Neural networks utilize a distributed processing approach to computation, in which many simple processing elements, or neurons, communicate with one another via a network. Information is stored in the network as a pattern of weights, and learning occurs during a training process in which changes are made to these weights. Neural networks are *trained* to behave in a desired fashion. Similar to humans, neural networks are capable of learning certain behaviors by being presented examples of those behaviors. Following training, neural networks are able to generalize to related but unseen behaviors.

Now let's look at the following aspects of neural network development for financial forecasting:

[15] Hecht-Nielsen, R. *Neurocomputing.* Reading, MA: Addison-Wesley Publishing Company, Inc., 1990.

[16] Aleksander, I., and H. Morton. *An Introduction to Neural Computing.* London: Chapman and Hall, 1990.

[17] Wasserman, P. D. *Neural Computing: Theory and Practice.* New York: Van Nostrand Reinhold, 1989.

- ◆ Paradigms

- ◆ Architecture

- ◆ Input data selection

- ◆ Preprocessing input data

- ◆ Fact selection

- ◆ Training and testing

- ◆ Implementation

Paradigms

Neural networks are applicable to many general problem areas within the financial industry, as well as in other industries. These areas include classification, filtering, autoassociation, pattern association, optimization, data compression, and prediction. It is important to identify the problems to be addressed before starting to develop a neural network application, since the proper choice of network paradigm is dependent on the problem definition for a specific application.

For example, paradigms like *differential competitive learning* and *counterpropagation* can be used for data-clustering tasks, while the *Hopfield network* and *brain state in a box* paradigms may be more appropriate for autoassociation, filtering, and pattern association. Each available paradigm has numerous variations, depending on how its parameters are selected. The problem domain of financial forecasting falls into the prediction category. For this application there are two often-used paradigms: *recurrent back-propagation networks* and *feed-forward back-propagation networks*. This chapter will focus on the latter, since it is probably the most widely used paradigm in financial analysis. Additionally, for every recurrent network there is a corresponding feed-forward network with identical behavior.[18]

Feed-Forward Back-Propagation Networks

A feed-forward network that trains by back-propagation of error throughout a multi-layered network is commonly referred to as a back-propagation, or back-prop, network. A typical back-prop network architecture is shown in Figure 3. In this type of network, time (temporal relationships) must be encoded into the facts presented to the network. To accomplish this a technique often referred to as taking a "snapshot" of the data is used to convert time-series data into a format necessary for training.

For example, to present facts that contain the differences in the closes for the past five weeks, a snapshot of the data must be created by constructing a fact with an input vector containing five values (one for each difference) and an output for the next week. This must be done for each fact-week to be presented to the network, effectively encoding the temporal information (data from the last five weeks) into the facts themselves.

---

[18] Hecht-Nielsen, R. *Neurocomputing*. Reading, MA: Addison-Wesley Publishing Company, Inc., 1990.

Figure 3. Simple feed-forward back-propagation network. A back-prop net using technical, fundamental, and intermarket data. The network trains by back-propagation of error throughout the network.

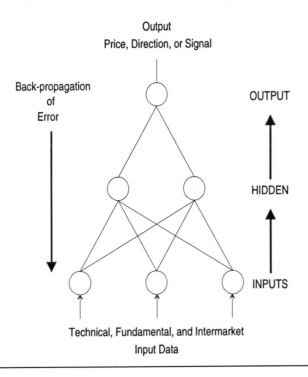

Output
Price, Direction, or Signal

Back-propagation
of
Error

OUTPUT

HIDDEN

INPUTS

Technical, Fundamental, and Intermarket
Input Data

Learning occurs in a feed-forward back-propagation network when it is given examples of inputs and expected outputs. For each output, the network computes an error measure between its generated output and the desired output. The error is typically averaged over the entire set of facts, then propagated backward through the network's layers, and used to alter the weight connections between neurons. The weights are changed in this manner to reduce the overall error associated with the network's outputs. As the training process continues, facts are presented to the network repeatedly in an effort to minimize the output error. While the error may be reduced to zero for simple problems, practical financial applications cannot be expected to achieve this level of accuracy, as will be discussed later in this chapter.

Architecture

Some decisions that must be made in reference to network architecture are:

♦ What transfer function should be used?

♦ How many inputs does the network need?

♦ How many hidden layers does the network need?

♦ How many hidden neurons per hidden layer?

♦ How many outputs should the network have?

Back-prop networks are comprised of an input layer and an output layer, usually separated by one or more "hidden" layers. The hidden layers are not directly accessible to the network's user. This arrangement, as represented in Figure 3, assumes that the layers are fully connected, which means that each neuron in the input layer is linked to each neuron in the hidden layer, with similar connections between the neurons in the hidden and output layers.

Each layer is comprised of neurons that send data to neurons in the next layer and receive data from neurons in the previous layer. The standard model is quite simple. For each neuron (see Figure 4), input data (I_0-I_n) is multiplied by the weight (W_0-W_n) associated with the connection to the neuron in the next layer. The products are summed, and the result is passed through a transfer function that maps the sum to a value in a specified interval, e.g., between zero and one. Each neuron's output is then multiplied by another weight and fed into the next neuron. If this neuron is in the output layer, as is the case in Figure 3, the output is not multiplied by a weight but is instead the network's output.

Figure 4.   An example of a hidden neuron.
Neural networks are composed of individual interconnected processing elements called neurons.

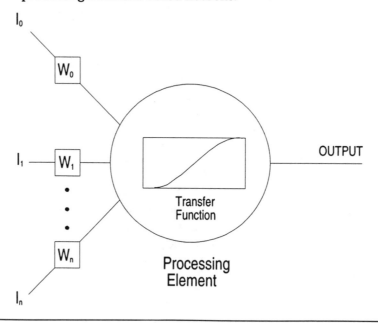

Transfer Functions

The transfer function, as mentioned earlier, maps a neuron's inputs to an output. A neuron's input signals are multiplied by their respective weights, summed, and then mapped via the transfer function to an output. It would not be appropriate, when modeling global financial markets, to use a transfer function that represents a line with a constant slope, or a discontinuous function, like those shown in Figure 5. Instead, the transfer function should be a nonlinear, continuously differentiable func-

Figure 5. Transfer functions.
Two transfer functions that may be used in a back-propagation
network, but not for modeling nonlinear systems.

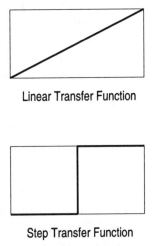

Linear Transfer Function

Step Transfer Function

tion, which allows the network to perform the necessary nonlinear modeling of inter-related financial markets.

The most commonly used nonlinear transfer functions include the logistic function (an example of which can be seen in Figure 4) and the tanh function, known as the hyperbolic tangent function. These functions are very similar to one another. The logistic function varies in height from zero to one, while the tanh function ranges from minus one to plus one.

Both of these functions can be used effectively in a back-prop network. Our research suggests that the tanh function trains slightly faster than the logistic function. Intuitively plausible reasons why this might be the case have been reported by other researchers.[19]

Layers and Neurons

In addition to the choice of transfer function, it must be decided how many layers and how many neurons in each layer will be used. These decisions are relatively straightforward with respect to the input and output layers. For instance, in order to predict the change in the close for a particular futures contract based on a 20-day moving average of closes plus a five-day moving average of the high and a five-day moving average of the low, the network would require three input neurons and one output neuron. An example of such a net was depicted in Figure 3.

For nonlinear problems, such as predicting future prices of a stock or commodity, a back-prop neural network needs at least one hidden layer. There are no simple rules for determining the proper number of hidden layers in a back-propagation net-

---

[19] Gallant, S. I. *Neural Network Learning and Expert Systems.* Cambridge, MA: The Massachusetts Institute of Technology, 1993.

work. While one layer is theoretically sufficient to approximate any nonlinear function's input-to-output mapping, networks can have more than one hidden layer. The best architectural configuration for a specific network application is usually arrived at through experimentation, since this facet of neural network development is more art than science. Experiments must be conducted to vary the number of hidden layers and hidden neurons to assess their influence on network performance. Complex problems typically require more hidden neurons. However, too many hidden neurons may cause "overfitting" to the training data, which should be avoided since it may contribute to poor network performance later on.

The more task-specific a neural network is, the more easily it can be trained. Therefore, it is often preferable to design networks that have only one output, rather than having one network with two or more outputs.

In neural network development, no individual design decision, such as selecting the number of hidden layers or neurons, entirely determines how well the network will perform. Choice of input data, data preprocessing techniques, optimization of training parameters, and choice of testing procedures are all important factors that affect network performance. Since optimizing network architecture is time-consuming, due to the size of the parameter space to be explored, this process should be automated. The remainder of this chapter will examine these issues in more detail, and will illustrate real-world examples to highlight common pitfalls that should be avoided during each phase of neural network development.

Input Data Selection

Questions that must be answered during the input data selection phase of network development include:

- What is the problem domain?

- What are the input sources?

- Should the input sources be technical, fundamental, intermarket, or a combination of the three?

Data selection must be performed judiciously to avoid the "garbage-in, garbage-out" syndrome often associated with computers. A neural network's performance is highly dependent on the quality and appropriateness of its input data. If relevant data inputs are not included, the network's performance will suffer needlessly. For this reason it is important to have a solid understanding of the financial markets and intermarket relationships within the context of global trading.

Following a specific market analysis theory or analytic perspective on the markets when selecting input data for a financial neural network application has its own implications. I posit that the financial markets are nonlinear, and possibly chaotic,[20, 21] that market inefficiencies exist, can be discerned quantitatively, and persist long

---

[20] Peters, E. E. *Chaos and Order in the Capital Markets: A New View of Cycles, Prices and Market Volatility.* New York: John Wiley & Sons, 1991.

[21] Peters, E. E. *Fractal Market Analysis: Applying Chaos Theory to Investment & Economics.* New York: John Wiley & Sons, 1994.

enough for traders to profit from them. Technical analysis suggests the use of only single-market technical data as inputs. Fundamental analysis focuses on economic factors that influence the target market. Neither of these traditional approaches alone is sufficient in today's global environment. Similarly, intermarket analysis that relies solely on the subjective and/or qualitative interpretation of several price charts cannot adequately model the simultaneous influence of multiple markets on a target market. By contrast, Synergistic Market Analysis, through the use of neural networks, combines these three methods of analysis into a multidimensional quantitative framework. Multiple data inputs reflecting a broad range of related markets and fundamental inputs can be used to discern the general tendencies and patterns between markets, and quantify these nonlinear relationships that affect a given market.

Now, to see how SMA can be implemented, let's look at a simple example of input data selection for a neural network designed to predict the following week's high and low for the Treasury bond market. First, technical price data on Treasury bonds is included to make general patterns and characteristics of the bond market apparent to the network. Then, related fundamental data, such as the federal funds rate, is included as additional inputs into the network. Finally, intermarket inputs are utilized. Sensitivity analysis, in which data inputs are varied, can be performed to help identify the best combination of intermarket and fundamental data to include as inputs.

For instance, in the case of VantagePoint, raw input data from the Treasury bond market—including open, high, low, close, volume, and open interest—is combined with similar data from eight related intermarkets—including the CRB Index, deutsche mark, Eurodollar, US Dollar Index, Japanese yen, S&P 500 Stock Index, crude oil, and gold. In addition, the daily Fed funds rate is included. Other VantagePoint systems incorporate intermarkets such as the FTSE and Nikkei stock indices as well as the Dow Jones Industrial and Utility Averages. Input selection and preprocessing is the subject of ongoing research by my firm, in an effort to improve network performance. Appendix 1 contains a simple case study that exemplifies the benefits of utilizing intermarket data.

Preprocessing Input Data

To facilitate neural network training, the selected raw input data must be preprocessed. Two widely used preprocessing methods, *transformation* and *normalization*, will now be discussed.

Transformation manipulates one or more raw data inputs to generate a single network input. Normalization is used to distribute data more evenly and scale it into an acceptable range for network usage. Decisions made during this phase are:

♦ What transformations should be applied to the data?

♦ Should these transformations include standard technical analysis indicators?

♦ How should the data be normalized?

As previously mentioned with respect to the selection of raw data inputs, domain knowledge is critical to the choice of preprocessing methods.

Transformation

For financial forecasting, commonly used technical indicators like moving averages can be utilized as transforms. The *noise* component within raw price data tends to obscure underlying relationships between input data sources and slow down the training process. Therefore, smoothing techniques such as moving averages, which help reduce the *noise* entering the network, are useful transforms.

In addition, two very simple preprocessing methods involve computing differences between, or ratios of, inputs. For example, when creating a neural net to predict the next week's Treasury bond close, various lengths of moving averages of the close can be used as inputs to the net. Additionally, moving averages of the ratio of the CRB Index to Treasury bond prices can be used as an intermarket input along with differences, or spreads, between Treasury bond prices and other related intermarkets. This helps to minimize the required number of input neurons and facilitates learning.

Normalization

The objective of data normalization is to ensure that the statistical distribution of values for each net input and output is roughly uniform. If this is not done, and an input with a normal distribution and a small variance is used, then the net will only see a small number of occurrences of facts away from the central tendency. The values should also be scaled to match the range of the input neurons. Therefore, in addition to any other transformations performed on network inputs, each should be normalized.

I will now discuss three useful methods of data normalization. The first is a simple linear method of scaling data. At a minimum, data must be scaled into the range used by the network's input neurons. This is typically in the range of minus one to one or zero to one. The scaling function involves finding the minimum and maximum values in a data set, setting these equal to the lower and upper values of the desired range, and scaling all intervening values based on the proportional change. This method scales input data into the appropriate range but does not increase its uniformity.

The second normalization method uses a statistical measure of central tendency and variance to help remove outliers, and spreads out the distribution of the data, typically increasing uniformity. This is done by altering, or clipping, data that is beyond a specified distance from the mean.

The third normalization method, the Mendelsohn histogram normalization (MHN) method, was developed by the *Predictive Technologies Group*, a research division of Mendelsohn Enterprises, Inc. This function performs several transformations on the data to minimize the standard deviation of the heights of the columns in the initial frequency distribution histogram.

Figure 6 depicts an example distribution, in the form of a histogram, in which the data is not uniformly distributed. To illustrate the effects of the three methods of normalization, each has been used to prepare this data as input to a neural net in the range zero to one. Figure 7 shows that a simple linear scaling of the data has no effect on the shape of the frequency distribution itself. Figure 8 shows the same original

Figure 6.   Example input distribution. A sample distribution of data for a single input neuron, in which the data are not uniformly distributed.

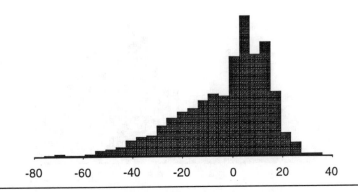

Figure 7.   Simple linear scaling. This normalization adjusts data into the range necessary for processing by a neural network but does not affect the uniformity of the distribution.

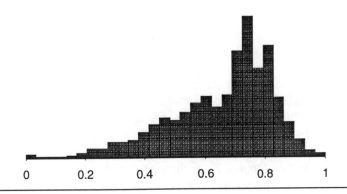

Figure 8.   Statistical normalization.
A standard method of increasing input data uniformity.

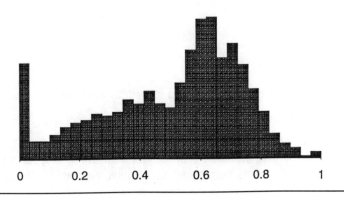

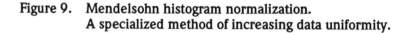

Figure 9.   Mendelsohn histogram normalization.
A specialized method of increasing data uniformity.

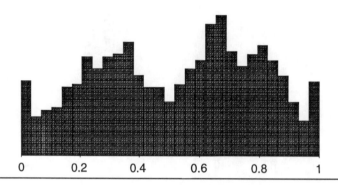

distribution normalized by the second method, in which two standard deviations are used to set the limits for the outliers so that the distribution becomes more uniform. Figure 9 shows that, after performing MHN on the data, the resulting distribution is the most uniformly distributed. There are various methods that can be used to normalize data, with some methods being more effective than others, depending on the data to be normalized.

Denormalization

During the testing phase of development, the output produced must be denormalized. Ideally, the normalization should be reversible with little or no loss in accuracy. Normalization methods that clip outlier values are sometimes not sufficiently reversible. For instance, if during training all output values greater than 75 are clipped by assigning them a value of 75, then, during testing if the net produces an output of 75, this simply indicates that the output is 75 *or more.* If this level of detail is acceptable for a specific application, then the normalization method used is sufficiently reversible.

After the architecture has been selected, and the raw data inputs have been chosen and preprocessed, fact sets must be created.

Fact Selection

This section examines:

- ♦ What is a fact?

- ♦ What is a fact set?

- ♦ How many fact sets should be used in training a network?

- ♦ What criteria should be used to select facts for the fact sets?

A *fact* is a single input vector and its associated output vector. A fact is typically represented as a row of numbers where the first n numbers correspond to n network inputs and the last m numbers correspond to m network outputs. If a network has been designed to predict the change in price of the Dow Jones Industrial Average (DJIA) one week in advance, based on the differences in the highs and the lows for the past five days and a moving average of the closes for the past 10 days, then each fact would be composed of a three-valued input vector and a single-valued output vector. The three input values would correspond to the differences in the highs and the lows for the past five days and a moving average of the closes for the past 10 days. The single-valued output vector would represent the change in the DJIA over the next week (see Figure 10).

Figure 10. Representation of a fact. A fact can be represented as two vectors— one input and one output.

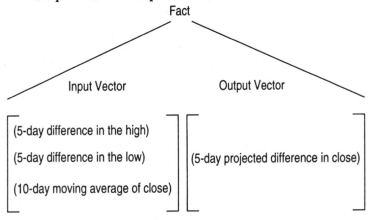

A *fact set* is a group of related facts. It is important to determine what data to include in a fact set, since it should represent the problem space to be modeled. For example, it must be decided whether or not to include S&P 500 data from October 1987 in a fact set. Since this data is not supported by a sufficient number of examples, the network may not be able to learn how to recognize it in the future. Additionally, its presence in the fact set might introduce a bias that could reduce the overall accuracy of the system during more typical trading periods.

Although internal technical data for a target market are readily available, related fundamental data are still not widely available through most data vendors. Likewise, relevant intermarket data may be unavailable, depending on when each of the related markets began trading. For instance, while Japanese yen futures began trading in 1972, the Nikkei 225 Index only started trading as a futures contract in 1990. To use both markets' data in a neural network application for currency predictions, the fact set would have to be shortened so that it starts in 1990. However, use of shortened data sets can result in significant market characteristics being missed. For example, over the past decade there has really not been a sustained bear market in the S&P 500. Therefore, a neural network trained only on recent data will not be able to adapt quickly to changing market conditions in the future such as would occur at the onset of the next bear market. Data availability and sufficient representation of various market conditions are important considerations in the choice of input data and fact selection.

Training and Testing Fact Sets

Once the fact set has been selected, it is divided into training and testing subsets. Back-propagation networks operate in two modes: a learning or training mode, and a recall or testing mode. In the *learning* mode, the network modifies the values of its weights to adapt its internal representation, in an effort to improve the mapping of inputs to outputs. In the *recall* mode the network is presented with new inputs and utilizes the representation it had previously learned to generate associated outputs without changing the weights. Since neural networks operate in these two modes, the facts should be separated into at least two subsets: a training set and a testing set. The training set's facts are used during learning, while the testing set's facts are used during recall. Performance comparisons of various networks on the test set are used to determine which net to select for use in the final application.

Various criteria can be used to determine the composition of the training and testing sets. First, they should be mutually exclusive, which means that a specific fact does not reside in both subsets. It also means that if two facts have the same input and output values, one of these facts should be deleted from the fact set before it is separated into subsets. Additionally, caution must be exercised when using commercial tools that automatically split the initial fact set. For example, in an 80/20 split of the initial fact set, some tools may place every fifth fact in the test set, as opposed to randomly assigning facts to each subset. If the facts are in chronological order before the split, all data representing one day of the week, such as a Monday or Friday, could be assigned to the test set, while the remaining data would be assigned to the training set. This can skew the network results. To avoid this, the order of the facts should be randomized before they are split into subsets.

Even when randomizing fact order and splitting into subsets, all facts with a specific characteristic might still be placed in one subset or the other. To prevent this, it is advisable to identify the most important characteristics thought to be associated with the data and determine the fact set's underlying distribution relative to these characteristics. Then the fact set can be split so that the training and testing subsets have similar distributions relative to these characteristics. Statistical analysis or clustering algorithms can be used to accomplish this. A careful analysis of the fact set will also allow outliers to be identified and eliminated.

Experimentation with a number of data-handling methods should be performed before selecting one. The Predictive Technologies Group has developed a training/testing regimen that splits the initial fact set into three mutually exclusive subsets, not just two. In addition to the standard training and testing sets, a second testing set, which includes examples of those facts thought to be most important in judging network performance, is utilized to compare various networks to one another.

Training and Testing

This section will examine the process of training and testing a back-propagation neural network. When performing these steps of network development, the following issues must be addressed:

- ♦ How should the initial weights be determined?

- ♦ What learning algorithm should be used?

- ◆ What is the learning rate? How should it be set?

- ◆ What is momentum? How should it be set?

- ◆ What is simulated annealing?

- ◆ What is overtraining? How can it be avoided?

- ◆ What metrics are appropriate for testing?

After the training fact set has been created, training can be initiated. First, the weights are initialized. Typically, relatively small random weights are used to initialize the network. As mentioned earlier, during training the weights are changed to allow the network to adapt its internal representation when modeling a problem. It is sometimes advisable to train the same network several times with different sets of initial weights, since they can affect network training and performance.

Learning Algorithms

Various learning algorithms can be used when performing back-propagation, which provide methods of minimizing the overall error associated with the network's output. They accomplish this by traversing the net's error surface, or error landscape. Since the landscape is immense, each algorithm attempts to minimize the overall error while evaluating as few points as possible on the error surface. This results in a trade-off between network performance and training time. If every point on the surface were to be evaluated through an exhaustive search, optimal performance would be assured. Since this would be impossible for all but the simplest problems, algorithms are utilized that produce acceptable solutions within a reasonable time.

The Gradient-Descent Algorithm

One of the most common algorithms used in back-propagation is the gradient-descent algorithm. Starting at an initial point on the error surface, it determines the gradient that quantifies the slope, or steepness, of the curvature of the error surface at that point. The algorithm uses this information by moving in the exact opposite direction by an amount proportional to the learning rate, a constant discussed later in this chapter. By utilizing this "downhill" movement along the error surface, the algorithm minimizes error.

Other learning algorithms include conjugate-gradients, Newton-Raphson, and Levenberg-Marquardt. However, no one algorithm is the best for all optimization problems.[22] They all require a starting point somewhere in the vicinity of the optimal point, and some degree of smoothness of the performance landscape. This is not true of genetic algorithms.

---

[22] Wolfe, M. A. *Numerical Methods for Unconstrained Optimization: An Introduction.* New York: Van Nostrand Reinhold, 1978.

Genetic Algorithms (GAs)

Genetic algorithms[23,24] use simple mechanisms, analogous to those used in genetics, to breed populations of superior solutions. Those that do well "breed" with other solutions to form new solutions. Solutions that perform poorly are culled.

Genetic algorithms are a robust class of optimization algorithms. They do not require any special initial conditions and make no requirements on the smoothness of the performance landscape.

Genetic algorithms can be used to train a net by evolving populations of weight matrices. In this case, back-propagation of errors is not needed. Only the forward-propagation of facts through the net and subsequent evaluation of the fact-errors is required.

Learning

The network "learns" during training by altering its weights, based on error information propagated backward throughout the network from the output layer. Error can be propagated, and weights changed, each time a fact is presented, after a subset of the facts has been presented, or after all facts have been presented. One cycle, in which all facts have been presented to the network, is referred to as an *epoch*. With each change in the weights' values, the network is taking a step on a multidimensional surface, which represents the overall error space. During training, the network traverses the surface in an attempt to find the lowest point, or minimum error. Weight changes are proportional to a training parameter called the *learning rate*.

Oscillation

The largest possible learning rate that does not result in oscillation should be selected. As a simple example of oscillation, imagine that a network's current weight values place it halfway down a valley on a two-dimensional error surface, as depicted in Figure 11. If the learning rate is too large, the network's next step might be to the other side of the valley, as opposed to moving toward the bottom. Then, the following step might return to the original side, so that the network tends to bounce back and forth from one side of the valley to the other without much movement toward the bottom, where the solution lies. Alternatively, with too small a learning rate, in which the steps that the network takes are very small, it could take too long to get to the bottom of the valley to arrive at a solution. Since each problem space has its own unique error surface, the learning rate must be varied to achieve the best balance between training time and overall error reduction for a specific application.

Momentum

Another training parameter, known as *momentum*, acts as a filter to reduce oscillation. It allows higher learning rates to be used to obtain solutions similar to those found with lower learning rates, thereby potentially decreasing the training time.

---

[23] Holland, J. H. *Adaptation in Natural and Artificial Systems.* Ann Arbor, MI: The University of Michigan Press, 1975.

[24] Goldberg, D. E. *Genetic Algorithms in Search, Optimization & Machine Learning.* Reading, MA: Addison-Wesley Publishing Company, 1989.

Figure 11. 2-D example of oscillation.
With the step size held constant, oscillation can occur.

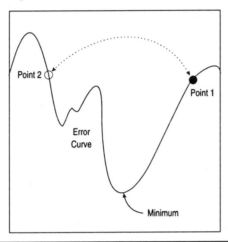

Learning rates and momentum should be adjusted through experimentation. Some development tools include additional parameters—such as temperature, gain, and noise—that can also be modified to affect training.

Simulated Annealing

Simulated annealing is a training method that simulates the process of annealing by including a temperature term which affects the learning rate. The temperature begins relatively high, allowing the network to move quickly over the error surface. Then, as training progresses the temperature decreases, so that learning slows as the network *cools* and settles upon a near-optimum solution. The use of simulated annealing also reduces the likelihood of oscillation. Figure 12 depicts a two-dimensional example of

Figure 12. Example of simulated annealing.
By reducing the learning rate over time, oscillation is less likely and better solutions may be found more quickly.

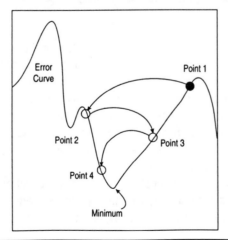

simulated annealing, in which the step size is reduced to avoid oscillation while finding a minimum point on the error surface.

Training and Testing Automation Necessary

The multidimensional space defined by all free parameters is known as the parameter-space of a back-propagation model. If it has only two free parameters, such as the learning rate and the momentum, then the parameter-space can be represented graphically in two dimensions, with the learning rate on one axis and the momentum on the other. Here, the parameter-space is composed of the quarter-plane defined by the positive values of the two parameters (see Figure 13).

Figure 13. 2-D parameter space.
A graphic depiction of the 2-D plane resulting from two free
parameters and the quarter-plane parameter space they create.

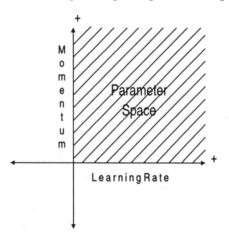

The goal is to find an optimal set of values for the parameters, whereby an optimally performing net is produced upon training with these values. This amounts to finding the "best" point in the parameter-space.

Brute Force

Brute force is perhaps the simplest way to find the optimal parameters, in which a large set of points in the parameter-space is examined. Assume that a third axis representing performance is defined. The three-dimensional space comprised of the learning rate, momentum, and performance can be viewed as creating a performance landscape. Each experiment identifies one point on the performance landscape. Once many points have been identified, the shape of the landscape becomes apparent (at least in this simple example). Now, the landscape can be used to guide the selection of trial parameter-space points.

After investigating the properties of the back-propagation paradigm, a practical sense of the size of its parameter-space can be appreciated. The training parameters may vary from node to node in the network and from epoch to epoch during training.

If a net has 100 trainable nodes and is trained for 1,000 epochs, then the two-dimensional example becomes 200,000-dimensional!

To further complicate matters, all possible initial (random weight) conditions, as well as the number of hidden layers and nodes, must be considered part of the parameter-space. In this light, the parameter-space is virtually infinite in extent.

Automation

The myriad decisions that must be made in the development of a neural network application makes automation of the training and testing process highly desirable. This is particularly true in selecting preprocessing, choosing the number of hidden layers and neurons, and setting training parameters. Tools such as genetic algorithms can be used to expedite parameter space searches. Genetic algorithms can be used to control only the free parameters, such as the learning rate and momentum within the traditional gradient-descent-based back-prop algorithm. Also, methods such as simulated annealing are useful for automating learning rate adjustments during training.

Avoid Overtraining

During training, a serious pitfall that must be avoided is *overtraining*. This is analogous to the common problem of *overoptimizing* rule-based trading systems. Overtraining occurs when a network has learned not only the basic mapping associated with the input and output data presented to it, but also the subtle nuances and even the errors specific to the training set. Through memorization, an overtrained network can perform very well on the training set, but will fail to do so on out-of-sample test data and later during actual trading. This is because the network is unable to *generalize* to new data.

Overtraining can be avoided through the use of an automated training/testing routine in which testing is an integral part of the training process. Network training is stopped periodically at predetermined intervals. The network then operates in recall mode on the test set to evaluate the network's performance on selected error criteria, after which training resumes.

This process continues iteratively, with interim results that meet selected error criteria retained for later analysis. When network performance on the test set begins to degrade, the best saved network configurations up to this point are further evaluated. In order to conduct a rigorous comparison of various networks as their architectures, raw data inputs, preprocessing, and training parameters are changed, a robust, automated training/testing methodology is necessary.

Error Measures

Network performance can be evaluated on test data according to various criteria. One commonly used error measure is called *average error*. Unfortunately, when judging network performance, this metric is not particularly useful, since the positive errors cancel the negative errors. A more useful error metric would be *average absolute error*. With this metric, the absolute value of the error for each fact in the test set is summed and then divided by the number of facts in the test set. Examples of other error measures based on the distance from the target value include *sum-of-squares error* and *root mean squared* (RMS) *error*.

Neural networks can even be used to judge the performance of other networks. One simple approach that we use to determine how much a net can still be improved is to train a second net that predicts the errors of the first net. If the second net learns to predict a significant percentage of the first net's errors, then the first net could still be improved. This method is referred to as iterative refinement, since it may be repeated indefinitely by adding more nets. There are other approaches that are useful for improving a net's performance, but most involve constructive algorithms applied during the training or retraining of an existing net.[25]

Expectations of Performance

Performance expectations for a financial forecasting application depend on one's viewpoint on the underlying market dynamics of the target market. For example, if a neural net is designed to forecast a completely random time series, then it should not be surprising if large prediction errors occur, since, by definition, such a time series is unpredictable.

While a given market is driven by both stochastic (random) and deterministic forces, only the latter are predictable. However, even chaos can be deterministically generated. As recent work at Los Alamos National Laboratory has shown, neural networks can predict such chaos quite well.[26,27]

Still, expectations must be realistic. The equity curve in Figure 21 (from the section "Hybrid Trading Systems") based on VantagePoint's predicted information, suggests that there is a sufficient degree of predictability within the markets to be profitable. Presently, the maximum achievable accuracy of financial forecasting is unknown. It is unrealistic to expect to achieve zero error, since this would require a model that accounts for events that are today deemed random. Nevertheless, simply because events are currently unpredictable does not mean that they are necessarily random. Indeed, each revision of VantagePoint over the past three years has been able to predict events that previously appeared to be stochastic noise. For the time being, it is unknown where the "ceiling" on performance accuracy is located.

Since many commercial network development tools have limited error metrics available, development and implementation of custom error functions is most desirable for serious network development.

Successful neural network applications for nontrivial problems require considerable talent and expertise in a number of disciplines, including market analysis, computer science, and applied mathematics. Even with extensive in-house research and development tools and the availability of numerous commercial tools, neural net development to implement Synergistic Market Analysis for financial forecasting is a time-consuming, labor-intensive task. Since a team effort is necessary for successful neural

---

[25] Gallant, S. I. Neural Network Learning and Expert Systems. Cambridge, MA: The Massachusetts Institute of Technology, 1993.

[26] Lapedes, A., and R. Farber. "Nonlinear Signal Processing Using Neural Network Prediction and System Modeling." Theoretical Division, Los Alamos National Laboratory, Report #: LA-UR-87-2662, 1987.

[27] Farmer, D. F. and J. J. Sidorowich, J. J. "Exploiting Chaos to Predict the Future and Reduce Noise," Version 1.2. Theoretical Division, and Center for Nonlinear Studies, Los Alamos National Laboratory, Report #: LA-UR-88-901, 1988.

network development, traders lacking such expertise can still benefit from this technology's ability to assess intermarket relationships through the application of fully developed and trained networks, such as VantagePoint. The main benefit of utilizing a pretrained neural network system is that traders can put this technology to use without having to first become rocket scientists.

Implementation

Now I would like to discuss how Synergistic Analysis can be implemented through the use of neural networks, and how they can be integrated within an overall trading strategy into two types of trading applications: information systems and trading systems. VantagePoint will be used as an example to illustrate how this can be accomplished. Finally, I will offer insights into future directions for use of artificial intelligence technologies to implement Synergistic Market Analysis in the financial forecasting arena.

Information Systems

Information systems that generate forecasts related to a specific target market, including price forecasts and predictions about market direction or turning points, can be implemented through the use of neural networks. Such information can be used alone or in conjunction with other analytic information available to the trader. Information systems can be comprised of a single neural network, or as in the case of VantagePoint, which utilizes five networks, a multinetwork hierarchically organized system. Traders need to collect daily data on the target market and related intermarkets by modem, in order to obtain predictions for the next day's trading.

VantagePoint has four networks, which are specifically designed and trained to make independent market forecasts of the high, low, short-term, and medium-term trends for use on the following trading day. Since these forecasts are independently derived, they can be used to confirm one another. Additionally, the outputs from the four networks are used as inputs into a fifth network, which predicts market turning points. A network architecture such as VantagePoint's, depicted in Figure 14, is referred to as *hierarchical.*

In this type of network configuration, predictions made by networks at the primary level of the hierarchy are incorporated as inputs into a network, or networks, at a secondary level. Such hierarchical architecture facilitates faster training, since all networks at the primary level of the hierarchy can be trained simultaneously, as each focuses solely on a single output.

VantagePoint's predictions can be visualized graphically with various chart overlays or in tabular form on its daily trading prediction report. When viewing the charts, users can select four different chart types, from bar charts to candlestick charts (see Figure 15). As many as eight different studies can be overlayed on each chart. These studies include forecasted information as well as information computed from these forecasts, to help traders utilize the information more effectively. Additionally, to customize the chart's appearance, a variety of user-adjustable parameters (see Figure 15) are available.

An example of a chart produced by the VantagePoint Treasury Bond System is shown in Figure 16, in which the predicted high and low values are plotted over the

Figure 14. Hierarchical neural network.
Here is a graphical depiction of a multinetwork architecture.

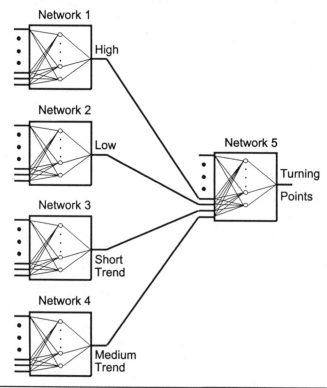

Figure 15. Chart preferences. This window allows users to display a variety of
studies and change the overall appearance of VantagePoint's charts.

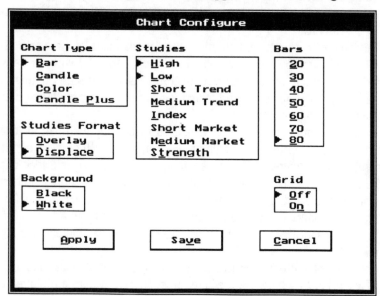

Figure 16. VantagePoint forecasts. Bar chart of the Treasury bond futures contract with predicted highs and lows.

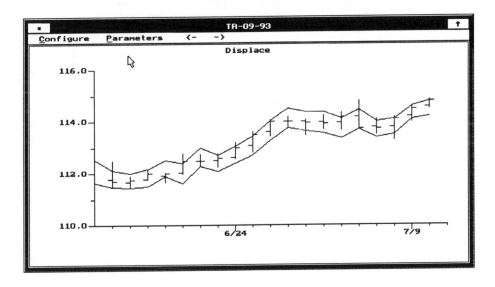

daily price bars. Such information is particularly useful in helping to determine entry and exit points for day trading or position holding. If the forecasted information on the daily report suggests that the next day will be an *up* day in the market, day traders might wait until the market trades down toward the predicted low, then enter a long position with a limit or market order. The reverse would involve entering a short position at or near the predicted high on a day expected to be a down day. Entering at these levels increases the potential for a profitable day trade. Two examples of this are shown from the March 1994 Treasury bond contract (see Figure 17). In the example on the left, the up arrow (indicating an expected upward trend in market direction) and the predicted low for tomorrow are generated on December 2, 1993. If a long position was entered on the open and exited at the close on December 3, 1993, based solely on the anticipated direction, a profit of 12 ticks ($375.00 before slippage and commission) would have been realized. If, instead, an entry to go long had been executed at the predicted low, with an exit at the close, a profit of 24 ticks ($750.00 before slippage and commission) would have been realized, doubling the profit.

The example on the right of Figure 17 shows the same concept in reverse. Instead of entering at the open and exiting at the close on an expected *down* day, a short trade could entered at the predicted high and exited at the close, resulting in a profit of 10 ticks ($312.50 before slippage and commission). Additionally, day traders can use the predicted high/low range to set exit points, rather than exiting at the close. In this scenario, on a day when the market direction is predicted to be *up,* a long position is entered at or near the predicted low, then closed out intraday at or near the predicted high. Similarly, short positions can be closed out intraday at or near the predicted low, rather than exited at the close.

Figure 17. **Improved day trading using forecasts.**
Synergistic neural systems, like VantagePoint, can be used to
forecast market direction and improve trade profitability.

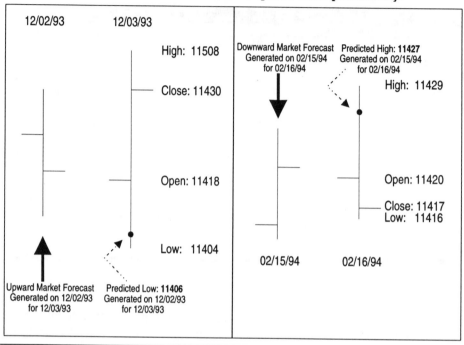

Using these strategies, entry trades may not get executed when the market does not make the entry objective indicated by the predicted high or low. However, the profitability of those trades that are executed can be substantial, with minimal risk since very tight stops can be used.

Position holders might apply the same principles in entering the market, using the predicted range on subsequent days to set daily stops. For example, if position holders are long Treasury bonds and the next day is expected to be an *up* day, they might set their stops for the next day a few ticks below its predicted low, which acts as a support level. This reduces the likelihood of getting stopped out during the day prematurely as the result of intraday market volatility, yet protects profits in the event of a severe intraday market downturn.

Position holders and day traders can use forecasted trends and changes in trend direction to their advantage. This information can be used alone or in conjunction with other market information to generate buy/sell signals. One still popular method of technical analysis is a moving-average crossover system. Typically, two or more moving averages are plotted on a chart. Buy and sell signals are generated when the short moving average crosses over or under the long moving average. The obvious limitation of this approach is that, by definition, moving averages are lagging indicators. As a result, they get whipsawed during sideways markets. Moving average systems also generate signals after market turning points have occurred, thus sacrificing profits at the beginning and end of a market move. Neural-network-generated trend forecasts can be used effectively by traders to reduce the lag associated with a traditional moving average crossover system. Instead of using a calculated value for today's short moving average, a forecasted moving average value for two to four days into the future can be used as the short moving average, in a crossover system. This reduces the lag, since the short moving average is now a prediction of its value *at a later point in time,* instead of today's calculated value. An example of a move captured by the crossover of a forecasted 10-day moving average four days in the future against a calculated 10-day moving average today is shown, as it would appear in VantagePoint, in Figure 18.

Figure 18. Forecasted moving average crossover.
Depicts the trend captured by a new method of crossover found in VantagePoint.

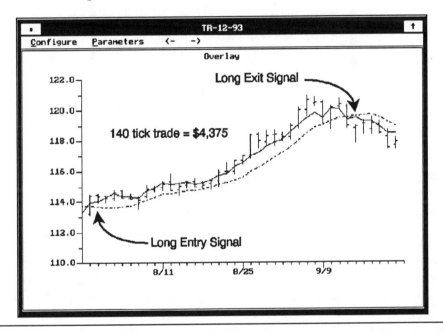

VantagePoint has adjustable parameters that allow users to customize the system to their style of trading. Figure 19 depicts a sample screen containing customizable parameters. Users can emphasize the importance placed on each of the predictions in affecting the Strength Index, which measures the strength of the impending move. This is done by altering the various "Weight" parameters. Signals that indicate the general market movement (up, down, or sideways) are then generated by filtering the Strength Index by the "Upper Strength Limit" and "Lower Strength Limit." In addition, other parameters can be set by traders to further customize VantagePoint's information.

Trading Systems

Neural networks can also be utilized in other ways. They can be trained to forecast trading signals. This is appealing, but has limitations that must be understood. Designing such a system requires that the trader who is actually going to use it be involved in its development. Since the network will generate its trading signals based on the

Figure 19. User parameters.
This window allows VantagePoint users to adapt the system to their personal trading style.

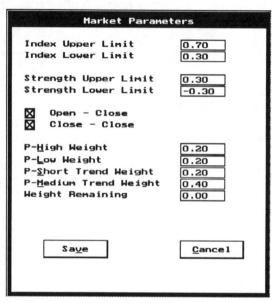

buy/sell points and the choice of selected input data and preprocessing performed during development, the signals must be consistent with the trader's style, risk propensity, investment time horizon, and capitalization.

Since traders have different trading styles, even with perfect hindsight no two traders would identify the same buy/sell points on historical data. Therefore, traders who are unable to tolerate large drawdowns would not develop a neural network that generates signals more appropriate for traders with larger capitalization or a higher risk propensity. Additionally, it is not easy to incorporate risk management considerations into a purely neural-network-based trading system. For this reason, a neural network is best utilized as an information system, or as part of a hybrid system, in conjunction with some sort of rule-based algorithms.

Hybrid Trading Systems

When used as part of a hybrid system, the neural network generates predictive information that can be used along with a set of rules that generate trading signals (see Figure 20).

This approach combines a front-end information system with a back-end rule-based system.[28] The rule-based portion of the system could range the gamut from relatively simple mathematical constructs to sophisticated expert systems. Regardless of how they are derived, the rules would need to be tailored to the trading style of the trader who will use the system.

---

[28] Gallant, S. I. *Neural Network Learning and Expert Systems.* Cambridge, MA: The Massachusetts Institute of Technology, 1993.

Figure 20: A hybrid trading system.
Depicts the flow of information through the model of a hybrid
trading system.

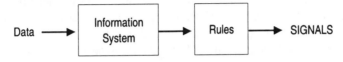

Now let us examine how an information system, such as VantagePoint, can be used as part of a hybrid trading system. VantagePoint would represent the box labeled "Information System" in Figure 20. For the box labeled "Rules," we have devised a simple set of rules that utilize VantagePoint's predicted information to generate buy and sell signals. This particular system uses just some of the information generated each day by VantagePoint's Treasury bond system, including the *short* and *medium* markets, which are two user-adjustable indicators based on the various forecasts produced by VantagePoint. The short and medium markets generate *up, down,* and *sideways* arrows on VantagePoint's charts, indicating the market trend direction for up to four trading days in the future.

If two up or down arrows occur within a specified window in the medium market, the system takes a long or short position, respectively, on the following day. Timing decisions concerning whether to enter at the open with a market order, or to use a limit order in conjunction with VantagePoint's predicted high and low for a more advantageous entry, are left to the trader's discretion. A full description of the details of this system can be found in Appendix 2 at the end of this chapter, along with a trade listing and summary of simulated trades made on the December 1992, March 1993, June 1993, September 1993, December 1993, March 1994, and June 1994 Treasury bond futures contracts, trading one contract at a time. Simulated trading of the system over these contract months (over 1.5 years of trading) resulted in the equity curve shown in Figure 21.

Figure 21. Equity curve.
Resulting from paper trading system from 09/01/92 to 04/15/94.

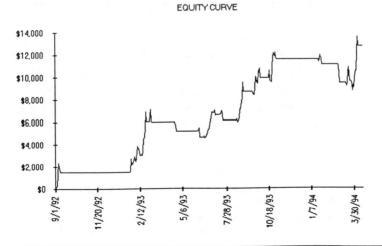

This chapter has briefly discussed all phases of neural network development, including decisions involving network architecture, input selection, preprocessing, fact selection, training, testing, and implementation. Each of these phases has been examined in the context of the recent globalization of the world's financial markets and the need to establish a synergistic framework to quantitatively assess technical, fundamental, and intermarket data. While an in-depth discussion of the development of an actual neural network system, such as VantagePoint, is beyond the scope of this chapter, a simple case study that utilizes some of VantagePoint's features can be seen in Appendix 2.

WHAT'S NEXT

Neural networks are an excellent tool for combining otherwise disparate technical, fundamental, and intermarket data within a quantitative framework for implementation of Synergistic Analysis. Through the use of neural networks, nonlinear patterns and intermarket relationships can be ascertained. In the global markets of the 1990s, it is dangerous to ignore this critical information by focusing only on a single market at a time. As market globalization accelerates and more traders recognize the benefit of a synergistic approach to global market analysis, technical analysis as it is currently practiced will become totally obsolete. Synergistic Analysis, combining technical, fundamental, and intermarket perspectives, will emerge as the preferred analytic framework for trading.

Still, it must be realized that neural network technology is just one of the tools applicable to the implementation of a synergistic trading strategy. Other related technologies, including expert systems and genetic algorithms, have a role to play in implementing Synergistic Analysis for financial forecasting. In fact, neural networks can be used to help extract primitive rules, which capture patterns that would not be apparent otherwise, for incorporation into an expert system.

Genetic algorithms are powerful search mechanisms that are well suited to optimizing neural network parameters. As mentioned earlier, during training, genetic algorithms can be used as training algorithms or to search the space of training parameters in an efficient manner. Genetic algorithms can also be used to automate the search for an optimal set of raw inputs and appropriate preprocessing, so that these tasks can be performed efficiently.[29]

The same technology incorporated into genetic algorithms has also been used in *classifier systems* and *genetic programming*. Classifier systems perform a type of machine learning that generates rules from examples. Genetic programming goes even further by automatically generating a program from a set of primitive constructs. In addition to genetic models, fuzzy logic,[30] wavelets, and chaos theory are also being applied in a multitude of domains including financial forecasting. Even virtual reality has applicability to financial analysis.

---

[29] Colin, A. M. "Neural Networks and Genetic Algorithms for Exchange Rate Forecasting." International Joint Conference on Neural Networks, Beijing, China, Nov. 1–5, 1992.

[30] Deboeck, G. J. "Neural, Genetic and Fuzzy Approaches to the Design of Trading Systems." The Second International Conference on Artificial Intelligence Applications on Wall Street, 1993.

Advancements in hardware are also affecting the speed at which various artificial intelligence technologies will be applied to financial market analysis, since these technologies are computationally intensive. In particular, massively parallel machines will be beneficial in this regard. Parallel processing machines work on different parts of a single problem simultaneously. As a result, the computing time associated with solving a particular type of problem is substantially reduced, once a suitable method of dividing the problem is devised. Neural networks and genetic algorithms are well suited to these parallel processing machines. With connectionist machines, accelerator boards, hypercube architectures, etc., hardware advancements will further facilitate the application of emerging software technologies to financial market analysis.

Although this chapter's focus has been on the application of SMA and neural networks to financial forecasting, their applicability goes far beyond this single arena. One area where my firm has been performing research is that of global asset allocation. Synergistic Analysis can be used to reduce diversifiable risk in global portfolio management by generating forecasts required by an asset allocation model. By using SMA and neural networks to increase forecasting accuracy, portfolios can be constructed and rebalanced that provide higher return for equivalent risk, or lower risk for equivalent return. Other technologies, such as expert systems, can be used to measure investor characteristics such as risk propensity.

Over the next decade, researchers will continue to explore the application of these technologies to financial market analysis and to develop complex hybrid systems. In the meantime, individual traders need to give more than just lip service to the globalization of markets and must move beyond the narrow focus of today's single-market analysis in order to analyze the interrelationships of markets and benefit from such information. Traders with the foresight to adopt a broader market perspective that encompasses today's intermarket global context will gain a competitive advantage over their competitors who continue to limit the focus of their analysis. The sooner traders adjust their thinking about technical analysis, and begin to benefit from more robust analytic methods and tools that employ a synergistic framework for intermarket global analysis, the more successful, disciplined, and confident their trading will become.

Easy-to-use software programs such as VantagePoint, which open the door of intermarket analysis to individual traders, while leaving the research and development of neural networks to professional developers, are an ideal way for traders to bridge the gap in their technical analysis arsenal and to begin benefiting immediately from global trading. In warfare, having more advanced weapons than one's opponent is a decided advantage. The same principle applies to the tools that traders use in the highly volatile global financial markets of this decade. Synergistic Analysis through the use of neural networks is one very powerful tool that should be part of every serious trader's arsenal.

The author would like to thank James T. Lilkendey, M. S., and Phillip Arcuri, Ph.D., of the Predictive Technologies Group, for their assistance in preparation of this chapter.
Synergistic Market Analysis, Market Synergy, Synergistic Analysis, and Synergistic Trading are trademarks of Lou Mendelsohn.

APPENDIX 1

The following is a simple case study that demonstrates the benefits of using intermarket data in addition to single-market data in neural networks. For each of four target markets (Treasury bonds, Eurodollar, Japanese yen, and S&P 500 Index) two sets of neural networks were developed to predict the change in the high from one trading day to the next. The first set's inputs consisted of single-market technical data only. The second set's inputs combined the inputs from the first set with seven additional intermarket inputs. Since the same procedures listed below were applied to all four of the target markets, the following discussion will be restricted to the Treasury bond market.

The following is a summary of the various phases of neural network development discussed earlier in this chapter and a brief look at the decisions made in each phase:

1. *Paradigm:* Feed-forward back-propagation was chosen, since it is one of the most common paradigms used in financial market analysis.

2. *Architecture:* The logistic transfer function was selected along with one hidden layer comprising five neurons.

3. *Input Data Selection:* Price, volume, and open interest data on the target market was used as the raw input to the first set of networks. The second set used seven additional intermarket inputs. For example, for the bonds the second set of nets included data from the CRB Index, the D-Mark, Eurodollar, U.S. dollar index, Japanese yen, the S&P 500 stock index, and the daily Fed funds rate.

4. *Preprocessing Input Data:* Minimal preprocessing, including differences in price data over various time periods, were used for both sets of nets. The second set's intermarket input preprocessing took only spreads between the target market and each of its related intermarkets. All inputs were normalized by clipping outliers beyond two standard deviations, and then linearly scaled.

5. *Fact Selection:* Approximately 1,200 fact days were selected spanning 1988-1993. Of these, 800 were used for training and 400 for testing.

6. *Training and Testing:* An automated training/testing regimen was utilized. For simplicity, the learning rate was held constant and momentum was not used. Testing was performed at set intervals, with the network evaluated on five different error measures. If performance, based on any of these metrics, yielded an improvement, then that network was saved. When training was completed for each target market, a total of 10 networks were found (five for each set), representing the best one for each error statistic. To simplify the presentation, only the results of average absolute error are shown in Table A-1.

7. *Implementation:* This type of simple network is useful as part of an information system. By predicting the high for the next trading day, it provides information that is useful in setting entry/exit stops and is an excellent

indicator of intraday resistance levels. Of course, for actual trading a more sophisticated network configuration such as VantagePoint's would be in order.

Table A-1 depicts the average absolute error of predictions for tomorrow's high on the test set data. The average absolute error is determined by computing the absolute value of the error for each fact in the test set, and then calculating the mean of all of the error values. The first column on the left shows the four target markets. The next column shows the error associated with the first set of networks that used only single-market data. The third column lists the error for the second set of nets that utilized intermarket data in addition to the single-market data. The fourth column presents the percent reduction in error achieved by including intermarket data for training. It is calculated by taking the difference between the error in column two and three and dividing by the value in column two.

Table A-1. Average absolute error when predicting tomorrow's high.
The average error is computed by first determining the absolute
value of the error for each fact in the test set and then determining
the mean of all the error values.

Target market	Average absolute error on high prediction		Percent reduction in average absolute error
	No intermarkets	Intermarkets	
Treasury bonds	7.34%	7.20%	1.9%
Eurodollar	7.04	6.83	3.0
Japanese yen	9.42	9.10	3.4
S&P 500 Index	7.65	7.15	6.5

These results illustrate that even the most minimal use of intermarket data is helpful in improving network performance. The network's average error was reduced by between 1.9 percent on Treasury bonds and 6.5 percent on the S&P 500 Index. In more sophisticated systems such as VantagePoint, utilizing extensive input data and preprocessing, the altering of training parameters, and the use of custom error functions, further increases in predictive accuracy are realized.

APPENDIX 2

HYBRID TREASURY BOND TRADING SYSTEM BASED ON VANTAGEPOINT

The following is a detailed description of a position-holding trading system on U.S. Treasury bond futures, utilizing predicted information generated by VantagePoint in conjunction with simple trading rules.

This system requires the following parameter values within VantagePoint:

1. Set the Index Upper Limit to 0.70

2. Set the Index Lower Limit to 0.30

3. Set the Strength Upper Limit to 0.70

4. Set the Strength Lower Limit to -0.70

5. Set the P-High Weight to 0.50

6. Set the P-Low Weight to 0.50

No signals should be taken until the first day of the month, three months prior to expiration. For example, for the Treasury bond 06-94 contract, no signals should be taken until 03/01/94.

Entry Rules

1. LONG: If the report indicates a TURN UP (up arrow) in the Medium Market and the Short Market is TURN UP, UP MODE, or SIDEWAYS, then look for a second TURN UP (up arrow) in the Medium Market within the last four trading days. If one exists, then enter a LONG position at tomorrow's open with a 25 tick protective stop. Intervening TURN DOWNS may be ignored. This position is then held until stopped out or one of the position-holding exit rules applies.

2. SHORT: If the report indicates a TURN DOWN (down arrow) in the Medium Market, the Index is 0.0, and the Short Market is TURN DOWN, DOWN MODE, or SIDEWAYS, then look for a second TURN DOWN (down arrow) in the Medium Market within the last four trading days. If one exists, then enter a SHORT position at tomorrow's open with a 25-tick protective stop. Intervening TURN UPS may be ignored. This position is then held until stopped out or one of the position-holding exit rules applies.

Exit Rules

1. Exit any positions at the close of the last trading day of the month prior to contract expiration. For example, for the Treasury bond 06-94 contract, positions would be exited at the close on the last trading day of 05/94.

2. LONG: If the current report has a TURN DOWN (down arrow) in the Medium Market, then exit long position tomorrow at the open.

3. SHORT: If the current report has a TURN UP (up arrow) in the Medium Market, then exit the short position tomorrow at the open.

Stop Movement Rules

1. If LONG: Tomorrow, move protective stop to 25 ticks below today's close unless existing stop is already higher, in which case the current protective stop should not be altered.

2. If SHORT: Tomorrow, move protective stop to 25 ticks above today's close unless exiting stop is already lower, in which case the current protective stop should not be altered.

Trading Log

Entry Date	Entry Action	Entry Price	Exit Date	Exit Action	Exit Price	Ticks from Trade	Cumulative
09/02/92	LONG	10418	09/10/92	Stopped Out	10604	50	50
01/22/93	LONG	10600	02/10/93	Stopped Out	10718	50	100
02/12/93	LONG	10728	02/24/93	Stopped Out	11030	98	198
03/04/93	LONG	11109	03/05/93	Stopped Out	11109	0	198
04/20/93	LONG	11215	04/22/93	Stopped Out	11122	-25	173
06/02/93	LONG	11021	06/04/93	Stopped Out	11005	-16	157
06/14/93	LONG	11124	07/07/93	Exit at Open	11325	65	222
07/15/93	LONG	11520	07/20/93	Stopped Out	11506	-14	208
08/16/93	LONG	11610	08/27/93	Stopped Out	11829	83	291
09/15/93	SHORT	11826	09/23/93	Exit at Open	11801	25	316
09/27/93	LONG	11821	09/29/93	Stopped Out	11907	18	334
10/15/93	LONG	12109	10/18/93	Stopped Out	12105	-4	330
10/19/93	SHORT	12031	10/29/93	Exit at Open	11903	60	390
01/19/94	LONG	11602	01/25/94	Stopped Out	11522	-12	378
02/25/94	SHORT	11115	02/28/94	Stopped Out	11208	-25	353
03/01/94	LONG	11112	03/01/94	Stopped Out	11019	-25	328
03/14/94	LONG	10830	03/18/94	Stopped Out	10904	6	334
03/23/94	LONG	10913	03/24/94	Stopped Out	10820	-25	309
03/25/94	SHORT	10802	04/05/94	Stopped Out	10401	129	438

Shaded rows indicate a loss.

Summary of Trading Results

Summary Information	
Time Period	09/01/92-04/15/94
Number Contracts Spanned	7
Number Trades	19
Number Winning Trades	11
Number Losing Trades	8
Percent Winning Trades	58%
Average Number Trades Per Contract	3
Maximum Consecutive Losing Trades	3
% LONG Trades	79%
% SHORT Trades	21%
Maximum Drawdown	81 ticks ($2,531.25)
Largest Winning Trade	129 ticks ($4,031.25)
Largest Losing Trade	-25 ticks ($781.25)
Average Winning Trade	53 ticks ($1,656.25)
Average Losing Trade	18 ticks ($562.50)
Gross Profit	438 ticks ($13,687.50)
Assumed Slippage and Commission per Trade	$50.00
Overhead Due to Slippage and Commission	$950.00
Net Profit (After Slippage and Commission)	$12,737.50

Hypothetical or simulated performance results have certain inherent limitations. Unlike an actual performance record, simulated results do not represent actual trading. Also, since the trades have not actually been executed, the results may have under- or overcompensated for the impact, if any, of certain market factors, such as lack of liquidity, market conditions, the time of execution, and the costs of execution, including brokerage commissions and other fees. Simulated trading programs in general are also subject to the fact that they are designed with the benefit of hindsight. No representation is being made that any account will or is likely to achieve profits or losses similar to those shown.

Chapter 6

DEVELOPING A MULTIPLE-INDICATOR MARKET TIMING SYSTEM: Theory, Practice, and Pitfalls[*]

Casimir C. Klimasauskas,
Financial Services Director
NeuralWare, Inc.

INTRODUCTION

This chapter describes the development of a multiple-indicator market timing system and provides all of the tools to create a complete system. It includes a description of the technologies used and some of the methods that were developed to attempt to overcome problems and deficiencies in the technology. It also explores pitfalls in using such a system and makes suggestions for the future.

The first section of this chapter describes the market timing problem and articulates the basic theory and mechanisms of genetic algorithms and the market timing problem to be solved. This section also describes pitfalls in using this system. The

---

*Major portions of this chapter are reproduced by permission from Advanced Technology for Developers, 103 Buckskin Court, Sewickley, Pennsylvania, 15143. Telephone (412) 741-7699. FAX (412) 741-6094. October-November-December 1993 special edition, Copyright © 1993 High-Tech Communications. All rights reserved.

127

second section provides a user's guide to the use of **macd3**, a genetic optimization program for market timing. The third section describes an Excel macro which can read the *output* files from the **macd3** program and generate a complete spreadsheet that can be extended daily to do trading. The final section provides an overview and example of the complete process.

MARKET TIMING AND GENETIC ALGORITHMS

Market Timing Problem

The eventual objective of this exercise is to build a system to trade S&P 500 futures. Several other approaches have been tested with varying degrees of success. These include trading systems proposed by a variety of individuals, neural networks, and genetic algorithms. Each system has its strengths and weaknesses. Though prior articles have investigated the use of genetic algorithms for market timing, this is an attempt to develop definitive answers to several key questions. In particular, it is essential to know that when a system is updated as part of a standard maintenance process, it will continue to provide a predictable level of performance. It is acceptable to miss the *best* performance in order to achieve *consistent* performance.

The basic approach to market timing described in this chapter is purely technical. This chapter assumes that the composite performance of the S&P 500 is chaotic. Based on this, there is some set of differential equations that combine together to create composite behavior of the market. One simple possible set of difference equations is represented by the Moving Average Convergence-Divergence oscillator (or MACD). This oscillator takes the difference of two moving averages, a fast one and a slow one. If the difference, fast minus slow, is positive, the market is moving up. If the difference is negative, the market is moving down. This signal is used to take an appropriate position in the market. An alternative to this method is to use exponential moving averages (EMACD) rather than simple moving averages. An exponential moving average weighs the most recent history more heavily than prior history. As with the MACD oscillator, the difference between a fast and slow exponential moving average is used as an indicator to take an appropriate position in the market. A third commonly used oscillator is Lane's Stochastics (%K and %D) [Eng 88]. All three of these methods will be used in combination to develop a market timing system.

Table 1 shows the performance of several individual MACD oscillators. The first column of the table shows the period of the *fast* moving average. The second column is the period of the *slow* moving average. The MACD signal is computed by taking the sign (+1 if greater than or equal to zero, or −1 if less than zero) of the fast average minus the slow average. Performance (profit or loss in dollars) for two non-overlapping time periods is computed in the last two columns. The trading strategy used was to close any current position and buy one S&P 500 at the current price if the MACD signal went from −1 to 1. If the MACD signal went from 1 to −1, the current position was closed, and one S&P 500 was sold short at the current price. For purposes of this table, transaction costs, drawdowns, and leverage were not considered. The training period consists of 288 trading days from 1/2/92 through 2/19/93. The test period consists of 100 trading days from 2/22/93 through

Table 1. Profit from a simple trading strategy using MACD oscillators. The highest profit was achieved with a fast average of three days against a slow average of seven days.

Fast	Slow	Train	Test	Fast	Slow	Train	Test
1	2	−38.10	8.90	4	15	−55.00	−37.20
1	3	−23.70	7.80	4	20	−64.70	−31.50
1	4	10.70	−19.20	4	25	−60.70	−17.80
1	5	−6.30	−1.60	5	6	−90.50	−26.60
1	6	1.90	−7.80	5	7	−63.70	−24.30
1	7	−18.70	−2.80	5	8	−19.50	−27.80
1	8	1.70	−7.00	5	9	−55.30	−40.20
1	9	9.90	−7.80	5	10	−65.70	−43.00
1	10	1.20	−6.10	5	15	−102.00	−41.60
1	15	−41.50	−13.70	5	20	−50.80	−28.10
1	20	−38.80	−14.50	5	25	−44.40	−29.40
1	25	−71.90	−20.30	6	7	12.30	−21.00
2	3	−13.10	0.80	6	8	−15.70	−31.20
2	4	−24.10	−14.80	6	9	−48.70	−36.90
2	5	−31.50	−18.10	6	10	−66.00	−37.20
2	6	−30.70	−8.40	6	15	−101.00	−26.30
2	7	−22.20	−6.70	6	20	−65.70	−13.20
2	8	0.70	−9.30	6	25	−54.10	−23.30
2	9	−11.10	−10.10	7	8	−34.10	−19.80
2	10	−12.60	−13.90	7	9	−65.50	−24.00
2	15	−50.40	−22.20	7	10	−134.10	−20.00
2	20	−58.80	−16.30	7	15	−98.00	−8.40
2	25	−52.40	−24.50	7	20	−58.80	−12.70
3	4	20.80	−7.60	7	25	−57.10	−13.00
3	5	46.80	−2.90	8	9	−64.40	−31.40
3	6	22.00	−3.60	8	10	−107.00	−23.30
3	7	52.50	−15.80	8	15	−100.30	0.00
3	8	42.50	−23.60	8	20	−55.20	−7.30
3	9	0.30	−21.60	8	25	−49.30	−12.00
3	10	−15.80	−24.30	9	10	−112.50	−17.60
3	15	−47.40	−31.80	9	15	−65.20	0.40
3	20	−72.70	−24.10	9	20	−39.30	−4.60
3	25	−41.00	−22.80	9	25	−41.70	2.30
4	5	2.50	−6.50	10	15	−61.80	1.50
4	6	−40.90	−13.40	10	20	−35.20	−7.70
4	7	4.30	−19.30	10	25	−46.50	−7.00
4	8	−15.80	−23.70	15	20	−38.90	−9.40
4	9	−54.40	−30.50	15	25	−51.00	−11.30
4	10	−84.90	−38.50	20	25	−48.30	−19.50

Figure 1. MACD oscillator with fast three-period moving average and slow seven-period moving average.

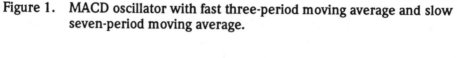
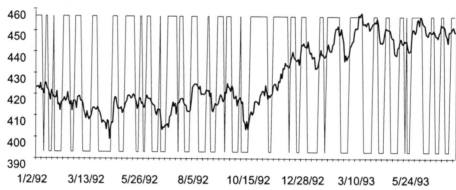

7/16/93. Data for holidays was eliminated from both training and test sets. These periods were selected, because prior experience showed that they were very hard to predict. Table 1 illustrates this with the generally abysmal performance for each of the oscillators.

Studying the results for the *best* MACD pair illustrates one of the key problems with this type of indicator: Lag. Figure 2 shows a blowup of one period in the training set where this is particularly apparent. The general trends are correct, but each transition is late, so that any gains from a change in the market are lost. Every one of the trades shown loses money. Single MACD oscillators work best when markets have strong trends.

Figure 2. A short period of time that illustrates the problems with MACD market timing signals.

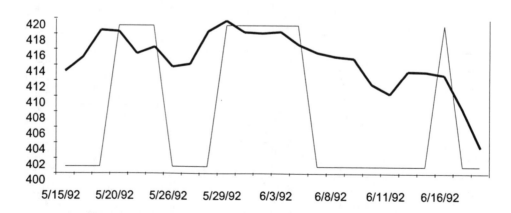

Another problem with MACD oscillators is that they do not generalize well. When a particular pair of moving averages is optimized for one period of time, the performance on a subsequent period of time has little relationship to the earlier one. This makes it very hard to trust an optimized moving average. Figure 3 is a scatter plot showing the performance on the training set (x-axis) against the performance on the test set (y-axis) for each of the pairs in Table 1.

Figure 3.   Scatter plot of performance on the training set (*x*-axis) versus performance on the test set (*y*-axis). The relationship between the two is very tenuous.

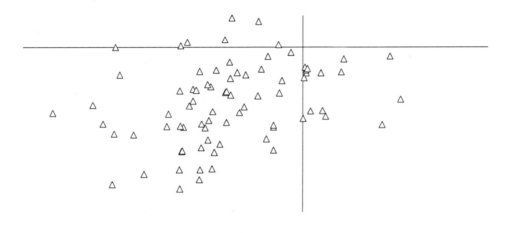

These same problems plague EMACD and stochastic oscillators, though in their own particular ways.

The challenge is to find a method for using MACD and other oscillators, where the parameters are based on the training period, yet they generalize consistently to the test period. The general approach is one suggested by Andrew Colin [Colin 1993] for currency trading. This approach takes several MACD oscillators and lets them vote for or against a long position. Each of the votes is "weighted." If the weighted majority are in favor, the position is long. If the majority are against, the position is short. The problem becomes finding the right set of weighting factors.

Genetic Algorithm Concepts

Though basic concepts of genetic algorithms have been discussed extensively elsewhere [Davis 1993, Deboeck 1994, Klimasauskas 1993, 1994, Koza 1993, 1994, Whitley 1991], this section introduces and combines several new concepts.

Genetic algorithms are classified, based on the type of problem they are optimizing. Binary genetic algorithms use binary encodings of the problem. Order-based genetic algorithms encode orderings for optimization. Real-valued genetic algorithms use floating point numbers for each of the genes. Linked-list genetic algorithms use tree-structures of functional components and variable-sized chromosomes. Hybrid genetic algorithms may use mixtures of these four types or other encodings that are specific to the problem. Within each of these broad categories, there are several subdivisions.

The primary focus of this section is on the real-valued genetic encoding that is most appropriate to this particular problem. Within the real-valued genetic algorithm, there are several variants and issues.

Every genetic algorithm has the same five components: selection method, breeding, evaluation, replacement, and migration. The relationship of each of these components is shown in the flowchart in Figure 4.

Figure 4.   Flowchart of the basic cycle of genetic evolution.

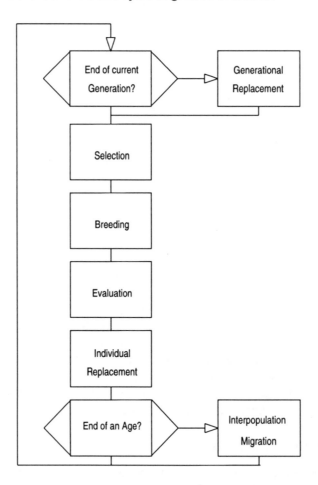

Each element in the population represents a point in space. It is assumed that each point in space represents a valid or potentially valid solution to the problem. Moreover, it is also assumed that each point in space can be evaluated and assigned a single number, which defines its fitness or score. The more desirable a solution, the larger the score. A solution or point in space is called a chromosome. The number of genes (or components to a vector or chromosome) defines the dimension of the space.

The selection process is the method used to select a point from the space. In order to arrive at an optimal solution, it is necessary to bias this selection process toward good solutions. Breeding is the method used to combine or modify components of a vector to create a new search point in the solution space. Once an offspring (new point in space) has been created, it must be evaluated. Once evaluated, it is re-inserted into the next generation. When sufficient cycles have been completed to populate the next generation, it becomes the current generation. The next new generation is seeded with elements from the new current population. Rather than one population, several independent populations are allowed to evolve. Occasionally, these populations exchange genetic material through a migration. These cycles continue until certain terminal conditions are met. Though these basic concepts have been described specifically for real-valued genetic algorithms, most apply to other types as well.

Selection Method. Spinning the roulette wheel is the traditional selection method. All of the others discussed are actually variants on it that modify how the score or fitness function is used in the selection process. The basic method of spinning the roulette wheel assumes that scores are all positive. In the most restricted case, scores must be in the range of zero to one. Unfortunately, this is not the case for most problems. Another issue is that when one score becomes particularly high, it tends to dominate the selection process, and this can lead to stagnation in the population. This kind of dominance, which leads to exploring the region around the most fit member by mutation, is not a problem if the current highest score is close to an optimum solution. Except in situations with one or a few global maxima, this rarely occurs.

In order to understand how the problem of negative or a few high scores is addressed, it is necessary to understand the basic mechanism involved. To illustrate this, consider the five chromosomes in Table 2. The total of their scores is 20. Chromosome 5 accounts for one-half of the total score. The scores of the chromosomes are shown graphically in the pie chart in Figure 5. The circumference of each segment of the pie is proportional to the score of the chromosome. The wheel (or pie) is spun, and whichever chromosome stops under the arrow is the one selected. The process of spinning is accomplished by picking a uniformly distributed random number between zero and one (.65 for example) and multiplying it by the sum of the scores (20). The result in this case is 13 (.65 x 20). Starting with the first chromosome, the scores are added up until they exceed this value. This occurs with chromosome 4 (10 + 4 = 14). In this spin, chromosome 4 is selected.

The "C" code below shows the basic concepts for spinning the roulette wheel. Assuming that all of the scores are greater than zero, the first "for" loop (lines 1–2) sums the scores over the entire population. This is equivalent to laying out all of the scores around the circumference of a circle. The next statement, line 3, multiplies a uniformly distributed random number between zero and one by the total of all scores in the population. This is equivalent to spinning the wheel. Now that the wheel has been spun, we need to find out in which chromosome it stopped. Lines 4–7 accomplish this by once again traversing the circumference of the wheel until the total distance traveled (CircumR) is equal or exceeds (line 6) the position where we stopped. Note that the "for" loop on line 4 takes as a maximum index (PopSizeS-1). This ensures that the value for "wxI" at the termination of the loop is always a legal index into the population.

```
1.  for( CircumR = 0., wxI = 0; wxI < PopSizeS; wxI++ )
2.        CircumR += Chrom[wxI]->ScoreF;
3.  SpinR = Rand01R() * CircumR;
4.  for( CircumR = 0., wxI = 0; wxI < (PopSizeS-1); wxI++ ) {
5.        CircumR += Chrom[wxI]->ScoreF;
6.        if ( CircumR >= SpinR ) break;
7.  }
```

As the wheel is spun repeatedly, the chromosomes are selected based on their proportion of the total score. In the scenario in Table 2, chromosome 1 is selected 5 percent of the time, and chromosome 5 is selected 10 times more often, or 50 percent of the time. When a population has very small (close to zero) as well as very large scores, the chromosomes with small scores are virtually never selected. This can lead to rapid loss of diversification and reduction in the efficiency of the search process.

One of the ways to overcome this is to add an offset to all of the scores so that the range of scores in proportion to the smallest score achieves a desired ratio. This can be used to increase the likelihood of selecting all of the chromosomes. In this example, the range of scores is 9, 10 is the maximum, and 1 is the minimum. This results in a ratio of range to minimum of 9 ((10-1)/1). To achieve a ratio of 1, a value of 8 needs to be added to each of the scores. The results are shown in the *Adjusted Score* column in Table 2. The minimum score is now 9, and the maximum score 18. The range is still 9 (18-9), but the ratio of range to minimum is 1 ((18-9)/9). Now the lowest-scoring chromosome is half as likely to be selected (15 percent vs. 30 percent) as the highest-scoring chromosome.

Table 2. **Five chromosomes in a population and their corresponding scores for a variety of selection mechanisms.**

Chromosome	Raw Score	Adjusted Score	Raw Rank	Adjusted Rank	Gaussian
5	10 (50%)	18 (30%)	5 (33%)	9 (26%)	38%
4	4 (20%)	12 (20%)	4 (27%)	8 (23%)	26%
3	3 (15%)	11 (18%)	3 (20%)	7 (20%)	18%
2	2 (10%)	10 (17%)	2 (13%)	6 (17%)	15%
1	1 (5%)	9 (15%)	1 (7%)	5 (14%)	3%
Total	20	60	15	35	100%

Modifying the code for spinning the roulette wheel to offset scores is shown below. In the loop from lines 2–8, the minimum score and maximum score, are computed along with the circumference. Line 1 sets the minimum score, maximum score, and circumference equal to the score of the first element in the population.

Figure 5. Five chromosomes as elements of a pie chart. The circumference of each pie section is proportional to the raw score (Table 2) of the corresponding chromosome.

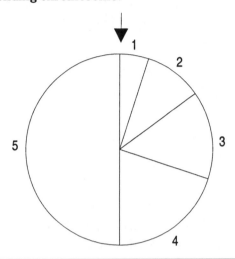

Figure 6. Frequency with which each chromosome is selected, based on the method selecting it.

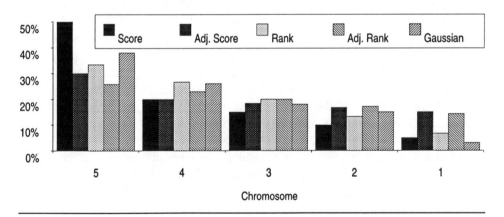

This eliminates the need to otherwise initialize them, or handle the special case of the first time through the loop. RatioF is the ratio for the range of the scores to the minimum score. Line 9 converts the actual minimum and maximum scores into an offset based on the target ratio. Line 10 handles the pathological case in which minimum and maximum are both equal. If they are both equal and happen to be zero, the first element of the population is always selected. Offsetting it by one then allows all members to be uniformly selected. Line 11 adjusts the circumference based on the offset. Lines 13–16 are equivalent to the prior code, but the adjusted scores (line 14) are used as the loop moves around the circumference of the wheel. When the loop exits, wxI is the index of the element selected.

1. MinScoreF = MaxScoreF = CircumR = Chrom[0]->ScoreF;
2. for(wxI = 1; wxI < PopSizeS; wxI++) {
3.   CircumR += Chrom[wxI]->ScoreF;/* find the circumference */
4.   if (Chrom[wxI]->ScoreF < MinScoreF)
5.   MinScoreF = Chrom[wxI]->ScoreF;
6.   if (Chrom[wxI]->ScoreF > MaxScoreF)
7.   MaxScoreF = Chrom[wxI]->ScoreF;
8. }
9. OffsetR = (MaxScoreF - MinScoreF) / RatioF - MinScoreF;
10. if (MaxScoreF == MinScoreF) OffsetR = 1.;
11. CircumR += PopSizeS * OffsetR;/* adjusted circumference */
12. SpinR = Rand01R() * CircumR;/* "spin" the wheel */
13. for(CircumR = 0., wxI = 0; wxI < (PopSizeS-1); wxI++) {
14.   CircumR += Chrom[wxI]->ScoreF + OffsetR;
15.   if (CircumR >= SpinR) break;/* exit where it stopped */
16. }

This same technique for offsetting scores can be used to handle negative scores. The method is exactly the same as described above. The use of a target ratio for the range of scores to the minimum adjusted score successfully addresses the problems of negative scores as well as the mixture of very small and large scores in the same population.

Another method for addressing the problem of range in scores is to use rank ordering and to select from the population based on rank. In this case, the least fit (lowest scoring) member of the population is assigned a rank of 1. The highest-scoring element of the population is assigned the highest rank. Raw rank biases selection heavily toward the most fit members of the population. This may cause premature loss of diversity. The same method of offsetting scores described above can be applied to rank to mitigate this problem. When adjusting the raw rank, setting the ratio to one less than the population size is equivalent to using the raw rank. The effects on selection rate for rank and adjusted rank are shown in Table 2.

Notice that adjusting the rank tends toward a uniform selection of chromosomes. Another way to address this problem is to use a *Gaussian* random number generator to select rank. Gaussian selection assumes that the population is sorted in order of decreasing fitness. The *Gaussian* column of Table 2 was generated using the sum of two random numbers. This is a quick and dirty technique based on the Central Limit Theorem, which says that when you add up enough zero-mean random numbers, the result is a Gaussian distribution. The Gaussian is folded and used as an index into a sorted population. In the code below, line 1 takes the sum of two uniformly distributed random numbers in the range zero to one. The average of the sum is 1., which is subtracted to change the expected average to zero. Taking the absolute value folds the two sides of the distribution into a single one, with most values close to zero, and fewer close to 1. Line 2 converts this into an index into the population. This works, assuming the population has been sorted in order of decreasing fitness.

1. CircumR = fabs(Rand01D() + Rand01D() - 1.);

2. wxI = CircumR * PopSizeS;

Finally, it is possible to select elements from the population on a purely uniform basis. The code for this is shown in the one line below. Uniform selection from the population has the effect of exploring quite a bit of space and may work well for problems with many local minima. However, using this method does not guarantee convergence to a solution, unless other criteria are met.

1. wxI = Rand01D() * PopSizeS;

The frequency with which each of the chromosomes is selected based on the selection method is shown graphically in Figure 6. The right method for each particular problem depends on the type of the problem.

Breeding. This is the process of producing a new point in the data space. The method used to accomplish this determines how the solution space is searched. There are two basic types of breeding: crossover and mutation. Conceptually, each chromosome represents a point in space. Mutation selects a point near an existing chromosome for further analysis. Crossover searches the space more broadly within the boundaries defined by two points in the space.

Crossover creates an offspring from two parents or points in space. Figure 7 shows two points selected from the population: (a, b, c) and (X, Y, Z), where the vector represents the chromosome, and each component of the vector represents a value of a gene. Depending on the crossover method used, the other points at the corners of the cube (or hypercube) are the potential offspring.

Figure 7. Diagram showing the possible outcomes from uniform crossover between (a, b, c) and (X, Y, Z).

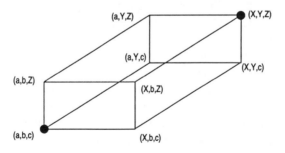

There are three basic crossover mechanisms: one-point, two-point, and uniform crossover. Holland's foundational work on binary genetic algorithms [Holland 75] used one-point crossover. Two-point and uniform crossover were later additions to the technology.

In one-point crossover, a point within the chromosome is selected. All material to the left of that point comes from the first parent, and all material from the other side comes from the second parent. For chromosomes with three genes, there are two possible crossover points: between the first two elements, and the last two elements. The possibilities for one-point crossover with (a, b, c) and (X, Y, Z) are: (a, Y, Z), (a, b, Z), (X, b, c), and (X, Y, c). This represents four of the possible six vertices on the cube in Figure 7. The other two vertices, (X, b, Z) and (a, Y, c), are not possible outcomes with one-point crossover. These are portions of the solution space that must be searched using other elements of the population.

The "C" code below illustrates how one-point crossover may be implemented. In lines 1–2, the parents are copied to the offspring. In line 3, a crossover point is selected between zero and (due to rounding) the total number of genes minus one. This ensures that at least one element in the offspring will be swapped. In lines 4–8, all of the values of the genes from the crossover point forward are swapped.

```
1. memcpy( (void *)ChOf1TP, (void *)ChPar1TP, sizeof(*CHOf1TP) );

2. memcpy( (void *)ChOf2TP, (void *)Chpar2TP, sizeof(*CHOf2TP) );

3. xp1I = Rand01D() * NGenesS;

4. for( wxI = xp1I; wxI < NGenesS; wxI++ ) {

5.     vD = ChOf1TP->GeneF[wxI];

6.     ChOf1TP->GeneF[wxI] = ChOf2TP->GeneF[wxI];

7.     ChOf2TP->GeneF[wxI] = vD;

8. }
```

Two-point crossover was developed to enhance the portion of space searched by one-point crossover. With two-point crossover, two points within the chromosome are selected at random. All of the material between the first and the second point (with wrap-around the end) come from the first parent, and the remainder from the second. This makes all of the six vertices possible outcomes from the crossover operation. However, when working in higher dimensional spaces, two-point crossover is only capable of creating offspring that have contiguous groups of common elements. This is analogous to the problem with one-point crossover in a population with three genes in each chromosome.

In the "C" code below, two crossover points are selected, xp1I and xp2I (lines 3–4). Since the random number generator can never output a value of exactly 1.0, and positive floating point numbers are rounded down toward zero in "C", xp1I and xp2I will both be less than NGenesS. In line 5, the two crossover points are swapped so that xp1I is always less than or equal to xp2I. This simplifies the following code and has the effect that if it is necessary to swap them, it is equivalent to swapping the offspring. The loop in lines 6–10 swaps all of the genetic material between xp1I and xp2I, inclusive. This guarantees that the offspring will differ from the parents in at least one position.

```
1. memcpy( (void *)ChOf1TP, (void *)ChPar1TP, sizeof(*CHOf1TP) );

2. memcpy( (void *)ChOf2TP, (void *)Chpar2TP, sizeof(*CHOf2TP) );

3. xp1I = Rand01D() * NGenesS;
```

```
4.   xp2I = Rand01D() * NGenesS;
5.   if ( xp1I > xp2I ) { wxI = xp1I; xp1I = xp2I; xp2I = wxI; }
6.   for( wxI = xp1I; wxI <= xp2I; wxI++ ) {
7.        vD = ChOf1TP->GeneF[wxI];
8.        ChOf1TP->GeneF[wxI] = ChOf2TP->GeneF[wxI];
9.        ChOf2TP->GeneF[wxI] = vD;
10. }
```

One problem that has been observed for both one-point and two-point crossover is that as a population matures and becomes less diverse, it is possible to select a crossover point that produces offspring identical to the parents! This happens when the portion of the gene which is selected to "cross-over" is identical in both parents. One remedy for this is to compare both parents, starting at each end. The index of the first gene to differ between them starting from the left is the left index. The index of the first gene to differ starting from the right is the right index. The crossover point is selected so that it is *between* these two endpoints. Since the crossover point cannot include the endpoints, this guarantees that the offspring differ in at least one position from both of the parents. If there is only one gene or element between the parents that differs, the first parent is mutated to produce an offspring.

Uniform crossover is capable of creating offspring that represent any of the vertices of the cube. In uniform crossover, elements of the offspring are selected randomly with equal probability from each of the parents. The author has run several tests in which the probability of selecting elements from one parent or the other was determined by their scores. Neither this nor other methods of selecting which parent to select an element from were as successful as equally likely selection from both parents. Though many engineers continue to prefer to use one- or two-point crossover, a growing number of researchers have published results that indicate that uniform crossover provides solutions more quickly.

As described above, uniform crossover randomly picks which elements to swap. In the code below, if the test on line 4 is true, the genetic material is swapped. Otherwise, it is unchanged.

```
1.   memcpy( (void *)ChOf1TP, (void *)ChPar1TP, sizeof(*CHOf1TP) );
2.   memcpy( (void *)ChOf2TP, (void *)Chpar2TP, sizeof(*CHOf2TP) );
3.   for( wxI = 0; wxI < NGenesS; wxI++ )
4.        if ( Rand01D() > 0.5 ) {
5.             vD = ChOf1TP->GeneF[wxI];
6.             ChOf1TP->GeneF[wxI] = ChOf2TP->GeneF[wxI];
7.             ChOf2TP->GeneF[wxI] = vD;
8.        }
```

Average crossover is actually a variant on one-point, two-point, and uniform crossover. With average crossover, when an element is selected from the second parent for inclusion in the offspring, the average of the genes from each parent are used

Figure 8.   Each of the vertices of these two rectangles represents one of the 13 possible solutions for uniform average crossover.

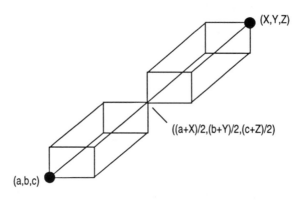

in the offspring. This is geometrically equivalent to selecting the solution from the vertices of the two rectangles shown in Figure 8. The vertices of these rectangles are the points at which two or more diagonals of the rectangle in Figure 7 intersect. This makes it possible to move closer to a solution, particularly as a population matures. For one particular problem, Davis [Davis 1993] has found that 5 percent average crossover provided maximum speedup for solving a particular problem.

Mutation comes in two variants. The first is called *creep*. It aptly describes what happens to the components of a real-valued chromosome. Elements are randomly chosen for mutation. Those selected to mutate are incremented or decremented by a small amount. This results in generating an offspring close to the parent. It is a method of locally searching the space. Whitley [Whitley 1991] has experimented with dynamically adjusting the ratio of mutation to crossover based on the fitness of the chromosome. The assumption is that if the chromosome is very fit, it is close to an optimal solution, and mutation is the primary method for getting to that final solution. Figure 9 shows the effective portion of space searched by creep. It is a rectangle around the selected point.

Figure 9.   Mutation by creep explores a rectangle around the selected point in space.

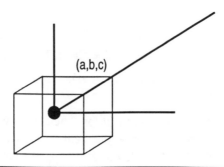

With creep, the resulting values are always "clipped" so that they fall within a legal range for values of genes. For ratio or asymmetric encodings, this is 0 to 1. For multiplicative norm or symmetric encodings, this range is −1 to +1.

Code to implement creep is shown below. For each gene in the chromosome, a random number between zero and one is generated and compared to the probability of mutating one gene (line 2). If the random number is less, the individual gene is mutated. A random number in the range −1 to 1 is selected and multiplied by the maximum limit for creeping a particular element. This is added to the current value for that gene (line 3). If it exceeds limits (−1 to 1 or 0 to 1 as required), it is rescaled by adding or subtracting 1 as needed (lines 4–5).

```
1.  for( wxI = 0; wxI < NGenesI; wxI++ )
2.        if ( Rand01D() < ProbMutOneD ) {
3.              NewD = RandD(-1.,1.) * CreepLimitD + ChOf1TP->GeneF[wxI];
4.              if ( NewD > 1. ) NewD -= 1.;
5.              if ( NewD < -1. ) NewD += 1.;
6.              ChOf1TP->GeneF[wxI] = NewD;
7.        }
```

The second variant on mutation is randomization. This type of mutation replaces selected elements of the chromosome with random values. This is equivalent to fixing certain dimensions of the solution, and randomly picking a new point in the other dimensions. It can help mature populations break the mold and explore other parts of the solution space, while maintaining some of the knowledge that has been acquired.

As with creep, only selected genes are randomized. Genes are selected for randomization by the same method used for creep. A random number between zero and one is selected and compared to the probability of mutating a single gene. If the random number is less, the gene is replaced with a random value.

```
1.  for( wxI = 0; wxI < NGenesI; wxI++ )
2.        if ( Rand01D() < ProbMutOneD )
3.              ChOf1TP->GeneF[wxI] = RandD(-1., 1.);
```

Once a new solution has been created by crossover or mutation, it may need to be normalized. There are two primary methods for normalization that are applicable to the market timing problem: Ratio-based and multiplicative normalization.

Multiplicative normalization rescales all of the elements in the chromosome so that the sum of their absolute values is equal to one. The current sum of the absolute values is computed (lines 1–2 below). To rescale them to sum to one, the multiplier 1 / sum is used (line 3). Each of the genes is multiplied by this value (lines 4–5).

```
1.  for( SumD = 0., wxI = 0; wxI < NGenesI; wxI++ )
2.        SumD += fabs(ChOf1TP->GeneF[wxI]);
3.  MultD = 1./SumD;
4.  for( wxI = 0; wxI < NGenesI; wxI++ )
5.        ChOf1TP->GeneF[wxI] *= MultD;
```

Ratio normalization is somewhat more complex. It assumes that the original parents were both properly normalized. It then rescales only the unswapped portion of the chromosome. To see how this is done, consider the following:

Let

S = sum of absolute values of swapped items.
U = sum of absolute values of unswapped items.
K = multiplier for unswapped values.

Then when we are done, $(S + K * U)$ must equal 1. Solving for K yields: $K = (1 - S) / U$. Each of the unswapped values is multiplied by this number. Several special cases arise that need to be handled individually to ensure that numeric overflow or other computational problems do not arise.

Several methods for constructing offspring have been discussed. The author's own experience is that no one of them is always right. Most often, a blend of several methods operating on the same population provides the best solution to a particular problem.

Evaluation. Once one or two offspring have been created and normalized in the breeding process, it is necessary to evaluate, score, or measure their fitness. This is one of the areas where the author has found the most significant potential for affecting the quality of a solution.

Three basic methods were investigated for evaluating performance, and five sub-methods. The three basic methods were: profit, trades (which includes profit), and accuracy in matching the output to an ideal target.

The evaluation process first involves computing a trading signal. Each chromosome contains a set of weights. Each weight corresponds to a particular oscillator. Three types of oscillators are supported: MACD, EMACD, and stochastic. The trading signal is computed by comparing each pair of components for the oscillator. If the fast component is above the slow, the weight associated with that oscillator is added into the signal. If the converse is true, the weight associated with that component is subtracted from the signal. If the composite signal is above a small positive threshold, a long position is taken (or maintained). If the composite signal is below a small negative threshold, a short position is taken (or maintained). Otherwise, an out-of-market position is taken (or maintained). The total of all net transactions is the profit associated with this set of weights. For purposes of computing profit, a transaction penalty is applied at the end of each transaction. This penalty discourages very frequent trading. The number of profitable and unprofitable trades are counted separately.

Profit is simply the penalized profit as computed over the transactions. *Trades* was initially the ratio of profitable to unprofitable trades. This was later modified to use a signed value and multiply by penalized profit. The exact code for this is shown in the *macd3.c* program listing. Though it may seem somewhat strange, *trades* is attempting to construct a measure that links consistency in profitable trades and profit together. *Accuracy* in synthesizing an ideal trading signal was computed by counting the number of times that the current and ideal signals matched.

A variant on this process was inspired from some of the ideas and observations by Pardo in his book [Pardo 1992]. In this variant the primary evaluation period is divided into several overlapping subregions. Each of these is evaluated independently, and the results are combined in one of several ways: Actual (one region only), average, minimum, average of two lowest scores, minimum + average, minimum + last. These were developed heuristically with the objective of achieving better overall performance over the entire training set, with the hope that it would result in better overall performance on the out-of-sample test set.

The process by which these various measures were developed may be of interest to the reader. Initially, profit was selected as the evaluation function. As it turns out, profit on the training set had no relationship to profit on the test set. So, the data was divided into several overlapping regions, and the minimum profit was taken as the fitness function. The use of overlapping regions ensured that there was enough data to compute a valid measure. Taking the minimum attempted to force the algorithm toward a solution that was good everywhere, rather than a few good calls. This resulted in solutions with moderate profits, many losing trades, and a few big winners. To address this problem, the idea of constructing an ideal trading signal and comparing the synthesized signal to the ideal one was tested. It turns out that this did not work very well. Scores in the range of 70 percent correct (minimum) were readily achieved, but the system lost lots of money: It was almost always too early or late in calling the turns in the market. The next step in the evolution of the evaluation function was to construct a measure that took into account the ratio of profitable to unprofitable trades. By itself, it did not work very well, since it did not differentiate between profitable and unprofitable solutions with the same ratio. This problem was solved by multiplying the ratio by the penalized profit. This latter actually turned out to be quite good for generating solutions that worked well on both the training and test sets. However, consistency from the training to the test set was still a problem. The minimum + last and minimum + average were both attempts to address that. The minimum + last turned out to be the best on the whole for constructing solutions that provided moderately consistent results on the training set, and which worked well on the test set. Later testing on different data demonstrated that this method, tuned to this particular data set, did not work well otherwise [Everly 93]. This observation led to further studies as described later in this section. Reviewing all of these results, another technique was developed that averaged the two lowest scores from each of the periods. This had the effect of improving the convergence of the populations, providing slightly better differentiation between solutions. That is the story of how these various combinations of unlikely measures came about. All of them have been left as part of the code described below to facilitate your own exploration of these or your own variants on them.

Perhaps the most important lesson to be learned from this exercise is that the nature of the evaluation function is crucial in achieving the desired results. It requires creativity on the part of the developer to select the right evaluation function for each problem.

The evaluation function had a tremendous impact on the types of solutions discovered. Each different evaluation method tended toward a specific kind of solution, which varied little from run to run, regardless of random seed, mixture of genetic operators, or other factors.

When a chromosome has been evaluated, several authors have suggested that performing local optimization on the chromosome can provide incremental benefits on the ultimate result. Initially, a very simple local optimization method was tested in which each of the weights in the chromosome was jiggled slightly in the positive or negative direction. Whichever one provided a gain in performance was kept and repeated. This method was later replaced by a more systematic Dynamic Hill Climbing local search technique [de la Maza 1994]. Three levels of local optimization were implemented: none, global, and local. Global optimization modified only the *best* chromosome in each population. Local optimization attempted to optimize every new chromosome. *None* made no attempts whatever at optimizing the chromosome.

Contrary to what the author expected, optimization had little effect on the solutions. Global optimization tended to produce mediocre solutions. Local optimization took a very long time (five days on a Sun SPARCStation) and produced a moderately good (though not the best) solution. Neither the original nor the Dynamic Hill Climbing techniques provided much advantage nor consistency. This appears to be largely caused by the very flat evaluation function: The evaluation method uses profit. There is no means to tell the optimizer which of two solutions with the same profit is better. This is an area for further research.

Handling of holidays had a quite interesting effect on the system. Initially, whenever data was not available, the day was dropped from the file. This usually happened during holidays. It was noted that in December of one year, the trading signals that had been lagging by one day from optimum started calling the turning points exactly. One day was lost at the end of November for Thanksgiving day. As a consequence, a new data set was prepared that filled in missing trading days with the closing price from the prior day. This actually improved the performance of both the MACD and the genetically developed oscillators! With a little thought, you can see why this might happen.

It is important to note that fitting MACD oscillators together to identify market turning points is actually a quite difficult problem. Computing the trading signal by multiplying the sign of the difference between the fast and slow moving average by the weight associated with that fast-slow pair introduces discontinuities into the trading signal as a function of the input data. Further thresholding the trading signal introduces more discontinuities. The effects of timing compound with the changes in price to produce numerous local minima in the solution space. The net result is that this is a very difficult problem to solve, even with a genetic algorithm. For this reason, the author believes that the nature of the fitness function is extremely important to obtaining good solutions.

Individual Replacement. Whenever a new element is created as the result of breeding, it is added to the new population. Two populations are always maintained: a current or existing population and a new population. The current or existing population is used to pick breeding material. The results of breeding are added to the new population.

When an element is added to the new population, it is always inserted into a sorted list so that the new population has the most fit at the top and the least fit at the bottom of the list. If a new element is identical to an existing element, it is ignored. If the new population is nominally full, the least fit member of the new population is dropped to make room for the new one.

If a population has a maximum of 30 elements in it, a generation is complete when 30 offspring have been generated and added to it.

Generational Replacement. A hybrid generational replacement method was implemented. The nature of the hybrid was suggested by several observations.

Pure generational replacement always starts with a new population that is completely empty. All of the offspring generated during the generation are added to the new population. Pure generational replacement tends to lose the *best* performing chromosome from generation to generation, but maintains good population diversity.

Rank-ordered replacement starts with the existing current population and inserts new elements into it, dropping the least fit element each time. Rank-ordered replacement always retains the best performing member of the population, but can lose its diversity as the population fills with offspring similar to the best member of the population.

The hybrid approach developed starts each new generation with some portion of the best from the current generation. Setting this proportion to zero leads to pure generational replacement. Setting this proportion to 100 percent leads to a rank-ordered replacement algorithm. In tests, at 50 percent, the populations seemed to wander, and the expected improvement in average fitness was slow to materialize. At 100 percent (rank-ordered replacement), the populations rapidly converged to variants of the best element, and failed to explore the space effectively. Brief experimentation led to 70 percent as optimum for this problem. The new population is maintained in rank order, and as new elements are added to it, the least fit member of the population is dropped. New elements are added to the population until the population has been potentially completely replenished. This not only maintained genetic diversity through the evolutionary process, but it also provided a mechanism for *stuck* populations to diversify through mutation.

In summary, the basic algorithm for updating the population is

1. Copy a portion of the best members of the current population to the new one.

2. Breed to create a new offspring.

3. If the offspring is identical to an existing member of the new population, ignore it and repeat (2).

4. Determine where the offspring fits in the hierarchy of fitness in the new population, and insert it. If the new population is full, drop the least fit element.

5. Repeat steps 2, 3, and 4 for as many times as there are elements in the population.

Migration. As already mentioned, one of the characteristics of populations is that they tend toward uniformity or lack of diversity. When the same problem is solved several times, quite different solutions can emerge. One of the ways to address this is to let several populations evolve simultaneously, and at the end of every *age*, let them swap a small amount of genetic material.

Swapping of genetic material is accomplished by combining a sample, say 10 percent of the best of each population and sorting it. The best few elements of this sorted list are migrated or used to update each of the populations. The effect of this is to cross-pollinate the populations. Often this cross-pollination leads almost immediately to a better solution to the problem. Initially, migrations were tested at 10 and 20 generations. This did not allow enough time for each population to explore its own potential solutions. Some experimentation led to 50 as a good value for this problem. Initial migration rates of 20 percent were tested, and led to clone populations. This was finally reduced to 10 percent, where good results were achieved. These are not necessarily optimal rates.

One of the problems with migration is that swapping the best solutions from each population tended to cause each of the populations to look the same. Thinking about the search mechanisms, it became apparent that migration was a method for maintaining diversity. With this in mind, a random migration algorithm was developed that randomly selects two populations to swap genetic material. The material swapped is selected using the standard roulette wheel selection method. This had a very positive effect on the overall solutions, and increased performance and consistency. This is the default in the program.

MACD Performance

Several tests were done with parameters to attempt to achieve the objectives of building a profitable MACD trading system where performance on the training set generalized well to the test set. The effort met with modest success. One aspect of the problem that was a bit surprising is that the final solution was highly dependent on the evaluation function. Table 3 shows the results for four different runs that were done with the default parameters in the program. Each of the systems made approximately the same number of trades, profits, and losses. Figure 10 shows the trading signals during the test period for each of the four runs. The top trace is the closing price of the S&P 500.

All of these were generated using the same parameters, but different initial random number seeds. Several prior runs confirm that this is the general solution that the system tends to produce.

Table 3.   **Results of letting four runs with different random seeds search until convergence.**

Run	Train Profit	Loss	Net	Trades +/−	Test Profit	Loss	Net	Trades +/−
bchk0143	219	−28	191	44/14	55	−5	50	11/4
bchk0268	201	−26	175	44/8	42	−9	33	12/5
bchk0345	239	−34	205	49/9	41	−7	34	11/3
bchk0422	206	−39	167	37/15	41	−18	23	8/8

Figure 10. Actual trading signals for each of the runs are shown at the bottom of the graph. The trace at the top is the closing price of the S&P 500.

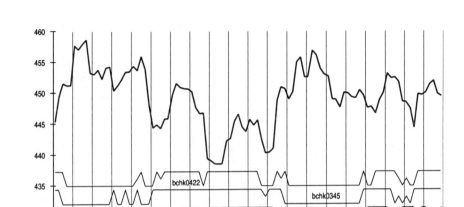

Even though the statistics show that the final systems were consistently profitable, looking closer at the solution indicates that the timing of buy and sell signals incurs substantial unrealized drawdowns. For many individuals, this makes the results very difficult to trade. Though it was not tried, it might be possible to generate more tradable signals by maximizing the average profit per trade. This might be a way to force it to generate more-profitable trades, while limiting the number of trades generated.

The good news is that the algorithm evolved a set of coefficients for the MACD oscillators that were profitable on both the test and training sets. The bad news is that the timing required to achieve those levels of performance was very exacting, and the strategies resulted in substantial unrealized drawdowns.

It was these insights, and the observation that most of the MACD oscillators were not used in a solution, that led to the further development of the types of indicators used. Three basic changes were made to the program. First, rather than generating all possible combinations of MACD oscillators given a set of moving averages, the user specifies the nature of each oscillator. Second, in addition to standard moving averages, truncated exponential moving averages and stochastics were added to the repertoire of oscillators. Third, a special summary was developed that back- and forward-tests the composite market timing signal. This led to certain very interesting phenomena.

Model Performance Evaluation

To begin with, think for a moment about what you might expect from a multiple oscillator trading signal. One possibility is that it would work well on the time period over which it was trained, and for a short time afterward. Performance would degrade when used both in the future and the past to close to chance. Figure 11 shows

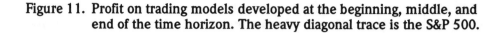

Figure 11. Profit on trading models developed at the beginning, middle, and end of the time horizon. The heavy diagonal trace is the S&P 500.

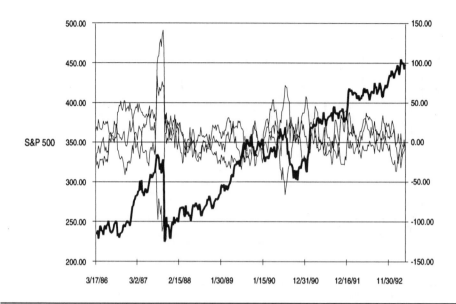

what happened when this idea was tested. Each of the graphs shows the profit for a 50-day period *forward* from the current date. The procedure for generating these graphs was to genetically construct a multiple oscillator trading signal. Eight indicators were used: EMA(3, 5), EMA(3, 10), EMA(5, 15), EMA(5, 20), EMA(5, 25), Stochastic(5, 5), Stochastic(10, 5), Stochastic(15, 5) where EMA(f, s) is the truncated period for the fast and slow exponential moving averages, and Stochastic(%K, %D) with period %K for the signal, and exponential smoothing period of %D. Each population consisted of 50 elements, and 10 populations evolved simultaneously. Each test was repeated seven times, using different random seeds each time. The *minimum 2* submethod was applied to optimizing profit. Each model used 250 trading days (approximately one year) of data. The results of each of the seven tests were typically quite consistent in performance. Each model was tested by starting at one date, using the model for 50 trading days forward, then closing out the position. This is the profit displayed for the current date. The process is moved forward five trading days in time and repeated. Figure 11 shows the results for three models developed using data at the beginning, middle, and end of the historical data period.

To better understand what is happening with the models, the individual results of two trading models are explored in depth. The first model, Figure 12, was developed on 250 trading days of data starting at 3/17/86. As expected, it performs well over the period on which it was developed, approximately 3/86 through 2/87. It is also the best or one of the best performing models for 10 to 15 weeks at the end of 1990, 1991, and 1992. Also notice that its performance drops drastically in the period immediately following the training window. This model seems to do well in sideways or trading markets.

Figure 12. The heavy trace is the performance (profit) of the model trained
on data from 3/17/86 for 250 trading days. The top and bottom
traces are the best and worst profit of all models. Each tick mark
represents 10 weeks.

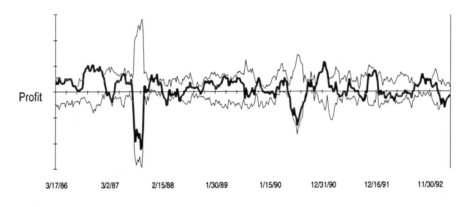

The second model, Figure 13, was developed on a window from 1/90 through
12/90. As expected, it was the best model for the middle of its training window. It
was also the best model through the turbulent period at the end of 1987 and early
1991. This model seems to do well with strongly trending markets.

Figure 13. The heavy trace is the performance (profit) of the model trained
on data from 1/15/90 for 250 trading days. The top and bottom
traces are the best and worst profit of all models. Each tick mark
represents 10 weeks.

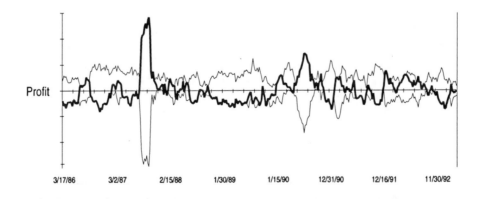

One of the questions that these graphs raised is to what extent this same phenomenon occurs in other markets. [Every 1994] and [Keller 1994] explored this for
Getty Oil and 30-year bonds. Similar effects were seen in both securities. Figure 14
shows the results of two models for 30-year bonds. Again, each model has phases
during which it works well, and others where it works poorly. The transitions between phases can be quite rapid.

Figure 14. **Profit from two models trained at diverse times (1/79, 12/90) used to trade 30-year bonds. The heavy trace at the bottom is the price of the bonds.**

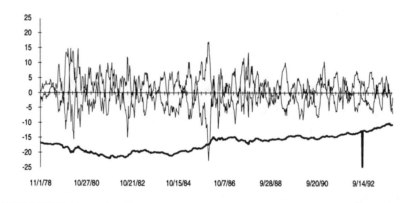

The profit from two models trained on Getty Oil are shown in Figure 15. Notice the same patterns emerging as with the S&P 500 and Treasury bonds. For Getty Oil, it is interesting to see that some models track well in terms of profit at times, and others are diametrically opposite.

Figure 15. **Profit from two models trained at diverse times used to trade Getty Oil. Both of the models were trained on 250 days, the first starting 3/88, the other starting 3/90. The graph covers 3/87 through 3/92.**

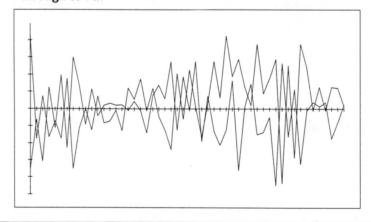

These graphs suggest several possible conclusions. First, no one model will always work well. Second, performance may drop precipitously with little warning. Third, model performance is highly related to market dynamics. A model may work well at widely separated times if the market dynamics are similar. Similar phenomena have been seen in developing neural-network-based stock picking systems. Models trained on one historical period may work well for days or weeks following, then precipitously fail. This often results in losses that reduce the total performance.

These results are not surprising. However, they do lead to certain interesting suggestions for the design of mechanical trading systems. The primary tactic that they suggest is to train several models on historical data, and then find a way to *predict* when a shift in market dynamics is about to occur, and if possible, which type of model is appropriate. This may be possible using the performance of a large ensemble of models trained on a variety of historical periods as input to a neural network that is trained to predict market shifts.

Summary

Several novel technologies were introduced to solve the multiple MACD / EMACD / Stochastic problem. The evaluation function was the most important single factor in finding a good solution that generalized well. Taking the minimum of the performance over several periods was one of the keys to this. A hybrid generational replacement approach appeared to work better than either pure generational replacement or rank-ordered replacement. Using a mixture of standard crossover as well as average crossover showed incremental benefits as well. Cross-population migrations between as many as 10 populations resulted in more rapid and consistent convergence. Rather than ratio-based normalization, multiplicative normalization with symmetric (positive and negative) weights worked best.

There are two primary areas for further investigation. First is the nature of the evaluation function. Particularly for purposes of local optimization, an evaluation function that produces a grade on how well the "profit" was achieved would facilitate potentially better solutions. Second, it is essential to develop a method to predict changes in market dynamics. One approach is to use the fine-grained historical performance on several models as inputs with a custom-designed training signal that indicates when a phase shift is about to occur. Finally, a variety of minor technical issues may improve performance. For example, it may be helpful to include various probabilities with which different types of breeding are engaged. One issue here is that as the populations become more uniform (less diverse), the primary method for evolution is through mutation (creep and randomization). It may be that some adaptive mechanism similar to the one Whitley [Whitley 1991] uses in rank-ordered evolution might be appropriate.

THE MACD3 PROGRAM

Overview

This program started out as minor modifications to one described in *Artificial Intelligence in Finance*, a special edition published by Miller Freeman under the *AI Expert* banner. It [Klimasauskas 1993] described a genetic algorithm for developing a set of coefficients for combining MACD oscillators. Deficiencies in the algorithm led to a complete rewrite of the code, and new implementation of all the algorithms [Klimasauskas 1994]. Pursuing various issues for improving the technique led to the program described below.

Enhancements to the program include the use of the command line interpreter previously introduced in *Advanced Technology for Developers*. This makes an interactive interface much easier, more extensible, and more flexible, and provides for nested batch capabilities as well.

As a step to making it possible for an individual to actually use the results of this genetic algorithm for trading, an Excel macro *BuildSystem* found in *macd3.xlm* was developed. This macro reads in a file created by *macd3* and generates all of the moving averages and weighted oscillators to compute a long-out-sell signal. The formulas are set up in a way that makes it easy to add new data and use the system. A spreadsheet generated by *BuildSystem* can be updated by the macro *UpdateFormulas*, also found in *macd3.xlm*.

The Symmantec C 6.0 was used for developing the program. The 386 flat model makes it possible to construct up to 10 populations of 50 members each, 4,000 data points, and 512 indicators. This takes about 170 K of memory plus 240 K for the program itself (total 420 K). The author was quite pleased with the Symmantec C 6.0 compiler and development system. One of its advantages is that it makes it possible to run a DOS program in a window on the screen while working on other projects in Word or Excel. The symbolic debugging capabilities are excellent, even with optimizations turned on. It also provides the best capabilities for viewing data and walking through a program that I have ever seen. (This includes several workstation compilers, Borland C, and Microsoft C compilers.) The code in *macd3* is quite vanilla C and should compile easily under Microsoft, Borland, or other popular C compilers. It has been compiled on the Sun SPARCstation (both C1.0 and SPARCWorks), the HP 9000/700, and the IBM RS-6000.

Under DOS, both *macd3* and *fincmd* were compiled with the following options: Unsigned characters (-Jm), large code and large data (-mx), in-line floating point (-f), fast floating point (-ff), 386 target machine (-3). The make, link, project, and related files for *macd3* are included on the source disk. A 386 with math coprocessor or 486 DX is required to run the program.

The basic commands for the interface are described in general, then more specifically. Philosophically, the command line interface is designed to allow parameters to be set or queried, as well as commands to be run. To find out the value of a particular parameter, type a question mark in front of the name. For example, to see the current value for the random number seed, type "?seed" at the prompt. To see the values of all variables that begin with "s," type "?s" at the prompt. To see the values of all variables, type "?" at the prompt. For the syntax of what is expected as input to a particular variable, type the variable name *followed* by a question mark. For example, to see what is expected as an argument to the variable seed, type "seed?" at the command prompt. In general, only the number of letters required to disambiguate one variable or command name from another are required. If a request for syntax is ambiguous—for example, "s?"—all variables that ambiguously match are displayed in a list. For the syntax of all variable input, type "??" at the prompt. The various modes are summarized below.

?name	value of that variable
?	value of all variables
name?	syntax expected
??	syntax of all variables

The names for most of the variables have been selected so that they are easy to remember (or hopefully so). They have been grouped together below based on their usage.

Model/Ideal Trader. This set of parameters describes the model itself. These parameters define how the trading signal is computed and converted to a long-out-short command.

indicator creates a new oscillator. It takes two arguments, which define the fast and slow components of the oscillator. Moving averages, exponential moving averages, and stochastics are supported. The type of the fast transform (S or K for stochastic, M for moving average, or E for exponential moving average) is followed by the period in trading days (no space between). This is followed by a space or comma. The type of the slow transform (S or K for stochastic, D for smoothed stochastic, M for moving average, or E for exponential moving average) is followed by the period in trading days (no space between). The following combinations are valid:

Fast	Slow
M	M or E
E	M or E
S, K	S, K, or D

Examples:

> indicator e3 e5
> indicator e5 m10
> indicator s15 d5
> indicator s5 s30

tradepenalty is the percentage of the transaction price that is attributed to the trade for transaction costs. It is always input as a fraction (.01 = 1 percent). The transaction costs are applied at only one side of the transaction. This value helps to prevent the system from zeroing in on trades that result in very small gains or losses. It tends to push toward larger trades over a longer period of time. Typical values are 0.002 (0.2 percent).

Example:

> tra .002

outofmarket defines a band for the trading signal that will cause an out-of-market signal. Normally, if the trading signal is positive, a long position is taken. If it is negative, a short position is taken. If out-of-market is nonzero, any trading signal within this distance of zero will be considered an out-of-market signal rather than a long or short signal. Typical values are zero or 0.01.

Example:

> out 0.01

searchwindow is used together with *tradepenalty* in constructing an ideal trading signal. Once a signal has been estimated using smoothed prices, it is jiggled forward and backward in time to see if it might result in a more profitable trade. The "search window" is the number of days it searches. A typical value is 3 (+ / − 3 days).

Example:

search 3

Selection Method. *Macd3* supports a variety of selection methods. The two key parameters are the scoring method, and the way in which an offset is computed to rescale the scores.

score determines the scoring method. This takes only a literal, which describes which method will be used for converting the fitness of a chromosome into a score for selection purposes. The methods supported are:

score uses the score returned by the evaluation function directly.

gaussianrank selects elements from the population, assuming that they are sorted by decreasing fitness, using a Gaussian distribution. The fitness returned by the evaluation function is used implicitly in sorting the population.

rank uses the ranking in the population directly. The most fit element in the population is assigned the highest (largest) rank.

uniform picks all elements of the population with the same probability.

Example:

score sco

selectionrange takes a floating-point value, which is used to normalize the scores. It applies only when *score* or *rank* are used for the scoring function. It is ignored for *gaussianrank* and *uniform*. It is used to compute an offset, which is added to each of the raw scores so that the ratio (Maximum Score − Minimum Score) / (Adjusted Minimum Score) is equal to the selection range. A typical value is 1. When the selection range is equal to 1, the range of scores is equal to the adjusted minimum score. This ensures that both fit and unfit members of the population have a reasonable probability of selection.

Example:

select 1.0

Breeding. There are several parameters that are associated with how one or two parents are conjoined or mutated to form an offspring. The first set of five parameters determines what operation will be performed to generate the offspring. They should nominally sum to one. The method for constructing an offspring is the same as for selecting an element of the population using score, where score is the probability of the method. Each of the five methods is assigned a separate probability. They are:

px1point is the probability of performing a single-point crossover, typically 0.1.

px2point is the probability of performing two-point crossover, typically 0.1.

pxuniform is the probability of performing uniform crossover, typically 0.2.

pmcreep is the probability of performing mutation by creep, typically 0.35.

pmrand is the probability of performing mutation by randomization, typically 0.25.

pxaverage is the probability that when one-point, two-point, or uniform crossover is selected, rather than swapping two genes, the average of the two genes is used in both offspring. A typical value for this is 0.05.

mutoneprob is the probability that for a chromosome undergoing mutation (creep or randomization), an individual gene is modified. A typical value for this is 0.5.

mutcreeplimit is the maximum amount that the value of a gene selected for modification will be changed. This is multiplied by a random number between minus one and one to generate the actual delta, which is applied to the gene.

Example:

```
px1 10%
px2 10%
pxu 20%
pmcr 25%
pmr 35%
pxav 0.05
mutone 50%
mutcre 0.2
```

NOTE: percentages can be entered as "23%" or 0.23. These are both equivalent as far as the input routine is concerned. Any number that is followed by a percent sign is automatically divided by 100.

After offspring are generated, they may be normalized: *normalization* specifies the method used to renormalize the chromosome. There are four methods:

ratio uses the methods for ratio-based genetic algorithms to renormalize. These were described in detail above. Genes always have values in the range zero to one.

multiplicative computes a rescaling factor and multiplies each of the genes by this so that the sum of absolute values is equal to one. Genes always range from minus one to plus one.

symmetric requires that all genes have values in the range minus one to one.

asymmetric requires only that all genes have values in the range zero to one.

Example:

```
norm mult
```

optimization may be applied to a new offspring. There are three methods of optimization: *local,* which optimizes every new offspring; *global,* which optimizes the best of each population; and *none,* which performs no optimization at all.

Example:

```
optim none
```

Evaluation Method. After a new offspring is created, it must be evaluated.

evaluation sets the method for evaluating performance of the ensemble of MACD oscillators. Three methods have been implemented: *profit, trades,* and *target: profit* computes the profit over a period of time, taking transaction costs into account; *trades* uses a heuristic formula that includes the ratio of profitable to unprofitable trades and profit into a single number; *target* evaluates performance against an ideal trading signal.

subevaluation determines how the evaluation method is applied to the training set; *actual* uses the actual value over the entire data period. Each of the other methods divides the training data into two or more overlapping periods. Performance is measured over each of these periods and combined using one of four methods: *average* takes the average of the performance in the subperiods; *minimum* takes the minimum of the subperiods (this was designed to attempt to force more uniform performance over a range of conditions); *minaverage* adds the average to the minimum. This was used when still trying to develop a heuristic formula for combining trades and profit. *minlast* is the average of the minimum and performance on the last subperiod of the training window. This was an attempt to improve generalization. *min2* takes the average of the two lowest scores. This is used to give more shape to the evaluation function. (This is the default.)

periods defines the number of periods used in subevaluation.

Example:

        eval trades
        subev minlast
        periods 5

Individual Replacement. Each population has a certain number of elements, or chromosomes. When enough unique items have been added to replace an entire population, a generation is complete.

members defines the total number of iterations, and the total number of elements, or chromosomes, in a complete population.

Example:

        members 30

Generational Replacement. Occurs when a population is full. A new population is started by copying some portion of the best of the current population to seed the new one.

populationseed is the fraction of the current population copied to start a new generation. When set to zero, this is effectively generational replacement. When set to one, it is equivalent to rank-ordered replacement. A value of 0.7 provided enough flexibility that the system continued to evolve, but not so much that it wandered.

Example:

        population 70%

Migration. Periodically, isolated populations exchange genetic material. This is migration.

isles is the number of isolated populations that evolve. When set to one, this is the same as a genetic algorithm without migration. Values of 5 to 10 seemed to work well on this problem.

migration is the portion of each population that migrates and can be replaced as a result of migration. When this is too small, very little happens. When it is too large (greater than 0.1), the populations become clones of each other.

genpermigration determines the frequency with which migrations occur. If this is too small, populations do not have a chance to explore local solutions. Good values seemed to be in the range of 30–70.

randommigration set to 1 (default) indicates that migrations are to occur randomly. When a random migration occurs, genetic material is randomly selected from each population with a bias based on their fitness. Otherwise migrations occur a fixed number of generations apart, and the best of each population are intermixed.

rmigrationrate is the probability of a random migration. It is typically set to 0.02, which causes a migration approximately every 50 generations.

Example (fixed migrations):

    isles 10
    migration 10%
    genpermigration 50

or Example (random migrations):

    isles 10
    migration 10 percent
    randommigration 1
    rmigrationrate 0.02

General. These parameters set global values and take various actions.

datafile is the name of the input data file. The format of the data file is shown below. Lines that are blank or begin with an "!" are considered comment lines. If it is not possible to convert the first field to a valid date, or the second field to a valid number, the record is ignored. All fields after the second one are ignored. The format of each input line is:

    mm/dd/yy pppp.pp

where "mm/dd/yy" is the date, and "pppp.pp" is the price. The file format does not support fractional prices (e.g., 5 3/8). Fields are separated by spaces or tabs.

Example:

    datafile sp500b.dat

runcode is used to set default names for the log file and save file. The runcode takes a letter as its argument. The default names are "bch?log.txt" for the batch file, and "bch?0000.txt" for the save files.

Example:

    runcode 'a'

logfile is used to record commands and status messages. It is regularly closed and reopened, so that if the computer crashes, or power goes out, a reasonably recent record of activity is available. As the system evolves, it prints out a status line with tab-separated data values (suitable for importing into Excel). The format of these status lines is:

g p trb tra trw ptrb ptra ptrw ptsb ptsa ptsw

Where:

g is the current generation.
p is the population number.
trb is the fitness of the best element.
tra is the average fitness of the population.
trw is the worst fitness in the population.
ptrb is the profit for the most fit element.
ptra is the average profit for the population.
ptrw is the profit for the least fit element.
ptsb is the profit on the test for the most fit element.
ptsa is the average profit on the test set.
ptsw is the profit on the test for the least fit element.

Other status messages identify when weights are saved and migrations occur. For debugging purposes, messages also show the number of allocations / deallocations and the maximum memory used.

Example:
logfile bchalog.txt

savefile is the root name of the file to save populations to. This name should have at least three zeros prior to the file name extension. This number is incremented each time a new chromosome is saved. The format of a save file is described below.

Indicators Genes Score Train-Profit Test-Profit
fit1 fper1 f1w1 f1w2 f1w3 ...
sit1 sper1 s1w1 s1w2 s1w3 ...
fit2 fper2 f2w1 f2w2 f2w3 ...
sit2 sper2 s2w1 s2w2 s2w3 ...
G1 G2 G3 .. Gn
1-pt 2-pt Uniform Creep Random
Sub-periods Score1 Score2 ... ScoreN

Data-Pts
date1 price1 signal1 position1 ideal1
date2 price2 signal2 position2 ideal2

...

Indicators is the number of indicators in this run. **Genes** is the number of genes in the chromosome (one more than indicators). There is one gene for each oscillator (indicator), and one extra as a *bias*. **Score** is the fitness associated with this chromosome. **Train-Profit** is the profit over the entire training period, exclusive of transaction costs. **Test-Profit** is the profit over the test period, exclusive of transaction costs.

fit1 is the type of the fast component of the first indicator; **sit1** is the type of the slow component of the first indicator. Type codes are: 1 = Moving average; 2 = Truncated exponential moving average; 3 = Stochastic (%K); 4 = Smoothing of stochastic (%D) (only valid as a slow type). **fper1** and **sper1** are the periods for fast and slow, respectively. **f1w1, f1w2, f1w3, ...** are the weights for computing the moving average, exponential moving average, or smoothing for the stochastic. They are ignored for stochastic %K. There is one pair of fast / slow definitions for each indicator.

G1, G2, ..., Gn are the values for each of the genes in the chromosome.

1-pt, 2-pt, Uniform, Creep, Random are the counts of the number of times each of these methods was used in the current population. This was for debugging purposes.

Subperiods is the number of subperiods that the training period is divided into for purposes of computing a score. **Score1, Score2, ..., ScoreN** are the actual scores from each of the subperiods. This is sometimes interesting to look at.

Data-Pts are the number of data points in the combined training and test sets. The data itself follows. **date1, date2** are the dates for the first and second respective rows. The format of the date is "mm/dd/yy." **price** is the decimalized price. **signal** is the signal computed by the evaluation function. **position** is the position that results from thresholding the signal. One is long. Zero is out. Minus one is short. **ideal** is the position computed by the ideal trading signal generator.

Tabs are used to separate each of the data fields so that the file is easily imported into Excel, Quattro, and other spreadsheets.

Example:

savef bcha0000.txt

seed is the number used to initialized the random number seed. Each time the random number generator is initialized, this is reset to zero. If you want to test the evolution of two populations with the same random seed, it is necessary to set it prior to each *go* command.

Example:

seed 175933

referencetest is *yes* or *no*. It determines if a series of evaluations are done on chromosomes in which only a single gene is set to one, and all others zero. This is used to compute the effectiveness of single MACD oscillators. This was used to generate Table 1.

Example:

reference no

frequency2save is how often the best chromosome of all populations is saved. After saving the best element of all populations, that element is processed through a local optimizer, which attempts to make it just a little better. The results of that tweaking are also saved. The purpose of periodically saving the best element of all populations is that it provides a method to see how the solutions evolved. In the example below, the best solution from all populations is saved every five generations. Setting the frequency to zero disables intermediate saves.

Example:

freq 5

statistics is used to test the model over a large number of overlapping periods. It takes three arguments: The start of the first period, the size of the test window, and the number of days to increment to the next test window. Statistics are written to the "summary.txt" file. In the example below, the first test window starts at the 50th trading day and runs for 50 trading days. The next test window starts five trading days later.

Example:

statistics 50,50,5

skippoints, trainpoints, and *testpoints* all work together. *skippoints* is used to specify the number of trading days to skip prior to the start of the training period. It can be used to start training at various offsets within the data file. *trainpoints* specifies the number of trading days to use for training purposes. *testpoints* specifies the number of test points for validating the model's performance. In the example below, 250 trading days are used to develop a trading model, 100 are used to compute the "test profit." Training starts 50 trading days after the start of the data. NOTE: It is important to make sure that *skip* is set to a number large enough that all moving averages, stochastics, etc., can be computed properly prior to the first training day. So, if you have a 25-day %K followed by a 5-day %D, *skip* must be set to at least 29.

Example:

trainpoints 250
testpoints 100
skip 50

go takes two arguments. The first is the maximum number of generations to run for. The second optional parameter is the number of generations without a new *champion.* The program will continue iteration until one or both of these conditions are met. The second parameter stops the process when no better solution is found after the specified number of iterations. The default for this is 100 generations.

Example:

go 500
go 2000, 50

batch provides a batch file capability. This is quite convenient for setting up long runs to test out various parameters. Batch files have exactly the same syntax and format as if commands were entered directly from the command line. Batch files can be nested, but each requires an open file.

Example:

batch batch.run

The file *batch.run* might contain the following commands to test the effects of several random numbers (5001, 21955, and 19565) on the evolution of a solution. Data is from the file *sp500b.dat* and the best solutions are periodically saved to files that are incremented from *bcha0000.txt*.

```
log bchalog.txt
data sp500b.dat
save bcha0000.txt
seed 5001
go 500,100
seed 21955
go 500,100
seed 19565
go 500,100
```

quit terminates the program when entered interactively and/or exits a batch file.

Example:

```
quit
```

It is also possible to run a series of batch files from the command line. This is done by placing the names of the batch files on the command line after the program name.

A complete listing of the *macd3* program is shown in Listing 1. The source for *fincmd.c* and *fincmd.h* are not shown, but are provided on the source disk. The source disk also contains the Excel macro (described below), the data files used (*sp500.dat* with holidays eliminated, and *sp500b.dat* with holidays copying the prior price), and Symmantec C 6.0 project and make files.

Future Exploration

One avenue to explore is modifying the data input routine to accept the output of several oscillators, already prethresholded. This would make it possible for the user to construct strength, volume, or intermarket oscillators and optimize how they should work together. The modified input routine would generate the bit values used in the evaluation routine directly.

EXCEL DEPLOYMENT

Overview

One of the most popular tools for financial modeling is the Excel spreadsheet from Microsoft. This program supports a wide range of technologies, which makes it easy to develop and model systems. For this reason, it was selected as the deployment vehicle.

A macro was written that takes a saved chromosome (as described under *save-file*), and builds a spreadsheet, complete with all of the formulas required to compute the moving averages and oscillators, weight them, and combine them into a trading signal.

Using the Macro

The macro in Listing 2 is called *macd3.xlm.* When loaded, it has two large buttons in the middle of the screen. Pressing the top button with the left mouse button causes an *open* dialog box to appear on the screen. This dialog box will display all of the text files (.txt) in the selected directory. It also has input of tab-separated text preset as the options.

Select the file that you want to convert, and press "OK." The file will be loaded into a sheet and selected portions of it copied to a new sheet for further processing. Formulas to compute the moving averages, weighted oscillators, and trading signal are inserted into the sheet. Computing %D requires a special macro, which is shown in Listing 4. This macro function **must** be part of the same macro as shown in Listing 2. After the new spreadsheet is created, the original input file is closed, and a dialog prompts you to save the new sheet.

The new spreadsheet uses the following columns:

A—date which corresponds to the price

B—closing price of the security

C—weighted result of the first indicator

D—weighted result of the second indicator ...

..—weighted sum of oscillator outputs

+1—trading signal: 1 = long; 0 = out; −1 = short

The actual construction of the new spreadsheet is quite straightforward, and it should be no problem for most Excel users.

Adding More Data

Once a system is working well, more data can be added using a quite simple procedure. Proceed to the row immediately below the bottom row of data in column A. Add the new date and price in columns A and B, respectively. Several new rows can be added at the bottom if desired. Select columns D through the rightmost end of the sheet in the last nonblank row. Copy this to the corresponding positions in the new rows. The formulas are designed to use relative or absolute referencing where appropriate, so all of the computations will work correctly.

Another method to use to update the spreadsheet is to use the macro *Update-Formulas* in the *macd3.xlm* macro sheet. To use this, start Excel, load the macro sheet, and press the lower button (or run the macro *UpdateFormulas*). You will be prompted to select an input file. This should be an Excel spreadsheet previously created with the *BuildSystem* macro (top button). The selected sheet is loaded. When loaded, it is tested to see that it has the right *magic number* in the second row, first column. Passing this test, it searches until the end of the first data column, then searches backward for the last row of formulas. It copies the last row of formulas and pastes them in to match the data. Finally, it saves the spreadsheet. This macro is shown in Listing 3.

After recomputing the spreadsheet, the new trading signals are in the last column.

APPLICATION EXAMPLE

Overview

This section attempts to summarize the entire process into a few easy steps. The result of following these steps is a genetically optimized multiple-oscillator trading signal. As mentioned in the disclaimer, neither the author, nor Advanced Technology for Developers, nor the publisher warrant that this will work, make money, not lose money, or do anything useful at all. Look again at Figure 10. Each of the best trading signals incurred substantial drawdowns, even though they nominally made money without any commissions. Reader beware. We make no warranties or representations.

The primary steps are shown in the flowchart in Figure 16.

Figure 16. Flowchart of the process of using the *macd3* program.

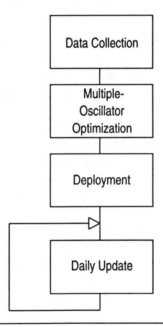

Data Collection. This phase requires obtaining historical data and converting it to the proper format. A variety of software packages are available which can access data from CompuServe,® Reuters, Dow Jones, and other sources. Though the S&P 500 was used for this example, other time series can be used as well. The data source must be able to acquire the data with decimalized pricing (no fractions). Most services support decimalized as well as fractional pricing. Typically 250-500 days (1–2 years) of historical data is required. To some extent, the amount required depends on how long you want the test period to be.

As a step toward building a system that is rapidly deployed, collect all of the data through Friday evening. Develop the model over the weekend, and start working with it on Monday. This approach will minimize the amount of subsequent data that must be collected.

For some types of data—bonds, for example—it is essential to make sure that the data is adjusted for expiration dates, dividend dates, or other factors that might have an artificial impact on price.

As described earlier in the text, one of the issues in preparing the data is addressing holidays and missing data days. The author observed that using the last price for these days worked better at first blush than eliminating them. This may be worth testing further.

Finally, the data needs to be stored in a text file. The data file input routine was written so that it can accept Excel text format (tab-separated price and data fields) or space separated data fields. Leading spaces are ignored. Only the first two data fields, a date and a price, are used by the input program. All other data on a line are ignored.

One data file, *sp500.dat,* is provided on the source disk. It contains S&P 500 closing prices from 1/6/86 through 6/18/93. The batch file *sprun.ini* is also provided. This contains the parameters used for creating the models shown in the graphs above.

Multiple-Oscillator Optimization. Once the data is prepared, the best way to proceed is to set up a batch file with several runs to find the best parameters for your data. It is very important at this point to establish consistent naming conventions and to keep a notebook describing the results at each step. When testing out an idea, make sure to try several random number seeds. This will help you identify if the solution is spurious or represents a valid global minimum. The key parameters to test are the evaluation method and submethod, the scoring mechanism, mutation (creep and randomization) rates, and population size. This is more or less the order to try the different parameters.

One note of caution, the S&P 500 is, relatively speaking, a very predictable time series. The time series for certain specific equities, many commodities, bonds, etc., are much harder to predict. Pick your problem well.

Looking at the log file will help you identify the names of the saved files. The listing below shows the batch file used to construct the runs shown in Figure 10. This batch file (bchk.run) was used to test the default parameters with four different random number seeds.

```
log bchklog.txt
save bchk0000.txt
seed 5102
go 500
seed 21965
go 500
seed 19845
go 500
seed 6753
go 500
```

Deployed System Construction. Once the weights or coefficients associated with each oscillator have been computed, the *macd3.xlm* macro can be used to read one of the saved files and construct a tradable spreadsheet. Using this macro requires loading it into Excel (version 4.0 for Windows), and pressing the top button in the macro sheet with the left mouse button.

Ongoing Operation. New data can be added daily to the system by editing the Excel spreadsheet built above. Copying the formulas down makes it easy to compute the new trading signals. Alternatively, load the macro sheet *macd3.xlm,* and press the bottom button. Follow the prompts from there.

Special Issues. One of the key issues is picking a tradable system. This may be somewhat problematic. Despite all of the effort that the author took to try to develop a way to maximize generalization, and though it did improve, it is still not very good. Performance on the training set is not a very good indicator of how well the system will perform on the test set. This still needs more work.

That is the process. The source code has been provided so that you can test your own ideas. I am interested in knowing to what degree others find this helpful. My own objective is ultimately to develop a system that can effectively call turning points in the markets, primarily from technical analysis. If the fractal market hypothesis is correct, this should be possible with a relatively high degree of accuracy.

Summary

This chapter defined an objective of building a market timing system using multiple MACDs optimized with a genetic algorithm. In the process of development, the author was moderately successful in finding a system to profitably trade the training period with some degree of generalization to the test period. An Excel macro was developed to facilitate deployment. The entire process was summarized in an example.

REFERENCES

Colin, Andrew. "Solving Ratio Optimization Problems With a Genetic Algorithm." *Advanced Technology for Developers.* High-Tech Communications, 103 Buckskin Court, Sewickley, Pennsylvania, 15143. FAX: (412) 741-6094. May 1993, pp. 1–7.

Davis, Lawrence. "Survivable Network Design With Hybrid Genetic Algorithms." *Advanced Technology for Developers.* High-Tech Communications, 103 Buckskin Court, Sewickley, Pennsylvania, 15143. FAX: (412) 741-6094. July 1993, pp. 8–12.

Deboeck, Guido J. *Trading on the Edge: Neural, Genetic, and Fuzzy Systems for Chaotic Financial Markets.* New York: John Wiley and Sons, 1994.

de la Maza, Michael, and Deniz Yuret. "Dynamic Hill Climbing." *AI Expert.* Miller Freeman, 600 Harrison Street, San Francisco, California, 94107. (415) 905-2200. March 1994, pp. 26–31.

Eng, William F. "Lane's Stochastics." *Technical Analysis of Stocks, Options, and Futures.* Chicago: Probus Publishing Co., 1988, pp. 91–113.

Everly, Robert. Personal communication. All of the possible evaluation functions were tested with each of four starting seeds. The results were quite ambiguous with respect to which provided the *best* system based on their ability to generalize.

Everly, Robert. Personal communication. Test results from applying this program to Getty Oil as shown.

Holland, J. H. *Adaptation in Natural and Artificial Systems: An Introductory Analysis with Applications to Biology, Control, and Artificial Intelligence.* 2d ed. Cambridge, MA: MIT Press, 1992.

Keller, William. Personal communication. Test results from 30-year Treasury bonds were provided by Mr. Keller.

Klimasauskas, Casimir C., "GAs Build a Better Market Timing System." *Artificial Intelligence in Finance.* San Francisco: Miller Freeman, 1993, pp. 12f.

Klimasauskas, Casimir C., "Developing a Multiple MACD Market Timing System." *Advanced Technology for Developers.* High-Tech Communications, 103 Buckskin Court, Sewickley, Pennsylvania, 15143. FAX: (412) 741-6094. December 1994, pp. 1f.

Koza, John R., *Genetic Programming.* Cambridge, MA: MIT Press, 1993.

Koza, John R. *Genetic Programming II.* Cambridge, MA: MIT Press, 1994.

Pardo, Edward. *Design, Testing, and Optimization of Trading Systems.* New York: John Wiley & Sons, 1992.

Whitley, D., S. Dominic, and R. Dos. "Genetic Reinforcement Learning with Multi-layered Neural Networks," in R. Beleu and L. Booker (eds.) *Proceedings of the Fourth International Conference on Genetic Algorithms.* San Diego, CA: Morgan Kaufman, 1991, pp. 562–569.

Note: All of the source code for the macd3 program, the command line interface, the Excel macro, and make files are available from High-Tech Communication for $60. Request the MACD3 disk.

Listing 1. The *macd3* Program

```
/* 09:21 04-Jan-94 (macd3.c) Program to Optimize MACD Timing signal */

#define TESTING      /* testing & writing article (undef for regular use) */

/*
    30-May-94 CCK
        Add additional information to summary output
        Integrate fixes for RS6000
    11-May-94 CCK
        Evaluate performance over several time-slices for post analysis
        & interpretation
    02-May-94 CCK
        Create specific indicators (rather than automatic)
        Random migrations (vs scheduled)
        Set "skip", "train" and "test" points
        Skip saving if best chromosome has not changed
    06-Jan-94 CCK
        Added "bias" term to voting
        Revised insertion for identical scores to use serial number
    05-Jan-94 CCK
        Worked on local optimization & performed various tests
    04-Jan-94 CCK
        Do not insert duplicates into the population
        Add "termination" criteria of X-gen with no improvement
        Modify findbest to take into account serial & score
    02-Jan-94 CCK
        Split up Evaluation method & sub-method
    28-Dec-93 CCK
        Originally Written (initial debugging done)
*/

/***************************************************************************
 *                                                                         *
 *    Genetically Optmized MACD Timing System                              *
 *                                                                         *
 ***************************************************************************
    Strategy:
    1) Define the problem structure so that multiple populations can
       be devised.
    2) Set the number of items that "migrate" between populations at
       set intervals. Also, set the number of members of the existing
       population which form the seed of the next generation.

    Issues to Address:
        Over optimization of the coefficients
    */

#define INITFILE    "macd3.ini"   /* default initialization file */

#if defined(SUN) || defined(sun4)
#if !defined(UNIX)
#define UNIX
#endif
#endif

#if defined(UNIX)
#define signed                    /* no signed chars */
#define BIG                       /* use large sized blocks to test! */
#define FAR                       /* no fars */
#define FAST register             /* fast variable */

#define ARGS(x) ()                /* no proto-types */
#define A0 ()
#define A1(t1,v1) \
( v1 ) t1 v1;
#define A2(t1,v1,t2,v2) \
(v1,v2) t1 v1; t2 v2;
#define A3(t1,v1,t2,v2,t3,v3) \
(v1,v2,v3) t1 v1; t2 v2; t3 v3;
#define A4(t1,v1,t2,v2,t3,v3,t4,v4) \
(v1,v2,v3,v4) t1 v1; t2 v2; t3 v3; t4 v4;

#else                             /* NOT UNIX */
#define FAR far
#define FAST                      /* fast variable */
#define ARGS(x) x
#define A0 ( void )
```

```
#define A1(t1,v1) ( t1 v1 )
#define A2(t1,v1,t2,v2) (t1 v1,t2 v2)
#define A3(t1,v1,t2,v2,t3,v3) (t1 v1,t2 v2,t3 v3)
#define A4(t1,v1,t2,v2,t3,v3,t4,v4) (t1 v1,t2 v2,t3 v3,t4 v4)
#endif

#define ASof(x) (sizeof(x)/sizeof(x[0]))      /* size of an array */

#include <stdio.h>
#include <stdlib.h>
#include <time.h>
#include <math.h>
#include "fincmd.h"

#if defined(BIG)
#define MAXPOP   100              /* maximum population size */
#define MAXGRP   50               /* maximum number of groups (populations) */
#define MAXDATA 4096         /* maximum number of data points */
#define MAXSUB   20          /* max number of sub-sets for computing score */
#define MAXIND 512          /* max number of indicators */
#else
#define MAXPOP   50               /* maximum population size */
#define MAXGRP   16               /* maximum number of groups (populations) */
#define MAXDATA 1024         /* maximum number of data points */
#define MAXSUB   8           /* max number of sub-sets for computing score */
#define MAXIND 256          /* max number of indicators */
#endif

typedef struct _idef {          /* indicator definition */
    char       IDFModeC;        /* fast mode */
    unsigned char IDFDurUC;     /* fast duration */
    char       IDSModeC;        /* slow mode */
    unsigned char IDSDurUC;     /* slow duration */
} IDEF;

          /* WARNING: if these change, make corresponding changes to macd3.xlm */
#define IDFM_MA      1              /* moving average */
#define IDFM_EMA     2              /* exponential moving average */
#define IDFM_STOCH   3              /* stochastic */
#define IDFM_SMTH    4              /* ema smoothing of prior field */

typedef struct _drow {          /* one row of data */
    short    DIdealPosS;        /* ideal position -1,0,1 */
    short    DCurPosS;          /* current position -1,0,1 */
    float    DSignalF;          /* current signal (value) */
    long     DDateL;            /* date */
    float    DPriceF;           /* price of security on this date */
    signed char DIndCA[MAXIND>>3];   /* storage for indicator flags */
} DROW;

typedef struct _chrom {             /* chromosome */
    long       CSerialL;            /* serial number of this chrom */
    signed char CPopIDS;            /* population ID of origin */
    signed char CCurPopIDS;         /* current population ID */
    short      COriginS;            /* method of origin */
    float      CTrainF;             /* profit on training portion */
    float      CTestF;              /* profit on test portion */
    float      CScoreF;             /* score for this chromosome */
    float      CSubScoreF[MAXSUB];  /* scores for sub-sets */
    float      CWtsFA[MAXIND];      /* genes (real-valued) */
} CHROM;


typedef struct _pop {           /* one population */
    long      PopSerialL;       /* population serial number */
    short     PopIDS;           /* population ID code */
                                /* --- Selection Method --- */
    short     SelMethodS;       /* selection method */
#define SELSCORE    1           /*    select based on score */
#define SELGRANK    2           /*    select using gaussian rank */
#define SELRANK     3           /*    select using rank as score */
#define SELUNIF     4           /*    select uniformly */
    double    SelRangeD;        /*    range of scores as % of minimum score */
                                /*    This is used to compute an "offset" */
                                /*    when selecting a chromosome from the */
                                /*    population. */
                                /*    --- Crossover & Mutation Rates --- */
    double    ProbXAVGD;        /*    prob of using average (vs replacement) */
                                /*    =0, replace only; =1, average only. */
    double    ProbChildD[5];    /*    probabilities for creating a child: */
#define CHILD1PT    0           /*      child by single point crossover */
```

```
#define CHILD2PT      1        /*  child by two point crossover */
#define CHILDUNIF     2        /*  child by uniform crossover */
#define CHILDCREEP    3        /*  child by creep mutation */
#define CHILDRAND     4        /*  child by randomization */

#define ProbX1PtD  ProbChildD[CHILD1PT]     /* one-point x-over */
#define ProbX2PtD  ProbChildD[CHILD2PT]     /* two-point x-over */
#define ProbXUnifD ProbChildD[CHILDUNIF]    /* uniform x-over */
#define ProbMCreepD ProbChildD[CHILDCREEP]  /* creep */
#define ProbMRandD ProbChildD[CHILDRAND]    /* random mutation */

    double    MutOneProbD;       /* probability of mutating a single gene */
    double    MutOneLimitD;      /* limit on how much it is mutated */
                                 /* --- Optimization --- */
    short     OptMethodS;        /* optimization method */
#define OPTNONE       1          /*  no optimization at all */
#define OPTLOCAL      2          /*  local for evelution purposes ONLY */
#define OPTGLOBAL     3          /*  globally update the gene itself */
#define OPTFORCE      4          /*  force optimization (internal only) */
    short     NormMethS;         /* normalization method */
#define NORMRATIO     1          /*  ratio-based GA */
#define NORMMULT      2          /*  multiplicative post-norm */
#define NORMSYMM      3          /*  -1..1 no normalization */
#define NORMASYM      4          /*  0..1 no normlaization */
                                 /* --- Evalutaion Method --- */
    short     EvalMethodS;       /* evelution method */
#define EVALPROFIT    1          /*  profit */
#define EVALTARGET    2          /*  target */
#define EVALTRADES    3          /*  number of trades */
    short     EvalSubMethS;      /* sub-method */
#define EVALAVG       1          /*  average */
#define EVALMIN       2          /*  minimum */
#define EVALMIN2      3          /*  average of two smallest scores */
#define EVALMINAVG    4          /*  min + average */
#define EVALMINLAST 5            /*  max( min, last) */
#define EVALACTUAL  6            /*  actual */
    short     EvalPeriodsS;      /* number of periods to divide data into */
                                 /* --- Replacement --- */
    double    SeedSizeD;         /* percent of "best" copied to new pop (0..1) */
                                 /*  1=do pure Rank-order GA; 0=Generational GA */
                                 /* --- Population --- */
    short     NGenesS;           /* number of genes used (out of max) */
    unsigned  ChromSizeU;        /* actual chromosome size (bytes) */
    short     SzPopMaxS;         /* max size of either population */
    short     SzCurPopS;         /* size of "current" population */
    short     SzNewPopS;         /* size of "new" (under construction) population */
    short     NewAddsS;          /* number of "additions" to new population */
    CHROM FAR * FAR *CurPopTPP;  /* current population */
    CHROM FAR * FAR *NewPopTPP;  /* new (under construction) population */
    CHROM FAR  *PopTP[MAXPOP*2]; /* pointers to data for both populations */
} POP;

/* --- Trading Positions --- */

#define POS_SHORT     (-1)       /* short */
#define POS_OUT       ( 0)       /* out of the market */
#define POS_LONG      ( 1)       /* long */

/* --- Global Data Declarations --- (initialized in InitParmV().) */

FILE  *LogFP        = {0};       /* W output for logging data */
long   LogModL      = {10};      /* I modulo for logging */

double TradePenaltyF = {0.0};    /* I trading penalty */
double OutLimitF     = {0.0};    /* I band for "out of market" */

int   NDataPtsI     = {0};       /* W number of data points */
int   ISDataXI      = {0};       /* W index of first in-sample point */
int   ISDataNI      = {0};       /* W number of in-sample points */
int   XPDataXI      = {0};       /* W index of first x-post sample point */
int   XPDataNI      = {0};       /* W number of x-post points */
DROW FAR *DataTP[MAXDATA]= {0};  /* W pointers to data & MA's */

int   EVStartI      = { 50};     /* I Evaluation Start Index */
int   EVSizeI       = {100};     /* I size of each item */
int   EVIncrI       = { 50};     /* I increment */

int   PtsSkipI      = {0};       /* I input points to skip */
int   PtsTrainI     = {0};       /* I points to train on */
int   PtsTestI      = {0};       /* I points to test on */
```

```
int    NIndsI        = {0};          /* W number of indicators */
static IDEF Inds[MAXIND] = {0};      /* work indicators */

long   IterCntL      = {0};          /* W iteration counter */

char   DataFile[40]  = {0};          /* I input data file */
char   LogFile[40]   = {0};          /* I log file */
char   SaveFile[40]  = {0};          /* I chromosome file */
char   BatchFile[40] = {0};          /* I current batch file */

POP    IsleT[MAXGRP+1] = {0};        /* W individual populations */
int    NGrpI         = {0};          /* I actual number of groups */
int    GenPerMigI    = {0};          /* I generations per migration */
int    GenCtrI       = {0};          /* W generations since last mig. */
int    GenRandI      = {0};          /* I =1, random data for migration */
double RandMigRateD  = {0};          /* I Random migration rate */
double MigSizeD      = {0};          /* I size of migration (1=all) */

int    RunGensI      = {0};          /* I generations to run */
int    RunTermI      = {0};          /* I gen w/o improvement -> term */
double BestScoreF    = {0.};         /* W best score */
long   RandSeedL     = {0};          /* I random number seed */
int    DoRefTestI    = {0};          /* I do reference tests */
int    SaveFreqI     = {0};          /* I save frequency */

int    SrchWindowI   = {0};          /* I search window for ideal trader */

long   OffMethL[6]   = {0};          /* W offspring methods */

#define RUNCODE 'a'                  /* modifier for log & output file names */
int    RunCodeI      = {RUNCODE};    /* I Run code */
char   GBuf[512]     = {0};          /* global data buffer */
char   IBuf[32]      = {0};          /* indicator buffer */
char   IBuf2[32]     = {0};          /* second field buffer */

static char Bits[8] = {0x80, 0x40, 0x20, 0x10, 0x08, 0x04, 0x02, 0x01 };

/* --- Work Buffer --- */

static float M1F[256]  = {0.};       /* first multipliers */
static float M2F[256]  = {0.};       /* second multipliers */
static float BFR[256]  = {0.};       /* work buffer */

/* --- Forward Refereces --- */

void EvalV  ARGS((CHROM FAR *, POP FAR *,int));
int CMDBatch ARGS((char *, long, FILE *));

/************************************************************************
 *                                                                     *
 *    DisclaimV() - Disclaimer & Title                                 *
 *                                                                     *
 ************************************************************************
 */

char *DisclaimerCP[] = {
"The hypothetical computer simulated performance results provided are\n",
"believed to be accurately presented. However, they are not guaranteed as\n",
"to accuracy or completeness and are subject to change without any notice.\n",
"Hypothetical or simulated performance results have certain inherent\n",
"limitations.  Unlike an actual performance record, simulated results\n",
"do not represent actual trading. Since, also, the trades have not actually\n",
"been executed, the results may under or over compensate for the impact,\n",
"if any, of certain market factors such as liquidity. Simulated trading\n",
"programs in general are also subject to the fact that they are designed with\n",
"the benefit of hindsight. No representation is being made that any account\n",
"will, or is likely to achieve profits or losses similar to those shown. All\n",
"investments and trades carry risks.\n",
"       # # # # # # # # # # # # # # # # # # #\n",
"This code is supplied to customers of Advanced Technology for Developers for\n",
"their own personal use. Distribution, re-sale, or other commercial uses\n",
"are expressly forbidden.\n",
"       # # # # # # # # # # # # # # # # # # #\n"
"Copyright (c) 1993-1994 High-Tech Communications. All rights reserved.\n",
"       # # # # # # # # # # # # # # # # # # #\n",
0
};

void DisclaimV A0
{
  int     wxI;       /* work index into the title */
```

```
  char    *sp;       /* work string */

  for( wxI = 0; (sp = DisclaimerCP[wxI]) != (char *)0; wxI++ ) {
    fputs( sp, stdout );
    if ( LogFP ) fputs( sp, LogFP );
  }

  fflush( stdout );
  if ( LogFP ) fflush( LogFP );

  return;
}
/*************************************************************************
 *                                                                       *
 *    RRand() - real-valued random number                                *
 *                                                                       *
 *************************************************************************
  Derived from Numerical Recipes "ran3" (Knuth Algorithm).
 */
#define MSEED   161803398L    /* base seed */
#define MBIG    1000000000L   /* largest possible number */
#define MZ      0             /* minimum size */

static long    RandMA[56]  = {0}; /* work array */
static short   Randp1      = {0}; /* first pointer */
static short   Randp2      = {0}; /* second pointer */

void RandSeedV A1(          /* set random seed */
long,      SeedL )         /* initial Seed */
{
  long    mj, mk, ml;      /* work variables */
  int     i, j;            /* work indicies */

  ml = SeedL < 0? -SeedL:SeedL;             /* positive seed */
  mk = 1;
  RandMA[55] = mj = (MSEED - ml) % MBIG;    /* initial "seed" for ma[55] */
  for( i = 1; i <= 54; i++ ) {              /* initialize rest of the table */
    j = (21 * i) % 55;
    RandMA[j] = ml = mk;
    mk = mj - mk;
    if ( mk < MZ ) mk += MBIG;              /* keep all positive */
    mj = ml;
  }
  for( j = 1; j <= 4; j++ )                 /* warm up the generator */
    for( i = 1; i <= 55; i++ ) {
      ml = (RandMA[i] -= RandMA[1 + (i+30) % 55 ]);
      if ( ml < MZ ) RandMA[i] += MBIG;
    }
  Randp1 = 0;          /* set initial pointer values */
  Randp2 = 31;
  RandMA[0] = 1;       /* clear "unitialized" flag */

  return;
}


long RandL A0         /* 0..MBIG uniform distributed values */
{
  FAST long  ml;      /* work / return value */

  if ( RandMA[0] == 0 ) RandSeedV(0L);    /* force initizliation */

  if ( ++Randp1 == 56 ) Randp1 = 1;       /* wrap pointers around */
  if ( ++Randp2 == 56 ) Randp2 = 1;

  ml = RandMA[Randp1] - RandMA[Randp2];   /* generate new number subtractively */
  if ( ml < MZ ) ml += MBIG;              /* make it positive */
  RandMA[Randp1] = ml;                    /* save it for later */
  return( ml );                           /* return long value */
}

double Rand01D()        /* 0..1 uniform distributed random number */
{ return( ((double)RandL())*(1./((double)MBIG)) ); }

#define RandRD( Min, Max ) (Rand01D() * ((Max)-(Min)) + (Min))
```

```
/***********************************************************************
 *                                                                     *
 *     Str2DateL() - Convert a data string to internal format          *
 *     Date2StrCP() - Convert an internal date format to string        *
 *                                                                     *
 ***********************************************************************
 */

long Str2DateL A1(      /* convert a date string to a long */
FAST char *,   dCP )    /* date pointer */
{
    long     dL;           /* return date */
    short    dy,mo,yr;     /* components */
    int      c;            /* work char */

    dy = mo = 0; yr = 0x19;

    for( ; '0' <= (c = *dCP) && c <= '9'; dCP++ )
      mo = (mo << 4) | (c & 0xf);
    if ( *dCP != 0 ) dCP++;

    for( ; '0' <= (c = *dCP) && c <= '9'; dCP++ )
      dy = (dy << 4) | (c & 0xf);
    if ( *dCP != 0 ) dCP++;

    for( ; '0' <= (c = *dCP) && c <= '9'; dCP++ )
      yr = (yr << 4) | (c & 0xf);

    dL = (((long)yr&0xffffL)<<16) | ((mo & 0xff)<<8) | (dy & 0xff);

    return( dL );
}

char *Date2StrCP A1(      /* convert long to internal date format */
long,      dL )           /* date to convert */
{
    static char dbf[12] = {0};      /* temp to generate date */
    sprintf( dbf, "%02x/%02x/%02x",
      (int)((dL>>8)&0xff), (int)(dL & 0xff), (int)((dL>>16) & 0xff) );
    return( &dbf[0] );
}

/***********************************************************************
 *                                                                     *
 *     MsgER() - Error message handler                                 *
 *                                                                     *
 ***********************************************************************
 */

int MsgER A1(
char *,      buf )             /* message buffer */
{
    fputs( buf, stdout );      /* send message to user */
    fflush( stdout );
    if ( LogFP ) {             /* send to log file & temp-close */
      fputs( buf, LogFP );
      fclose( LogFP ); LogFP = fopen( LogFile, "a" );
    }
    return( -1 );
}

/***********************************************************************
 *                                                                     *
 *     MemGetVP() - get memory & keep track of it                      *
 *     MemFreeV() - free memory & keep track of it                     *
 *     MemStatsV() - print out memory statistics                       *
 *                                                                     *
 ***********************************************************************
   These routines were designed to help track memory allocation problems.
 */

long   MemAlcdL    = {0};       /* memory allocated */
long   MemFreeL    = {0};       /* memory freed */
long   MemAlCntL   = {0};       /* allocation count */
long   MemFrCntL   = {0};       /* memory free count */

long   MaxMemL     = {0};       /* max memory allocated */
long   MaxMemCntL  = {0};       /* max allocations */
long   CurMemL     = {0};       /* current memory allocated */
long   CurMemCntL  = {0};       /* current memory count */
```

```
void FAR *MemGetVP A1(         /* allocate memory */
unsigned,     SizeU )    /* amount to allocate */
{
  FAST unsigned FAR *rp; /* return pointer */

  rp = (unsigned *)malloc( SizeU + 2*sizeof(*rp) );  /* allocate memory */
  if ( rp != (unsigned *)0 ) {
    MemAlcdL += (long)SizeU;        /* add in memory */
    MemAlCntL++;                    /* count it */
    rp[0] = SizeU;                  /* save size */
    rp += 2;                        /* start of data */

    CurMemL  = MemAlcdL - MemFreeL;        /* net memory */
    CurMemCntL = MemAlCntL - MemFrCntL;    /* net allocations */
    if ( CurMemL  > MaxMemL  ) MaxMemL  = CurMemL;
    if ( CurMemCntL > MaxMemCntL ) MaxMemCntL = CurMemCntL;
  }
  return( (void *)rp );            /* failed */
}


void MemFreeV A1(        /* free memory */
FAST void FAR *, p )     /* data pointer to free */
{
  unsigned FAR *rp;      /* pointer to free */

  rp = (unsigned *)p;
  if ( rp != (void *)0 ) {
    rp -= 2;                 /* back out overhead */
    MemFreeL += (long)rp[0];     /* account for freed memory */
    MemFrCntL++;                 /* count it */
    free( (void *)rp );          /* free it */

    CurMemL  = MemAlcdL - MemFreeL;        /* net memory */
    CurMemCntL = MemAlCntL - MemFrCntL;    /* net allocations */
    if ( CurMemL  > MaxMemL  ) MaxMemL  = CurMemL;
    if ( CurMemCntL > MaxMemCntL ) MaxMemCntL = CurMemCntL;
  }
  return;
}


void MemStatsV A0       /* print out memory statistics */
{
  sprintf( GBuf, "%ld (max %ld) allocated in %ld (max %ld) segments.\n",
    CurMemL, MaxMemL, CurMemCntL, MaxMemCntL );
  MsgER( GBuf );
  return;
}

/************************************************************************
 *                                                                      *
 *   GenMultVecV() - Generate coefficients for MA / EMA                 *
 *                                                                      *
 ************************************************************************
 These coefficients are used to compute the MA, EMA, %D values.
 A truncated series is used for EMA to stabilize results. When the
 standard convex average is used for EMA, results change if data is
 removed from or added to the start of the file.
 */

void GenMultVecV A3(
float *,     rvFP,      /* return vector */
int,        perI,       /* period */
int,        TypeI )     /* type */
{
  int    xI;            /* index */
  int    EmaFlagI;      /* EMA Flag */
  double    k, kc;      /* multipliers */
  double    s, f;       /* sum & multiplicative factor */

  EmaFlagI = (TypeI == IDFM_EMA || TypeI == IDFM_SMTH)? 1:0;
  if ( EmaFlagI )
    k = 2./((double)perI);       /* EMA multiplier */
  else k = 1./(double)perI;      /* MA multiplier */

  kc = 1.-k;                     /* convex compliment */
  s = 0.;                        /* sum */
  for( xI = perI; --xI >= 0; ) {
    rvFP[xI] = k;                /* EMA multiplier */
    s    += k;                   /* prior multiplier */
```

```
    if ( EmaFlagI ) k *= kc;        /* adjust EMA multiplier */
  }

  if ( EmaFlagI ) {
    f = 1./s;                       /* scale so sum is 1. */
    for( xI = perI; --xI >= 0; )
      rvFP[xI] *= f;
  }

  return;
}
/***********************************************************************
 *                                                                     *
 *    SaveChromI() - Save a Chromosome to a data file                  *
 *                                                                     *
 ***********************************************************************
  Format: # of Indicators\t# of Genes\tScore\tTest
      tf pf v v v v    - fast indicator
      ts ps v v v v... - slow indicator
      WT\tWT\t...\n

    tf, ts = type of fast (slow) indicator
        (1=MA, 2=EMA, 3=Stoch (%K), 4=%D)
    pf, ps = period for fast (slow) indicator.
 */

void IncFileNameV A1(
char *,       fnCP )        /* file name to fix */
{
  char     *CP;             /* work pointer */

  for( CP = fnCP; CP[1] != 0 && CP[1] != '.'; )
    CP++;                   /* skip to end of name */

  while( CP >= fnCP && '0' <= *CP && *CP <= '9' ) {
    if ( *CP == '9' ) *CP-- = '0'; /* increment the file name */
    else { (*CP)++; break; }
  }
  return;
}


int SaveChromI A2(         /* save a chromosome */
char *,       fnCP,        /* file name to save to */
CHROM FAR *,  chTP )       /* chromosome to save */
{
  POP FAR     *popTP;      /* current population */
  char FAR    *CP;         /* character pointer to "fix" name */
  FILE        *oFP;        /*output file pointer */
  int         wxI;         /* work index */
  int         exI;         /* end index */
  int         cxI;         /* current index into chrom */
  int         j;           /* work int */
  DROW FAR    *drTP;       /* row of data */

  popTP = &IsleT[chTP->CCurPopIDS];       /* population */
  IncFileNameV( fnCP );                   /* update file name */

  if ( (oFP = fopen( fnCP, "w" )) == (FILE *)0 ) {
    sprintf( GBuf, "Could not open output file <%s>\n", fnCP );
    MsgER( GBuf );
    return( -1 );
  }

  fprintf( oFP, "%d\t%d\t%.6g\t%.6g\t%.6g\n",
      NIndsI, popTP->NGenesS, chTP->CScoreF, chTP->CTrainF, chTP->CTestF );

  exI = NIndsI-1;
  for( wxI = 0; wxI <= exI; wxI++ ) {
    cxI = Inds[wxI].IDFDurUC & 0xff;
    fprintf( oFP, "%d\t%d", Inds[wxI].IDFModeC, cxI );
    GenMultVecV( &BFR[0], cxI, Inds[wxI].IDFModeC );
    for( j = 0; j < cxI; j++ )
      fprintf( oFP, "\t%.6g", BFR[j] );
    fprintf( oFP, "\n" );

    cxI = Inds[wxI].IDSDurUC & 0xff;
    fprintf( oFP, "%d\t%d\t", Inds[wxI].IDSModeC, cxI );
    GenMultVecV( &BFR[0], cxI, Inds[wxI].IDSModeC );
    for( j = 0; j < cxI; j++ )
      fprintf( oFP, "\t%.6g", BFR[j] );
```

```
      fprintf( oFP, "\n" );
   }

   exI = popTP->NGenesS-1;
   for( wxI = 0; wxI <= exI; wxI++ )
      fprintf( oFP, "%.6g%s", chTP->CWtsFA[wxI], wxI < exI? "\t":"\n" );

   /* --- The following code saves data for testing and building an
         Excel spreadsheet to trade. --- */

   EvalV( chTP, popTP, 0 );   /* reset local data */

   fprintf( oFP, "%ld\t%ld\t%ld\t%ld\t%ld\n",
      OffMethL[0], OffMethL[1], OffMethL[2], OffMethL[3], OffMethL[4] );
   fprintf( oFP, "%d", (exI = popTP->EvalPeriodsS) );
   if ( exI > 1 )                /* sub-scores */
      for( wxI = 0; wxI < exI; wxI++ )
         fprintf( oFP, "\t%.6g", chTP->CSubScoreF[wxI] );
   fprintf( oFP, "\n\n\n" );       /* leave room for excel macro */

   fprintf( oFP, "%d\n", NDataPtsI ); /* acutal scores */
   for( wxI = 0; wxI < NDataPtsI; wxI++ ) {
      drTP = DataTP[wxI];
      fprintf( oFP, "%s\t%.6g\t%.6g\t%d\t%d\n",
         Date2StrCP( drTP->DDateL ), drTP->DPriceF,
         drTP->DSignalF, drTP->DCurPosS, drTP->DIdealPosS );
   }

   fclose( oFP );
   return( 0 );
}

/************************************************************************
 *                                                                      *
 *    FindBestTP() - Find best chromosome in all of the islands         *
 *                                                                      *
 ************************************************************************
 */

CHROM FAR *FindBestTP AO     /* find best chromosome of all pops */
{
   FAST int        wxI;       /* work index */
   FAST CHROM FAR *chTP;      /* chromosome */
   FAST CHROM FAR *wchTP;     /* working chromosome */
   FAST POP  FAR  *wpopTP;    /* working population */

   chTP = (CHROM *)0;
   for( wxI = 1; wxI <= NGrpI; wxI++ ) {
      wpopTP = &IsleT[wxI];
      if ( wpopTP->SzNewPopS > 0 )  wchTP = wpopTP->NewPopTPP[0];
      else                wchTP = wpopTP->CurPopTPP[0];

      if ( wxI == 1 ||              /* first one */
         wchTP->CScoreF > chTP->CScoreF || /* better or earlier */
         (wchTP->CScoreF == chTP->CScoreF && wchTP->CSerialL < chTP->CSerialL) ) {
         chTP = wchTP;
      }
   }

   return( chTP );
}

/************************************************************************
 *                                                                      *
 *    SelectI() - Select a Chromosome from the Population                *
 *                                                                      *
 ************************************************************************
   returns: Index of the item selected in the current population.

   NOTE: This routine assumes that the current population is ALWAYS
   kept in order with the most fit element as the first, and all
   others following.

   Score-based selection:
      Scores are "offset" so that (max - min)/re-scaled min
      is popTP->SelRangeD. This makes it possible to insure that the
      most fit members of the population are not the only ones which
      are selected.

   Rank-based Gaussian selections
      generates a "cheap" gaussian and folds it so that it is most dense
```

```
        toward zero, and less dense toward 1.

    Score is rank
        uses scores from 1..SzPopI. These are assigned as scores based on
        rank (highest rank is best score). The roulette wheel is spun just
        as in score-based selection.

    Uniform selection
        makes all elements in the population equally likely.
   */


int SelectI A2(
FAST POP FAR *, popTP,          /* population to select from */
int,            parent1I )      /* first parent (-1 = n/c) */
{
    FAST CHROM FAR * FAR *chTPP; /* pointer to current population */
    FAST CHROM FAR *chTP;        /* pointer to current chromosome */
    FAST double     CircumR;     /* circumference */
    FAST double     MinR, MaxR;  /* minimum value */
    FAST double     OffsetR;     /* offset */
    FAST double     wD;          /* work value */
    FAST int        chXI;        /* chromosome index */
    FAST int        SzPopI;      /* size of the current population */
    FAST int        selXI;       /* selected index */

    selXI = 0;
    chTPP = popTP->CurPopTPP;       /* current population */
    SzPopI = popTP->SzCurPopS;      /* active elements in current pop */
    do {
      switch( popTP->SelMethodS ) {
      case SELSCORE:                    /* standard roulette based on score */
        MinR = MaxR = CircumR = chTPP[0]->CScoreF; /* first score */
        for( chXI = 1; chXI < SzPopI; chXI++ ) {
          wD = chTPP[chXI]->CScoreF;             /* current score */
          CircumR += wD;
          if ( wD < MinR ) MinR = wD;            /* smallest value */
          if ( wD > MaxR ) MaxR = wD;            /* largest value */
        }
        if ( MinR == MaxR )               /* all have the same score */
          goto DoUnif;                    /* very unlikely */

        wD = popTP->SelRangeD;          /* ratio for (max-min)/min */
        if ( wD < 1.e-3 ) wD = 1.0;         /* default value */
        OffsetR = (MaxR - MinR) / wD - MinR;    /* offset to add */
        CircumR += OffsetR * SzPopI;     /* revised circumference */
        wD = Rand01D() * CircumR;        /* spin the wheel */
        for( CircumR = 0., chXI = 0; chXI < (SzPopI-1); chXI++ ) {
          CircumR += (chTPP[chXI]->CScoreF + OffsetR);
          if ( CircumR >= wD ) break;
        }
        selXI = chXI;
        break;

      case SELGRANK:      /* roulette based on rank (gaussian distribution) */
        wD = fabs( Rand01D() + Rand01D() - 1. );
        selXI = SzPopI * wD;
        break;

      case SELRANK:       /* use rank as score */
        MinR = 1.;          /* minimum rank */
        MaxR = SzPopI;      /* maximum rank */
        CircumR = ((double)(SzPopI + 1) * SzPopI) * 0.5;

        wD = popTP->SelRangeD;          /* ratio for (max-min)/min */
        if ( wD < 1.e-3 ) wD = 1.0;             /* default value */
        OffsetR = (MaxR - MinR) / wD - MinR;    /* offset to add */
        CircumR += OffsetR * SzPopI; /* revised circumference */
        wD = Rand01D() * CircumR;       /* spin the wheel */
        for( CircumR = 0., chXI = 0; chXI < (SzPopI-1); chXI++ ) {
          CircumR += ((SzPopI - chXI) + OffsetR);
          if ( CircumR >= wD ) break;
        }
        selXI = chXI;
        break;

      case SELUNIF:       /* uniform selection */
      DoUnif:
        selXI = Rand01D() * SzPopI;
        break;
      }
```

```
      if ( selXI > (SzPopI-1) ) selXI = SzPopI - 1;
      if ( selXI < 0        ) selXI = 0;
   } while( selXI == parent1I );    /* make sure it is "unique" */

   return( selXI );        /* selected parent */
}

/***************************************************************************
 *                                                                         *
 *    IdealSignalV() - Compute "ideal" signal with penalty function        *
 *                                                                         *
 ***************************************************************************
 */

void IdealSignalV A2(             /* compute ideal trading signal */
double,      PenaltyD,            /* minimum change in price (%) */
FAST int,    SrchWinI )           /* search window for optimization */
{
   FAST int    sXI, cXI, eXI;     /* start, current, end indicies */
   FAST int    wXI;               /* window index */
   FAST int    lXI;               /* look ahead index */
   FAST int    CPosI;             /* current ideal position */
   FAST int    LPosI;             /* last position */
   FAST int    tsI, teI;          /* trade start / end indicies */
   FAST int    cttI;              /* current trade type */
   FAST float  CPriceF;           /* current price */
   FAST float  LPriceF;           /* look-ahead price */
   FAST float  NPriceF;           /* next "price" */
   FAST float  HighF, LowF;       /* highest difference, lowest difference */
   FAST float  ThreshF;           /* threshold */
   FAST DROW FAR *drTP;           /* data row pointer */
   FILE        *oFP;              /* work output file */

   /* --- Basic Idea: Compute average for next point over +/-2 periods.
    * if the result is greater than for the current one, go long.
    * otherwise, go short. later look for long-short-long or
    * short-long-short in a single step & eliminate them.
    */

   sXI   = 1;                     /* start index */
   eXI   = NDataPtsI - 4;         /* last data value */
   LPosI = POS_OUT;               /* last position value */
   for( cXI = 0; cXI < sXI; cXI++ )
    DataTP[cXI]->DIdealPosS = POS_OUT;

   NPriceF = 0.2* ( DataTP[0]->DPriceF +    /* 5-day MA */
             DataTP[1]->DPriceF +   /* current point */
             DataTP[2]->DPriceF +
              DataTP[3]->DPriceF +
               DataTP[4]->DPriceF);

   for( cXI = sXI;; ) {
   CPriceF = DataTP[cXI]->DPriceF; /* current price */
   if ( NPriceF > CPriceF )    CPosI = POS_LONG;
   else if ( NPriceF < CPriceF ) CPosI = POS_SHORT;
   else                CPosI = POS_OUT;
   DataTP[cXI]->DIdealPosS = CPosI;

   cXI++;
   if ( cXI >= eXI ) break;

   NPriceF += 0.2 * (DataTP[cXI+3]->DPriceF - DataTP[cXI-2]->DPriceF);
   }

   while( cXI < NDataPtsI )
   DataTP[cXI++]->DIdealPosS = POS_OUT;

   /* --- Take another pass through and "clean up" long-short-long issues --- */

   eXI = NDataPtsI-1;
   for( cXI = 1; cXI < eXI; cXI++ ) {
   LPosI = DataTP[cXI-1]->DIdealPosS;
    if ( LPosI == DataTP[cXI+1]->DIdealPosS &&
       LPosI != DataTP[cXI ]->DIdealPosS )
       DataTP[cXI]->DIdealPosS = LPosI;
   }

   /* --- Look at each transition & find the ideal transition +/- 1 day --- */

   eXI = NDataPtsI - (SrchWinI+1);
   CPosI = DataTP[SrchWinI]->DIdealPosS;
```

```
   for( cXI = SrchWinI; cXI < eXI; cXI++ ) {
     LPosI = CPosI;
     CPosI = DataTP[cXI]->DIdealPosS;
     if ( LPosI == POS_SHORT && CPosI == POS_LONG ) {
       /* --- Short to long transition --- *7
       LPriceF = DataTP[cXI]->DPriceF;   /* lowest price */
       sXI    = cXI;                /* index for lowest price */
       for( lXI = cXI-SrchWinI; lXI <= cXI+SrchWinI; lXI++ ) {
         if ( DataTP[lXI]->DPriceF < LPriceF ) {
           LPriceF = DataTP[lXI]->DPriceF; /* new low */
           sXI    = lXI;
         }
       }
       /* --- sXI is minimum price index: go long at this point --- */
       for( lXI = cXI-SrchWinI; lXI <= cXI+SrchWinI; lXI++ )
         DataTP[lXI]->DIdealPosS =
         lXI < sXI? POS_SHORT:POS_LONG;
       CPosI = DataTP[cXI]->DIdealPosS;
     } else if ( LPosI == POS_LONG && CPosI == POS_SHORT ) {
       /* --- Long to short transition --- */
       LPriceF = DataTP[cXI]->DPriceF;   /* highest price */
       sXI    = cXI;                /* index for highest price */
       for( lXI = cXI-SrchWinI; lXI <= cXI+SrchWinI; lXI++ ) {
         if ( DataTP[lXI]->DPriceF > LPriceF ) {
           LPriceF = DataTP[lXI]->DPriceF; /* new high */
           sXI    = lXI;
         }
       }
       /* --- sXI is maximum price index: go long at this point --- */
       for( lXI = cXI-SrchWinI; lXI <= cXI+SrchWinI; lXI++ )
         DataTP[lXI]->DIdealPosS =
         lXI < sXI? POS_LONG:POS_SHORT;
       CPosI = DataTP[cXI]->DIdealPosS;
     }
   }

   /* --- Look at a position & determine if it should be eliminated based on
    *     sub-optimal returns --- */

   eXI = NDataPtsI-1;
   CPosI = DataTP[0]->DIdealPosS;
   tsI = teI = -1;             /* no trades yet */
   cttI = POS_OUT;            /* no position yet */
   for( cXI = -1; cXI < eXI; cXI++ ) {
     LPosI = CPosI;
     CPosI = DataTP[cXI]->DIdealPosS;
     if ( LPosI != CPosI ) {
       teI = cXI;             /* position of end of trade */
       cttI = CPosI;          /* current position */
       if ( tsI > 0 ) {       /* start of this trade is live */
         LPriceF = DataTP[tsI]->DPriceF;
         CPriceF = DataTP[teI]->DPriceF - LPriceF;
         if ( fabs(CPriceF) < PenaltyD * LPriceF ) {   /* CCK/RDE */
           if ( DataTP[tsI-1]->DIdealPosS == cttI ) {
             for( lXI = tsI; lXI < teI; lXI++ )
               DataTP[lXI]->DIdealPosS = cttI;
           } else {
             for( lXI = tsI; lXI < teI; lXI++ )
               DataTP[lXI]->DIdealPosS = POS_OUT;
           }
         }
       }
       CPosI = DataTP[cXI]->DIdealPosS;
     }
     tsI = teI;          /* start of new trade */
   }
 }

#if defined(TESTING)
   if ( (oFP = fopen( "datadump.txt", "w" )) == (FILE *)0 ) {
     MsgER( "Could not open <datadump.txt> for output\n" );
     return;
   }
   for( cXI = 0; cXI <= eXI; cXI++ ) {
     drTP = DataTP[cXI];
     fprintf( oFP, "%s\t%.6g\t%d\t",
       Date2StrCP( drTP->DDateL ), drTP->DPriceF, drTP->DIdealPosS );
     for( wXI = 0; wXI < NIndsI; wXI++ )
       fprintf( oFP, "%d%s", (drTP->DIndCA[wXI>>3] & Bits[wXI&7])? 1:0,
       (wXI+1) < NIndsI? "\t":"\n" );
   }
   fclose( oFP );
```

```
#endif
  return;
}
/**************************************************************************
 *                                                                        *
 *    GenSignalV() - Compute signals based on user requests               *
 *                                                                        *
 **************************************************************************
 */

void GenSignalV()
{
  int       idx;         /* index into the "Inds" table */
  int       rx, r;       /* row index */
  int       p1, p2;      /* periods */
  IDEF      *defp;       /* def pointer */
  DROW FAR *drp;         /* row pointer */
  float     ll, hh, cl;  /* low, high, close */
  double    v1, v2;      /* multiplicative value */
  float     *fp;         /* float ptr */
  int       ibf, abf;    /* buffer */

  ibf = -1;                             /* work buffer index */
  for( rx = 0; rx < ASof(BFR); rx++ ) BFR[rx] = 0.;
  for( idx = 0; idx < NIndsI; idx++ ) {
    defp = &Inds[idx];                  /* definition */
    p1 = defp->IDFDurUC & 0xff;
    if ( defp->IDFModeC != IDFM_STOCH )
      GenMultVecV( M1F, p1, defp->IDFModeC );
    p2 = defp->IDSDurUC & 0xff;
    if ( defp->IDSModeC != IDFM_STOCH )
      GenMultVecV( M2F, p2, defp->IDSModeC );

    for( rx = 0; rx < NDataPtsI; rx++ ) {
      v1 = v2 = 0.;                     /* weighted sum */
      if ( rx >= (p1-1) && rx >= (p2-1) ) {
        switch( defp->IDFModeC ) {   /* --- First Series --- */
        case IDFM_MA:
        case IDFM_EMA:
          fp = &M1F[0];
          for( r = rx - p1; ++r <= rx; )
            v1 += *fp++ * DataTP[r]->DPriceF;
          break;

        case IDFM_STOCH:
          ll = hh = cl = DataTP[rx]->DPriceF;
          for( r = rx - p1; ++r < rx; ) {
            v1 = DataTP[r]->DPriceF;
            if ( v1 > hh ) hh = v1;
            if ( v1 < ll ) ll = v1;
          }
          v1 = (cl - ll)/(hh - ll + 1.e-15);
          break;
        }

        if ( ++ibf >= p2 ) ibf = 0;
        BFR[ibf] = v1;

        switch( defp->IDSModeC ) {   /* --- Second Series --- */
        case IDFM_MA:
        case IDFM_EMA:
          fp = &M2F[0];
          for( r = rx - p2; ++r <= rx; )
            v2 += *fp++ * DataTP[r]->DPriceF;
          break;

        case IDFM_STOCH:
          ll = hh = cl = DataTP[rx]->DPriceF;
          for( r = rx - p2; ++r < rx; ) {
            v1 = DataTP[r]->DPriceF;
            if ( v2 > hh ) hh = v2;
            if ( v2 < ll ) ll = v2;
          }
          v2 = (cl - ll)/(hh - ll + 1.e-15);
          break;

        case IDFM_SMTH:
          if ( (rx - p1) < p2 ) {
            v2 = v1;
            break;          /* not enough data yet */
```

```
                    }
                    fp = &M2F[0];
                    if ( (abf = ibf+1) >= p2 ) abf = 0;
                    for( r = p2; --r >= 0; ) {
                        v2 += *fp++ * BFR[abf];
                        if ( ++abf >= p2 ) abf = 0;
                    }
                    break;
                }
            }
            drp = DataTP[rx];                    /* current row */
            if ( v1 > v2 ) drp->DIndCA[ idx>>3 ] |= Bits[ idx & 0x7 ];
            else           drp->DIndCA[ idx>>3 ] &= ~Bits[ idx & 0x7 ];
        }
    }
    return;
}

/*************************************************************************
 *                                                                       *
 *    EvalSignalV() - Evaluate the output signal at all points           *
 *                                                                       *
 *************************************************************************
 */

void EvalSignalV A1( CHROM FAR *, chTP )
{
    FAST float  SigF;             /* output signal */
    FAST int    PosI;             /* position */
    FAST unsigned dxU;            /* data index */
    FAST unsigned fmxU, smxU;     /* fast / slow moving average index */
    FAST unsigned ndpU, nmaU;     /* data pts, moving averages */
    FAST DROW FAR *drTP;          /* data row pointer */
    FAST float FAR *chFP;         /* chromosome data pointer */
    FAST float FAR *mFP;          /* moving average pointer */
    float       cF;               /* chromosome value */
    float       fmF;              /* value of fast moving average */

    ndpU = (unsigned)NDataPtsI;
    nmaU = (unsigned)NIndsI;
    for( dxU = 0; dxU < ndpU; dxU++ ) {
        drTP = DataTP[dxU];                      /* current data row to evaluate */
        chFP = &chTP->CWtsFA[0];                 /* chromosome itself */
        SigF = 0;
        for( fmxU = 0; fmxU < nmaU; chFP++, fmxU++ ) {
            if ( (drTP->DIndCA[ fmxU >> 3 ] & Bits[ fmxU & 0x7 ]) != 0 )
                SigF += *chFP;
            else SigF -= *chFP;
        }
        SigF += *chFP;              /* bias */
        if (    SigF >  OutLimitF )  PosI = POS_LONG;
        else if ( SigF < -OutLimitF ) PosI = POS_SHORT;
        else                 PosI = POS_OUT;
        drTP->DSignalF = SigF;      /* update signal in data */
        drTP->DCurPosS = PosI;      /* update position in data */
    }
    return;
}

/*************************************************************************
 *                                                                       *
 *    EvalStepD() - evaluate the chromosome over one segment of data     *
 *                                                                       *
 *************************************************************************
    NOTE: assumes DCurPosS has been properly set up prior to calling
    this routine.
 */

double EvalStepD A4(
double,      TradePenaltyD,   /* trading penalty */
int,         EvMethI,         /* evauation method */
int,         StXI,            /* start data index */
int,         NI )             /* data points */
{
    int      EnXI;            /* end position */
    FAST int NewPosI;         /* new position */
    FAST int CurPosI;         /* current position */
    FAST int dXI;             /* data index */
    FAST DROW FAR *drTP;      /* data row pointer */
    FAST float ProfitF;       /* profit */
    FAST float PurchF;        /* purchase price */
```

```
     FAST float   wF;              /* work float */
     float        PflF, PfsF;      /* long / short penalty function */
     int          HitsI, TotI;     /* hits / total days */
     int          NProfI,NLossI;   /* profitable trades / losing trades */

     EnXI = StXI + NI - 1;         /* last data point */
     if ( EvMethI == EVALPROFIT || EvMethI == EVALTRADES ) {
       PflF   = 1. + TradePenaltyD;       /* bought higher (long) */
       PfsF   = 1. - TradePenaltyD;       /* sold lower (short) */
       ProfitF = 0.;
       CurPosI = POS_OUT;
       PurchF = 0.;
       NProfI = NLossI = 0;
       for( dXI = StXI; dXI <= EnXI; dXI++ ) {
         drTP = DataTP[dXI];               /* current data point */
         NewPosI = drTP->DCurPosS;            /* current signal */
         if ( CurPosI != NewPosI || dXI == EnXI ) {
           switch( CurPosI ) {
           case POS_LONG: wF = (drTP->DPriceF - PurchF * PflF); break;
           case POS_OUT:  wF = 0;                       break;
           case POS_SHORT: wF = (PurchF * PfsF - drTP->DPriceF);  break;
           }
           if (   wF > 0. )   NProfI++;
           else if ( wF < 0. )   NLossI++;
           ProfitF += wF;
           CurPosI = NewPosI;
           PurchF = drTP->DPriceF;
         }
       }

       if ( EvMethI == EVALTRADES ) {
         if ( NProfI >= NLossI ) {
           ProfitF = ( ((double)NProfI)/(NLossI==0? 0.1:(double)NLossI) ) *
                  (ProfitF > 0.0? ProfitF:1.0);
         } else {
           ProfitF = -(((double)NLossI)/(NProfI == 0? 0.1:(double)NProfI)) *
                  (ProfitF < 0.0? -ProfitF:1.0);
         }
       }
       return( (double)ProfitF );

     } else if ( EvMethI == EVALTARGET ) {

       HitsI = TotI = 0;
       for( dXI = StXI; dXI <= EnXI; dXI++ ) {
         drTP = DataTP[dXI];
         if ( drTP->DCurPosS == drTP->DIdealPosS ) HitsI++;
         TotI++;
       }
       return( ((double)HitsI) / ((double)TotI) );

     } else return( -1. );     /* error ! */
}

/***********************************************************************
 *                                                                     *
 *    EvalV() - Evaluate a Chromosome & set the fitness                *
 *                                                                     *
 ***********************************************************************
   If multiple periods are used, evaluate each one separately & average
   the results together. Otherwise, just compute the fitness once.
 */

void EvalV A3(
FAST CHROM FAR *, chTP,            /* chromosome to evaluate */
POP FAR *,       popTP,           /* population description */
int,             LogFlagI )       /* =1,log output results */
{
  int       MethI;               /* evaluation method */
  int       SMethI;              /* sub-method: avg, min, actual */
  int       sXI, NI;             /* start index, number of days */
  int       eXI;                 /* evaluation period */
  double    AvgD;                /* average of scores */
  double    MinD;                /* smallest score */
  double    MinPrvD;             /* prior minimum */
  double    LastD;               /* last test */

  EvalSignalV( chTP );                   /* evaluate the signal */
  MethI = popTP->EvalMethodS;            /* basic method */
  SMethI = popTP->EvalSubMethS;          /* sub-method */
  switch( SMethI ) {
```

```
    default:
    case EVALACTUAL:                    /* actual score */
      chTP->CScoreF = EvalStepD( TradePenaltyF, MethI, ISDataXI, ISDataNI );
      break;

    case EVALAVG:                       /* average */
    case EVALMIN:                       /* minimum */
    case EVALMIN2:                      /* average of two lowest scores */
    case EVALMINAVG:                    /* min + average */
    case EVALMINLAST:                   /* max( min, last ) */
      sXI = ISDataXI;
      AvgD = 0.;
      MinD = MinPrvD = 0.;
      NI  = ((double)ISDataNI) / (popTP->EvalPeriodsS * 0.5 + 0.5);
      for( eXI = 0; eXI < popTP->EvalPeriodsS; eXI++ ) {
        LastD = EvalStepD( TradePenaltyF, MethI, sXI, NI );
        chTP->CSubScoreF[eXI] = LastD;
        AvgD += LastD;

        if (    eXI == 0 ) {
          MinD = MinPrvD = LastD;
        } else if ( LastD < MinD ) {
          MinPrvD = MinD; MinD = LastD;
        } else if ( LastD < MinPrvD ) {
          MinPrvD = LastD;
        }

        sXI += NI/2;
      }
      AvgD /= popTP->EvalPeriodsS;
      switch( SMethI ) {
      case EVALAVG:      chTP->CScoreF = AvgD;                          break;
      case EVALMIN:      chTP->CScoreF = MinD;                          break;
      case EVALMIN2:     chTP->CScoreF = 0.5 * (MinD + MinPrvD);        break;
      case EVALMINAVG:   chTP->CScoreF = MinD>0.? (MinD+AvgD)*.5:MinD;  break;
      case EVALMINLAST:  chTP->CScoreF = MinD>0.? (MinD+LastD)*.5:MinD; break;
      }
    }

  chTP->CTrainF = EvalStepD( 0., EVALPROFIT, ISDataXI, ISDataNI );
  chTP->CTestF = EvalStepD( 0., EVALPROFIT, XPDataXI, XPDataNI );

  if ( LogFlagI ) {
    sprintf( GBuf, "EvalD\t%ld\t%.6g\t%.6g\n", chTP->CSerialL, chTP->CScoreF, chTP-
>CTestF );
    MsgER( GBuf );
  }

  return;
}
/***********************************************************************
 *                                                                     *
 *    EvalStatsV() - Compute Statistics for summary data               *
 *                                                                     *
 ***********************************************************************
 */

void EvalStatsV A2(
FAST CHROM FAR *,    chTP,          /* chromosome to evaluate */
FILE *,              oFP )          /* output file pointer */
{
  int            sXI, eXI;   /* start / end index */

  EvalSignalV( chTP );           /* evaluate the signal */
  fprintf( oFP, "\t%s", Date2StrCP( DataTP[EVStartI]->DDateL ) );
  for( sXI = EVStartI; (sXI + EVSizeI) <= NDataPtsI; sXI += EVIncrI ) {
    fprintf( oFP, "\t%.6g",
      EvalStepD( 0., EVALPROFIT, sXI, EVSizeI ) );
  }

  return;
}

/***********************************************************************
 *                                                                     *
 *    NormChromV() - Normalized the Chromosome                         *
 *                                                                     *
 ***********************************************************************
 This is used during initialization to multiplicatively normalize
 the elements of a chromosome to 1.
 */
```

```
void NormChromV A3(          /* normalize a chromosome */
CHROM FAR *,    chTP,        /* chromosome to normalize */
int,            NGenesI,     /* number of genes to worry about */
int,            MethodI )    /* method to use to normalize */
{
  FAST float FAR *fp1;       /* weights in the chromosome */
  FAST int   txI;            /* work index */
  FAST double w;             /* work sum / multiplier */

  fp1 = &chTP->CWtsFA[-1];
  txI = NGenesI;
  switch( MethodI ) {
  case NORMRATIO:            /* ratio normalization */
    for( w = 1.e-8, fp1++; --txI >= 0; fp1++ )
      w += fabs(*fp1);
    goto MultNormCom;

  case NORMMULT:             /* multiplicative normalization */
    for( w = 1.e-8, fp1++; --txI >= 0; fp1++ ) {
      if ( fabs(*fp1) > w ) w = fabs(*fp1);
    }
  MultNormCom:
    if ( fabs( 1. - w ) > 1.e-6 ) {
      fp1 = &chTP->CWtsFA[-1];  /* re-normalize */
      txI = NGenesI;
      w   = 1. / w;
      while( --txI >= 0 )
        *++fp1 *= w;
    }
    break;

  case NORMASYM:            /* assymetric limiting */
    while( --txI >= 0 ) {
      w = *++fp1;
      if (    w > 1. ) *fp1 = 1.;
      else if ( w < 0. ) *fp1 = 0.;
    }
    break;

  case NORMSYMM:            /* symmetric limiting */
    while( --txI >= 0 ) {
      w = *++fp1;
      if (    w > 1. ) *fp1 = 1.;
      else if ( w < -1. ) *fp1 = -1.;
    }
    break;
  }

  return;
}

/************************************************************************
 *                                                                      *
 *    DHCOptI() - Optimize a vector with Dynamic Hill Climbing (DHC)     *
 *                                                                      *
 ************************************************************************
  Direction Vector Number:

     0..popTP->NGenesS-1 represents a single component to change
     -1 is the sum of the last two vectors

  Initially, all of the vectors are set to small positive random numbers.

  waCHT - work chromsome (best is stored back over chTP)
  index                      -2 = conjugate negative vector
  index                      -1 = conjugate positive vector
  index 0...NGenesS-1        positive unit vector
  index NGenesS..2*NGenesS-1 negative unit vector
*/

static CHROM waCHT = {0};   /* work a chromosome (LocalOptI) */
static CHROM wbCHT = {0};   /* work b chromosome (OptStepI, DHC) */

static float DHCdvf[MAXPOP+MAXPOP] = {0};   /* unit direction vectors */
static float DHCcpvf[MAXPOP]       = {0};   /* conjugate pos vector */
static float DHCcnvf[MAXPOP]       = {0};   /* conjugate neg vector */

int DHCOptI A2(      /* Dynamic Hill Climbing */
CHROM FAR *,  chTP,     /* chromosome to optimize */
POP FAR *,    popTP )   /* population it is part of */
{
```

```
FAST float  *fp1, *fp2;          /* work pointer */
int         NGenesI;             /* number of genes */
int         xm1, xm2;            /* index of genes at t-1, t-2 */
float       dm1, dm2;            /* delta at t-1, t-2 */
float       w;                   /* work float */
int         xlg, xlgp;           /* index of largest magnitude */
float       mag, mult;           /* magnitude of vector */
float       magcp, magcn;        /* size of pos/neg conjugate vector */
int         cgct;                /* conjugate count */
int         txI;                 /* test index */
int         exI;                 /* end index */
int         patI, iterI;         /* patence and iterations */
int         MaxPatI;             /* max patience */
int         betterCt;            /* better count */
float       best, best0;         /* best score */
float       EpsF;                /* epsilon */

NGenesI = popTP->NGenesS;            /* number of genes to process */
exI = NGenesI+NGenesI;               /* end index */

MaxPatI = 20 * NGenesI;              /* patience */
iterI   = 50 * NGenesI;              /* max iterations */
EpsF    = 0.002;                     /* nominal epsilon */
switch( popTP->NormMethS ) {
case NORMMULT: EpsF = EpsF / sqrt((double)NGenesI); break;
case NORMRATIO: EpsF = EpsF / ((double)NGenesI);    break;
case NORMSYMM: EpsF = EpsF * 0.5;            break;
case NORMASYM:                       break;
}
mag = 1.;                            /* initialization range */
patI = MaxPatI;                      /* current patience */

fp1 = &DHCdvf[0]-1;                  /* direction vector */
for( txI = NGenesI; --txI >= 0; ) *++fp1 = mag;
mag = 0.-mag;
for( txI = NGenesI; --txI >= 0; ) *++fp1 = mag;

fp1 = &DHCcpvf[-1];                  /* conjugate vectors */
fp2 = &DHCcnvf[-1];
for( txI = NGenesI; --txI >= 0; ) {
  *++fp1 = 0.; *++fp2 = 0.;
}
magcp = magcn = 0.;                  /* zero length conjugate */
xm1   = xm2 = -3;                    /* prior vectors */
dm1   = dm2 = 0.;                    /* prior magnitudes */
cgct  = 0;                           /* zero non-conj prior vectors */

/* --- Set a Base-line for Performance --- */

best = best0 = chTP->CScoreF;        /* score on train set */
betterCt = 0;                        /* better count */
xlgp = -3;                           /* no prior */

for(;;) {

  /* --- Pick the largest, start with gradient vector --- */

  if ( magcn > magcp ) { xlg = -2; mag = magcn; }
  else               { xlg = -1; mag = magcp; }
  fp1 = &DHCdvf[0];                  /* unit direction vector */
  for( txI = 0; txI < exI; txI++, fp1++ ) {
    if ( (w = fabs(*fp1)) > mag ) {
      mag = w;                       /* size of largest */
      xlg = txI;                     /* index of largest */
    }
  }

  /* --- Construct the Work Vector --- */

  memcpy( (void *)&wbCHT, (void *)chTP, popTP->ChromSizeU );
  if ( xlg < 0 ) {      /* largest is conjugate vector */
    /* --- Merge in the Conjugate vector --- */
    fp1 = xlg< -1? (&DHCcnvf[0]-1):(&DHCcpvf[0]-1);
    fp2 = &wbCHT.CWtsFA[0] -1;
    for( txI = NGenesI; --txI >= 0; )
      *++fp2 += *++fp1;
  } else {            /* largest is work vector */
    /* --- Merge in individual vector --- */
    wbCHT.CWtsFA[xlg<NGenesI? (xlg):(xlg-NGenesI) ] +=
      DHCdvf[xlg];
  }
```

```
      /* --- Evalute it --- */

      NormChromV( &wbCHT, NGenesI, popTP->NormMethS );     /* normalize it */
      EvalV( &wbCHT, popTP, 0 );                    /* evaluate it */
      if ( wbCHT.CScoreF > best ) {

        /* --- Found Something Better !! --- */

        memcpy( (void *)chTP, (void *)&wbCHT, popTP->ChromSizeU );
        best = chTP->CScoreF;
        betterCt++;
        patI = MaxPatI;                    /* current patience */

        /* --- Determine how to update conjugate vector --- */

        if ( xlg < 0 ) {
          cgct = 0;              /* conjugate count */
        } else {
          dm2 = dm1; dm1 = DHCdvf[xlg];
          xm2 = xm1; xm1 = xlg>NGenesI? (xlg-NGenesI):xlg;
          cgct++;
          if ( cgct >= 2 ) {
            /* --- Re-generate the conjugate vectors --- */
            fp1 = &DHCcnvf[0]-1;
            fp2 = &DHCcpvf[0]-1;
            for( txI = NGenesI; --txI >= 0; ) {
              *++fp1 = 0.; *++fp2 = 0.;
            }
            DHCcpvf[xm1] = dm1; DHCcnvf[xm1] = -dm1;
            DHCcpvf[xm2] = dm2; DHCcnvf[xm2] = -dm2;
            magcn = magcn = sqrt( dm1*dm1 + dm2*dm2 );
          }
        }

        /* --- If same direction, double the vector --- */

        if ( xlg == xlgp ) {
          mult = 2.;   /* same twice, double vector size */
          goto MultVec;
        }

      } else {
        /* --- Evaluates worse, reduce magnitude of genes --- */
        mult = 0.5;

        /* --- Adjust magnitude of the vector --- */
      MultVec:
        if ( xlg < 0 ) {
          if ( xlg < -1 ) {
            fp1 = &DHCcnvf[0]-1;     /* negative direction vector */
            magcn *= mult;
          } else {
            fp1 = &DHCcpvf[0]-1;     /* positive direction vector */
            magcp *= mult;
          }
          for( txI = NGenesI; --txI >= 0; )
            *++fp1 *= mult;          /* normalize the conjugate */
        } else {
          DHCdvf[xlg] *= mult;  /* adjust unit vector in half */
        }
      }
      xlgp = xlg;

      if ( mag < EpsF || --iterI < 0 || --patI < 0 )
        break;               /* terminal conditions */
    }
    sprintf( GBuf, "Optimized: mag=%.4f/%.4f Iter=%d Pat=%d best=%.7g/%.7g\n",
      mag, EpsF, iterI, patI, best, best0 );
    MsgER( GBuf );

    return( betterCt );
}

/*****************************************************************************
 *                                                                          *
 *    LocalOptI() - Perform "local" optimization on the chrom.              *
 *                                                                          *
 *****************************************************************************
 NOTE: This process may be VERY time-consuming, and requires many
 evaluations of the chromosome for each step.
 */
```

```
int LocalOptI A4(      /* perform local optimization & Evaluate Chrom */
CHROM FAR *,    chTP,         /* chromosome to evaluate */
POP FAR *,      popTP,        /* population descriptor */
int,            OptMethI,     /* optimization method */
int,            LogFlagI )    /* =0, no logging */
{
   CHROM FAR    *rfTP;        /* reference to work from */
   int          gxI;          /* gene index */
   int          ImprvI;       /* improvement count */
   int          i;            /* work value */
   double       DeltaD;       /* change in weight */
   double       ROD;          /* ref 0 score */

   NormChromV( chTP, popTP->NGenesS, popTP->NormMethS );
   EvalV( chTP, popTP, LogFlagI );         /* initial evaluation */
   if ( OptMethI != OPTFORCE ) {
      if ( OptMethI == OPTNONE || popTP->SzNewPopS < 2 )
         return( 0 );          /* done */

      if ( OptMethI == OPTGLOBAL &&
         chTP->CScoreF <= popTP->NewPopTPP[0]->CScoreF )
         return( 0 );          /* only optimize "best" */
   }

   /* --- Copy the Chromosome over & try "tweaking" it --- */

   rfTP = &waCHT;                        /* golden result */
   memcpy( (void *)rfTP, (void *)chTP, popTP->ChromSizeU );
   ROD = rfTP->CScoreF;                  /* starting score */
   ImprvI = DHCOptI( rfTP, popTP );   /* opt by DHC */

   if ( rfTP->CScoreF > ROD || ImprvI > 0 ) {
      memcpy( (void *)chTP, (void *)rfTP, popTP->ChromSizeU );
      sprintf( GBuf, "Optimized score to %.7g from %.7g\n", rfTP->CScoreF, ROD );
   } else sprintf( GBuf, "Could not improve score of %.7g\n", ROD );
   MsgER( GBuf );

   return( 1 );     /* optimized */
}

/************************************************************************
*                                                                      *
*    BreedTP() - Create an offspring & return a pointer                 *
*                                                                      *
*************************************************************************
   There are five possible methods of procreation:
      1) 1-point crossover
      2) 2-point crossover
      3) uniform crossover
      4) mutation by creep
      5) mutation by randomization
   One of these methods is selected, and parents are then chosen.
   All results are re-normalized so that the values sum to 1.
*/

static CHROM w1CHT = {0};          /* work 1 chromosome */
static CHROM w2CHT = {0};          /* work 2 chromosome */

CHROM FAR *BreedTP A2(
FAST POP FAR *, popTP,                 /* population to work from */
int,            LogFlagI )            /* flag to log results */
{
   FAST int     ProXI;               /* index for method of procreation */
   FAST double  CircumR;             /* circumference */
   FAST double  SpinR;               /* result of spinning the wheel */
   FAST double  wD;                  /* work double */
   FAST double  S1D,S2D, U1D,U2D;    /* swapped & unswapped sum */
   FAST double  MinD, MaxD;          /* min/max for randomization & creep */
   FAST int     wxI;                 /* work index */
   FAST int     p1XI, p2XI;          /* indices of the parents */
   FAST int     x1I, x2I;            /* crossover points */
   FAST int     sxI, exI;            /* start, end of "unique" portion of genes */
   FAST int     DoAvgI;              /* =1, do average crossover */
   FAST int     NGenesI;             /* number of genes in each chrom */
   FAST int     UGenesI;             /* unique genes */
   FAST CHROM FAR *RtnCHTP;          /* return pointer */
   static char  SrcC[MAXIND] = {0};  /* source of the result */

   NGenesI = popTP->NGenesS;          /* number of genes actually used */

   for( CircumR = 0., wxI = 0; wxI < ASof(popTP->ProbChildD); wxI++ )
```

```
   CircumR += popTP->ProbChildD[wxI];    /* sum of "probabilities" */
SpinR = Rand01D() * CircumR;             /* spin the wheel */
for( CircumR = 0., ProXI = 0; ProXI < ASof(popTP->ProbChildD)-1; ProXI++ ) {
   CircumR += popTP->ProbChildD[ProXI];  /* add in current score */
   if ( CircumR >= SpinR ) break;        /* found it */
}

/* --- Special test to see if the population is "big" enough --- */

if ( popTP->SzCurPopS < 3 )
   ProXI = CHILDRAND;                     /* too few elements */

/* --- Select the parent(s) --- */

p1XI = SelectI( popTP, -1 );             /* first parent */
if ( ProXI == CHILD1PT || ProXI == CHILD2PT || ProXI == CHILDUNIF )
   p2XI = SelectI( popTP, p1XI );        /* second parent */
else p2XI = p1XI;                        /* same if mutating */
memcpy( (void *)&w1CHT, (void *)popTP->CurPopTPP[p1XI], popTP->ChromSizeU );
memcpy( (void *)&w2CHT, (void *)popTP->CurPopTPP[p2XI], popTP->ChromSizeU );

/* --- Find "unique" portion of the genes --- */

if ( p1XI != p2XI ) {

   for( sxI = 0; sxI < NGenesI; sxI++ )
      if ( w1CHT.CWtsFA[sxI] != w2CHT.CWtsFA[sxI] ) break;
   if ( sxI >= NGenesI ) goto Same;

   for( exI = NGenesI-1; exI > sxI; exI-- )
      if ( w1CHT.CWtsFA[exI] != w2CHT.CWtsFA[exI] ) break;

   if ( (exI - sxI) < 2 ) {
Same:  /* differ by 2 or fewer positoins: shake things up */
      ProXI = CHILDRAND;
      p2XI = p1XI;
   }
}

if ( p1XI == p2XI ) {    /* NOTE: May now be same from above */
   sxI = 0; exI = NGenesI-1;
}
UGenesI = exI - sxI + 1;        /* unique genes */

/* --- Create offspring --- */

switch( popTP->NormMethS ) {
default:
case NORMRATIO:
case NORMASYM:    MinD = 0.; MaxD = 1.; break;
case NORMMULT:
case NORMSYMM:    MinD = -1.; MaxD = 1.; break;
}

OffMethL[ ProXI ]++;
memset( (void *)&SrcC[0], 0, sizeof(SrcC) );     /* clear working memory */
switch( ProXI ) {
case CHILD1PT:
   x1I = (RandL() % (UGenesI-1))+sxI+1;  /* crossover point */
   for( ; x1I <= exI; x1I++ ) SrcC[x1I] = 1;
   break;

case CHILD2PT:
   x1I = (RandL() % UGenesI) + sxI;
   do {
      x2I = (RandL() % UGenesI) + sxI;
   } while( x2I == x1I );
   if ( x2I < x1I ) { wxI = x2I; x2I = x1I; x1I = wxI; }
   for( ; x1I <= x2I; x1I++ ) SrcC[x1I] = 1;
   break;

case CHILDUNIF:
   for( ; sxI <= exI; sxI++ )
      if ( Rand01D() > 0.5 ) SrcC[sxI] = 1;
   break;

case CHILDCREEP:
   for( ; sxI <= exI; sxI++ )
      if ( Rand01D() < popTP->MutOneProbD ) {
         wD = w1CHT.CWtsFA[sxI] + (Rand01D() * 2. - 1.) * popTP->MutOneLimitD;
         while ( wD < MinD ) wD += 1.;
```

```
            while ( wD > MaxD ) wD -= 1.;
            w1CHT.CWtsFA[sxI] = wD;
            SrcC[sxI] = 1;
          }
      break;

    case CHILDRAND:
      for( ; sxI <= exI; sxI++ )
        if ( Rand01D() < popTP->MutOneProbD ) {
          w1CHT.CWtsFA[sxI] = RandRD( MinD, MaxD );
          SrcC[sxI] = 1;
        }
      break;
  }

  /* --- Determine if 'average' or standard crossover --- */

  DoAvgI = Rand01D() > popTP->ProbXAVGD? 0:1;

  /* --- Find the length of swapped & unswapped portions --- */

  S1D = S2D = U1D = U2D = 0.;
  for( wxI = 0; wxI < NGenesI; wxI++ ) {
    if ( SrcC[wxI] == 0 ) {                /* un-swapped */
      U1D += fabs(w1CHT.CWtsFA[wxI]);
      U2D += fabs(w2CHT.CWtsFA[wxI]);
    } else {                               /* swap & compute */
      if ( p1XI != p2XI ) {
        if ( DoAvgI ) {
          w1CHT.CWtsFA[wxI] = w2CHT.CWtsFA[wxI] =
            (0.5 * w1CHT.CWtsFA[wxI] + w2CHT.CWtsFA[wxI]);
        } else {
          wD = w1CHT.CWtsFA[wxI];
          w1CHT.CWtsFA[wxI] = w2CHT.CWtsFA[wxI];
          w2CHT.CWtsFA[wxI] = wD;
        }
      }
      S1D += fabs(w1CHT.CWtsFA[wxI]);
      S2D += fabs(w2CHT.CWtsFA[wxI]);
    }
  }

  /* --- Compute factors to "normalize" the results --- */
  /*  Handle pathological cases, then in priority, re-scale the */
  /*  unswapped, swapped, and both sets of elements */

  switch( popTP->NormMethS ) {
  case NORMRATIO:        /* ratio-based */
    if     ( S1D < .0001 ) { S1D = 0.; U1D = 1./(U1D>1.e-4? U1D:1.); }
    else if ( U1D < .0001 ) { U1D = 0.; S1D = 1./(S1D>1.e-4? S1D:1.); }
    else if ( S1D < .99  ) { S1D = (1. - S1D)/U1D; S1D = 1.; }
    else if ( U1D < .99  ) { S1D = (1. - U1D)/S1D; U1D = 1.; }
    else           { S1D = U1D = 1./(S1D + U1D); }

    if     ( S2D < .0001 ) { S2D = 0.; U2D = 1./(U2D>1.e-4? U2D:1.); }
    else if ( U2D < .0001 ) { U2D = 0.; S2D = 1./(S2D>1.e-4? S2D:1.); }
    else if ( S2D < .99  ) { U2D = (1. - S2D)/U2D; S2D = 1.; }
    else if ( U2D < .99  ) { S2D = (1. - U2D)/S2D; U2D = 1.; }
    else           { S2D = U2D = 1./(S2D + U2D); }

    for( wxI = 0; wxI < NGenesI; wxI++ ) {
      if ( SrcC[wxI] == 0 ) {              /* un-swapped */
        w1CHT.CWtsFA[wxI] *= U1D;
        w2CHT.CWtsFA[wxI] *= U2D;
      } else {                             /* swapped */
        w1CHT.CWtsFA[wxI] *= S1D;
        w1CHT.CWtsFA[wxI] *= S2D;
      }
    }
    break;

  case NORMMULT:        /* multiplicative norm */
    if ( S1D < .0001 && U1D < .0001 ) S1D = 1.;
    else              S1D = 1./(S1D + U1D);
    if ( S2D < .0001 && U2D < .0001 ) S2D = 1.;
    else              S2D = 1./(S2D + U2D);
    for( wxI = 0; wxI < NGenesI; wxI++ ) {
      w1CHT.CWtsFA[wxI] *= S1D;
      w2CHT.CWtsFA[wxI] *= S2D;
    }
```

```
    break;

  default:
  case NORMSYMM:
  case NORMASYM:
    break;
  }

  /* --- Evaluate the off-spring & return the "best" --- */

  RtnCHTP = &w1CHT;
  LocalOptI( &w1CHT, popTP, popTP->OptMethodS, LogFlagI );
  if ( p1XI != p2XI && Rand01D() > 0.5 ) {  /* sometimes pick worst */
    LocalOptI( &w2CHT, popTP, popTP->OptMethodS, LogFlagI );
    if ( w2CHT.CScoreF > w1CHT.CScoreF )
      RtnCHTP = &w2CHT;
  }

  popTP->PopSerialL++;                /* next generation */
  RtnCHTP->CSerialL = popTP->PopSerialL;  /* generation */
  RtnCHTP->CPopIDS  = popTP->PopIDS;      /* population ID */
  RtnCHTP->CCurPopIDS = popTP->PopIDS;
  RtnCHTP->COriginS = ProXI;          /* origin */

  return( RtnCHTP );
}

/************************************************************************
 *                                                                      *
 *   UpdatePopI() - Insert a chromosome into the population              *
 *                                                                      *
 ************************************************************************
  The new item to be inserted into the population is passed along with
  the pointer to the population itself. If there is room, the new
  item is added. If not, the "worst" element in the population is
  dropped to make room.
 */

int UpdatePopI A2(
FAST POP FAR *, popTP,              /* population */
FAST CHROM FAR *, chTP )            /* chromosome to insert */
{
  FAST int     ixI;                 /* insert index */
  FAST int     sxI, exI;            /* start / end indicies */
  FAST float   wF;                  /* work value */
  FAST float   FitnessF;            /* fitness of new element */
  FAST long    SerialL;             /* current serial number */
  FAST CHROM FAR * FAR *wcTPP;      /* work pointer */
  FAST CHROM FAR *nTP;              /* pointer to where new item goes */
  FAST float FAR *nFP;              /* new pointer */
  FAST float FAR *rFP;              /* reference pointer */

  if ( popTP->SzNewPopS < 1 ) {
    memcpy( (void *)popTP->NewPopTPP[0], (void *)chTP, popTP->ChromSizeU );
    popTP->SzNewPopS = 1;           /* one element in population */
    popTP->NewAddsS = 1;            /* new item added to population */
    return( 0 );                    /* inserted w/o dropping */
  }

  /* --- Binary Search for Insertion point --- */

  FitnessF = chTP->CScoreF;         /* new fitness */
  SerialL = chTP->CSerialL;         /* new serial number */
  sxI = 0; exI = popTP->SzNewPopS-1; /* start / end */
  for(; sxI <= exI;) {              /* binary search for position */
    ixI = (sxI + exI) >> 1;         /* mid-point */
    nTP = popTP->NewPopTPP[ixI];    /* current test item */
    wF = nTP->CScoreF;              /* current fitness */
    if (   FitnessF < wF ) sxI = ixI+1; /* goes below */
    else if ( FitnessF > wF ) exI = ixI-1; /* goes above */
    else {                          /* same, use serial */
      if (   SerialL > nTP->CSerialL ) sxI = ixI+1; /* below */
      else if ( SerialL < nTP->CSerialL ) exI = ixI-1; /* above */
      else              break;  /* same */
    }
  }

  /* --- Check for Duplicate & skip insertion --- */

  if ( sxI < popTP->SzNewPopS ) {       /* internal insertion */
    nTP = popTP->NewPopTPP[sxI];        /* insertion point */
```

```
      if ( FitnessF == nTP->CScoreF && chTP->CTestF == nTP->CTestF ) {
        nFP = &chTP->CWtsFA[0];              /* compare genes */
        rFP = &nTP->CWtsFA[0];
        for( ixI = popTP->NGenesS; --ixI >= 0; )
          if ( fabs(*nFP++ - *rFP++) > 1.e-4 )
            goto DoInsert;                   /* not the same, insert */
        return( -1 );                        /* duplicate */
      }
  DoInsert:
      ;
  }

  /* --- Push the list down & insert the new element --- */

  if ( popTP->SzNewPopS < popTP->SzPopMaxS )
    popTP->SzNewPopS++;                      /* increase population size */
  exI = popTP->SzNewPopS - 2;                /* ptr to last "usable" item */

  wcTPP = &popTP->NewPopTPP[exI];            /* end of list */
  nTP   = wcTPP[1];                          /* save pointer */
  memcpy( (void *)nTP, (void *)chTP, popTP->ChromSizeU );
  if ( sxI <= exI ) {
    /* --- Insert into middle of the list --- */
    for( ixI = exI; ixI >= sxI; ixI--, wcTPP-- )
      wcTPP[1] = wcTPP[0];                   /* copy reverse order */
    wcTPP[1] = nTP;                          /* insert new item */
  }
  nTP->CCurPopIDS = popTP->PopIDS;  /* set current pop id */

  popTP->NewAddsS++;                         /* new item added to population */
  return( sxI );                             /* return insertion point */
}

/****************************************************************************
 *                                                                        *
 *    SwapPopsV() - Swap Populations                                      *
 *                                                                        *
 ****************************************************************************
 */

void SwapPopsV A1(             /* swap new & current populations */
FAST POP FAR *, popTP )        /* popuation to swap pools */
{
  FAST CHROM FAR * FAR *cTPP;  /* temp for swapping */
  FAST int    itemsI;          /* items to copy to new population */
  FAST int    wxI;             /* work index */

  /* --- Swap the Population pointers themselves --- */

  cTPP        = popTP->NewPopTPP;
  popTP->NewPopTPP = popTP->CurPopTPP;
  popTP->CurPopTPP = cTPP;
  popTP->SzCurPopS = popTP->SzNewPopS;
  popTP->SzNewPopS = 0;
  popTP->NewAddsS = 0;

  /* --- Copy over a portion of the population as a "seed" --- */

  if ( (itemsI = (int)(popTP->SeedSizeD * popTP->SzCurPopS)) > 0 ) {
    if ( itemsI > popTP->SzCurPopS ) itemsI = popTP->SzCurPopS;
    for( wxI = 0; wxI < itemsI; wxI++ )
      memcpy( (void *)popTP->NewPopTPP[wxI],
          (void *)popTP->CurPopTPP[wxI], popTP->ChromSizeU );
    popTP->SzNewPopS = itemsI;
  }

  return;
}

/****************************************************************************
 *                                                                        *
 *    RandMigrateV() - Cause a Random migration among populations         *
 *                                                                        *
 ****************************************************************************
 1) Called ONLY when it is time for two populations to mix
 2) Populations to mix are randomly picked.
 3) Material from each is randomly picked and sent to the other
 */

void RandMigrateV A2(
FAST POP FAR *,   IslesTP,            /* pointer to list of islands */
```

```
FAST int,          NIslesI )        /* number of islands */
{
  int              Is1, Is2;        /* island numbers */
  int              mx1, mx2;        /* max of pop 1 & 2 */
  int              mg1, mg2;        /* number to migrate from each */
  int              s;               /* selected gene */
  FAST int         cXI, rXI;        /* work indicies */
  FAST POP FAR     *p1, FAR *p2;    /* populations */
  FAST int         nCandI;          /* total candidates */
  FAST int         pCandI;          /* candidates from each population */
  FAST int         SzMaxPopI;       /* larges pop size */
  CHROM FAR *CandsTP[2*MAXPOP+1];   /* candidate list */

  switch( NIslesI ) {
  case 0:
  case 1:   return;                 /* nothing to do */
  case 2:   Is1 = 0; Is2 = 1; break;  /* only one pair */
  default:
    Is1 = RandL() % NIslesI;        /* pick a population */
    do {
      Is2 = RandL() % NIslesI;            /* and a second random one */
    } while( Is1 == Is2 );
  }
  Is1++; Is2++;
  sprintf( GBuf, "Random Migration: Is1=%d Is2=%d\n", Is1, Is2 );
  MsgER( GBuf );
  p1 = &IslesTP[Is1];       /* population pointers */
  p2 = &IslesTP[Is2];

  mx1 = p1->SzNewPopS;      /* max size of this population */
  mg1 = mx1 * MigSizeD;     /* candidates to use */
  mg1 = (mg1 < 1? 1:(mg1 > mx1? mx1:mg1));

  mx2 = p2->SzNewPopS;      /* max size of this population */
  mg2 = mx2 * MigSizeD;     /* candidates to use */
  mg2 = (mg2 < 1? 1:(mg2 > mx2? mx2:mg2));
  nCandI = 0;
  for( cXI = 0; cXI < mg1; cXI++ ) {
    CandsTP[nCandI++] = p1->NewPopTPP[(s=SelectI( p1, -1 ))];
  }
  for( cXI = 0; cXI < mg2; cXI++ ) {
    CandsTP[nCandI++] = p2->NewPopTPP[(s=SelectI( p2, -1 ))];
  }

  nCandI = 0;
  for( cXI = 0; cXI < mg1; cXI++ )
    UpdatePopI( p2, CandsTP[nCandI++] );
  for( cXI = 0; cXI < mg2; cXI++ )
    UpdatePopI( p1, CandsTP[nCandI++] );

  return;
}

/**************************************************************************
 *                                                                       *
 *    MigrateV() - Cause a migration among populations                   *
 *                                                                       *
 **************************************************************************
  1) Each population contributes some number of elements to a "migration".
  2) The candidates are collected in a list which is sorted by score.
  3) The final list is integrated into each new population.
 */

void MigrateV A2(
FAST POP FAR *, IslesTP,         /* pointer to list of islands */
FAST int,      NIslesI )         /* number of islands */
{
  FAST int        PopXI;         /* population index */
  FAST int        cXI;           /* chromosome index */
  FAST int        sxI, exI, ixI; /* indicies for insertion */
  FAST float      FitnessF;      /* fitness of candidate */
  FAST float      wF;            /* work fitness */
  FAST int        nCandI;        /* total candidates */
  FAST int        pCandI;        /* candidates from each population */
  FAST int        SzMaxPopI;     /* larges pop size */
  FAST CHROM FAR  *chTP;         /* work chromosome pointer */
  FAST POP FAR    *popTP;        /* pointer to current population */
  CHROM FAR  *CandsTP[MAXPOP+1]; /* candidate list */

  if ( NIslesI <= 1 )
    return;                      /* nothing to do ! */
```

```
    nCandI = 0;                        /* list is empty */
    memset( (void *)&CandsTP[0], 0, sizeof(CandsTP) );
    for( PopXI = 1; PopXI <= NIslesI; PopXI++ ) {
      popTP    = &IslesTP[PopXI];       /* current population */
      SzMaxPopI = popTP->SzNewPopS;     /* max size of this population */
      pCandI   = SzMaxPopI * MigSizeD;  /* candidates to use */
      pCandI   = (pCandI < 1? 1:(pCandI > SzMaxPopI? SzMaxPopI:pCandI));

      for( cXI = 0; cXI < pCandI; cXI++ ) {
        chTP = popTP->NewPopTPP[cXI];    /* current candidate */
        if ( nCandI < 1 ) {
          CandsTP[nCandI++] = chTP;      /* first item in list */
          continue;
        }

        FitnessF = chTP->CScoreF;        /* score of item to insert */
        if ( FitnessF < CandsTP[nCandI-1]->CScoreF ) {
          /* --- Goes at the end of the list --- */
          if ( nCandI < ASof(CandsTP) )
            CandsTP[nCandI++] = chTP;
          continue;
        }

        sxI = 0; exI = nCandI-1;         /* start / end */
        for(; sxI <= exI;) {             /* binary search for position */
          ixI = (sxI + exI) >> 1;            /* mid-point */
          wF = CandsTP[ixI]->CScoreF;        /* current fitness */
          if ( FitnessF < wF ) sxI = ixI+1;  /* goes below */
          else               exI = ixI-1;    /* goes above */
        }

        if ( nCandI < ASof(CandsTP) ) nCandI++;    /* still room at end */
        for( exI = nCandI-2; exI >= sxI; exI-- )  /* make room */
          CandsTP[exI+1] = CandsTP[exI];
        CandsTP[exI+1] = chTP;           /* insert the new item */
      }
    }

    /* --- Merge the appropirate number of "top" candidates into the populations --- */

    MsgER( "Migrating...\n" );
    for( PopXI   = 1; PopXI <= NIslesI; PopXI++ ) {
      popTP    = &IslesTP[PopXI];          /* current population */
      SzMaxPopI = popTP->SzCurPopS;        /* max size of this population */
      pCandI   = SzMaxPopI * MigSizeD;    /* candidates to use */
      if ( pCandI > SzMaxPopI ) pCandI = SzMaxPopI;
      if ( pCandI > nCandI   ) pCandI = nCandI;

      for( cXI = 0; cXI < pCandI; cXI++ ) {
        chTP = CandsTP[cXI];             /* current candidate */
        if ( chTP->CCurPopIDS == PopXI )
          continue;              /* already there */
        UpdatePopI( popTP, chTP );       /* merge it into new population */
      }
    }

    return;
  }

/**************************************************************************
 *                                                                       *
 *    FreeAllPopsI() - Free all memory associated with populations       *
 *                                                                       *
 **************************************************************************
 */

int FreeAllPopsI A0
{
  FAST int    PopXI;        /* population index */
  FAST POP FAR *popTP;      /* population pointer */
  FAST int    chXI;         /* chromosome index */

  for( PopXI = 1; PopXI < ASof(IsleT); PopXI++ ) {
    popTP = &IsleT[PopXI];        /* current population */
    for( chXI = 0; chXI < ASof(popTP->PopTP); chXI++ )
      if ( popTP->PopTP[chXI] != (CHROM *)0 )
        MemFreeV( (void *)popTP->PopTP[chXI] );
    memset( (void *)popTP, 0, sizeof(*popTP) );
  }
  return( 0 );
}
```

```
/************************************************************************
 *                                                                      *
 *    InitOnePopI() - Initialize one Population                         *
 *                                                                      *
 ************************************************************************
   Allocates all memory and sets up a new population.
 */

int InitOnePopI A3(              /* create a population */
FAST POP FAR *, RefTP,           /* pointer to "reference" population */
FAST POP FAR *, PopTP,           /* pointer to "blank" population */
FAST int,    PopIDI )            /* population ID */
{
   FAST CHROM FAR *cTP;          /* working item pointer */
   FAST unsigned SizeU;          /* size to allocate for a chrom */
   FAST int   wxI;               /* population index */
   FAST int   ixI, jxI, gxI;     /* item index */
   FAST float evalF;             /* result of evaluating Chromosome */
   CHROM   wCT;                  /* work chromomsome */
   FAST double MinD, MaxD;       /* min / max for normalization */

   cTP  = (CHROM *)0;            /* force a valid value to make compiler happy */
   SizeU = sizeof(CHROM) -       /* size of each chromosome */
      sizeof(cTP->CWtsFA) + RefTP->NGenesS * sizeof(cTP->CWtsFA[0]);
   if ( RefTP->SzPopMaxS > MAXPOP ) RefTP->SzPopMaxS = MAXPOP;
   RefTP->ChromSizeU = SizeU;             /* store for ref too */

   sprintf( GBuf, "Population (%d) with (%d) elements (%d) Genes (length %d bytes)\n",
      PopIDI, RefTP->SzPopMaxS, RefTP->NGenesS, SizeU );
   MsgER( GBuf );

   /* --- Clear the data structure & fill it with initial values --- */

   memset( (void *)PopTP, 0, sizeof(*PopTP) );      /* zap it */
   PopTP->PopSerialL   = 1L;                        /* starting serial number */
   PopTP->PopIDS       = PopIDI;                    /* population ID */
   PopTP->SelMethodS   = RefTP->SelMethodS; /* selection method */
   PopTP->SelRangeD    = RefTP->SelRangeD;  /* selection range */
   memcpy(  (void *)PopTP->ProbChildD,  (void *)RefTP->ProbChildD,  sizeof(PopTP-
>ProbChildD) );
   PopTP->MutOneProbD  = RefTP->MutOneProbD;  /* prob of mutating a gene */
   PopTP->MutOneLimitD = RefTP->MutOneLimitD; /* creep limit */
   PopTP->OptMethodS   = RefTP->OptMethodS;   /* optimization method */
   PopTP->NormMethS    = RefTP->NormMethS;    /* normalization method */
   PopTP->EvalMethodS  = RefTP->EvalMethodS;  /* evaluation method */
   PopTP->EvalSubMethS = RefTP->EvalSubMethS; /* sub-method */
   PopTP->EvalPeriodsS = RefTP->EvalPeriodsS; /* number of "periods" for eval */
   PopTP->SeedSizeD    = RefTP->SeedSizeD;    /* portion of old pop to copy to new */
   PopTP->NGenesS      = RefTP->NGenesS;      /* number of genes */
   PopTP->ChromSizeU   = SizeU;               /* size of each chromosome */
   PopTP->SzPopMaxS    = RefTP->SzPopMaxS;    /* max population size */
   PopTP->SzCurPopS    = 0;                   /* nothing in current population yet */
   PopTP->SzNewPopS    = 0;                   /* nothing in new population yet */
   PopTP->NewAddsS     = 0;                   /* no new additions yet */
   PopTP->CurPopTPP    = &PopTP->PopTP[0];    /* current population */
   PopTP->NewPopTPP    = &PopTP->PopTP[PopTP->SzPopMaxS]; /* new population */
   /* --- Allocate memory for current & new populations --- */

   for( wxI = 0; wxI < 2*PopTP->SzPopMaxS; wxI++ ) {
      if ( (cTP = (CHROM *)MemGetVP( SizeU)) == (CHROM *)0 ) {
         sprintf( GBuf,
            "\nInsufficient room to allocate item (%d) in population (%d)\n", wxI, PopTP-
>PopIDS );
         MsgER( GBuf );
         return( -1 );
      }
      PopTP->PopTP[wxI] = cTP;          /* master list */
   }
   /* --- Set up initial values for the new population --- */

   switch( PopTP->NormMethS ) {
   default:
   case NORMRATIO:
   case NORMASYM:   MinD = 0.; MaxD = 1.; break;
   case NORMMULT:
   case NORMSYMM:   MinD = -1.; MaxD = 1.; break;
   }

   memset( (void *)&wCT, 0, sizeof(wCT) );    /* clear work area */
   for( PopTP->NewAddsS = 0; PopTP->NewAddsS < PopTP->SzPopMaxS; ) {
      wCT.CSerialL  = 0;                 /* from initialization */
```

```
    wCT.CPopIDS  = PopTP->PopIDS;        /* population ID */
    wCT.CCurPopIDS = PopTP->PopIDS;
    wCT.COriginS = 0;                    /* initialization */
    for( ixI = 0; ixI < PopTP->NGenesS; ixI++ )
      wCT.CWtsFA[ixI] = RandRD(MinD,MaxD);/* start with random values */
    NormChromV( &wCT, PopTP->NGenesS, PopTP->NormMethS );  /* normalize it */
    LocalOptI( &wCT, PopTP, PopTP->OptMethodS, 0);      /* evaluate it */
    UpdatePopI( PopTP, &wCT );          /* insert it into "new" */
  }

  return( 0 );              /* done successfully */
}

/***************************************************************************
 *                                                                         *
 *    InitAllPopsI() - Initialize All Populations                          *
 *                                                                         *
 ***************************************************************************
 */

int CheckParmsI A1( int, ckF )      /* check population data */
{
  FAST POP FAR *rpTP;        /* reference population */
  FAST int      wI;          /* work integer */
  FAST int      ChangesI;    /* changes made */

  rpTP = &IsleT[0];

  /* --- Sanity Checks --- */

  ChangesI = 0;

  wI = rpTP->SelMethodS;
  if ( !(wI == SELSCORE || wI == SELGRANK || wI == SELRANK || wI == SELUNIF ) ) {
    rpTP->SelMethodS = SELSCORE; ChangesI++; }
  if ( !(0.1 <= rpTP->SelRangeD && rpTP->SelRangeD < 100.) ) {
    rpTP->SelRangeD = 1.0; ChangesI++; }
  if ( !(0.0 <= rpTP->ProbXAVGD && rpTP->ProbXAVGD <= 1.0) ) {
    rpTP->ProbXAVGD = 0.05; ChangesI++; }
  for( wI = 0; wI < ASof(rpTP->ProbChildD); wI++ )
    if ( !(0.0 <= rpTP->ProbChildD[wI] && rpTP->ProbChildD[wI] <= 1.0 ) ) {
      rpTP->ProbChildD[wI] = 0.2; ChangesI++; }
  if ( !(0.0 < rpTP->MutOneProbD && rpTP->MutOneProbD <= 1.0) ) {
    rpTP->MutOneProbD = 0.2; ChangesI++; }
  if ( !(0.001 <= rpTP->MutOneLimitD && rpTP->MutOneLimitD <= 1.0) ) {
    rpTP->MutOneLimitD = 0.2; ChangesI++; }
  wI = rpTP->OptMethodS;
  if ( !(wI == OPTNONE || wI == OPTLOCAL || wI == OPTGLOBAL) ) {
    rpTP->OptMethodS = OPTNONE; ChangesI++; }
  wI = rpTP->NormMethS;
  if ( !(wI == NORMRATIO || wI == NORMMULT || wI == NORMSYMM || wI == NORMASYM) ) {
    rpTP->NormMethS = NORMMULT; ChangesI++; }
  wI = rpTP->EvalMethodS;
  if ( !(wI == EVALPROFIT || wI == EVALTARGET || wI == EVALTRADES) ) {
    rpTP->EvalMethodS = EVALPROFIT; ChangesI++; }
  wI = rpTP->EvalSubMethS;
  if ( !(wI == EVALAVG || wI == EVALMIN || wI == EVALMIN2 || wI == EVALMINAVG ||
      wI == EVALMINLAST || wI == EVALACTUAL) ) {
    rpTP->EvalSubMethS = EVALMINLAST; ChangesI++; }
  if ( !(0 <= rpTP->EvalPeriodsS && rpTP->EvalPeriodsS <= MAXSUB) ) {
    rpTP->EvalPeriodsS = MAXSUB / 2; ChangesI++; }
  if ( !(0.0 <= rpTP->SeedSizeD && rpTP->SeedSizeD <= 1.0) ) {
    rpTP->SeedSizeD = 0.1; ChangesI++; }
  if ( !(0 < rpTP->NGenesS && rpTP->NGenesS <= MAXIND) ) {
    if ( ckF == 0 ) {
      sprintf( GBuf, "Illegal number of genes (%d)\n", rpTP->NGenesS );
      MsgER( GBuf );
    }
    return(-1);        /* error! */
  }
  if ( !( 3 <= rpTP->SzPopMaxS && rpTP->SzPopMaxS <= MAXPOP ) ) {
    rpTP->SzPopMaxS = 10; ChangesI++; }

  return( ChangesI );
}


int InitAllPopsI A1(         /* set up all populations */
FAST int,    NPopsI )        /* number of populations to create */
{
```

```
FAST POP    FAR *rpTP;       /* reference population */
FAST int    wI;              /* work integer */
FAST int    ChangesI;        /* changes made */

FreeAllPopsI();              /* free any "pending" populations */

/* --- Check moving averages & data loaded --- */

if ( NDataPtsI < 25 ) {
  MsgER( "Too few data points or data file was not loaded\n" );
  return( -1 );
}

if ( NIndsI < 2 ) {
  MsgER( "Too few moving indicators or none specified\n" );
  return( -1 );
}
rpTP = &IsleT[0];
rpTP->NGenesS = NIndsI        /* number of oscillators */
          + 1;        /* plus bias */

/* --- Sanity Checks --- */

ChangesI = 0;
if ( NPopsI >= ASof(IsleT) ) { ChangesI++; NPopsI = ASof(IsleT)-1; }
if ( NPopsI < 1      ) { ChangesI++; NPopsI = 1;          }
ChangesI += CheckParmsI( 0 );

if ( ChangesI > 0 ) {
  sprintf( GBuf, "Warning: %d parameters 'adjusted'\n", ChangesI );
  MsgER( GBuf );
}

/* --- Allocate the populations --- */

MsgER( "Initializing populations\n" );
for( NGrpI = 0; NGrpI < NPopsI; ) {
  NGrpI++;
  if ( InitOnePopI( rpTP, &IsleT[NGrpI], NGrpI ) )
    return( -1 );        /* error !! */
}
MsgER( "...Done\n" );

  return( ChangesI );    /* ok or warning */
}

/****************************************************************************
 *                                                                         *
 *   OneGenV() - Compute one Generation on all populations                 *
 *                                                                         *
 ****************************************************************************
 */

void OneGenV A0      /* cycle through one generation */
{
  FAST int     PopXI;         /* populatin index */
  FAST POP FAR *popTP;        /* pointer to current pop */
  FAST double  wD, xD, tD;    /* work value */
  FAST int     wxI;           /* work index */
  FAST CHROM FAR *chTP;       /* current chromosome */
  FAST CHROM FAR *achTP;      /* alt chromosome */

  for( PopXI = 1; PopXI <= NGrpI; PopXI++ ) {
    popTP = &IsleT[PopXI];    /* current population */
    if ( popTP->NewAddsS >= popTP->SzPopMaxS )
      SwapPopsV( popTP );     /* swap populations */

    while( popTP->NewAddsS < popTP->SzPopMaxS )
      UpdatePopI( popTP, BreedTP( popTP, 0 ) );

    if ( LogFP != (FILE *)0 ) {
      /* --- Compute statistics: Best, Worst, average --- */
      for( wD = xD = tD = 0., wxI = 0; wxI < popTP->SzNewPopS; wxI++ ) {
        chTP = popTP->NewPopPP[wxI];
        wD += chTP->CScoreF;
        xD += chTP->CTrainF;
        tD += chTP->CTestF;
      }
      wD /= popTP->SzNewPopS;
      xD /= popTP->SzNewPopS;
      tD /= popTP->SzNewPopS;
```

```
        achTP = popTP->NewPopTPP[0];     /* best */
                        s   p   r   i   n   t   f   (       G   B   u   f   ,
"%ld\t%d\t%.4g\t%.4g\t%.4g\t%.4g\t%.4g\t%.4g\t%.4g\t%.4g\n",
            IterCntL, popTP->PopIDS,          /* global generation & ID */
            achTP->CScoreF, wD, chTP->CScoreF,     /* working scores */
            achTP->CTrainF, xD, chTP->CTrainF,     /* working profit */
            achTP->CTestF, tD, chTP->CTestF );     /* test profit */
        MsgER( GBuf );
    }

  }
  return;
}

/***************************************************************************
 *                                                                         *
 *   MultiGenV() - Run multiple Generations & Migrations                   *
 *                                                                         *
 ***************************************************************************
 */

void MultiGenV A2(
FAST int,     NGenI,      /* # of generations to run */
FAST int,     ModGenI )   /* modulo for "saving" */
{
    FAST int    wxI;         /* work index */
    FAST int    SvCtrI;      /* save counter */
    FAST CHROM FAR *chTP;    /* best chromosome in populations */
    FAST int    TermCtrI;    /* termination counter */
    CHROM FAR   *schTP;      /* best saved chrom */

    if ( GenPerMigI < 1 )
      GenPerMigI = 1;

    schTP = (CHROM FAR *)0;
    SvCtrI = 0;
    TermCtrI = -1;
    for( wxI = NGenI; --wxI >= 0; ) {
      if ( GenRandI ) {                      /* random migration */
        if ( Rand01D() < RandMigRateD )
          RandMigrateV( &IsleT[0], NGrpI );
      } else {                               /* full migration */
        if ( GenCtrI++ >= GenPerMigI ) {
          MigrateV( &IsleT[0], NGrpI );  /* perform migration */
          GenCtrI = 1;               /* reset migration ctr */
        }
      }

      OneGenV();                      /* step one generation */
      chTP = FindBestTP();            /* find best chrom */
      if ( ++TermCtrI > 0 ) {         /* if not initial cond: */
        if ( chTP->CScoreF == BestScoreF ) {
          if ( TermCtrI > RunTermI )  /* score is same */
            return;                   /* termination cond met */
        } else if ( chTP->CScoreF > BestScoreF )
          TermCtrI = 0;               /* reset counter */
      }
      BestScoreF = chTP->CScoreF;

      IterCntL++;                     /* track iterations */
      if ( ModGenI > 0 && SvCtrI++ >= ModGenI ) {
        SvCtrI = 1;
        if ( schTP != (CHROM FAR *)0 &&
             schTP->CSerialL == chTP->CSerialL &&
             schTP->CPopIDS == chTP->CPopIDS ) {
          sprintf( GBuf, "...Saving aborted, since same as prior\n" );
          MsgER( GBuf );
        } else {
          SaveChromI( SaveFile, chTP );
          memcpy( (void *)&w1CHT, (void *)chTP, sizeof(w1CHT) );
          LocalOptI( &w1CHT, &IsleT[0], OPTFORCE, 0 ); /* optimize it */
          if ( (&w1CHT)->CScoreF != chTP->CScoreF )
            SaveChromI( SaveFile, &w1CHT );
          else IncFileNameV( SaveFile );
          sprintf( GBuf,
            "...Saving Optimized (%.6g/%.6g/%.6g) vs (%.6g/%.6g/%.6g) in <%s>\n",
            w1CHT.CScoreF, w1CHT.CTrainF, w1CHT.CTestF,
            chTP->CScoreF, chTP->CTrainF, chTP->CTestF,
            SaveFile );
          MsgER( GBuf );
```

```
            if ( w1CHT.CScoreF > chTP->CScoreF &&
                 w1CHT.CScoreF <= chTP->CScoreF * 1.1 )
                memcpy( (void *)chTP, (void *)&w1CHT, IsleT[0].ChromSizeU );
        }
        schTP = chTP;
    }
  }
  return;
}

/***********************************************************************
 *                                                                     *
 *    ReadDataI() - Read Data from the input file                      *
 *                                                                     *
 ***********************************************************************
  Format expected: Date price...
 */

int ReadDataI A1( char *, fnCP )     /* read input data file */
{
    FILE       *iFP;            /* input file pointer */
    DROW FAR   *dTP;            /* row work pointer */
    double      wD;             /* work double */
    long        DateL;          /* current date */
    unsigned    SizeU;          /* size of a row of data */
    int         UsableDataI;    /* usable data points */
    int         imx, i;         /* work indicies to find start point */
    char       *sp, *ap;        /* work pointers */
    char        date[12];       /* work date */
    char        lbuf[80];       /* line buffer */

    /* --- try opening the input file --- */

    if ( NIndsI < 2 ) {
        sprintf( GBuf, "Too few (%d) indicators to work with.\n",
          NIndsI );
        MsgER( GBuf );
        return( -1 );
    }

    if ( (iFP = fopen( fnCP, "r" )) == (FILE *)0 ) {
        sprintf( GBuf, "Could not open input file <%s>\n", fnCP );
        MsgER( GBuf );
        return( -2 );
    }
    sprintf( GBuf, "Reading input data file <%s>", fnCP );
    MsgER( GBuf );

    dTP  = (DROW *)&wD;     /* make compiler happy */
    SizeU = sizeof(DROW)    /* actual size of data used */
          - sizeof(dTP->DIndCA)
          + ( (NIndsI+8) * sizeof(dTP->DIndCA[0]) ) / 8;
    NDataPtsI = 0;          /* nothing yet */
    for(;;) {
        if ( (sp = fgets( lbuf, sizeof(lbuf), iFP )) == (char *)0 )
            break;               /* end of file */

        while( *sp && *sp <= ' ' ) sp++;    /* skip leading spaces */
        if ( *sp == 0 || *sp == ';' || *sp == '!' )
            continue;               /* skip "blank" lines */

        for( ap = &date[0]; *sp > ' '; sp++ )
            if ( ap < &date[11] ) *ap++ = *sp;
        *ap = 0;                /* copy date */
        if ( (DateL = Str2DateL( date )) <= 0x19000000L )
            continue;               /* bad date, skip record */

        wD = strtod( sp, &ap );        /* convert price */
        if ( *ap > ' ' ) {
            sprintf( GBuf, "Error processing line: %s", lbuf );
            MsgER( GBuf );
            continue;
        }

        if ( NDataPtsI >= MAXDATA ) {
            sprintf( GBuf, "Too many data records. Ignored after %d.\n",
              NDataPtsI );
            MsgER( GBuf );
            break;
        }
```

```
     if ( (dTP = (DROW *)MemGetVP( SizeU )) == (DROW *)0 ) {
       sprintf( GBuf, "Error allocating (%d) bytes for data item %d\n",
         SizeU, NDataPtsI );
       MsgER( GBuf );
       return( -3 );
     }
     memset( (void *)dTP, 0, SizeU );      /* clear out data */
     dTP->DDateL = DateL;                   /* save date */
     dTP->DPriceF = wD;                     /* set price */
     DataTP[NDataPtsI++] = dTP;             /* save pointer */
   }
   fclose( iFP );                           /* close input file */
   GenSignalV();                            /* compute signals */
   strcpy( GBuf, "...Done\n" );
   fputs( GBuf, stdout ); fflush( stdout );
   if ( LogFP ) fputs( GBuf, LogFP );

   /* --- Compute starting & end points --- */

   for( i = imx = 0; i < NIndsI; i++ ) {
     if ( Inds[i].IDFDurUC > (unsigned)imx ) imx = Inds[i].IDFDurUC;
     if ( Inds[i].IDSDurUC > (unsigned)imx ) imx = Inds[i].IDSDurUC;
   }
   imx--;                                   /* min pts to skip */

   if ( imx < PtsSkipI ) imx = PtsSkipI;    /* points to skip */
   ISDataXI = imx;                          /* start of training data */
   UsableDataI = NDataPtsI - imx;           /* usable data */
   if ( PtsTrainI > 0 ) {                   /* user specified training pts */
     ISDataNI = PtsTrainI;
     if ( ISDataNI > UsableDataI )          /* see if enough data */
       ISDataNI = UsableDataI;              /* limit to what we have */
   } else {
     ISDataNI = UsableDataI / 2;            /* use half of it */
   }

   XPDataXI = ISDataXI + ISDataNI;          /* start of x-ante data */
   XPDataNI = NDataPtsI - XPDataXI;         /* all that is left */
   if ( PtsTestI > 0 && XPDataNI > PtsTestI )
     XPDataNI= PtsTestI;                    /* limit max test data */

   return( 0 );
}

/****************************************************************************
 *                                                                          *
 *    FreeDataI() - Free all memory used for data                           *
 *                                                                          *
 ****************************************************************************
 */

int FreeDataI A0
{
  int     dXI;        /* data index */

  for( dXI = 0; dXI < ASof(DataTP); dXI++ )
    if ( DataTP[dXI] != (DROW *)0 )
      MemFreeV( (void *)DataTP[dXI] );

  memset( (void *)&DataTP[0], 0, sizeof(DataTP) );
  NDataPtsI = 0;

  return( 0 );
}

/****************************************************************************
 *                                                                          *
 *    InitParmsV() - Set initial parameters                                 *
 *                                                                          *
 ****************************************************************************
 */

void InitParmsV A0
{
  FAST POP FAR          *p;          /* pointer to the reference pop */

  /* --- Global Control Variables --- */

  LogModL             = 10;          /* sampling period for logging */
  TradePenaltyF       = 0.002;       /* 1% penalty on each round-trip */
  OutLimitF           = 0.01;        /* band for "out-of-market" */
```

```
XPDataNI            = 50;          /* test data points */
NIndsI              = 0;           /* no indicators yet */
strcpy( DataFile, "sp500.dat" );   /* initial data file */
strcpy( LogFile, "bch_log.txt" );  /* log file */
strcpy( SaveFile, "bch_0000.txt" ); /* save file */
LogFile[3]          = RunCodeI;    /* insert run-code into names */
SaveFile[3]         = RunCodeI;
NGrpI               = 10;          /* one population */
MigSizeD            = 0.1;         /* portion of poulation to migrate */
RandMigRateD        = 0.02;        /* random migration rate */
GenPerMigI          = 50;          /* generations per migration */
GenRandI            = 1;           /* use random migration */
RunGensI            = 1000;        /* generations to iterate for */
RunTermI            = 100;         /* term if no improvement in 100 gen */
BestScoreF          = 0.;          /* score on "best" of generation */
RandSeedL           = 10925L;      /* initial random number seed */
SrchWindowI         = 3;           /* search window for ideal trader */
DoRefTestI          = 0;           /* typically do reference tests */
SaveFreqI           = 0;           /* how often to save */

/* --- Population Parameters --- */

memset( (void *)&IsleT[0], 0, sizeof(IsleT) );    /* clear out population data */
p = &IsleT[0];                     /* reference population */
p->SelMethodS       = SELSCORE;    /* selection method */
p->SelRangeD        = 1.0;         /* 50-50 split on spin */
p->ProbXAVGD        = 0.05;        /* 5% chance of using average x-over */
p->ProbX1PtD        = 0.10;        /* one-point x-over */
p->ProbX2PtD        = 0.10;        /* two-point x-over */
p->ProbXUnifD       = 0.20;        /* uniform x-over */
p->ProbMCreepD      = 0.35;        /* creep */
p->ProbMRandD       = 0.25;        /* random mutation */
p->MutOneProbD      = 0.50;        /* probability of mutating a single gene */
p->MutOneLimitD     = 0.2;         /* limit on how much it is mutated */
p->OptMethodS       = OPTNONE;     /* optimization method */
p->NormMethS        = NORMMULT;    /* normalization method */
p->EvalMethodS      = EVALPROFIT;  /* evalution method */
p->EvalSubMethS     = EVALMIN2;    /* sub-method */
p->EvalPeriodsS     = 5;           /* number of periods to divide data into */
p->SeedSizeD        = 0.7;         /* percent of "best" copied to new pop (0..1) */
p->NGenesS          = 0;           /* number of genes used (out of max) */
p->SzPopMaxS        = 30;          /* max size of either population */
memset( (void *)&OffMethL[0], 0, sizeof(OffMethL) );

return;
}

/******************************************************************************
*                                                                            *
*    PrintParmsV() - Print out parameters                                    *
*                                                                            *
******************************************************************************
*/

static char *SelLit[] = { "", "Score", "GRank", "Rank", "Uniform" };
static char *NormLit[] = { "", "Ratio", "Mult", "Symm", "Asym" };
static char *EvalLit[] = { "", "Profit", "Target", "Trades" };
static char *SEvalLit[]= { "", "Average", "Minimum", "Min2",
                  "Min+Avg", "Min+Last", "Actual" };
static char *OptLit[] = { "", "None", "Local", "Global" };
static char *IDFMLit[] = { "", "m", "e", "s", "d" };

void PrintParmsV A1(             /* print out parameters for run */
FILE *,     oFP )               /* print output file */
{
  unsigned long timeL;         /* current time */
  char    *sp;                 /* string pointer */
  POP     *p;                  /* population reference pointer */
  int     wxI;                 /* work index */
  char    tbuf[40];            /* time buffer */

  time( (time_t *)&timeL );
  strcpy( tbuf, ctime( (time_t *)&timeL ) );
  for( sp = &tbuf[0]; *sp >= ' '; ) sp++;
  *sp = 0;

  p = &IsleT[0];               /* reference population */

  fprintf( oFP, "\nParameters at: %s\n", tbuf );
  fprintf( oFP, "%20.3f Trade Penalty\n", TradePenaltyF );
  fprintf( oFP, "%20d Search Window for ideal trader\n", SrchWindowI );
```

```
      fprintf( oFP, "%20.3f Tolerance for 'out-of-market'\n", OutLimitF );
      fprintf( oFP, "%20d Test points (out of %d total)\n", XPDataNI, NDataPtsI );
      fprintf( oFP, "%20s Data File\n%20s Log File\n%20s Save File\n",
              DataFile, LogFile, SaveFile );
      fprintf( oFP, "%20d Indicators\n", NIndsI );
      for( wxI = 0; wxI < NIndsI; wxI++ )
        fprintf( oFP, "           %s%d %s%d\n"
          IDFMLit[Inds[wxI].IDFModeC], Inds[wxI].IDFDurUC & Oxff,
          IDFMLit[Inds[wxI].IDSModeC], Inds[wxI].IDSDurUC & Oxff );
      fprintf( oFP, "%20d Populations\n", NGrpI );
      fprintf( oFP, "%20d Migration flag: =1, random; =0, fixed\n", GenRandI );
      fprintf( oFP, "%20.3f Probability of migrating (random only)\n",
              RandMigRateD );
      fprintf( oFP, "%20.3f Portion of population that migrates\n%20d    Fixed
Generations\n",
              MigSizeD, GenPerMigI );
      fprintf( oFP, "%20d Generations per run (%d to terminate)\n%20ld Random seed
(initial)\n\n",
              RunGensI, RunTermI, RandSeedL );
      fprintf( oFP, "%20d Data points to skip (%d of %d)\n",
        PtsSkipI, ISDataXI, NDataPtsI );
      fprintf( oFP, "%20d Data points to train (%d to %d)\n",
        PtsTrainI, ISDataXI, ISDataXI+ISDataNI-1 );
      fprintf( oFP, "%20d Data points to test (%d to %d)\n",
        PtsTestI, XPDataXI, XPDataXI+XPDataNI-1 );

      fprintf( oFP, "%20s Selection Method\n", SelLit[p->SelMethodS] );
      fprintf( oFP, "%20.3f (Max Score - Min Score) / Min Score ratio\n", p->SelRangeD );
      fprintf( oFP, "%20.3f Probability of Average (vs std) crossover\n", p->ProbXAVGD );
      fprintf( oFP, "%20.3f  1-point crossover\n", p->ProbX1PtD );
      fprintf( oFP, "%20.3f  2-point crossover\n", p->ProbX2PtD );
      fprintf( oFP, "%20.3f  Uniform crossover\n", p->ProbXUnifD );
      fprintf( oFP, "%20.3f  Creep mutation\n",   p->ProbMCreepD );
      fprintf( oFP, "%20.3f  Random mutation\n",  p->ProbMRandD );
      fprintf( oFP, "%20.3f Probability of Mutating one gene (Limit %.3f)\n",
              p->MutOneProbD, p->MutOneLimitD );
      fprintf( oFP, "%20s Optimization method\n", OptLit[p->OptMethodS] );
      fprintf( oFP, "%20s Normalization Method\n", NormLit[p->NormMethS] );
      strcpy( tbuf, EvalLit[p->EvalMethodS] );
      strcat( tbuf, ": " );
      strcat( tbuf, SEvalLit[p->EvalSubMethS] );
      fprintf( oFP, "%20s Evaluation Method\n", tbuf );
      fprintf( oFP, "%20d  Periods per evaluation\n", p->EvalPeriodsS );
      fprintf( oFP, "%20.3f Portion of current population to seed new one with\n",
              p->SeedSizeD );
      fprintf( oFP, "%20d Maximum population size\n", p->SzPopMaxS );

      fflush( oFP );
      return;
}

/***********************************************************************
*                                                                     *
*    RefScoreV() - Compute reference scores for single MACD pairs      *
*                                                                     *
***********************************************************************
*/

void RefScoreV A0
{
    FAST POP  FAR   *popTP;    /* fake population */
    FAST CHROM FAR *chTP;      /* work chromosome */
    FAST int   fxI, sxI;       /* fast & slow indices */
    FAST int   cxI;            /* current chromosome index */
    char       wsn[80];        /* work save name */

    chTP = &w1CHT;             /* work chromosome */
    chTP->CCurPopIDS = 1;      /* current population owner */
    popTP = &IsleT[1];         /* first population for "reference" */
    strcpy( wsn, SaveFile );   /* temp for file name */
    for( cxI = 0; wsn[cxI] != 0; cxI++ )
      if ( '0' <= wsn[cxI] && wsn[cxI] <= '9' )
        wsn[cxI] = '0';

    for( cxI = 0; wsn[cxI] != 0; cxI++ )
      if ( '0' <= wsn[cxI] && wsn[cxI] <= '9' ) {
        wsn[cxI] = 'r';        /* reference */
        break;
      }

    for( cxI = 0; cxI < popTP->NGenesS; cxI++ )
```

```
        chTP->CWtsFA[cxI] = 0.;           /* clear out all */

     for( cxI = 0, fxI = 0; fxI < NIndsI; fxI++ ) {
        chTP->CWtsFA[cxI] = 1.;      /* only one oscillator */
        EvalSignalV( chTP );        /* evaluate the signal */
        chTP->CScoreF = EvalStepD( 0., EVALPROFIT, ISDataXI, ISDataNI );
        chTP->CTestF = EvalStepD( 0., EVALPROFIT, XPDataXI, XPDataNI );
        sprintf( GBuf, "\t%s%d\t%s%d\t%.6g\t%.6g\n",
          IDFMLit[Inds[fxI].IDFModeC], Inds[fxI].IDFDurUC & 0xff,
          IDFMLit[Inds[fxI].IDSModeC], Inds[fxI].IDSDurUC & 0xff,
          chTP->CScoreF, chTP->CTestF );
        MsgER( GBuf );              /* write stats to log file */
        SaveChromI( wsn, chTP );    /* save chrom & data */
        chTP->CWtsFA[cxI] = 0.;     /* reset weight */
        cxI++;                      /* next oscillator */
     }
     return;
  }

/**************************************************************************
 *                                                                       *
 *    CMDRunCode() - Set Run-Code in Current File Names                   *
 *                                                                       *
 **************************************************************************
 */

int CMDRunCode A3(        /* Set up files with a particular run code */
char *,     cmdP,         /* pointer to command table */
long,       cntL,         /* # of items converted */
FILE *,     eFP )         /* error file pointer */
{
  strcpy( LogFile, "bch_log.txt" ); /* log file */
  strcpy( SaveFile, "bch_0000.txt" ); /* save file */
  LogFile[3]    = RunCodeI;   /* insert run-code into names */
  SaveFile[3]   = RunCodeI;

  return( 0 );
}

/**************************************************************************
 *                                                                       *
 *    CMDInd() - Parse indicator line                                    *
 *                                                                       *
 **************************************************************************
 */

int CMDInd A3(     /* Parse indicator line */
char *,     cmdP,     /* pointer to command table */
long,       cntL,     /* # of items converted */
FILE *,     eFP )     /* error file pointer */
{
  int     mf, ms, pf, ps;    /* mode & period */
  int     c;                 /* work char */
  char    *sp, *dp;          /* work pointers */

  strcat( &IBuf[0], " " );
  strcat( &IBuf[0], &IBuf2[0] );
  sp = &IBuf[0];
  mf = ms = -1;              /* nothing yet */
  pf = ps = 0;
  for( sp = &IBuf[0]; *sp && *sp <= ' '; )
    sp++;                    /* update pointer */

  switch( *sp ) {            /* work char */
  default:
    fprintf( eFP, "Illegal Fast type <%c>. Must be E, M, S[K]\n", *sp );
    goto Error;
  case 'E': case 'e': mf = IDFM_EMA;  break; /* EMA */
  case 'M': case 'm': mf = IDFM_MA;  break; /* moving averages */
  case 'S': case 's':                 /* stochastics */
  case 'K': case 'k': mf = IDFM_STOCH; break;
  }
  sp++;
  while( *sp && *sp <= ' ' ) sp++;     /* skip leading spaces */
  while( '0' <= *sp && *sp <= '9' )
    pf = pf * 10 + ((*sp++) - '0');    /* merge in next digit */

  while( *sp && *sp <= ' ' ) sp++;     /* skip spaces */
  switch( *sp ) {                      /* work char */
  default:
    fprintf( eFP, "Illegal Slow type <%c>\n", *sp );
```

```
         goto Error;
    case 'E': case 'e': ms = IDFM_EMA;  break; /* EMA */
    case 'M': case 'm': ms = IDFM_MA;   break;  /* moving average */
    case 'S': case 's':                         /* stochastics */
    case 'K': case 'k': ms = IDFM_STOCH; break;
    case 'D': case 'd': ms = IDFM_SMTH; break; /* %D stochastic */
    }
    if ( mf == IDFM_STOCH && (ms != IDFM_SMTH && ms != IDFM_STOCH) ) {
      fprintf( eFP,
      "Only Smoothing (D) & Stochastic (K or S) can be used for Slow signal with
stochastic.\n" );
      goto Error;
    }
    if ( mf != IDFM_STOCH && ms == IDFM_SMTH ) {
      fprintf( eFP, "Smoothing (D) can only be used with Stochastic.\n" );
      goto Error;
    }
    sp++;
    while( *sp && *sp <= ' ' ) sp++;          /* skip leading spaces */
    while( '0' <= *sp && *sp <= '9' )
      ps = ps * 10 + ((*sp++) - '0');         /* merge in next digit */
    while( *sp && *sp <= ' ' ) sp++;
    if ( *sp != 0 ) goto Error;

    if ( NIndsI >= ASof(Inds) )
      goto Error;                             /* too many items */

    Inds[NIndsI].IDFModeC = (char)mf;
    Inds[NIndsI].IDFDurUC = (unsigned char)pf;
    Inds[NIndsI].IDSModeC = (char)ms;
    Inds[NIndsI].IDSDurUC = (unsigned char)ps;
    NIndsI++;

    return( 0 );
Error:
    return( -1 );
}

/***************************************************************************
 *                                                                         *
 *    CMDRunI() - Run the current set of GA parameters                     *
 *                                                                         *
 ***************************************************************************
 */

static int RandInitedI = {0};

int CMDRun A3(         /* RDE added; plot data columns */
char *,       cmdP,            /* pointer to command table */
long,         cntL,            /* # of items converted */
FILE *,       eFP )            /* error file pointer */
{
    FILE      *afp;            /* alt file pointer */
    int       wxI;             /* generation index */
    unsigned long   tL;        /* time to run */
    unsigned long   wL;        /* work long */
    CHROM FAR      *chTP;      /* work chrom */

    if ( RandInitedI == 0 || RandSeedL != 0 ) {
      RandSeedV( RandSeedL );
      RandSeedL  = 0;
      RandInitedI = 1;
    }

    IterCntL = 0;                        /* no iterations yet */
    GenCtrI = 0;                         /* no generations yet */
    if ( LogFP != (FILE *)0 )
      fclose( LogFP );                   /* close it just in case */
    LogFP = fopen( LogFile, "a" );       /* try to open log file */
    time( (time_t *)&tL );               /* current time */

    DisclaimV();
    FreeDataI();                         /* make sure data is clear */
    if ( ReadDataI( DataFile ) != 0 )
      goto Error;
    MemStatsV();                         /* size of data */

    MsgER( "Computing ideal trading signal..." );
    IdealSignalV( TradePenaltyF, SrchWindowI ); /* compute Ideal Trading Signal */
    MsgER( "Done\n" );
```

```
    CheckParmsI( 1 );                   /* check parameters */
    PrintParmsV( stdout );              /* show parameters */
    if ( LogFP ) {
      PrintParmsV( LogFP );
      fclose( LogFP );
      LogFP = fopen( LogFile, "a" );
    }

    if ( RunGensI > 0 ) {
      if ( InitAllPopsI( NGrpI ) < 0 )     /* set up populations */
        goto Error;

      MemStatsV();                      /* memory statistics */
      if ( DoRefTestI ) {
        MsgER( "Generating reference scores\n" );
        RefScoreV();                    /* MUST be done after init pops */
        MsgER( "...Done\n" );
      }
      MultiGenV( RunGensI, SaveFreqI );   /* iterate */
      chTP = FindBestTP();                /* find best chrom */
      SaveChromI( SaveFile, chTP );       /* save the best */
      sprintf( GBuf, "Best chromosome saved in <%s>\n", SaveFile );
      MsgER( GBuf );
    }

    if ( (afp = fopen( "summary.txt", "a" )) != (FILE *)0 ) {
      fprintf( afp, "%s\t%d\t%d\t%d\t%d\t%.6g\t%.6g\t%ld\t%d\t%s",
        Date2StrCP( DataTP[PtsSkipI]->DDateL ),
        IsleT[0].EvalPeriodsS, PtsSkipI, PtsTrainI, PtsTestI,
        chTP->CScoreF, chTP->CTrainF, chTP->CTestF,
        chTP->CSerialL, chTP->CPopIDS, SaveFile );
      EvalStatsV( chTP, afp );
      fprintf( afp, "\n" );
      fclose( afp );
    }

    FreeDataI();             /* release data */
    FreeAllPopsI();          /* release populations */
    MemStatsV();             /* verify proper memory management */
    time( (time_t *)&wL );
    sprintf( GBuf, "%ld seconds elapsed time\n", wL-tL );
    MsgER( GBuf );
    if ( LogFP ) { fclose( LogFP ); LogFP = fopen( LogFile, "a" ); }
    return( 0 );

Error:
    FreeDataI();
    FreeAllPopsI();
    MemStatsV();             /* just in case */
    time( (time_t *)&wL );
    sprintf( GBuf, "%ld seconds elapsed time\n", wL-tL );
    MsgER( GBuf );
    if ( LogFP ) { fclose( LogFP ); LogFP = fopen( LogFile, "a" ); }
    return( -1 );
}

/***********************************************************************
 *                                                                     *
 *              Batch File Capability                                  *
 *                                                                     *
 ***********************************************************************/
--- DoCommandsI() --- Execute commands from the command line
until "quit" is encountered. Provide for recursive calls
from other routines to switch to alternate command tables &
sub-functions.
*/

FILE  *inputFP = {stdin};  /* current command line input */
int   QuitI  = {0};        /* parameter to terminate parsing */

/* --- CMDQuit() --- Terminate the program. */

int CMDQuit A3(
char *,     cmdP,          /* pointer to command table */
long,       cntL,          /* # of items converted */
FILE *,     eFP )          /* error file pointer */
{ QuitI = 1; return( 0 ); }

int DoCommandsI A3(        /* execute commands */
CMD *,      ct,            /* command table */
char *,     PromptSP,      /* prompt */
```

```
FILE *,      inFP )        /* input file pointer */
{
  int      rc;             /* return code */
  char     *sp;            /* string pointer */
  char     *wsp;           /* work string pointer */
  char     buf[80];        /* work buffer */
  int      QuitSaveI;      /* save old quit flag */
  int      CommentI;       /* blank or comment line */

  QuitSaveI = QuitI;
  for( QuitI = 0; QuitI == 0 ;) {
    fputs( PromptSP, stdout );
    fputs( "> ", stdout );
    fflush( stdout );
    sp = fgets( buf, sizeof(buf), inFP );
    if ( sp == (char *)0 ) {
      QuitI = 1;
      sp = "!<eof>";
    } else {
      for( wsp = sp; *wsp > 0; wsp++ )
        if ( *wsp < ' ' ) *wsp = ' ';
    }

    if ( inFP != stdin ) {
      fputs( sp, stdout );
      fputs( "\n", stdout );
      fflush( stdout );
    }

    for( wsp = sp; *wsp <= ' '; ) wsp++;
    CommentI = ( *wsp == '!' || *wsp == 0 )? 1:0;
    wsp = sp;
    if ( LogFP ) {
      fprintf( LogFP, "%s> %s\n", PromptSP, sp );
      if ( !CommentI ) {
        rc = ParseLineI( &wsp, &ct[0], LogFP, 1 ); /* syntax check */
        wsp = sp;
        fclose( LogFP ); LogFP = fopen( LogFile, "a" );
      }
    }
    if ( !CommentI ) {
      rc = ParseLineI( &wsp, &ct[0], stdout, 1 ); /* syntax check */
      if ( rc == 0 ) {
        wsp = sp;
        rc = ParseLineI( &wsp, &ct[0], stdout, 0 );
        fclose( LogFP ); LogFP = fopen( LogFile, "a" );
      }
    }
    if ( LogFile[0] != 0 && LogFP == (FILE *)0 )
      LogFP = fopen( LogFile, "a" );   /* try opening log file again */
  }
  QuitI = QuitSaveI;
  return( 0 );
}

/***************************************************************************
 *                                                                         *
 *    Command Table for setting variables                                  *
 *                                                                         *
 ***************************************************************************
 */

LIT LITScore[] = { { "score",  SELSCORE  }, { "gaussianrank", SELGRANK },
        { "rank",   SELRANK  }, { "uniform"    SELUNIF }, {0} };
LIT LITOpt[]  = { { "none",   OPTNONE  }, { "local",    OPTLOCAL },
        { "global", OPTGLOBAL }, {0} };
LIT LITNorm[] = { { "ratio", NORMRATIO }, { "multiplicative", NORMMULT },
        { "symmetric", NORMSYMM },{ "asymmetric",  NORMASYM }, {0} };
LIT LITEval[] = { { "profit", EVALPROFIT }, { "target", EVALTARGET },
        { "trades", EVALTRADES }, {0} };
LIT LITSEval[] = { { "actual", EVALACTUAL }, { "average", EVALAVG },
        { "minimum", EVALMIN }, { "min2smallest", EVALMIN2 },
        { "minaverage", EVALMINAVG }, { "minlast", EVALMINLAST }, {0} };
LIT LITyn[]   = { { "yes", 1 }, { "no", 0 }, {0} };

INPUT INStats[] = {
 IVAL( EVStartI, IO_INT|IO_DSP|IO_OPT, FMT_INTU, 0 ),
 IVAL( EVSizeI, IO_INT|IO_DSP|IO_OPT, FMT_INTU, 0 ),
 IVAL( EVIncrI, IO_INT|IO_DSP|IO_OPT, FMT_INTU, 0 ),
 INUL
};
```

```
INPUT INRun[] = {
 IVAL( RunGensI, IO_INT|IO_DSP, FMT_INTU, 0 ),
 IVAL( RunTermI, IO_INT|IO_DSP|IO_OPT, FMT_INTU, 0 ),
 INUL
};

INPUT INInd[] = {
 ISTR( IBuf, IO_STR|IO_DSP ),
 ISTR( IBuf2, IO_STR|IO_DSP|IO_OPT ),
 INUL
};

CMD ct[] = {
 { "datafile",       "Input data file",
                     0, ISTR( DataFile, IO_FNM ) },
 { "logfile",        "Log file name",
                     0, ISTR( LogFile, IO_FNM ) },
 { "savefile",       "Save file (end with zeros: sv0000)",
                     0, ISTR( SaveFile, IO_FNM ) },
 { "runcode",        "Set root name for log/save files",
                     CMDRunCode, IVAL( RunCodeI, IO_INT, FMT_INTU, 0 ) },
 { "seed",           "Initial random seed",
                     0, IVAL( RandSeedL, IO_INT, FMT_INTU, 0 ) },
 { "tradepenalty",   "Penalty applied to each round-trip trade",
                     0, IVAL( TradePenaltyF, IO_FLT,FMT_FLT3,0 ) },
 { "searchwindow",   "Search window for ideal trader",
                     0, IVAL( SrchWindowI, IO_INT, FMT_INTU, 0 ) },
 { "outofmarket",    "Band for 'out-of-market'",
                     0, IVAL( OutLimitF,  IO_FLT,FMT_FLT3,0 ) },
 { "indicator",      "Indicator to compute {EMK}ff {EMKD}ss",
                     CMDInd, ILIST( INInd, IO_DSP ) },
 { "isles",          "Populations to generate",
                     0, IVAL( NGrpI, IO_INT, FMT_INTU, 0 ) },
 { "randommigration","=1, Random Migrations; otherwise fixed",
                     0, IVAL( GenRandI, IO_INT, FMT_INTU, 0 ) },
 { "rmigrationrate", "Probability of random migration",
                     0, IVAL( RandMigRateD, IO_FLT, FMT_FLT5, 0 ) },
 { "migration",      "Size of migration (portion of population)",
                     0, IVAL( MigSizeD, IO_FLT,FMT_FLT3, 0 ) },
 { "genpermigration","Generations per migration",
                     0, IVAL( GenPerMigI, IO_INT,FMT_INTU, 0 ) },
 { "skippoints",     "Number of input data points to skip",
                     0, IVAL( PtsSkipI, IO_INT,FMT_INTU, 0 ) },
 { "trainpoints",    "Number of points to use for training",
                     0, IVAL( PtsTrainI, IO_INT,FMT_INTU, 0 ) },
 { "testpoints",     "Number of points to use for testing",
                     0, IVAL( PtsTestI, IO_INT,FMT_INTU, 0 ) },
 { "score",          "Scoring method",
                     0, IVAL( IsleT[0].SelMethodS, IO_INT|IO_LITONLY,FMT_INTU, LITScore ) },
 { "selectionrange", "Ratio of score-range to score min",
                     0, IVAL( IsleT[0].SelRangeD, IO_FLT, FMT_FLT3, 0 ) },
 { "pxaverage",      "Prob average crossover",
                     0, IVAL( IsleT[0].ProbXAVGD, IO_FLT, FMT_FLT3, 0 ) },
 { "px1point",       "Prob of 1-point crossover",
                     0, IVAL( IsleT[0].ProbX1PtD, IO_FLT, FMT_FLT3, 0 ) },
 { "px2point",       "Prob of 2-point crossover",
                     0, IVAL( IsleT[0].ProbX2PtD, IO_FLT, FMT_FLT3, 0 ) },
 { "pxuniform",      "Prob of uniform crossover",
                     0, IVAL( IsleT[0].ProbXUnifD, IO_FLT, FMT_FLT3, 0 ) },
 { "pmcreep",        "Prob of creep mutation",
                     0, IVAL( IsleT[0].ProbMCreepD,IO_FLT, FMT_FLT3, 0 ) },
 { "pmrand",         "Prob of random mutation",
                     0, IVAL( IsleT[0].ProbMRandD, IO_FLT, FMT_FLT3, 0 ) },
 { "mutoneprob",     "Prob of mutating a single gene",
                     0, IVAL( IsleT[0].MutOneProbD,IO_FLT, FMT_FLT3, 0 ) },
 { "mutcreeplimit",  "Limit on value added when 'creeping' an element",
                     0, IVAL( IsleT[0].MutOneLimitD,IO_FLT,FMT_FLT3, 0 ) },
 { "optimization",   "Local optimization method",
                     0, IVAL( IsleT[0].OptMethodS, IO_INT|IO_LITONLY,FMT_INTU, LITOpt ) },
 { "normalization",  "Normalize chromosome method",
                     0, IVAL( IsleT[0].NormMethS, IO_INT|IO_LITONLY,FMT_INTU, LITNorm ) },
 { "evaluation",     "Evaluation method",
                     0, IVAL( IsleT[0].EvalMethodS, IO_INT|IO_LITONLY,FMT_INTU, LITEval ) },
 { "subevaluation",  "Way to combine evaluations",
                     0, IVAL( IsleT[0].EvalSubMethS, IO_INT|IO_LITONLY,FMT_INTU, LITSEval ) },
 { "periods",        "Periods in average (min) evaluation",
                     0, IVAL( IsleT[0].EvalPeriodsS, IO_INT, FMT_INTU, 0 ) },
 { "populationseed", "Portion of population to seed next generation",
                     0, IVAL( IsleT[0].SeedSizeD, IO_FLT, FMT_FLT3, 0 ) },
 { "members",        "Elements in each population",
                     0, IVAL( IsleT[0].SzPopMaxS, IO_INT, FMT_INTU, 0 ) },
```

```
{ "referencetest",   "Perform MA tests",
             0, IVAL( DoRefTestI, IO_INT|IO_LITONLY,FMT_INTS, LITyn ) },
{ "statistics",    "start index, size, increment [50,T00,50]",
             0, ILIST( INStats, IO_DSP ) },
{ "frequency2save",  "How often to save the files",
             0, IVAL( SaveFreqI, IO_INT, FMT_INTU, 0 ) },
{ "go",           "Run a generation",
             CMDRun, ILIST( INRun, IO_DSP ) },
{ "batch",         "Read input from a batch file",
             CMDBatch, ISTR( BatchFile, IO_DSP|IO_FNM ) },
{ "quit",         "Return to main menu",
             CMDQuit, IACTRO },
{ 0 }
};

/**********************************************************************
 *                                                                  *
 *            Batch File Capability                                 *
 *                                                                  *
 **********************************************************************
 */
int CMDBatch A3(          /* batch file processing */
char *,      cmdP,        /* pointer to command table */
long,        cntL,        /* # of items converted */
FILE *,      eFP )        /* error file pointer */
{ FILE    *inFP;          /* new input file pointer */
  FILE    *inSaveFP;      /* save existing file pointer */

  if ( (inFP = fopen( BatchFile, "r" )) == (FILE *)0 ) {
    fprintf( eFP, "Could not open batch file <%s>\n", BatchFile );
    return( -1 );
  }

  inSaveFP = inputFP;           /* save current pointer */
  inputFP = inFP;
  DoCommandsI( &ct[0], "batch", inputFP );
  fclose( inFP );
  inputFP = inSaveFP;

  return( 0 );
}

/**********************************************************************
 *                                                                  *
 *   Main() - driver program                                        *
 *                                                                  *
 **********************************************************************
 */
main A2( int, ac, char **, av )
{
  FILE    *inSaveFP;  /* input file pointer save */
  FILE    *inFP;      /* current input file */
  char    *sp;        /* work string pointer */
  int     wxI;        /* index to parse command line */

  QuitI = 0;
  InitParmsV();            /* set up all parameters */
  DisclaimV();
  NIndsI = 0;

  if ( ac == 1 ) {

    /* --- Interactive: Look for "init" file --- */

    if ( (inFP = fopen( INITFILE, "r" )) != (FILE *)0 ) {
      inSaveFP = inputFP;
      inputFP = inFP;
      DoCommandsI( &ct[0], "init", inputFP );
      fclose( inFP );
      inputFP = inSaveFP;
    }

    /* --- Perform Interactive Batch Commands --- */

    DoCommandsI( &ct[0], "Command", inputFP );
```

```
    } else {
      /* --- Batch Command File(s) on the Command Line --- */

      for( wxI = 1; wxI < ac; wxI++ ) {
        sp = av[wxI];
        if ( (inFP = fopen( sp, "r" )) != (FILE *)0 ) {
          inSaveFP = inputFP;
          inputFP = inFP;
          DoCommandsI( &ct[0], sp, inputFP );
          fclose( inFP );
          inputFP = inSaveFP;
        }
      }
    }

  exit( 0 );
}
```

Listing 2. An Excel macro to input a saved chromosome and construct a spreadsheet that computes the trading signal.

	Load the output of the MACD3 program & generates a spreadsheet to compute trading signals	
BuildSystem		
MagicValue	503177	
	=SET.NAME("MacroSheet",GET.CELL(32,MagicValue))	Name of this sheet
	=SET.NAME("OrgOpenSheet",OPEN?("*.txt",,1,1,,,,2,1,))	Open Input File to Analyze (read only)
	=SET.NAME("OrgCell",ACTIVE.CELL())	Top left corner of text file
	=IF(NOT(OrgOpenSheet))	Check if file opened
	= ALERT("Could not open input file",2)	"Alert" the user to the problem
	= SET.NAME("OrgCell",0)	Clear Sheet Reference
	= HALT()	
	=END.IF()	
	=SET.NAME("NewOpenSheet",NEW(1))	Create a new work sheet
	=SET.NAME("NewCell",ACTIVE.CELL())	Top left corner of new sheet
	=IF(ISERROR(FIND("!",REFTEXT(OrgCell))))	
	= ALERT("Name of Original Sheet < "&REFTEXT(OrgCell)&" > is illegal",2)	
	= SET.NAME("OrgCell",0)	Clear sheet references
	= SET.NAME("NewCell",0)	
	= HALT()	
	=END.IF()	
	=SET.NAME("OrgSheet",LEFT(REFTEXT(OrgCell),FIND("!",REFTEXT(OrgCell))-1))	
	=IF(ISERROR(FIND("!",REFTEXT(NewCell))))	
	= ALERT("Name of new sheet < "&REFTEXT(NewCell)&" > is illegal",2)	
	= SET.NAME("OrgCell",0)	Clear sheet references
	= SET.NAME("NewCell",0)	
	= HALT()	
	=END.IF()	
	=SET.NAME("NewSheet",LEFT(REFTEXT(NewCell),FIND("!",REFTEXT(NewCell))-1))	
	=IF(OR(ROW(OrgCell)<>1,COLUMN(OrgCell)<>1))	Sanity Check
	= ALERT("Internal Error: OrgCell is not in top left corner!",2)	
	= HALT()	
	=END.IF()	
	=IF(OR(ROW(NewCell)<>1,COLUMN(NewCell)<>1))	Sanity Check
	= ALERT("Internal Error: NewCell is not in top left corner!",2)	
	= HALT()	
	=END.IF()	

	=FORMULA.GOTO(OFFSET(NewCell,1,0,1,1))	
	=FORMULA(MagicValue)	
	=SET.NAME("IndCount",DEREF(OrgCell))	Number of indicators to work with
	=SET.NAME("DurRange",OFFSET(OrgCell,1,1,2*IndCount,1))	Range for Durations
	=SET.NAME("DurMax",MAX(DurRange))	Maximum Duration
	=SET.NAME("Ind1Range",OFFSET(NewCell,DurMax+2,2,1,1))	Lower Left Corner of First Indicator Range
	=SET.NAME("Ind2Range",OFFSET(Ind1Range,DurMax+1,0,1,1))	Lower Left Corner of Second Indicator Range
	=SET.NAME("DataTop",OFFSET(Ind2Range,1,-1,1,1))	Top Left Corner of Data
	=SET.NAME("DataOrg",OFFSET(OrgCell,7+2*IndCount,0,1,1))	
	=SET.NAME("DataRows",DEREF(OFFSET(DataOrg,-1,0,1,1)))	Data Rows
	=SET.NAME("OrgWeights",OFFSET(OrgCell,1+2*IndCount,0,1,IndCount+1))	Weight Range
	=SET.NAME("NewWts",OFFSET(NewCell,1,2,1,1))	New Range
	=FORMULA.GOTO(OFFSET(DataOrg,0,0,DataRows,2))	Date & Data
	=COPY()	
	=FORMULA.GOTO(OFFSET(DataTop,0,-1,1,1))	Destination
	=PASTE()	
	=FORMULA.GOTO(OrgWeights)	Copy the Weights over to where they belong
	=COPY()	
	=FORMULA.GOTO(NewWts)	
	=PASTE()	
	=CALCULATION(3)	Manual Calculation Mode
	=FOR("Ind",0,IndCount-1)	Loop through each indicator & generate code
	= SET.NAME("Ind1Ref",OFFSET(Ind1Range,0,Ind,1,1))	Ref to first indicator
	= SET.NAME("IndRef",OFFSET(OrgCell,1+2*Ind,0,1,1))	First Column of First Indicator
	= SET.NAME("IndType",DEREF(IndRef))	Type code for first indicator
	= SET.NAME("IndLen",DEREF(OFFSET(IndRef,0,1,1,1)))	Length of indicator
	= FORMULA.GOTO(OFFSET(IndRef,0,2,1,IndLen))	Select the data
	= COPY()	To clip board
	= FORMULA.GOTO(OFFSET(Ind1Ref,1-IndLen,0,1,1))	Place to paste it
	= PASTE.SPECIAL(3,1,FALSE,TRUE)	Coefficients are in place
	= SET.NAME("Coef1Range",NewSheet&"!r"&TEXT(ROW(Ind1Ref)-IndLen+1,"#")&"c"&TEXT(COLUMN(Ind1Ref),"#")&":r"&TEXT(ROW(Ind1Ref),"#")&"c"&TEXT(COLUMN(Ind1Ref),"#"))	Formula Range for First Set of Coefficients

	=	SET.NAME("Data1Range",NewSheet&"!r["&TEXT(1-IndLen,"#")&"]c["&TEXT(-1-Ind,"#")&"]:rc["&TEXT(-1-Ind,"#")&"]")	Formula Range for corresponding data
	=	IF(IndType=3)	
	=	SET.NAME("Expr1","("&NewSheet&"!rc["&TEXT(-1-Ind,"#")&"]-min("&Data1Range&"))/(max("&Data1Range&")-min("&Data1Range&")+1.e-15)")	Stochastic
	=	ELSE()	
	=	SET.NAME("Expr1","sumproduct("&Data1Range&","&Coef1Range&")")	EMA/MA
	=	END.IF()	
	=	SET.NAME("Ind2Ref",OFFSET(Ind2Range,0,Ind,1,1))	Ref to first indicator
	=	SET.NAME("IndRef",OFFSET(OrgCell,2+2*Ind,0,1,1))	First Column of Second Indicator
	=	SET.NAME("IndType",DEREF(IndRef))	Type code for second indicator
	=	SET.NAME("IndLen",DEREF(OFFSET(IndRef,0,1,1,1)))	Length of indicator
	=	FORMULA.GOTO(OFFSET(IndRef,0,2,1,IndLen))	Select the data
	=	COPY()	To clip board
	=	FORMULA.GOTO(OFFSET(Ind2Ref,1-IndLen,0,1,1))	Place to paste it
	=	PASTE.SPECIAL(3,1,FALSE,TRUE)	Coefficients are in place
	=	SET.NAME("Coef2Range",NewSheet&"!r"&TEXT(ROW(Ind2Ref)-IndLen+1,"#")&"c"&TEXT(COLUMN(Ind2Ref),"#")&":r"&TEXT(ROW(Ind2Ref),"#")&"c"&TEXT(COLUMN(Ind2Ref),"#"))	Formula Range for First Set of Coefficients
	=	SET.NAME("Data2Range",NewSheet&"!r["&TEXT(1-IndLen,"#")&"]c["&TEXT(-1-Ind,"#")&"]:rc["&TEXT(-1-Ind,"#")&"]")	Formula Range for corresponding data
	=	IF(IndType=3)	
	=	SET.NAME("Expr2","("&NewSheet&"!rc["&TEXT(-1-Ind,"#")&"]-min("&Data2Range&"))/(max("&Data2Range&")-min("&Data2Range&")+1.e-15)")	Stochastic
	=	ELSE.IF(IndType=4)	
	=	SET.NAME("Expr2",MacroSheet&"!StochD("&Data1Range&","&Coef2Range&")")	Smoothed Stochastic
	=	ELSE()	
	=	SET.NAME("Expr2","sumproduct("&Data2Range&","&Coef2Range&")")	EMA/MA
	=	END.IF()	
	=	SET.NAME("WtsRef",NewSheet&"!r"&TEXT(ROW(NewWts),"#")&"c"&TEXT(COLUMN(NewWts)+Ind,"#"))	Weight Reference
	=	SET.NAME("Expr"," =if("&Expr1&" > "&Expr2&","&WtsRef&",-"&WtsRef&")")	Final Expression
	=	FORMULA.GOTO(OFFSET(Ind2Ref,DurMax,0,1,1))	Select the target area
	=	FORMULA(Expr)	Write it!
	=	COPY()	
	=	FORMULA.GOTO(OFFSET(Ind2Ref,DurMax,0,DataRows-DurMax+1,1))	
	=	PASTE()	
	=NEXT()		
	=SET.NAME("WtsRef",NewSheet&"!r"&TEXT(ROW(NewWts),"#")&"c"&TEXT(COLUMN(NewWts)+IndCount,"#"))	Bias Reference
	=SET.NAME("Ind2Ref",OFFSET(Ind2Range,0,IndCount,1,1))	Destination

	=SET.NAME("Expr","="&WtsRef&"+sum(rc["&TEXT(-IndCount,"#")&"]:rc[-1])")	Expression
	=FORMULA.GOTO(OFFSET(Ind2Ref,DurMax,0,1,1))	Select the target area
	=FORMULA(Expr)	Write it!
	=COPY()	
	=FORMULA.GOTO(OFFSET(Ind2Ref,DurMax,0,DataRows-DurMax+1,1))	
	=PASTE()	
	=FORMULA(0.1,OFFSET(TEXTREF(WtsRef),0,1,1,1))	Min Range
	=FORMULA(-0.1,OFFSET(TEXTREF(WtsRef),1,1,1,1))	Max Range
	=SET.NAME("Ind2Ref",OFFSET(Ind2Range,0,IndCount+1,1,1))	Destination
	=SET.NAME("Expr","=if(rc[-1]>"&REFTEXT(OFFSET(TEXTREF(WtsRef),0,1,1,1))&",1,if(rc[-1]<"&REFTEXT(OFFSET(TEXTREF(WtsRef),1,1,1,1))&",-1,0))")	
	=FORMULA.GOTO(OFFSET(Ind2Ref,DurMax,0,1,1))	Select the target area
	=FORMULA(Expr)	Write it!
	=COPY()	
	=FORMULA.GOTO(OFFSET(Ind2Ref,DurMax,0,DataRows-DurMax+1,1))	
	=PASTE()	
	=CALCULATION(1)	
	=ERROR(FALSE)	Turn off error checking
	=ACTIVATE(OrgSheet)	Close Data sheet
	=IF(NOT(ISERROR(B191)),CLOSE())	
	=ERROR(TRUE)	Trun error checking back on
	=ACTIVATE(NewSheet)	
	=SAVE.AS?(LEFT(OrgSheet,LEN(OrgSheet)-3)&"xls",1,,1,)	Save the File
	=SET.NAME("StochData")	Clear References to other sheets
	=SET.NAME("StochCell")	
	=SET.NAME("StochCoef")	
	=SET.NAME("StochDataRef")	
	=SET.NAME("StochDataRow")	
	=SET.NAME("StochCell")	
	=SET.NAME("OrgCell")	
	=SET.NAME("NewCell")	
	=SET.NAME("DurRange")	
	=SET.NAME("Ind1Range")	
	=SET.NAME("Ind2Range")	
	=SET.NAME("DataTop")	
	=SET.NAME("DataOrg")	
	=SET.NAME("OrgWeights")	
	=SET.NAME("NewWts")	
	=SET.NAME("Ind1Ref")	
	=SET.NAME("Ind2Ref")	
	=SET.NAME("IndRef")	
	=HALT()	Done

Listing 3. An Excel macro to update a previously generated spreadsheet.

	Update Formulas when new data is added at the end of the sheet	
UpdateFormulas		
	=SET.NAME("UpdOpen",OPEN?("*.xls",,0,1,,,,2,1,))	Open Input File to Analyze
	=SET.NAME("UpdCell",ACTIVE.CELL())	Flag active cell
	=IF(NOT(UpdOpen))	Check if file opened
	= ALERT("Could not open input file to update",2)	
	= HALT()	
	=END.IF()	
	=FORMULA.GOTO(UpdCell)	Check for proper format
	=SELECT("r2c1")	
	=IF(ACTIVE.CELL() < > MagicValue)	
	= ALERT("Spread sheet just loaded is not proper format",2)	
	= HALT()	
	=END.IF()	
	=SELECT("r3c1")	Start of Data
	=SELECT.END(4)	Skip Blank Space
	=SELECT.END(4)	Skip to End of Data
	=SET.NAME("UpdLDR",ROW(ACTIVE.CELL()))	Row number of last data row
	=SELECT("rc3")	Bottom of formulas
	=IF(ISNUMBER(ACTIVE.CELL()))	
	= ALERT("Spreadsheet appears to have already been updated.",2)	
	= HALT()	
	=END.IF()	
	=SELECT.END(3)	Last formula
	=SET.NAME("UpdLFR",ACTIVE.CELL())	Row of last formula
	=SELECT.END(2)	Right most column
	=SET.NAME("UpdFormulas",OFFSET(UpdLFR,0,0,1,COLUMN(ACTIVE.CELL())-COLUMN(UpdLFR)+1))	
	=SET.NAME("UpdNewRange",OFFSET(UpdLFR,1,0,UpdLDR-ROW(UpdLFR),1))	
	=FORMULA.GOTO(UpdFormulas)	Select a row of formulas
	=COPY()	
	=FORMULA.GOTO(UpdNewRange)	Paste them into the new area
	=PASTE()	
	=CANCEL.COPY()	
	=SELECT("rc1")	Point back to first column
	=WINDOW.MAXIMIZE()	
	=SAVE()	Save the file
	=HALT()	

Listing 4. An Excel macro function required to compute %D stochastic.

	Compute Smoothed Stochastic	
StochD		Lane's D Stochastic
	=RESULT(1)	Result is a value
	=ARGUMENT("StochData",8)	Data Reference
	=ARGUMENT("StochCoef",8)	Coefficients
	=SET.NAME("StochRes",0)	Result
	=SET.NAME("StochDataRef",OFFSET(StochData,1-ROWS(StochCoef),0,ROWS(StochData),1))	Offset for first coef
	=SET.NAME("StochDataRow",OFFSET(StochDataRef,ROWS(StochData)-1,0,1,1))	Last Data Item
	=FOR.CELL("StochCell",StochCoef)	For each cell in coefficients
	= SET.NAME("StochRes",StochRes+DEREF(StochCell)*(DEREF(StochDataRow)-MIN(StochDataRef))/(MAX(StochDataRef)-MIN(StochDataRef)+0.000000000000001))	Accumulate result
	= SET.NAME("StochDataRef",OFFSET(StochDataRef,1,0,ROWS(StochDataRef),1))	Next data block
	= SET.NAME("StochDataRow",OFFSET(StochDataRow,1,0,1,1))	Next data item
	=NEXT()	
	=RETURN(StochRes)	Return result

If your  lays golden ,

**would you
sell it?**

Why would anyone offer to sell you a "million-dollar" trading system for peanuts? He'll likely profit more by selling it than using it! So what's a trader to do? Put aside those unprofitable systems-of-the-month and develop your own.

Analyze and forecast ... with tools used by professionals!

Proper data preprocessing greatly improves a trading system's performance. Large firms can afford having math professors preprocess their data. Can you?

We offer a line of preprocessing tools designed to cut HOURS of your labor down to seconds. For example, we have designed an ultra smooth, "zero lag" moving average. Note on the chart how it glides **through** the data rather than after it.. This filter is perfect for forecasts because, unlike some other low-lag moving averages, our filter uses only historical price data (no forward peeking).

We offer other advanced tools too, as well as training seminars and consulting services. For more details, see our company description in the back of this book.

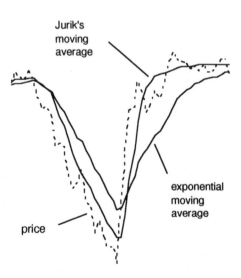

JURIK RESEARCH ◆ PO 2379, Aptos, CA ◆ 408-688-5893   FAX 408-688-8947

Chapter 7

TRADING THE S&P 500 WITH A NEURAL NETWORK

John Kean, Principal
KEAN ANALYTICS

INTRODUCTION

Recent years have seen a great deal of application of artificial intelligence methods to finance. In particular, neural networks have been applied to such diverse things as rating mortgage applicants, detecting credit-card fraud, and grading corporate bonds. But by far the greatest quest in neural net application in finance has been in price prediction.

Neural network software has a special mystique associated with it. This is because it imitates the learning mechanism of the brain while teaching itself the relationship between causal/diagnostic factors (inputs), and results (patterns). Conceptually, neural networks are composed of layers of processors that are connected to each other by variably weighted links. This is an approximation of the relationship between the neurons, dendrites, and synapses of biological systems.

The sort of network typically used in financial market prediction has three types of layers: First, an input layer through which preprocessed causal/diagnostic data is fed in; adjacent to this are one or more "hidden layers," which lie between the inputs and the third (output) layer. The resultant data, which is a response to the inputs, makes up the output layer. During training, the neural net seeks solutions to the relationships between the causal/diagnostic data and the resultant data by developing a cryptic set of variably weighted interconnections between the three layers.

Before starting out on any analysis, whether it be of financial markets, voting demographics, or submarine sonar returns, it's sensible to frame some questions. First, is it reasonable to assume that the variable to be predicted is nonrandom? For example, it's always amusing to see advertisements for methods purported to predict lottery numbers. These numbers are selected by processes that are designed to be random, and if they aren't, it's because somebody is rigging the game. By definition, it's impossible to predict a random process. With reference to the stock market, some academics have in the past claimed that price moves are indeed random, and that any analytical approach is doomed. After two decades, this assertion has been largely discounted. Nowadays, there is a general acceptance of the idea that while stock price moves are very hard to predict, they are related to fathomable evolving economic and market factors. These partially predictive relationships are occasionally overwhelmed by exogenous forces like surprise invasions, coups in great-power countries, and behind the scenes financial market manipulations. Since stock price moves are not an entirely random process, the market is a valid subject for analysis.

Second, positing nonrandomness, can we determine some causal/diagnostic factors that historically tended to be precursors to price changes? With a good historical financial database, it's not difficult to show that rough relationships do exist between elements like interest rates, earnings, dividends, and subsequent stock index changes. But can we somehow develop these various factors into a predictive system that works sufficiently well on data from the past?

Knowing that relationships and tendencies exist between variables is still a long way from achieving a predictive system that a trader or investor can apply with confidence and discipline. The nice thing about neural net analysis is that once provided with inputs, the process will repetitiously search for a set of patterns and relationships. In contrast, when developing an expert system, a human has to supply the basic rules that can then be modified and applied by the computer. Third, assuming we can develop a predictive method based on past relationships, how confident can we be that these relationships will continue to work in the future? All that can be realistically done with any predictive analysis is to improve the probability of success—not create a certainty of it. The best policy is to stick to sensible inputs. Anyone who watches the markets knows that all sorts of claims exist vis-a-vis the predictive value of things like planetary movements, Superbowl outcomes, and disparate statistical series. It's easy for otherwise sensible people to get caught up in pseudo-predictive relationships.

Recognize that there are an infinite number of trackable events going on in the world. It's certain that given this immeasurably large field to choose from, people will periodically turn up sets of coincidental nuances that appear to be Rosetta stones. If there is no fundamental reason for a relationship to exist between two variables, it's best to reject it as having any lasting value before involving it in the neural net training process.

SETTING UP A NEURAL NET FINANCIAL DATABASE

The first step in conducting a neural net analysis involves building a file of historical data to train the net on. Each line of the file contains historical inputs along with a corresponding index price level. In this discussion, our objective is to determine the valuation level of the S&P 500 stock index on a monthly basis.

Ideas vary widely on what factors are important in determining stock prices, but we'll stick to just four inputs, whose importance most people would be hard pressed to refute. These are: dividends, earnings, 3-month Treasury bill rates, and longest Treasury bond yields. Higher earnings and dividends should support higher stock prices. Conversely, higher interest rates undermine prices by drawing investment funds away from stocks and by dampening profits through lower sales and higher interest expenses.

There's no unique way of determining the optimum number of training observations, or time periods, to use in training. Too brief a time span will limit the scope of the lessons the neural net learns during training. On the other end of the scale, if you train over too long a period, the net will be burdened with learning archaic relationships. It's important to make the training span long enough to encompass a spectrum of situations. My bias is to train nets on at least two or three hundred observations. In this case, this allows us to include several bear and bull market episodes, thus constituting a good test of versatility.

A generic vulnerability of neural nets is that when confronted with material that is difficult to learn, they have a disposition to resort to memorization instead of comprehension. There's a big difference between these two forms of knowledge. Memorization is brittle and superficial, and as a type of knowledge, it is not enduring. Conversely, comprehension involves deciphering genuine relationships among variables, and thus has durability as long as those causal/diagnostic relationships persist. Needless to say, financial market prediction is a very difficult class of problem.

The memorization problem was combatted in the analysis later shown here by using Talon Development's "@Brain" neural net system, under a training option designed to defeat memorization. With this option, training progress is evaluated on error minimization in the user-specified testing data set (versus the training set). The testing inputs are not seen during the training runs, and are therefore not memorizable. Additionally, no less than one-third of the data was totally withheld from the training process, and the effectiveness of the trained neural nets on this out-of-sample data set was used as a criterion in evaluation.

DESCRIPTION OF THE NEURAL NET SETUP

As mentioned above, only four inputs to the neural net were used. The objective of the training was for the neural net to determine the S&P 500 valuation for a given level of earnings, dividends, Treasury bill rates, and Treasury bond yields. No clever technical analysis methods were used, and the input data wasn't preprocessed or trimmed for excursions. The neural net saw one-third of the rows as training data inputs and one-third as testing outputs. The other one-third of the data was totally withheld and was used to evaluate the final neural net's validity. This was a plain vanilla approach. The net was structured with the four previously mentioned inputs, a single hidden layer with two neurons, and an output layer comprised of a single continuous variable (the calculated valuation level of the S&P 500). The analysis covered 334 months, ending with April 1994.

Several training runs were made from different initial connection weightings, and resultant trained nets were analyzed for their usefulness. Once a neural net was done training, its validity was evaluated by using it in simulated trading. Every month was traded, with a long signal being defined as the actual S&P 500 price being below the neural net calculated price. A short signal was defined as the reverse of the above situation. Trading evaluations were carried out by taking statistical correlations between the series of trade results, and the series of available returns (i.e., as if each trade had been a winner). These statistical correlations were made for each category of data: the training set, the testing set, and the out-of-sample set. (The trades of the selected net are listed in Table 1). Correlations of +.3 and above were considered favorable.

If a net looked good from the standpoint of its trade correlations, the next step was to evaluate it from a functional standpoint. Using April 1994 numbers, each of the four inputs was individually varied from minus through plus 20 percent its actual value in calculating the neural net's output, while holding the other inputs constant. The results for the chosen net are shown in Figures 1 through 4.

Figure 1 shows the effect on the neural-net-calculated S&P 500 valuation of varying the longest Treasury bond yield from around 5.75 percent to about 8.75 percent. As might be expected, higher bond yields result in a lower S&P 500 level, in a nearly linear fashion. A similar relationship is shown in Figure 2 for 3-month Treasury bill rates. Figures 3 and 4 show that higher dividends and earnings relate to higher S&P 500 levels, as expected, but with some departure from linearity. Inspecting the range of *y*-axis values shows that valuation over these minus to plus 20 percent ranges is dependent on dividend level, Treasury bond yield, 3-month Treasury bill rate, and earnings level, in order of descending importance.

This step of looking at neural nets from their functional aspects rather than just their error minimization stats and trading characteristics can be important. Several nets that looked good otherwise, failed the functional common sense test. In several cases, the function test showed higher dividends and/or earnings leading to higher S&P 500 levels up to a certain point, and then further increases leading to lower price

**Figure 1.   T-bond yields versus neural net output.
Values for end of April 1994.**

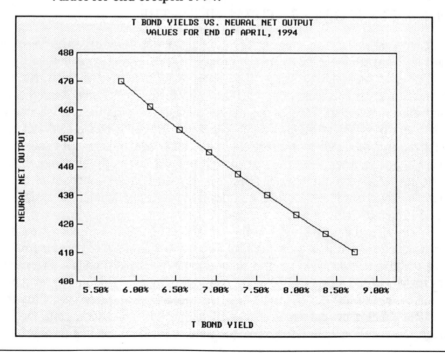

**Figure 2.   T-bill rates versus neural net output.
Values for end of April 1994.**

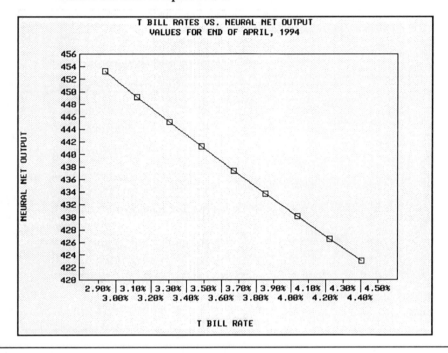

**Figure 3.   Dividends versus neural net output.
Values for end of April 1994.**

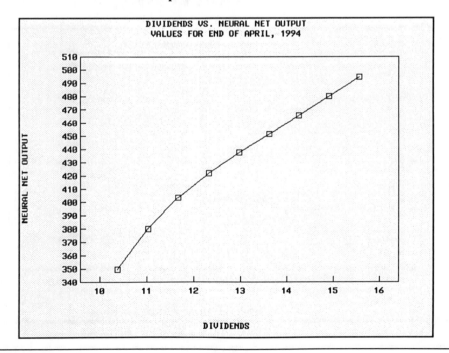

Figure 4.   Earnings versus neural net output.
            Values for end of April 1994.

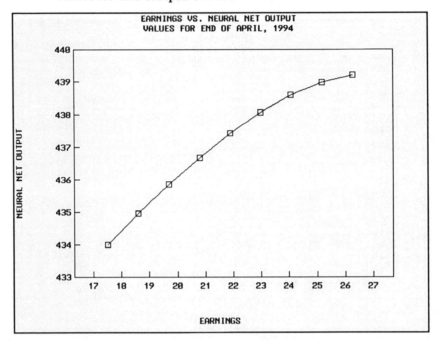

Figure 5.   S&P 500 valuation model trading.

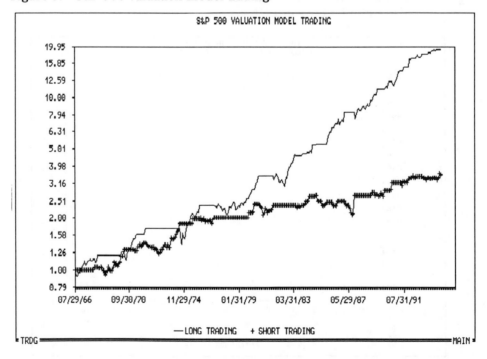

levels. Even in the convoluted world of financial markets, this is a nonstarter. When training and evaluating neural nets, it's best to remember that these things have no common sense or knowledge of the world outside of the data they are exposed to. In the quest to minimize the error of their outputs over a given set of data, some unrealistic relationships can be generated.

The selected net's trading is shown in Figure 5, and can be compared to the course of the S&P 500 index over the period (shown in Figure 6). The trading results were respectable. The rate of return per annum for combined long and short trading was 16.4 percent, excluding dividends when long. The annualized long trading return was 11.4 percent; the short trading return was 4.7 percent. The trading analysis required a trade during every one of the 334 months covered, and 62.35 percent were winners. The gain over the 12-month period ending with April 1994 was 13.78 percent. Not bad for a plain vanilla treatment!

Figure 6.   S&P 500 stock index.

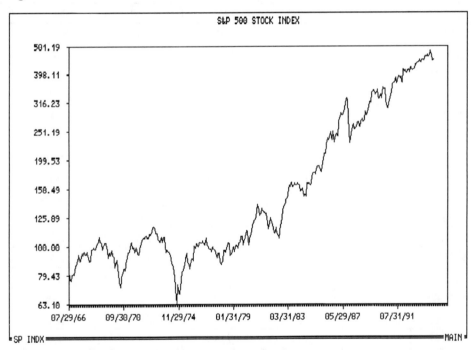

Table 1. List of simulated trades in this analysis.

Date	Available Trade Gain	Trade Gain/Loss	Test Data Set	Train Data Set	Out-of-Sample Data Set
08/31/66	7.78%	–7.78%	–7.78%	NA	NA
09/30/66	0.70%	–0.70%	NA	–0.70%	NA
10/31/66	4.75%	4.75%	NA	NA	4.75%
11/30/66	0.31%	0.31%	NA	0.31%	NA
12/30/66	0.15%	–0.15%	NA	NA	–0.15%
01/31/67	7.82%	7.82%	7.82%	NA	NA
02/28/67	0.20%	0.20%	NA	0.20%	NA
03/31/67	3.94%	3.94%	3.94%	NA	NA
04/28/67	4.22%	4.22%	NA	NA	4.22%
05/31/67	5.24%	–5.24%	NA	NA	–5.24%
06/30/67	1.75%	1.75%	NA	1.75%	NA
07/31/67	4.53%	4.53%	4.53%	NA	NA
08/31/67	1.17%	–1.17%	–1.17%	NA	NA
09/29/67	3.28%	3.28%	NA	3.28%	NA
10/31/67	2.91%	–2.91%	NA	NA	–2.91%
11/30/67	0.11%	0.11%	NA	0.11%	NA
12/29/67	2.63%	2.63%	2.63%	NA	NA
01/31/68	4.59%	4.59%	NA	NA	4.59%
02/29/68	3.12%	–3.12%	–3.12%	NA	NA
03/29/68	0.94%	0.94%	NA	NA	0.94%
04/30/68	8.19%	8.19%	NA	8.19%	NA
05/31/68	1.10%	–1.10%	–1.10%	NA	NA
06/28/68	0.90%	–0.90%	NA	–0.90%	NA
07/31/68	1.88%	1.88%	NA	NA	1.88%
08/30/68	1.13%	–1.13%	NA	NA	–1.13%
09/30/68	3.71%	–3.71%	NA	–3.71%	NA
10/31/68	0.72%	–0.72%	–0.72%	NA	NA
11/29/68	4.58%	–4.58%	NA	NA	–4.58%
12/31/68	4.34%	4.34%	4.34%	NA	NA
01/31/69	0.83%	0.83%	NA	0.83%	NA
02/28/69	4.97%	4.97%	NA	4.97%	NA
03/31/69	3.33%	–3.33%	–3.33%	NA	NA
04/30/69	2.10%	–2.10%	NA	NA	–2.10%
5/30/69	0.22%	0.22%	NA	NA	0.22%
6/30/69	5.88%	5.88%	5.88%	NA	NA

Date	Available Trade Gain	Trade Gain/Loss	Test Data Set	Train Data Set	Out-of-Sample Data Set
07/31/69	6.40%	6.40%	NA	6.40%	NA
08/29/69	3.85%	−3.85%	−3.85%	NA	NA
09/30/69	2.57%	2.57%	NA	2.57%	NA
10/31/69	4.24%	−4.24%	NA	NA	−4.24%
11/28/69	3.66%	3.66%	3.66%	NA	NA
12/31/69	1.90%	1.90%	NA	1.90%	NA
01/30/70	8.28%	8.28%	NA	NA	8.28%
2/27/70	5.27%	5.27%	NA	NA	5.27%
3/31/70	0.15%	−0.15%	NA	−0.15%	NA
04/30/70	9.95%	9.95%	9.95%	NA	NA
05/29/70	6.10%	−6.10%	NA	−6.10%	NA
06/30/70	5.00%	−5.00%	NA	NA	−5.00%
7/31/70	7.33%	7.33%	7.33%	NA	NA
08/31/70	4.45%	4.45%	NA	4.45%	NA
09/30/70	3.30%	3.30%	NA	NA	3.30%
10/30/70	1.14%	−1.14%	−1.14%	NA	NA
11/30/70	4.74%	4.74%	4.74%	NA	NA
12/31/70	5.68%	5.68%	NA	NA	5.68%
1/29/71	4.05%	4.05%	NA	4.05%	NA
02/26/71	0.90%	−0.90%	NA	NA	−0.90%
3/31/71	3.68%	3.68%	3.68%	NA	NA
04/30/71	3.63%	3.63%	NA	3.63%	NA
05/31/71	4.34%	4.34%	NA	4.34%	NA
06/30/71	0.07%	−0.07%	−0.07%	NA	NA
07/30/71	4.31%	4.31%	NA	NA	4.31%
8/31/71	3.48%	−3.48%	−3.48%	NA	NA
09/30/71	0.70%	0.70%	NA	0.70%	NA
10/29/71	4.36%	4.36%	NA	NA	4.36%
11/30/71	0.25%	−0.25%	−0.25%	NA	NA
12/31/71	8.62%	8.62%	NA	NA	8.62%
1/31/72	1.50%	−1.50%	NA	−1.50%	NA
02/29/72	2.75%	−2.75%	NA	NA	−2.75%
3/31/72	0.59%	−0.59%	−0.59%	NA	NA
04/28/72	0.44%	−0.44%	NA	−0.44%	NA
05/31/72	1.70%	−1.70%	NA	NA	−1.70%
6/30/72	2.23%	2.23%	2.23%	NA	NA

Date	Available Trade Gain	Trade Gain/Loss	Test Data Set	Train Data Set	Out-of-Sample Data Set
07/31/72	0.23%	–0.23%	NA	–0.23%	NA
08/31/72	3.33%	–3.33%	NA	–3.33%	NA
09/29/72	0.49%	0.49%	NA	NA	0.49%
10/31/72	0.92%	–0.92%	–0.92%	NA	NA
11/30/72	4.36%	–4.36%	–4.36%	NA	NA
12/29/72	1.17%	–1.17%	NA	–1.17%	NA
01/31/73	1.74%	1.74%	NA	NA	1.74%
2/28/73	3.90%	3.90%	NA	3.90%	NA
03/30/73	0.14%	0.14%	NA	NA	0.14%
4/30/73	4.25%	4.25%	4.25%	NA	NA
05/31/73	1.92%	1.92%	1.92%	NA	NA
06/29/73	0.66%	0.66%	NA	NA	0.66%
7/31/73	3.66%	–3.66%	NA	–3.66%	NA
08/31/73	3.81%	3.81%	3.81%	NA	NA
09/28/73	3.86%	–3.86%	NA	–3.86%	NA
10/31/73	0.13%	0.13%	NA	NA	0.13%
11/30/73	12.85%	12.85%	NA	NA	12.85%
12/31/73	1.63%	–1.63%	–1.63%	NA	NA
01/31/74	1.01%	1.01%	NA	1.01%	NA
02/28/74	0.36%	0.36%	0.36%	NA	NA
03/29/74	2.38%	2.38%	NA	2.38%	NA
04/30/74	4.06%	4.06%	NA	NA	4.06%
5/31/74	3.47%	3.47%	NA	NA	3.47%
6/28/74	1.49%	1.49%	1.49%	NA	NA
07/31/74	8.44%	8.44%	NA	8.44%	NA
08/30/74	9.03%	–9.03%	NA	–9.03%	NA
09/30/74	11.93%	–11.93%	–11.93%	NA	NA
10/31/74	16.30%	16.30%	NA	NA	16.30%
11/29/74	5.32%	–5.32%	NA	NA	–5.32%
12/31/74	2.02%	–2.02%	–2.02%	NA	NA
01/31/75	12.28%	12.28%	NA	12.28%	NA
02/28/75	5.99%	5.99%	NA	NA	5.99%
3/31/75	2.17%	2.17%	2.17%	NA	NA
04/30/75	4.73%	4.73%	NA	4.73%	NA
05/30/75	4.41%	4.41%	NA	4.41%	NA
06/30/75	4.43%	4.43%	4.43%	NA	NA

Date	Available Trade Gain	Trade Gain/Loss	Test Data Set	Train Data Set	Out-of-Sample Data Set
07/31/75	7.26%	7.26%	NA	NA	7.26%
8/29/75	2.11%	−2.11%	NA	−2.11%	NA
09/30/75	3.46%	−3.46%	NA	NA	−3.46%
10/31/75	6.16%	6.16%	6.16%	NA	NA
11/28/75	2.47%	2.47%	NA	2.47%	NA
12/31/75	1.15%	−1.15%	−1.15%	NA	NA
01/30/76	11.83%	11.83%	NA	NA	11.83%
2/27/76	1.15%	1.15%	NA	1.15%	NA
03/31/76	2.98%	−2.98%	NA	NA	−2.98%
4/30/76	1.11%	1.11%	1.11%	NA	NA
05/31/76	1.46%	1.46%	1.46%	NA	NA
06/30/76	3.93%	−3.93%	NA	−3.93%	NA
07/30/76	0.81%	0.81%	NA	NA	0.81%
8/31/76	0.52%	0.52%	NA	0.52%	NA
09/30/76	2.21%	−2.21%	−2.21%	NA	NA
10/29/76	2.27%	2.27%	NA	NA	2.27%
11/30/76	0.78%	0.78%	NA	NA	0.78%
12/31/76	4.99%	−4.99%	−4.99%	NA	NA
01/31/77	5.32%	5.32%	NA	5.32%	NA
02/28/77	2.21%	2.21%	NA	NA	2.21%
3/31/77	1.40%	−1.40%	NA	−1.40%	NA
04/29/77	0.02%	0.02%	0.02%	NA	NA
05/31/77	2.36%	−2.36%	NA	NA	−2.36%
6/30/77	4.54%	4.54%	NA	4.54%	NA
07/29/77	1.62%	−1.62%	−1.62%	NA	NA
08/31/77	2.10%	−2.10%	−2.10%	NA	NA
09/30/77	0.25%	−0.25%	NA	NA	−0.25%
10/31/77	4.34%	−4.34%	NA	−4.34%	NA
11/30/77	2.70%	2.70%	NA	2.70%	NA
12/30/77	0.28%	0.28%	0.28%	NA	NA
01/31/78	6.15%	−6.15%	NA	NA	−6.15%
2/28/78	2.48%	−2.48%	−2.48%	NA	NA
03/31/78	2.49%	2.49%	NA	NA	2.49%
4/28/78	8.54%	8.54%	NA	8.54%	NA
05/31/78	0.48%	0.48%	0.48%	NA	NA
06/30/78	1.81%	−1.81%	NA	−1.81%	NA

Date	Available Trade Gain	Trade Gain/Loss	Test Data Set	Train Data Set	Out-of-Sample Data Set
07/31/78	5.39%	5.39%	NA	NA	5.39%
8/31/78	2.59%	2.59%	2.59%	NA	NA
09/29/78	0.73%	−0.73%	NA	−0.73%	NA
10/31/78	9.16%	−9.16%	NA	NA	−9.16%
11/30/78	1.66%	1.66%	1.66%	NA	NA
12/29/78	1.49%	1.49%	NA	NA	1.49%
1/31/79	3.97%	3.97%	NA	3.97%	NA
02/28/79	3.65%	−3.65%	NA	−3.65%	NA
03/30/79	5.52%	5.52%	5.52%	NA	NA
04/30/79	0.17%	0.17%	NA	NA	0.17%
5/31/79	2.63%	−2.63%	−2.63%	NA	NA
06/29/79	3.87%	3.87%	NA	NA	3.87%
7/31/79	0.87%	0.87%	NA	0.87%	NA
08/31/79	5.31%	5.31%	NA	NA	5.31%
9/28/79	0.00%	0.00%	0.00%	NA	NA
10/31/79	7.37%	7.37%	NA	7.37%	NA
11/30/79	4.26%	4.26%	NA	4.26%	NA
12/31/79	1.68%	1.68%	NA	NA	1.68%
1/31/80	5.76%	5.76%	5.76%	NA	NA
02/29/80	0.44%	0.44%	NA	NA	0.44%
3/31/80	11.33%	11.33%	NA	11.33%	NA
04/30/80	4.11%	4.11%	4.11%	NA	NA
05/30/80	4.66%	4.66%	4.66%	NA	NA
06/30/80	2.70%	2.70%	NA	2.70%	NA
07/31/80	6.50%	6.50%	NA	NA	6.50%
8/29/80	0.58%	−0.58%	NA	−0.58%	NA
09/30/80	2.45%	−2.45%	NA	NA	−2.45%
10/31/80	1.58%	−1.58%	−1.58%	NA	NA
11/28/80	9.29%	−9.29%	NA	−9.29%	NA
12/31/80	3.51%	3.51%	3.51%	NA	NA
01/30/81	4.79%	4.79%	NA	NA	4.79%
2/27/81	1.31%	−1.31%	NA	NA	−1.31%
3/31/81	3.48%	−3.48%	−3.48%	NA	NA
04/30/81	2.40%	2.40%	NA	2.40%	NA
05/29/81	0.17%	0.17%	NA	0.17%	NA
06/30/81	1.05%	1.05%	NA	NA	1.05%

Date	Available Trade Gain	Trade Gain/Loss	Test Data Set	Train Data Set	Out-of-Sample Data Set
7/31/81	0.22%	0.22%	0.22%	NA	NA
08/31/81	6.62%	6.62%	6.62%	NA	NA
09/30/81	5.38%	−5.38%	NA	NA	−5.38%
10/30/81	4.91%	4.91%	NA	4.91%	NA
11/30/81	3.66%	3.66%	NA	NA	3.66%
12/31/81	3.01%	−3.01%	NA	−3.01%	NA
01/29/82	1.75%	−1.75%	−1.75%	NA	NA
02/26/82	6.05%	−6.05%	−6.05%	NA	NA
03/31/82	1.02%	−1.02%	NA	NA	−1.02%
4/30/82	4.00%	4.00%	NA	4.00%	NA
05/31/82	3.92%	−3.92%	NA	NA	−3.92%
6/30/82	2.03%	−2.03%	−2.03%	NA	NA
07/30/82	2.30%	−2.30%	NA	−2.30%	NA
08/31/82	11.60%	11.60%	NA	NA	11.60%
9/30/82	0.76%	0.76%	NA	0.76%	NA
10/29/82	11.04%	11.04%	11.04%	NA	NA
11/30/82	3.60%	3.60%	NA	NA	3.60%
12/31/82	1.52%	1.52%	NA	1.52%	NA
01/31/83	3.31%	3.31%	3.31%	NA	NA
02/28/83	1.89%	1.89%	1.89%	NA	NA
03/31/83	3.32%	3.32%	NA	3.32%	NA
04/29/83	7.50%	7.50%	NA	NA	7.50%
5/31/83	1.24%	−1.24%	NA	−1.24%	NA
06/30/83	3.40%	−3.40%	NA	NA	−3.40%
7/29/83	3.41%	3.41%	3.41%	NA	NA
08/31/83	1.12%	−1.12%	−1.12%	NA	NA
09/30/83	1.01%	−1.01%	NA	NA	−1.01%
10/31/83	1.54%	1.54%	NA	1.54%	NA
11/30/83	1.74%	1.74%	NA	NA	1.74%
12/30/83	0.89%	0.89%	0.89%	NA	NA
01/31/84	0.92%	0.92%	NA	0.92%	NA
02/29/84	4.05%	4.05%	NA	NA	4.05%
3/30/84	1.35%	1.35%	1.35%	NA	NA
04/30/84	0.54%	0.54%	NA	0.54%	NA
05/31/84	6.30%	6.30%	6.30%	NA	NA
06/29/84	1.75%	1.75%	NA	1.75%	NA

Date	Available Trade Gain	Trade Gain/Loss	Test Data Set	Train Data Set	Out-of-Sample Data Set
07/31/84	1.65%	−1.65%	NA	NA	−1.65%
8/31/84	10.63%	10.63%	NA	10.63%	NA
09/28/84	0.35%	−0.35%	NA	NA	−0.35%
10/31/84	0.01%	0.01%	0.01%	NA	NA
11/30/84	1.53%	1.53%	NA	NA	1.53%
12/31/84	2.24%	2.24%	2.24%	NA	NA
01/31/85	6.90%	−6.90%	NA	−6.90%	NA
02/28/85	0.86%	−0.86%	NA	−0.86%	NA
03/29/85	0.29%	0.29%	NA	NA	0.29%
4/30/85	0.46%	0.46%	0.46%	NA	NA
05/31/85	5.14%	−5.14%	−5.14%	NA	NA
06/28/85	1.19%	−1.19%	NA	NA	−1.19%
7/31/85	0.49%	0.49%	NA	0.49%	NA
08/30/85	1.21%	1.21%	1.21%	NA	NA
09/30/85	3.60%	3.60%	NA	NA	3.60%
10/31/85	4.25%	4.25%	NA	4.25%	NA
11/29/85	6.51%	6.51%	NA	NA	6.51%
12/31/85	4.51%	4.51%	NA	4.51%	NA
01/31/86	0.24%	−0.24%	−0.24%	NA	NA
02/28/86	7.15%	7.15%	NA	7.15%	NA
03/31/86	5.01%	−5.01%	−5.01%	NA	NA
04/30/86	1.44%	1.44%	NA	NA	1.44%
5/30/86	5.02%	5.02%	NA	NA	5.02%
6/30/86	1.39%	−1.39%	−1.39%	NA	NA
07/31/86	6.23%	6.23%	NA	6.23%	NA
08/29/86	7.12%	7.12%	7.12%	NA	NA
09/30/86	8.54%	−8.54%	NA	NA	−8.54%
10/31/86	5.47%	5.47%	NA	5.47%	NA
11/28/86	2.15%	2.15%	2.15%	NA	NA
12/31/86	2.83%	−2.83%	NA	−2.83%	NA
01/30/87	13.18%	13.18%	NA	NA	13.18%
2/27/87	3.56%	−3.56%	−3.56%	NA	NA
03/31/87	2.57%	−2.57%	NA	NA	−2.57%
4/30/87	1.16%	1.16%	NA	1.16%	NA
05/29/87	0.60%	−0.60%	−0.60%	NA	NA
06/30/87	4.57%	−4.57%	NA	−4.57%	NA

Date	Available Trade Gain	Trade Gain/Loss	Test Data Set	Train Data Set	Out-of-Sample Data Set
07/31/87	4.60%	−4.60%	NA	NA	−4.60%
8/31/87	3.38%	−3.38%	NA	NA	−3.38%
9/30/87	2.48%	2.48%	2.48%	NA	NA
10/30/87	27.82%	27.82%	NA	27.82%	NA
11/30/87	8.53%	−8.53%	NA	NA	−8.53%
12/31/87	7.29%	7.29%	7.29%	NA	NA
01/29/88	4.04%	4.04%	NA	4.04%	NA
02/29/88	4.18%	4.18%	4.18%	NA	NA
03/31/88	3.33%	−3.33%	NA	−3.33%	NA
04/29/88	0.94%	0.94%	NA	NA	0.94%
5/31/88	0.32%	0.32%	0.32%	NA	NA
06/30/88	4.33%	4.33%	NA	4.33%	NA
07/29/88	0.54%	−0.54%	NA	NA	−0.54% f
8/31/88	3.86%	−3.86%	−3.86%	NA	NA
09/30/88	3.97%	3.97%	NA	NA	3.97%
10/31/88	2.60%	2.60%	NA	2.60%	NA
11/30/88	1.89%	−1.89%	NA	NA	−1.89%
12/30/88	1.47%	1.47%	NA	1.47%	NA
01/31/89	7.11%	7.11%	7.11%	NA	NA
02/28/89	2.98%	2.98%	NA	2.98%	NA
03/31/89	2.08%	2.08%	NA	NA	2.08%
4/28/89	5.01%	5.01%	5.01%	NA	NA
05/31/89	3.39%	−3.39%	NA	−3.39%	NA
06/30/89	0.80%	0.80%	0.80%	NA	NA
07/31/89	8.84%	8.84%	NA	NA	8.84%
8/31/89	1.53%	−1.53%	NA	−1.53%	NA
09/29/89	0.66%	0.66%	NA	NA	0.66%
10/31/89	2.58%	2.58%	2.58%	NA	NA
11/30/89	1.63%	−1.63%	NA	−1.63%	NA
12/29/89	2.10%	−2.10%	NA	NA	−2.10%
1/31/90	7.39%	7.39%	7.39%	NA	NA
02/28/90	0.85%	0.85%	NA	0.85%	NA
03/30/90	2.43%	2.43%	2.43%	NA	NA
04/30/90	2.69%	−2.69%	NA	NA	−2.69%
5/31/90	9.20%	9.20%	NA	NA	9.20%
6/29/90	0.90%	0.90%	NA	0.90%	NA

Date	Available Trade Gain	Trade Gain/Loss	Test Data Set	Train Data Set	Out-of-Sample Data Set
07/31/90	0.53%	0.53%	0.53%	NA	NA
08/31/90	10.41%	10.41%	NA	NA	10.41%
9/28/90	5.12%	−5.12%	−5.12%	NA	NA
10/31/90	0.67%	−0.67%	NA	−0.67%	NA
11/30/90	5.99%	5.99%	NA	5.99%	NA
12/31/90	2.48%	2.48%	NA	NA	2.48%
1/31/91	4.15%	4.15%	4.15%	NA	NA
02/28/91	6.73%	6.73%	NA	6.73%	NA
03/29/91	2.22%	2.22%	NA	NA	2.22%
4/30/91	0.03%	−0.03%	−0.03%	NA	NA
05/31/91	3.71%	−3.71%	NA	NA	−3.71%
6/28/91	5.03%	5.03%	NA	5.03%	NA
07/31/91	4.49%	4.49%	4.49%	NA	NA
08/30/91	1.93%	−1.93%	NA	NA	−1.93%
9/30/91	1.95%	1.95%	NA	1.95%	NA
10/31/91	1.17%	−1.17%	−1.17%	NA	NA
11/29/91	4.59%	4.59%	NA	NA	4.59%
12/31/91	11.16%	11.16%	11.16%	NA	NA
01/31/92	2.03%	2.03%	NA	2.03%	NA
02/28/92	0.96%	0.96%	NA	NA	0.96%
3/31/92	2.23%	2.23%	NA	2.23%	NA
04/30/92	2.71%	−2.71%	−2.71%	NA	NA
05/29/92	0.10%	−0.10%	−0.10%	NA	NA
06/30/92	1.77%	1.77%	NA	1.77%	NA
07/31/92	3.94% '	3.94%	NA	NA	3.94%
8/31/92	2.40%	−2.40%	−2.40%	NA	NA
09/30/92	0.91%	0.91%	NA	NA	0.91%
10/30/92	0.21%	0.21%	NA	0.21%	NA
11/30/92	3.03%	3.03%	NA	NA	3.03%
12/31/92	1.00%	−1.00%	−1.00%	NA	NA
01/29/93	0.70%	−0.70%	NA	−0.70%	NA
02/26/93	1.04%	−1.04%	−1.04%	NA	NA
03/31/93	1.84%	−1.84%	NA	−1.84%	NA
04/30/93	2.61%	2.61%	NA	NA	2.61%
5/31/93	2.27%	2.27%	NA	NA	2.27%
6/30/93	0.08%	−0.08%	NA	−0.08%	NA

Date	Available Trade Gain	Trade Gain/Loss	Test Data Set	Train Data Set	Out-of-Sample Data Set
07/30/93	0.53%	−0.53%	−0.53%	NA	NA
08/31/93	3.44%	3.44%	3.44%	NA	NA
09/30/93	1.01%	1.01%	NA	NA	1.01%
10/29/93	1.94%	1.94%	NA	1.94%	NA
11/30/93	1.29%	−1.29%	−1.29%	NA	NA
12/31/93	1.01%	1.01%	NA	1.01%	NA
01/31/94	3.15%	−3.15%	NA	NA	−3.15%
2/28/94	3.10%	3.10%	NA	3.10%	NA
03/31/94	4.80%	4.80%	NA	NA	4.80%
4/29/94	1.14%	−1.14%	−1.14%	NA	NA

Chapter 8

TRADING GOLD STOCKS WITH A NEURAL NET

John Kean, Principal
KEAN ANALYTICS

INTRODUCTION

This chapter applies the same methods used in Chapter 7 to trading gold stocks. The analysis of gold stocks is an inherently difficult task. Amongst the universe of stocks, some of the most variable are the golds. In addition to the often high volatility of the price of the gold mineral itself, factors like new finds, labor strikes, and host country politics add another mercurial layer to valuation. We will lessen this last set of considerations somewhat by analyzing a collection of these stocks in the form of a gold stock mutual fund, rather than fixing on a single company.

In addressing the nonrandomness of this collection of stocks, there follows a listing of statistical correlations between the Fidelity Select American Gold stock fund (FSAG fund) and three variables of potential explanatory interest: the 3-month Treasury bill interest rate, the 30-year Treasury bond yield, and, of course, gold prices. The term "gold stocks" suggests that a nonrandom relationship should exist between these stocks and gold, and indeed the correlation coefficient supports this. The correlations were conducted over 275 weeks of data, ending May 5, 1994.

Correlation coefficient of:

FSAG fund to 3-month Treasury bill rate: −.21
FSAG fund to gold prices: +.51
FSAG fund to 30-year Treasury bond yield: −.58

It's evident that gold stock prices should be heavily influenced by gold, but it's somewhat less obvious that long-term interest rates would have an even higher absolute value of correlation coefficient. A likely explanation is that rises in interest rates over the period have been anticipated as choking off future inflation, thus hurting gold and gold stock prices. Also, higher interest rates will, to some extent, draw money away from other areas of investment, including gold and gold stocks. Last, and probably least, gold speculators and gold mining companies have interest expenses, which rise with rates.

EVALUATING THE RESULTS

The financial database, neural net setup, and training were handled in the same manner described in the previous chapter.

The input to output relationships are shown in Figure 1, 2, and 3. Figure 1 shows the selected neural net's response to a span of gold prices, at the May 5, 1994, level of T-bill and T-bond rates. Notice how the outputs take off when gold prices exceed the low 300s. Many of the nets generated during training showed this effect, and it may be a function of gold mine profitability versus gold prices. In the literature, there are references that many mines are of low to negative profitability with gold prices less than the low 300s. If a mine's operations became unprofitable, it would shut down, but its stock shouldn't go to zero because of its assets and because of the chance that gold prices would again rise to profitable mining levels.

The neural-net-determined relationship of FSAG fund's value versus T-bond yields is shown in Figure 2. Higher T-bond yields have, over the period analyzed, been associated with lower gold stock prices. Figure 3 shows a similar relationship for T-bill rates, but with a more subdued effect.

A comparison of the selected neural net's outputs with the actual FSAG fund price levels is displayed in Figure 4. There are often some fairly major differences between the two, and this is emphasized in the Figure 5, which focuses on the

Figure 1.   Gold price versus neural net output. Values fixed at 5/4/94.

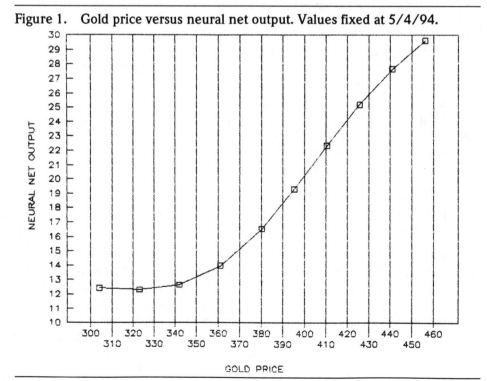

GOLD PRICE

Figure 2. T-bond yield versus neural net output. Values fixed at 5/4/94.

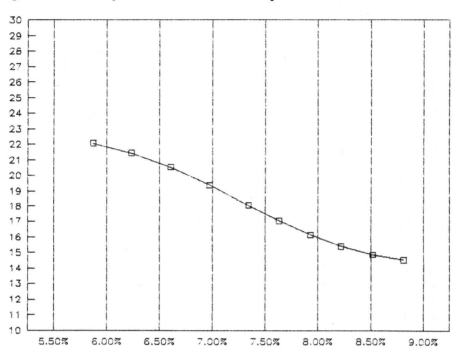

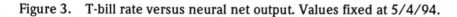

Figure 3. T-bill rate versus neural net output. Values fixed at 5/4/94.

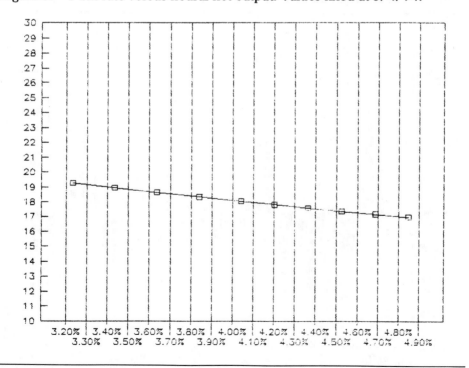

Figure 4. Gold stock fund versus neural net output.

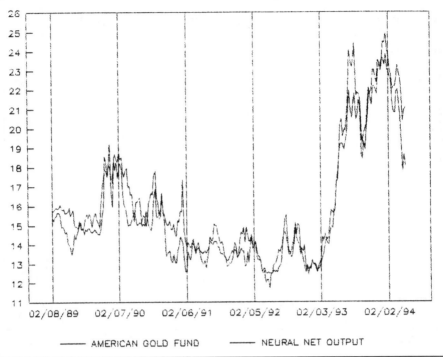

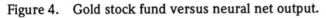

Figure 5. Neural net output/gold fund price.

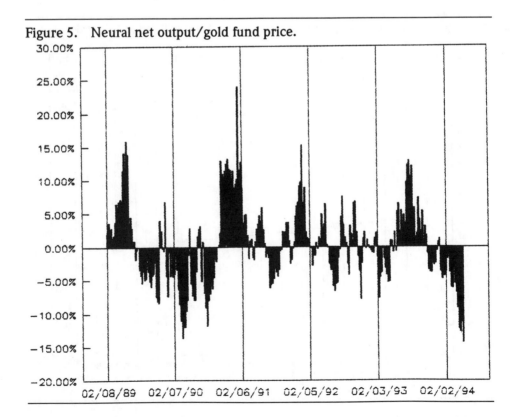

percentage difference between the neural net's theoretical valuation and the current price. Excursions above the zero percent line indicate, at least in theory, a condition of undervaluation, which will eventually be rectified by price rises and/or valuation changes. In the same way, values below the zero line indicate the fund's price is too high.

The next step was to test the usefulness of these "out-of-value" indications by simulated trading. The neural net outputs were used in an expert system that evaluated the degree of "out-of-valueness" and whether FSAG fund prices were responding by closing the gap. Trading evaluations were carried out by taking statistical correlations between the series of trade results, and the series of available returns (i.e., as if each trade had been a winner). These statistical correlations were made for each category of data: the training set, the testing set, and the out-of-sample set.

This analysis suggests an approach for trading a very volatile sector of stocks. The results didn't support trading every nit and nuance of imbalance between the actual and theoretical value, but rather offered a step up to a framework within which to conduct profitable trading.

Table 1.   List of simulated trades in this analysis.

Date	Available Trade Gain	Trade Gain/Loss	Test Data Set	Train Data Set	Out-of-Sample Data Set
02/15/89	1.10%	−1.10%	NA	−1.10%	NA
02/22/89	1.25%	NA	NA	NA	NA
03/01/89	0.32%	0.32%	0.32%	NA	NA
03/08/89	1.10%	1.10%	NA	1.10%	NA
03/15/89	0.00%	NA	NA	NA	NA
03/22/89	0.96%	NA	NA	NA	NA
03/29/89	3.81%	NA	NA	NA	NA
04/05/89	0.07%	NA	NA	NA	NA
04/12/89	0.40%	−0.40%	−0.40%	NA	NA
04/19/89	1.75%	NA	NA	NA	NA
04/26/89	0.41%	NA	NA	NA	NA
05/03/89	3.89%	−3.89%	−3.89%	NA	NA
05/10/89	0.99%	NA	NA	NA	NA
05/17/89	0.72%	NA	NA	NA	NA
05/24/89	2.74%	NA	NA	NA	NA
05/31/89	2.75%	NA	NA	NA	NA
06/07/89	4.91%	4.91%	NA	NA	4.91%
06/14/89	1.58%	−1.58%	−1.58%	NA	NA
06/21/89	1.68%	NA	NA	NA	NA
06/28/89	1.31%	1.31%	NA	NA	1.31%

Date	Available Trade Gain	Trade Gain/Loss	Test Data Set	Train Data Set	Out-of-Sample Data Set
07/05/89	2.31%	NA	NA	NA	NA
07/12/89	0.46%	NA	NA	NA	NA
07/19/89	1.98%	NA	NA	NA	NA
07/26/89	0.13%	NA	NA	NA	NA
08/02/89	1.55%	NA	NA	NA	NA
08/09/89	2.53%	NA	NA	NA	NA
08/16/89	0.91%	NA	NA	NA	NA
08/23/89	1.16%	NA	NA	NA	NA
08/30/89	1.30%	NA	NA	NA	NA
09/06/89	0.90%	NA	NA	NA	NA
09/13/89	3.56%	NA	NA	NA	NA
09/20/89	2.42%	−2.42%	NA	NA	−2.42%
09/27/89	2.03%	NA	NA	NA	NA
10/04/89	0.39%	NA	NA	NA	NA
10/11/89	2.37%	NA	NA	NA	NA
10/18/89	0.86%	0.86%	0.86%	NA	NA
10/25/89	1.85%	NA	NA	NA	NA
11/01/89	7.07%	NA	NA	NA	NA
11/08/89	6.73%	NA	NA	NA	NA
11/15/89	1.94%	NA	NA	NA	NA
11/22/89	3.35%	NA	NA	NA	NA
11/29/89	0.50%	−0.50%	−0.50%	NA	NA
12/06/89	1.35%	NA	NA	NA	NA
12/13/89	3.36%	NA	NA	NA	NA
12/20/89	0.72%	NA	NA	NA	NA
12/27/89	2.89%	NA	NA	NA	NA
01/03/90	1.63%	1.63%	NA	NA	1.63%
01/10/90	7.21%	NA	NA	NA	NA
01/17/90	1.14%	NA	NA	NA	NA
01/24/90	1.34%	NA	NA	NA	NA
01/31/90	0.76%	NA	NA	NA	NA
02/07/90	2.74%	NA	NA	NA	NA
02/14/90	1.86%	NA	NA	NA	NA
02/21/90	0.38%	NA	NA	NA	NA
02/28/90	3.95%	NA	NA	NA	NA
03/07/90	1.25%	1.25%	NA	NA	1.25%
03/14/90	1.82%	NA	NA	NA	NA

Date	Available Trade Gain	Trade Gain/Loss	Test Data Set	Train Data Set	Out-of-Sample Data Set
03/21/90	0.50%	NA	NA	NA	NA
03/28/90	5.40%	NA	NA	NA	NA
04/04/90	0.35%	−0.35%	−0.35%	NA	NA
04/11/90	2.64%	NA	NA	NA	NA
04/18/90	0.12%	−0.12%	NA	NA	−0.12%
04/25/90	5.60%	NA	NA	NA	NA
05/02/90	3.09%	3.09%	NA	3.09%	NA
05/09/90	6.51%	NA	NA	NA	NA
05/16/90	0.06%	NA	NA	NA	NA
05/23/90	0.93%	NA	NA	NA	NA
05/30/90	0.55%	NA	NA	NA	NA
06/06/90	4.69%	NA	NA	NA	NA
06/13/90	4.96%	4.96%	NA	4.96%	NA
06/20/90	1.01%	NA	NA	NA	NA
06/27/90	0.73%	−0.73%	−0.73%	NA	NA
07/03/90	4.95%	NA	NA	NA	NA
07/11/90	2.74%	NA	NA	NA	NA
07/18/90	5.44%	NA	NA	NA	NA
07/25/90	1.74%	NA	NA	NA	NA
08/01/90	1.83%	NA	NA	NA	NA
08/08/90	0.54%	NA	NA	NA	NA
08/15/90	5.49%	NA	NA	NA	NA
08/22/90	1.83%	NA	NA	NA	NA
08/29/90	7.74%	NA	NA	NA	NA
09/05/90	1.73%	1.73%	NA	1.73%	NA
09/12/90	4.02%	NA	NA	NA	NA
09/19/90	1.84%	−1.84%	−1.84%	NA	NA
09/26/90	5.38%	NA	NA	NA	NA
10/03/90	6.07%	NA	NA	NA	NA
10/10/90	2.94%	NA	NA	NA	NA
10/17/90	11.73%	NA	NA	NA	NA
10/24/90	0.90%	NA	NA	NA	NA
10/31/90	0.59%	0.59%	0.59%	NA	NA
11/07/90	0.37%	0.37%	NA	0.37%	NA
11/14/90	3.81%	−3.81%	NA	NA	−3.81%
11/21/90	0.61%	NA	NA	NA	NA
11/28/90	3.30%	NA	NA	NA	NA

Date	Available Trade Gain	Trade Gain/Loss	Test Data Set	Train Data Set	Out-of-Sample Data Set
12/05/90	3.34%	−3.34%	NA	NA	−3.34%
12/12/90	0.08%	NA	NA	NA	NA
12/19/90	4.83%	4.83%	NA	4.83%	NA
12/26/90	1.90%	1.90%	NA	NA	1.90%
01/02/91	3.16%	3.16%	3.16%	NA	NA
01/09/91	0.97%	−0.97%	NA	−0.97%	NA
01/16/91	1.48%	NA	NA	NA	NA
01/23/91	5.92%	NA	NA	NA	NA
01/30/91	4.93%	NA	NA	NA	NA
02/06/91	1.36%	NA	NA	NA	NA
02/13/91	6.92%	6.92%	6.92%	NA	NA
02/20/91	2.35%	−2.35%	NA	−2.35%	NA
02/27/91	0.45%	NA	NA	NA	NA
03/06/91	4.47%	NA	NA	NA	NA
03/13/91	3.26%	NA	NA	NA	NA
03/20/91	3.23%	NA	NA	NA	NA
03/27/91	2.03%	NA	NA	NA	NA
04/03/91	3.18%	NA	NA	NA	NA
04/10/91	1.08%	NA	NA	NA	NA
04/17/91	3.48%	NA	NA	NA	NA
04/24/91	2.57%	NA	NA	NA	NA
05/01/91	1.28%	NA	NA	NA	NA
05/08/91	0.99%	NA	NA	NA	NA
05/15/91	1.54%	NA	NA	NA	NA
05/22/91	2.74%	−2.74%	NA	NA	−2.74%
05/29/91	4.22%	NA	NA	NA	NA
06/05/91	3.23%	3.23%	NA	3.23%	NA
06/12/91	4.43%	NA	NA	NA	NA
06/19/91	1.11%	NA	NA	NA	NA
06/26/91	0.07%	NA	NA	NA	NA
07/03/91	6.06%	NA	NA	NA	NA
07/10/91	0.46%	NA	NA	NA	NA
07/17/91	0.27%	NA	NA	NA	NA
07/24/91	2.61%	NA	NA	NA	NA
07/31/91	1.96%	1.96%	1.96%	NA	NA
08/07/91	1.75%	NA	NA	NA	NA
08/14/91	0.78%	NA	NA	NA	NA

Date	Available Trade Gain	Trade Gain/Loss	Test Data Set	Train Data Set	Out-of-Sample Data Set
08/21/91	1.34%	NA	NA	NA	NA
08/28/91	3.66%	NA	NA	NA	NA
09/04/91	0.97%	NA	NA	NA	NA
09/11/91	3.38%	NA	NA	NA	NA
09/18/91	0.23%	NA	NA	NA	NA
09/25/91	1.09%	1.09%	NA	NA	1.09%
10/02/91	0.23%	−0.23%	−0.23%	NA	NA
10/09/91	1.31%	NA	NA	NA	NA
10/16/91	2.28%	2.28%	NA	NA	2.28%
10/23/91	4.53%	NA	NA	NA	NA
10/30/91	1.21%	NA	NA	NA	NA
11/06/91	4.17%	NA	NA	NA	NA
11/13/91	0.68%	NA	NA	NA	NA
11/20/91	1.34%	NA	NA	NA	NA
11/27/91	1.25%	1.25%	NA	NA	1.25%
12/04/91	1.02%	−1.02%	−1.02%	NA	NA
12/11/91	0.00%	NA	NA	NA	NA
12/18/91	5.65%	NA	NA	NA	NA
12/24/91	0.70%	NA	NA	NA	NA
12/31/91	5.02%	5.02%	NA	5.02%	NA
01/08/92	3.97%	−3.97%	NA	NA	−3.97%
01/15/92	5.97%	NA	NA	NA	NA
01/22/92	3.47%	3.47%	NA	3.47%	NA
01/29/92	3.77%	NA	NA	NA	NA
02/05/92	0.80%	NA	NA	NA	NA
02/12/92	1.73%	NA	NA	NA	NA
02/19/92	2.48%	NA	NA	NA	NA
02/26/92	3.07%	3.07%	3.07%	NA	NA
03/04/92	0.07%	0.07%	NA	0.07%	NA
03/11/92	2.17%	NA	NA	NA	NA
03/18/92	3.37%	NA	NA	NA	NA
03/25/92	1.19%	NA	NA	NA	NA
04/01/92	0.96%	NA	NA	NA	NA
04/08/92	5.00%	NA	NA	NA	NA
04/15/92	1.42%	NA	NA	NA	NA
04/22/92	0.00%	0.00%	NA	NA	0.00%
04/29/92	3.46%	NA	NA	NA	NA

Date	Available Trade Gain	Trade Gain/Loss	Test Data Set	Train Data Set	Out-of-Sample Data Set
05/06/92	6.23%	NA	NA	NA	NA
05/13/92	0.24%	NA	NA	NA	NA
05/20/92	3.69%	NA	NA	NA	NA
05/27/92	0.54%	NA	NA	NA	NA
06/03/92	0.31%	NA	NA	NA	NA
06/10/92	2.22%	NA	NA	NA	NA
06/17/92	2.62%	NA	NA	NA	NA
06/24/92	0.58%	NA	NA	NA	NA
07/01/92	1.40%	NA	NA	NA	NA
07/08/92	1.52%	NA	NA	NA	NA
07/15/92	3.93%	NA	NA	NA	NA
07/22/92	0.41%	NA	NA	NA	NA
07/29/92	1.44%	−1.44%	NA	−1.44%	NA
08/05/92	2.64%	NA	NA	NA	NA
08/12/92	4.35%	NA	NA	NA	NA
08/19/92	0.60%	NA	NA	NA	NA
08/26/92	1.19%	NA	NA	NA	NA
09/02/92	3.00%	NA	NA	NA	NA
09/09/92	0.64%	NA	NA	NA	NA
09/16/92	6.08%	NA	NA	NA	NA
09/23/92	3.03%	NA	NA	NA	NA
09/30/92	1.74%	NA	NA	NA	NA
10/07/92	0.99%	NA	NA	NA	NA
10/14/92	3.93%	NA	NA	NA	NA
10/21/92	2.53%	NA	NA	NA	NA
10/28/92	1.02%	NA	NA	NA	NA
11/04/92	2.27%	NA	NA	NA	NA
11/11/92	7.96%	NA	NA	NA	NA
11/18/92	0.86%	0.86%	NA	NA	0.86%
11/25/92	2.44%	NA	NA	NA	NA
12/02/92	2.90%	NA	NA	NA	NA
12/09/92	0.55%	NA	NA	NA	NA
12/16/92	3.46%	NA	NA	NA	NA
12/23/92	1.37%	NA	NA	NA	NA
12/30/92	0.23%	NA	NA	NA	NA
01/06/93	0.77%	NA	NA	NA	NA
01/13/93	1.86%	NA	NA	NA	NA

Date	Available Trade Gain	Trade Gain/Loss	Test Data Set	Train Data Set	Out-of-Sample Data Set
01/20/93	0.39%	NA	NA	NA	NA
01/27/93	0.79%	NA	NA	NA	NA
02/03/93	3.20%	3.20%	NA	3.20%	NA
02/10/93	9.08%	NA	NA	NA	NA
02/17/93	1.73%	NA	NA	NA	NA
02/24/93	2.68%	NA	NA	NA	NA
03/03/93	1.86%	NA	NA	NA	NA
03/10/93	0.07%	NA	NA	NA	NA
03/17/93	1.33%	NA	NA	NA	NA
03/24/93	5.53%	NA	NA	NA	NA
03/31/93	3.15%	NA	NA	NA	NA
04/07/93	0.64%	NA	NA	NA	NA
04/14/93	0.13%	NA	NA	NA	NA
04/21/93	0.64%	NA	NA	NA	NA
04/28/93	9.71%	NA	NA	NA	NA
05/05/93	0.23%	NA	NA	NA	NA
05/12/93	7.96%	7.96%	7.96%	NA	NA
05/19/93	2.41%	NA	NA	NA	NA
05/26/93	0.37%	0.37%	NA	NA	0.37%
06/02/93	0.47%	−0.47%	−0.47%	NA	NA
06/09/93	1.25%	NA	NA	NA	NA
06/16/93	2.12%	NA	NA	NA	NA
06/23/93	2.12%	2.12%	2.12%	NA	NA
06/30/93	5.78%	5.78%	NA	5.78%	NA
07/07/93	5.28%	5.28%	NA	NA	5.28%
07/14/93	4.69%	−4.69%	−4.69%	NA	NA
07/21/93	1.82%	NA	NA	NA	NA
07/28/93	4.14%	NA	NA	NA	NA
08/04/93	1.82%	1.82%	1.82%	NA	NA
08/11/93	5.88%	−5.88%	NA	−5.88%	NA
08/18/93	0.73%	NA	NA	NA	NA
08/25/93	3.92%	3.92%	3.92%	NA	NA
09/01/93	1.40%	NA	NA	NA	NA
09/08/93	11.96%	NA	NA	NA	NA
09/15/93	1.02%	NA	NA	NA	NA
09/22/93	4.72%	NA	NA	NA	NA
09/29/93	1.97%	−1.97%	NA	NA	−1.97%

Date	Available Trade Gain	Trade Gain/Loss	Test Data Set	Train Data Set	Out-of-Sample Data Set
10/06/93	5.86%	NA	NA	NA	NA
10/13/93	3.59%	NA	NA	NA	NA
10/20/93	4.62%	4.62%	NA	NA	4.62%
10/27/93	0.55%	NA	NA	NA	NA
11/03/93	0.64%	NA	NA	NA	NA
11/10/93	4.64%	NA	NA	NA	NA
11/17/93	0.26%	NA	NA	NA	NA
11/24/93	2.30%	NA	NA	NA	NA
12/01/93	0.58%	0.58%	NA	NA	0.58%
12/08/93	5.09%	NA	NA	NA	NA
12/15/93	0.51%	NA	NA	NA	NA
12/22/93	1.79%	NA	NA	NA	NA
12/29/93	1.57%	NA	NA	NA	NA
01/05/94	4.88%	NA	NA	NA	NA
01/12/94	0.20%	NA	NA	NA	NA
01/19/94	1.84%	NA	NA	NA	NA
01/26/94	3.37%	NA	NA	NA	NA
02/02/94	0.84%	0.84%	NA	NA	0.84%
02/09/94	3.48%	NA	NA	NA	NA
02/16/94	1.01%	1.01%	NA	1.01%	NA
02/23/94	3.38%	NA	NA	NA	NA
03/02/94	0.72%	−0.72%	−0.72%	NA	NA
03/09/94	0.05%	NA	NA	NA	NA
03/16/94	1.76%	NA	NA	NA	NA
03/23/94	3.10%	NA	NA	NA	NA
03/30/94	1.68%	NA	NA	NA	NA
04/06/94	1.44%	NA	NA	NA	NA
04/13/94	2.48%	NA	NA	NA	NA
04/20/94	7.90%	7.90%	NA	7.90%	NA
04/26/94	2.72%	−2.72%	NA	NA	−2.72%
05/04/94	0.53%	NA	NA	NA	NA

Chapter 9

TRADING WITH AN AUTOMATIC TRAINING NETWORK

Joe Shepard,
Director of Software Development
RaceCom, Inc.

INTRODUCTION

To understand RaceCom's approach to neural networks, it is necessary to understand why we conceived the company. This explanation will begin with a simple interest in understanding learning. We'll end by explaining how Windows NT will allow neural networks to gather and train on live, tick-by-tick data. Along the way we'll delve into such areas as data reenforcing, generalizing, asking the right questions of neural networks, and knowing what the answers mean. But before we can explain where we are, we need to explain where and how we started. Just as many things in life begin in unexpected ways, our neural networks began with a mouse.

While in a psychology 101 class at Rochester Institute of Technology, I was assigned the task of demonstrating to the whole class how a living body learns. At first blush, this seemed a somewhat daunting task. With my usual flair for starting in the wrong way and using the wrong books, I slaved away on the quiet second floor of the RIT's library, reading books on brain organization, synapses, sensory inputs, and the related milieu. Each night I left the library and walked the half mile to my car. While bracing against the bitterly cold winter winds blowing across the open parking lot, I took comfort in the knowledge that soon I would have the understanding necessary to give a meaningful presentation.

The unpleasantness of spending winter nights away from hearth and home pursuing an understanding of the problem of learning was not completely offset by what I had uncovered, however. I could probably spit out facts about the brain like a Pez dispenser, but I didn't understand how this information all fit together. To me, it was like explaining the sensation of standing in front of a Van Gogh by describing the chemical makeup of paint. I was missing the essence of learning.

At that time I lived in a large old house on Lake Avenue that I rented from Eastman Kodak. The house had an aging, detached garage. This tired building with peeling red paint had two sets of doors that swung out instead of sliding up into the ceiling. I'd have to pull up to the garage, open the doors, and then drive the car in. There was no outside light switch, so the car's headlights were left on. This meant the inside of the garage was dark until the instant the door began to swing open.

On the fateful night, there was about 12 inches of new snow. Opening the door would also require moving a large amount of snow that was drifting against it. As I was freezing, I wanted the process over with quickly so I could get inside in front of the steam radiator. I grabbed the door and threw it open.

Just as I did, a mouse bolted across the floor. Startled by the headlights and the noise of the door, it instantly made for a narrow opening in the back wall. The movement was precise and totally without wasted effort. I was struck by the unerring course the mouse took. It did not hesitate or look for visual cues. The head snapped to the direction of the hole and it was off. The running away was doubtless instinctive, but running through that little hole was learned. It knew where it wanted to go and how to get there.

That night I grappled with how the mouse learned to head directly for that hole. Naturally, the mouse could have learned that the hole meant safety from watching other mice. Yet, if one backtracked through the mouse genealogy in that garage, a creature somewhere had to have learned what to do. How that learning occurred could give me a glimpse as to what learning really was.

The next morning before I left to stand watch over an 11x17-inch X-ray film scanning machine in Building 313, I wandered around the garage with a flashlight that had both weak batteries and an intermittent on/off switch. Between banging on the light and cursing the gods of winter that made the building so cold, I looked at the general layout of the garage to see if there was some physical pathway that lead to the hole, something that would show the logic of learning. As I studied the floor and the walls, the flashlight seemed to want to stay on less and less. In frustration, I slammed the butt down on the makeshift workbench. I hit an old doorbell someone had left. The crack of the bell echoed against the bare walls. In that instant, I had my answer.

After work, I went to a Radio Shack store for some simple electrical devices. Then to the pet store for two white mice and a birdcage. If I was right, I could demonstrate learning. It wasn't just the mouse's learning process I was struck with, it was also my own.

That weekend I fashioned an insulating bottom for the birdcage I had purchased. Next, I made a heavy cardboard piece to fit the bottom of the cage. In the center of this piece I taped a vertical barrier about 4 inches high.

On the left side of the barrier I wrapped a pair of bare copper wires. The wires were separated from each other by about 1/8 inch. In essence, there was no area on the left side of the cage barrier where a mouse could stand without coming into contact with the bare wires.

To supply voltage to the wires, I used a simple doorbell step-down transformer. I believe it was about 18 volts (18 V). The transformer output was fed to a large, three-position knife switch. I connected the wires on the floor of the birdcage to one side of the knife switch. The other side of the knife switch was wired to a doorbell—move the switch one way and the bell would ring; move it in the other direction, and the left side of the floor of the birdcage would become electrically charged. If the switch was straight up, nothing would happen.

I put the mouse in the cage and, with a pencil, prodded the creature over to the side of the floor that had the bare copper wires. I moved the knife switch so that the doorbell rang. The mouse ignored the bell. I then flipped the switch so that the 18 V was applied to the surface on which the mouse was standing. The mouse ran around wildly trying to get away from the harmless, yet irritating, voltage. It tried unsuccessfully many times to climb the cage. Finally, it scrambled over the barrier and was safely away from the electrified floor.

I repeated the process of forcing the mouse to the side of the cage with the exposed wires. I'd first ring the bell and then apply voltage to the floor. The mouse's learning progressed each time. It became less and less random in its choice of escape. Soon the instant the voltage was applied, the mouse headed for the barrier.

Within about 15 to 20 sequences of ringing the bell and then applying voltage, the mouse's learning had advanced to the point where the animal would scamper over the barrier when he heard the bell without waiting for the voltage. This little mouse had learned to associate the bell with the voltage. Further, he had learned the most efficient method of escaping the annoying voltage before it was applied. At this point, I must say that I learned later that this experiment was done by others before with similar results.

In examining the notes I took during the exercise, one point became clear. The mouse did not approach learning in a thoughtful way. It experimented with what appeared to be random selections. The choices that worked, such as climbing the barrier and reacting to the bell, were committed to memory. The choices that did not work, such as trying to climb the wires of the cage and ignoring the bell, were probably either discarded or committed to memory as bad choices.

There was demonstrable learning using the mouse, but what concerned me was I had no way of separating the precise areas that represented new learning. For instance, was the barrier similar to something the mouse had seen before? Further, there was a simplicity to learning that intrigued me. Probably due to my own mental immaturity, I committed this experiment to memory, did nothing more, and moved on with my own learning by trial and error.

Years later, another event shook me into returning to the mouse. It had to do with *The New York Times*. On rare occasions, I drove into Rochester on quiet Sunday mornings to pick up the *Times*. The ride was pleasant and the buzz of ethnic conversation at Worldwide News lent perspective to the world. This particular Sunday I happened upon an ad for the Mattle Horse Race Analyzer. It was a device handicappers could use to predict the order of finish of thoroughbred races. Looking at that ad shaped everything I've done since.

Thoroughbred handicapping really was of no interest to me in and of itself. What sparked my interest was that people were applying rudimentary algorithms to historical events in order to predict future events. In other words, they were trying to use what they had learned from observing past races to select the winners of future races. The learned knowledge was encoded into the algorithms stored in the device's memory.

The Mattle Horse Race Analyzer was in fact a hybrid calculator. Data was entered and the numbers of the top four choices for a particular race were returned as output. The accuracy was of little concern to me. It was more important that mathematical algorithms attempted to store knowledge.

I remembered looking at a sine wave on an oscilloscope knowing that I could write a formula accurately predicting the level of the wave at virtually any time in the future. Was this knowledge? I doubted it. The possible excursions of the voltage was known through observation. The rise and fall of the voltage was globally and locally stable. Any formula would simply describe the movement—not predict it.

A horse race would possess infinitely more variables than a sine wave. The physical condition of the horses, the track, the weather, racing luck—the dimensions of the problem seemed enormous and endless. I could not believe a simple calculator arriving in the '70s would be capable of handling the challenge. You would need incredibly complex formulae dealing with the myriad of conditions.

Then I remembered something that always amazed me even more. I played high school basketball and I can recall making a jump shot while falling back away from the basket. The ball hit nothing but net. To calculate the proper trajectory mathematically would be a serious challenge given my movement, the relationship of the basket, the aerodynamic resistance of the ball, and all the rest. I'm sure my mind didn't make all the needed calculations in the split second I had to shoot. How, then, was I able to learn how to do something that complex? The problem of learning had raised itself again in my mind and this time it was not going away.

The only reasonable way to delve into the problem of learning was to control both the method of learning and the testing of this learning. A computer was the logical choice. I felt computers were, and to a large extent still are, used as large graphic calculators. They were very good at collecting and manipulating data, but they didn't really learn.

Through investigation, I got wind of something people were excited about—the back-propagation neural network. It was referred to as a paradigm. *Paradigm* means either "an example" or "a concept that effectively explains a complex process." This example of a neural network could "learn" how to recognize patterns. In studying the back-propagation neural network, I was troubled by several aspects. The sigmoid function seemed out of place, for one thing. I remember thinking the transfer function reminded me of a poorly designed bass and treble control—something tagged on to get reasonable performance. Another problem was the network's requirement for normalized numbers either between +0.5 and −0.5 or 0.0 and 1.0. Also, it was immediately obvious that the middle neurodes and hidden layers could become a mechanism for memorizing. There was one other thing that troubled me.

The randomizing of numbers seemed critical. The random number generator in a computer was predictable. Without proper care, this predictable sequence of numbers could, in reality, be used by the network as a secondary way to store "knowledge." The learning process would be clouded if the network "expected" certain numbers.

Even with all these reservations I, nonetheless, decided to use the back-propagation in my studies involving the process of learning. There was nothing else available in my estimation.

After deciding on the network, I looked at another concern. There is a practical side to research. One must continue to live and provide for one's family's maintenance. This meant that I must involve myself in learning; neural networks would have to become my business.

In business, the first rule is to identify the customer. But who would be willing to buy a neural network to benefit their lives? After much investigation, I went back to what caused my renewed interest in learning—thoroughbred handicappers. They were eager to try new ways for picking winners. Thus, RaceCom, Inc., was born. We were going to sell handicapping software, but our ultimate goal was making computers learn.

There were still several other problems. For one, I didn't know how to program a computer. With a year's effort at night and on weekends, I felt I had become reasonably good enough to sell what I wrote.

Mathematics was still another challenge. The highest I'd ever climbed in mathematics training was calculus for business decisions. I did, however, have extensive statistics education. What mathematics I needed to know to create neural networks I would have to learn where and when I could.

Another problem was the customer. Handicappers are intelligent people, but most don't want to bother learning a concept as involved as neural networks. Handicapping to these people is enjoyable. They want to input data about the horse with as little effort as possible and get a projection in as little time as possible. They have zero tolerance for the frustrations often attendant on computer programs. Further, the projections have to be right or they won't be back. To solve all the customer's problems, I would have to design a program that was easy to use and deadly accurate.

The back-propagation could meet the needs of our customers reasonably well. The accuracy of the predictions was about 40 percent. In other words, a customer who put in enough historical races could make money at the track. But, the back-propagation showed then, as it still does, many problems. For one, if it wasn't able to learn, the middle neurodes and hidden layers had to be increased. If these elements were increased too much, the network memorized. Further, the customer would pay a penalty in increased training time.

I agonized over the back-propagation network. Even with all the improvements I read about and tested, it never met my goals of fast, accurate training. I read how the back-propagation and its variants could perform the spiral test and the exclusive-or test. My customers did not need to forecast spirals or solve logic gate problems. What they wanted was the winner in the fourth race at Belmont.

These people had limited computer power. The processors were slow by today's standards. Hard drive space was limited. And, most importantly, there was a finite amount of time available for our customers to spend operating a neural network. In other words, what was available in terms of time and machinery needed to be utilized properly.

Serving our customers' needs caused us to rethink neural networks. The idea of developing a neural network that performed a specific task well seemed reasonable.

My belief was that it is proper to develop neural networks that excel in a limited, application-specific environment. As you increase a neural network's ability to learn a wider range of problems, you tax the computer more. Years ago when we first started shipping neural networks, it took days to train some of the larger files. Computers ran at 4.77 MHz with an 8-bit bus, so that large training files posed a serious problem. To stay in business, the back-propagation neural network was not the answer. I needed to create a class of neural networks that were application-specific.

First, I had to create a neural network that was fast, easy to use, and filled the needs of my customers—handicappers. You can liken the complexity of a neural network to a polynomial formula. A wildly moving graph takes a wildly complex polynomial formula to describe it. Horse races, on the other hand, fit within a rather narrow range. In essence, I could reduce the complexity of the neural network until I had speed and accuracy that matched my customers' needs. Along the way I gave up the ability to learn spirals and exclusive-or gates. Not one of my customers ever lost money because the software wasn't able to forecast a spiral or a triangle wave.

To explain further, the data sets our neural networks faced then were limited. For instance, a horse could be expected to run a six-furlong race within a fairly narrow range of times. Thus, we could structure the neural network to take advantage of this range. Why make a neural network capable of learning an infinite time range when all we needed was about 30 seconds? If we limited what the network does, then we could concentrate on making it better and faster. Both a tractor trailer and a motorcycle will carry a dozen eggs, but which would do it faster and more efficiently? Again, this is an application-specific approach to developing neural networks.

Over the years we have continued to target neural networks at specific problems. The proof that this was a valid approach was driven home when a customer using our latest software ran 150 races at Hollywood Park and the software picked the winner 78 percent of the time. Or, when a new female customer was 13 out of 14 against the spread in pro football. She didn't know a field goal from a french fry. But when the Las Vegas casino's own handicapper was 5 out of 12, she was 10 out of 12. She doubled her money the first weekend and tripled it the second. Not once did she complain the network wasn't able to forecast a spiral or know the output of an exclusive-or logic gate. She just folded her winnings neatly and walked out of the casino.

Our customers experience success like that because RaceCom never was able to be in the sanitized world of the theoretical application of neural networks; neither could we ship our products to people with training in neural networks. If a particular neural network process worked, we used it. If it didn't, we abandoned it. The overriding concern that guided our path was consistent accuracy of forecasts in the shortest possible time. We had to produce software that paid the bills and made the customers happy.

We couldn't be just close in a horse race. Our software had to nail the winner day in and day out in all kinds of weather and at all kinds of tracks. Further, we had to deliver these winners with minimal effort on the user's part. In other words, for seven years we've had to make neural networks practical. This may explain why we've developed our own opinions about neural networks.

When we turned to financial investing, we brought our experience. RaceCom still believed people wanted a software that's easy to use. We also felt that customers would appreciate RaceCom's willingness to continually reevaluate current thinking. In our estimation, everything was open for improvement. Whether it was time bars or stochastics, if there was a better way, it would be used.

The ATN2 Neural Network

The ATN2 neural network is a highly successful paradigm we created to solve many of the problems facing our customers. It has speed, puts very limited demands on computer memory, and does not have the ability to memorize. The most important aspect of using this network is that we can control the representation of the problem. The ATN2 paradigm does not utilize a true hidden layer to accomplish mapping. Instead, a layer is created that consists of an enhanced representation of the input pattern. The representation is in a higher dimension than the original input space. Only one set of weights is created, and thus we have very short training times.

The ATN2 neural network was also the first network we created that was capable of completely organizing itself. In essence, "organizing" meant creating the enhanced representation of the problem to be solved.

Back-propagation neural networks can be, and are, designed with many user-defined features. Using all these controls, the user is expected to modify the neural network for optimal performance to solve a specific problem. The user is also required to understand the problem of memorizing.

The problem with this approach lies in the crippling effect this has on the rapid analysis of several different combinations of input and target data. If a trader wishes to see if the British pound has an effect on the S&P 500, it may require a complete reorganizing of the network. The normalizing would be changed, hidden layers and middle neurodes altered, and the multitude of complex training functions adjusted. Even for an experienced, trained neural network specialist, this is a time-consuming challenge. What's more, the setup process may have to be repeated many times before the network begins to perform well.

From the average customer's point of view, setting up a back-propagation neural network is an overwhelming problem. A customer who just purchased another company's general purpose back-propagation neural network called and was raving about all the flexibility he would have because of the multitude of network controls. He excitedly rattled off a long list of optional settings. We asked him a simple question: "Do you know what all those controls do?" He paused and then said, "No." "Do you know what even one of those controls does?" Again, "No." The back-propagation neural network he bought may have performed marvelously, but he simply didn't know how to make it work to do even the simplest forecast.

The ATN2, on the other hand, looks at the problem and modifies itself. The ATN2 is dynamically configured when the user presses the "Train" button. The beauty of this approach is that a new customer without any neural network experience can be training and forecasting within minutes of opening the software package. The altering of the ATN2 to see if the British pound had an effect of the S&P 500 would take less than 30 seconds. The complete retraining and testing process would require only a few minutes.

To explain the network setup, here is an excerpt from the electronic on-line help system:

INPUTS/INDICATORS

The Inputs dialog box will appear when either, "Inputs" from the "Neural Network" menu, or the Inputs Tool, is selected. This dialog box is used to create project files. A project file consists of data inputs and targets, which are set by the user. Once the inputs and targets are set and the project file is saved, the neural networks can then train on the data.

There are many options in setting up a project file, the first of which is data acquisition. This dialog box has the ability to read a number of different types of files. Whether you are getting your data from Computrac (*.DOP), or Tech Tools (*.TTD), it doesn't matter, as long as the type of data you are using is listed in the "List Files of Type:" list box. The types of data that can be read are shown in the "List Files of Type:" graphic.

You are not limited to using just one type of data. You can mix and match several different types. For example; you can take the Open/Hi/Lo/Close data out of a Computrac (*.DOP) file, take the same from a Tech Tools (*.TTD) file, and save this combination as a project file. As you can see you are not limited to one type of file. You are also not limited by the amount of files you can use for a project. Below are the steps necessary for creating a project file.

STEP 1: Click on "Neural Network" on the main menu bar. Click on "Inputs." The same can be accomplished by clicking on the Inputs Tool.

STEP 2: Select the type of file you are using from the "List Files of Type:" list box. To perform this function, click on the down arrow, which can be found on the right side of the "List Files of Type:" list box. Click on the type of file you wish to use. If you need to change the drive and/or directory, please do so. To change drives, CLick on the down arrow symbol, then click on the desired drive. To change directories, double-click on the top drive letter entry in the Directories list box. When the entire list of directories is displayed, double-click on the desired directory.

Before continuing with the steps, it is important for you to understand what we are trying to accomplish by setting up a project. For demonstration purposes let's say that you wanted to project the closing price for the Swiss franc. To do this you must first decide what other *indicator* might affect the price of the Swiss franc.

An indicator is a variable used to forecast the value or change in the value of another variable (as defined by the book *Every Investor's Guide To Wall Street Words*, by David L. Scott). For example, changes in the British pound, Eurodollar, Japanese yen, and deutsche mark could be used to forecast changes in the Swiss franc, or changes in the British pound, Eurodollar, Japanese yen, and Swiss franc could be used to forecast changes in the deutsche mark. The point here is that you will probably get better results if you use indicators that relate in some way. In this case we are dealing with all currencies.

We could probably agree that the price of wheat or beef carcasses would not affect the price of the Swiss franc. A more reasonable assumption would be either the British pound, Eurodollar, Japanese yen, deutsche mark, or a combination of any or all of these. What we mean by this is that you set up a project with indicators that best represent what might affect the changes in what you are trying to forecast, no matter what that might be.

In the following steps we will be setting up a project file that will forecast the closing price for the Swiss franc. This is just a guideline showing you the steps necessary in setting up a project file. All project files will be created using these steps, no matter what you are trying to forecast.

STEP 3: The next step is to add data that you would like to use as one of your indicators. Click on the file that contains the British pound data. Click on the "Open File" button. The same can be accomplished by double-clicking on the file.

STEP 4: The headings for the file will be displayed in the "Data Headings" box. Click on the headings you would like to include as part of your project. Only the data that exists in the headings you choose will be considered by the network. You can choose any combination of the headings listed but never select the ticker name or date. These must be, and are, taken care of internally by the software. In this case we will select the Open, High, Low, and Close headings.

In some cases your file will not have the standard headings such as Open, High, Low, and Close. It will have letters as headings, such as A, B, C, and D. This is most common if you are using Comma Separated (*.CSV), or Text Files (*.TXT). In these situations you would select the letter that contains the data you would like to add as part of your project. Most commonly the letter A represents the Date, B represents the Open, C represents High, D represents Low, E represents Close, and so on. To accomplish step 4, if your data is in this form, would be to select B, C, D, and E.

STEP 5: Add this as part of your project by clicking on the "Add Data" button.

STEP 6: Repeat steps 3–5 to include the Eurodollar, Japanese yen, deutsche mark, and Swiss franc data. Yes, you should always include what you are forecasting as part of your indicators.

STEP 7: This step involves adding the *target*. The target is what you are trying to forecast, in this case the closing price for the Swiss franc. You are not limited to the amount of targets you can forecast at one time. You can select Open, High, Low, and Close as the targets if you wish.

Now open the file that contains the target data. In this case the file that contains the Swiss franc data. Click on the Close heading. Click on the "Add Target" button.

STEP 8: The next step is to choose a data preprocessing method for each indicator. Click on the first indicator from the list in the "Current Inputs" box.

When the "Add Data" button is selected, the data are displayed in the "Current Inputs" list box. This is done so that you are able to see what indicators you have selected. If there is an indicator present that you do not want to include in your project, it can be deleted by selecting the indicator, then clicking on the "Delete Input" button. There are several things you must know about the "Current Inputs" list box:

1. The "Disconnect/Connect Inputs" button is mainly used for testing a particular set of indicators. Scenario: Let's say you have created a project file and trained it to 98 percent accuracy but would like it trained to a higher percent. You think that one or more of the indicators may be causing the network not to train to a higher percent. To test your theory you would like to disconnect (effectively cloaking) one or more of the indicators and train the file again to see if this does indeed solve the dilemma. You would also like to do this without deleting the indicator from the project. This is where the "Disconnect/Connect Inputs" button comes into play. To disconnect an indicator, you must first open the *.CDB file (project file) and scroll through the list of indicators. Click on the indicator you would like to disconnect. Then click on the "Disconnect/Connect Inputs" button. The same steps would be taken to reconnect the indicator. When an indicator is disconnected, it will look like this. Save the file when you are satisfied with the changes you've made.

2. We will now show you what the information presented with each indicator listed in the "Current Inputs" list box—C:\TT\BP___93A.TTDOpen[P-1][C-2]—represents. The first piece of data presented for all indicators will be the directory; in this case, C:\TT. The second piece of data will be the file name; in this case, BP___93A.TTD. The third piece of data will be the data heading; in this case, "Open." The fourth piece of data will be the data preprocessing method you've chosen, in this case, [P-1]. The number 1 represents the first method listed. The final piece of data is the data heading number, in this case [C-2]. C stands for column, 2 stands for the column number. In other words, if you were to open BP___93A.TTD into our spreadsheet the Open heading would be the second column of data in from the left.

Now choose a data preprocessing method. Repeat this step for each indicator listed. Use the instructions for this step to also choose a data preprocessing method for the target. The only difference would be that you substitute the word *target* wherever you see the word *indicator* or *input*.

STEP 9: Enter the *periods and periods ahead* information. Click in the "Periods" edit cell. Enter the number of periods you desire. Click in the "Ahead" edit cell. Enter the number of periods ahead you desire.

Each of the two cells must be filled with a number before a project file can be saved.

Periods: This number represents how the network will learn day-to-day relationships. The number 1 that you see in the graphic means that when the network trains, it will learn one-day relationships. You can look at it like this: If the network was training on data from 10/24/93, it would look at the data from 10/25/93, and determine the difference between the two days. It would then try to figure out why the change, if any, happened. The network does this for each and every piece of data. If numbers are higher than 1, the network changes how it looks at the data. If periods were set at five for example, the network would take a data chunk five days long, let's say

10/24/93, 10/25/93, 10/26/93, 10/27/93, and 10/28/93. While training, the network would take the data from 10/24/93, then determine the difference between that day and the data from 10/25/93. Once the network has dissevered these two dates, it takes the data from 10/24/93 and 10/26/93 and dissevers these two days; then 10/24/93, and 10/27/93, and so on. After the network has compared all the days with the data from 10/24/93 it takes the data from 10/25/93 and compares this data to all other dates and determines differences and tries to figure out why the differences happened. With the network set at five periods, you would force it to try and determine if one date in the 5-period chunk had anything to do with another's outcome.

Ahead: This number represents how many days into the future you would like the network to project. You should make this number the same as the periods.

STEP 10: Click on either "Linear," "Dates," or "Records." Before the network trains, it must first collect the data. It can collect the data in one of three ways:

DATES: Select this only if the data you are using are date-dependent. If the data you are using do not have dates anywhere in them, do not use this option. If this is selected, the network, while collecting data, will match dates from each file used in creating the project file and train only on this data. Let's say you are forecasting the Swiss franc. In the Swiss franc data file, there are data as far back as 6/2/93. Let's also say that the British pound data file, which is used as an indicator, has data as far back as 2/2/93. With this option selected, the network will ignore all data from 2/2/93 to 6/1/93 in the British pound file. The reason for this is that the dates must coincide. If the dates do not coincide, the network ignores extraneous data.

RECORDS: Select this option if the data files you are using do not have dates as part of the data. The data will be collected by the network in the same manner as it collects date-dependent data. The only difference is that instead of finding matching dates the network will find coinciding record numbers. For example, let's say that one of your data files has 1,000 records and another data file has 500 records. When the network collects data to ready it for training, only 500 records will be collected.

LINEAR: If you select this option, the network will collect all data whether the dates and/or records coincide or not.

STEP 11: The final step is to save the project file. Click on the "Save" button. The Save dialog box will appear. In the "File Name:" edit cell, enter a name for a CDB file. A suggestion would be to name the file so that you know what the file is. For example, if you are forecasting the closing price for Swiss Francs you would name the file SFC.CDB. Click on the "Ok" button. This CDB file is now ready to be trained.

Figure 1.   Select inputs/targets.

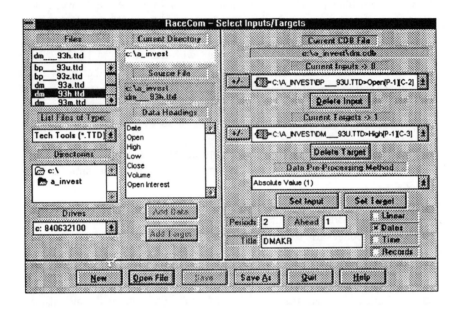

A New Neural Network

Conventional neural networks have neurodes that "fire," or produce an output, when the sum of the inputs to that neurode reach a specified level. It's like a light switch that takes four inch/ounces of force to turn on. If one person exerts all four inch/ounces of force, the light goes on. If eight people combine and each exerts 1/2 inch/ounce of force, the light goes on. How the total required force was developed is irrelevant. The light doesn't care.

A fuzzy neural network can be made to work differently. Let's take our eight people again. We might have a case where only one person exerts all the force necessary to turn on the light. The other seven exert no force because they really don't want the light on. With the conventional neural network, the light would go on even though this activation doesn't reflect the actual number of people who want the light on.

With the fuzzy neural network, we can design it in such a way that the force to turn on the light must come from a majority of people. Or, we can make the light not go to full brightness. We could have a brightness level that reflects not only the level of force being applied to the switch, but also the number of people applying force.

In our case, where only one person really wants the light on and the other seven do not, we could have the light go to 12.5 percent brightness. We could extend this process, for example, to the light on only if persons number three and number six also want the light on. But, adding these features, while interesting, means just another level of hard wiring computer instructions. We need to be more creative and imaginative.

Rather than building in these additional instructions, why not let the neural network learn the best way to set up the fuzzy neurodes. We could interlink other neural networks that would, in essence, create a map of the best way to fire the neurodes so that the output did not represent only the aggregate of the inputs but also the relative importance of each input source.

Further, we could create a 4x4 matrix transform for each neurode. Think of a 4x4 matrix as pattern of 16 light bulbs arranged 4 across and 4 down. If the bulbs can be in one of two states, either on or off, we have a total of 65,536 (2^{16}) possible patterns of lights.

Now, let's put a matrix like this between the incoming data and each neurode in our neural network. This 4x4 matrix would then function as a way of interpreting the incoming data before it's passed to the neurode; so we now have 65,536 ways we can structure the way each neurode reacts to incoming information.

The next step would be to dynamically alter the way we turn on the 16 light bulbs in each of our matrices. To do that, let's have another normal neural network's output act as a controller for the fuzzy neural network's matrices. As the standard network learns, it alters the matrix settings for each of the matrices. We could pass the fuzzy neural network's error back to the standard neural network so that it could benefit from what the fuzzy neural network has learned.

The only difference between our example and the actual Fuzzy 4x4 Neural-Net™ we developed is that we don't use simple on/off, two-state switches in our actual network. We use an 80-bit decimal number so that each matrix can assume $(1.2E +/- 4932)^{16}$ possible states. This is a number so long it extends into the next zip code. The end result of all this is a neural network that is adaptive not only in its ability to learn but also in the way it learns.

Quite candidly, the work we did on the ATN2 neural network, our 3D graphics, and the new Chaos Theory Option, made the Fuzzy 4x4 NeuralNet™ possible. Essentially, technology from one part of the company affected the progress in other areas. This is definitely a result of the synergy between disciplines.

A training session of the Fuzzy 4x4 NeuralNet is provided to demonstrate its ability. The normal reaction to this accuracy is to assume that the software is memorizing. The knowledge file for this training session was about 17K bytes. The data alone was nearly 100K bytes. This represents over a 5:1 reduction the network could not have memorized. Further, the fact that six errors were present showed the network was indeed using its gained knowledge.

Another reason for assuming the network is memorizing has to do with "mathematical noise." Learned people believe all market data contains noise—little random movements of 4 percent to 6 percent that make no sense. They consider the reason for this noise unknowable. We think that the reasons may be unknown, but they are not unknowable.

Test of Fuzzy 4x4 NeuralNets™

Learning Ability—One (1) cycle

Test parameters: Network allowed to set adjustments of fuzzy control elements. Chaos Theory module set on automatic. Network Interlink off.

Date	Open	High	Low	Close 5 Days Later TARGET	Close 5 Days Later OUTPUT	ERROR
dm___93u	8/17/93	$59.04	$59.15	$58.74	$59.44	$59.44
dm___93u	8/16/93	$58.50	$59.30	$58.48	$59.20	$59.20
dm___93u	8/13/93	$58.26	$58.37	$58.10	$59.55	$59.55
dm___93u	8/12/93	$58.09	$58.17	$57.79	$59.05	$59.05
dm___93u	8/11/93	$58.16	$58.24	$57.80	$59.37	$59.37
dm___93u	8/10/93	$58.58	$58.60	$58.01	$58.90	$58.90
dm___93u	8/09/93	$58.77	$58.90	$58.56	$59.17	$59.17
dm___93u	8/06/93	$58.19	$58.89	$58.12	$58.26	$58.26
dm___93u	8/05/93	$58.17	$58.25	$57.94	$58.12	$58.12
dm___93u	8/04/93	$58.17	$58.25	$57.94	$57.88	$58.12
dm___93u	8/03/93	$57.37	$58.61	$58.12	$58.05	$58.05
dm___93u	8/02/93	$57.49	$58.42	$57.48	$58.73	$58.73
dm___93u	7/30/93	$57.81	$57.31	$57.03	$58.79	$58.79
dm___93u	7/29/93	$57.80	$57.98	$57.09	$58.21	$58.21
dm___93u	7/28/93	$57.82	$57.97	$57.70	$58.21	$58.21
dm___93u	7/27/93	$57.79	$57.83	$57.58	$58.35	$58.35
dm___93u	7/26/93	$57.62	$57.73	$57.60	$58.34	$58.34
dm___93u	7/23/93	$57.87	$58.00	$57.76	$57.20	$57.20
dm___93u	7/22/93	$58.30	$58.36	$58.08	$57.14	$57.14
dm___93u	7/21/93	$58.56	$58.73	$58.42	$57.93	$57.93
dm___93u	7/20/93	$58.23	$58.55	$58.05	$57.60	$57.60
dm___93u	7/19/93	$58.06	$58.35	$58.06	$57.68	$57.68
dm___93u	7/16/93	$57.59	$57.94	$57.33	$57.87	$57.87
dm___93u	7/15/93	$57.97	$57.98	$57.52	$58.33	$58.33
dm___93u	7/14/93	$57.51	$57.96	$57.44	$58.57	$58.57
dm___93u	7/13/93	$57.60	$57.87	$57.53	$58.51	$58.51
dm___93u	7/12/93	$57.27	$57.48	$57.27	$58.25	$58.25
dm___93u	7/09/93	$57.76	$57.76	$57.54	$57.90	$57.90
dm___93u	7/08/93	$58.22	$58.35	$58.00	$57.70	$57.70
dm___93u	7/07/93	$58.38	$58.44	$57.97	$57.85	$57.85
dm___93u	7/06/93	$58.25	$58.52	$58.18	$57.77	$57.77
dm___93u	7/02/93	$58.57	$59.10	$58.26	$57.39	$57.39
dm___93u	7/01/93	$58.26	$58.60	$58.23	$57.67	$57.67
dm___93u	6/30/93	$58.70	$58.80	$57.98	$58.29	$58.29
dm___93u	6/29/93	$58.35	$58.77	$58.35	$58.06	$58.06
dm___93u	6/28/93	$57.93	$58.40	$57.91	$58.20	$58.20
dm___93u	6/25/93	$58.02	$58.43	$57.95	$58.46	$58.46
dm___93u	6/24/93	$57.97	$58.08	$57.82	$58.57	$58.57
dm___93u	6/23/93	$58.16	$58.66	$58.12	$58.08	$58.08
dm___93u	6/22/93	$58.63	$58.71	$58.24	$58.73	$58.73
dm___93u	6/21/93	$58.66	$58.77	$58.41	$58.31	$58.31

Date		Open	High	Low	Close 5 Days Later TARGET	Close 5 Days Later OUTPUT	ERROR
dm___93u	6/18/93	$59.46	$59.46	$58.73	$58.13	$58.13
dm___93u	6/17/93	$59.65	$59.90	$59.43	$58.04	$58.04
dm___93u	6/16/93	$60.09	$60.15	$59.51	$58.53	$58.53
dm___93u	6/15/93	$60.85	$61.10	$59.95	$58.39	$58.39
dm___93u	6/14/93	$60.92	$61.05	$60.70	$58.67	$58.67
dm___93u	6/11/93	$60.60	$61.20	$60.56	$58.90	$58.90
dm___93u	6/10/93	$60.37	$60.79	$60.30	$59.65	$59.65
dm___93u	6/09/93	$60.66	$60.71	$60.27	$59.69	$59.69
dm___93u	6/08/93	$60.92	$61.01	$60.79	$60.07	$60.07
dm___93u	6/07/93	$60.81	$61.09	$60.76	$60.73	$60.73
dm___93u	6/04/93	$61.90	$62.06	$60.68	$60.80	$60.80
dm___93u	6/03/93	$61.81	$61.84	$61.65	$60.68	$60.68
dm___93u	6/02/93	$62.01	$62.08	$61.71	$60.44	$60.44
dm___93u	6/01/93	$62.21	$62.26	$61.98	$60.81	$60.81
dm___93u	5/28/93	$61.88	$62.37	$61.86	$60.96	$60.96
dm___93u	5/27/93	$61.01	$61.66	$60.92	$60.70	$60.70
dm___93u	5/26/93	$60.69	$60.83	$60.40	$61.76	$61.76

Above is a fragment of a test of 223 days of the D-Mark.

This test was performed to illustrate the learning ability of the Fuzzy 4x4 NeuralNet™. We allowed the network to look at the data one time and then to output its results. The object was to see if the network could find a relationship between the Open/High/Low and the Close five days later. There were no additional data supplied to the network.

The actual training time was approximately 15 minutes on a 486DX 66 MHz computer. We limited the output to two decimal places. The only additional modification was formatting the output in Excel, which in essence did no more than put dollar signs in front of the numbers.

The Fuzzy 4x4 NeuralNet™ was allowed to completely configure itself with no outside control. Further, the Chaos Theory Option was placed in the automatic mode. As there were no additional networks being used, the Network Interlink function was disabled.

Out of 223 days, there was one day where the difference between the target and the output was $4.34. One day was $3.40. One day was $0.24. One day was $0.10. There were two days with $0.02 error, and there were 217 days with zero errors between the target and output.

Flexible Learning

There is another important aspect of the Fuzzy 4x4 NeuralNet™. It's called unlimited degrees of freedom.

Figure 2.   BP test test.

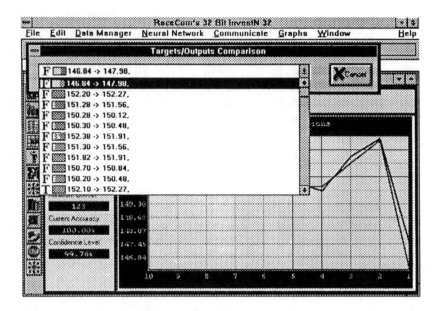

Let yourself take the place of a neural network as part of a little test. For this exercise, let's say you know nothing about traveling. Your job is to learn how best to travel between places so that we can use this knowledge to plan future trips. We'll begin by letting you figure how to get to New York City. But we're going to start by dropping you onto a randomly chosen spot somewhere within the continental United States. It may be in the middle of a desert, on top of a mountain, or in a lake. No matter where you start, you know your ultimate goal is New York City. Remember, though, what you learn about traveling will be applied to future destinations that we will keep secret for the moment.

If you started in Washington, D.C., you might jump on the 737 jet shuttle. You'd learn to go to the airport, buy a ticket, get on the plane, and fly to New York City. Case closed.

But, how many ways can you travel to New York City? While there may be a physical limit to the number of ways, there is no theoretical limit. In all cases, once you're within the designated city limits, you're in New York City. Your goal is accomplished, no matter how you got there. As a test, we drop you in Washington, D.C. again, and with your newly acquired knowledge you easily get back to New York City. If you were a neural network, you'd be considered trained and ready to tell us the best way to travel to other places.

Remember, you're fully trained because you've learned and we've tested you. To see if you are of any value, though, we test to see if you can get to a new destination, Byron, New York. You fail, unfortunately. Byron does not have a major airport that could handle a 737 jet. We should discard you because, obviously, you can't help us plan trips. You learned, but what you learned was of no value to us because you couldn't predict.

But wait. Let's change the way we evaluate you. First, we tell you that you were wrong. We tell you to get to New York from Washington again, but learn to do it a different way. This time you decide to take a boat from a dock on the Chesapeake and sail up to New York Harbor. Again, you've made it to New York. As a neural network, you're trained. But, when we test to see if you can get to Byron, New York, you fail. Byron is inland and has no water access. What you've learned is of no value to us even though you trained properly. It's not *if* you learned but *what* you learned.

The process is repeated over and over. We tell you to go back and try it again. Remember—we do not tell you anything about Byron, New York, during your training process. Everything about that destination is hidden from you at all times during training. The only thing you know is that what you learned was wrong. And each time you train you must try a different method of getting to New York City. Finally, after several attempts, you rent a car and drive to New York City. You could also rent a car and drive to Byron. So, what you've learned can be used to get to either destination. You are of value to us.

You can use the same analogy when thinking about training a neural network. Neural networks are initialized with random numbers. They are trained and then tested on specific data. They are considered trained if we can present the training information to them again and have them recognize the patterns correctly. This testing process is seriously flawed, however, if the neural network is to be used for predicting future events.

During training, the neural network deduced causal relationships between the inputs and targets from the training data. The idea is to ensure that these causal relationships are also applicable to unknown data. If the causal relationships don't apply to the unknown data, as was the case in our test on having you get to Byron, New York, the network is of little value for predicting.

With this discussion we've laid down the most fundamental problem with neural networks. The neural network has to be forced to learn the necessary relationships. If you consider learning using known targets as one level of supervision, learning causal relationships that have predictive value can be considered a higher level of supervision. We're forcing the network to be predictive.

Now, let's go back to you as a neural network. If you will recall, you were able to demonstrate flexibility with your learning. You could learn, or be taught, to solve the same problem in different ways. You have many degrees of freedom. The learning structure in your mind is adaptable. This flexibility is central to the success of the human race. If we weren't able to realize an apple on an upper branch is just as nourishing as an apple on a lower branch, we might starve.

For us to have a successful neural network, it must also be able to solve the same problem many ways. The problem we found is that most neural network paradigms have virtually zero flexibility. This cripples their ability.

A New Way to Use a Neural Network

Generalizing is the key to neural network performance. To illustrate, let's take what appears to be a simple problem. If we wanted to predict the D-mark for the next day, we might use the Open/High/Low/Close for both the D-mark and the Swiss franc for the past 200+ days. This gives us a total of eight (8) data inputs. Now let's assume these prices are globally stable within a $5.00 range. The possible combinations of these 8 inputs, each with a 500-penny range is 500^8. A neural network would have to see all $3.90625 * 10^{21}$ combinations to be certain of perfect predictions.

Neural network owners want to use easily obtained data to train their neural network. Further, they want to train it to a high level of accuracy and get perfect predictions in return. One could take the position that the user had to be educated on how best to use a neural network. Just as long as the neural network performed its duties, it would be up to the user to attend to the proper care and feeding. As a software developer, RaceCom looks at the problem differently. We feel it is our job to make the neural networks fit the needs of the user. To do this, we had to rethink many of the concepts surrounding neural networks, especially generalizing.

Generalize means "to infer or derive the underlying characteristics of historical data by looking at the specifics of that data." A neural network is expected to generalize. Neural networks that predict better than average are considered able to generalize, but we found this not to be the case. The crux of the problem lies in a common feature in neural networks—the exponential function. This function appeared to limit what many call mathematical noise. In fact, there have been tests of neural networks in which mathematical noise was deliberately introduced in order to properly simulate, in the eyes of the test creator, market information. We took a different approach.

It was, and still is, our belief that all historical financial data has value and should not be treated as part information and part noise. However, taking financial data in its unprocessed form will pose a problem for current neural networks in that the user is presenting precise data to the network. From this precise data, the user wants generalizations to be drawn. Further, the user will not accept the neural network as being trained unless the network reports back accurate training. RaceCom's next generation neural network, the Fuzzy 4x4 NeuralNet™, preprocesses data and limits its training states. Preprocessing data does not mean normalizing. Current networks must have normalized data within a range of values either between –0.5 and 0.5 or 0.0 and 1.0. To accomplish this normalizing, the data are divided by some number. For instance, if you're using the S&P 500 and the high is 460 and the low is 440, we have to stuff that range of numbers into an area between 1.0 and 0.0. The software would use a formula like (actual value – low value) * (1.0 / (high value – low value)). Substituting an arbitrary value of 450, our formula would look like (450 – 440) * (1 / (460 – 440)), with the answer being 0.5. Our value of 450 is 900 times larger than the number we're supplying the software. It is easy to see the loss of precision using this process.

The Fuzzy 4x4 NeuralNet™ does not require normalized inputs. Instead, we've devised a method whereby we've done away with the exponential (sigmoid) function. In fact, we've created a totally new concept. In one sense, the network itself generalizes by virtue of the way data is presented to it. It further generalizes its training because the number of possible output values is set for each individual target and input.

What this all means is that you can use precise data and get precise predictions. This approach also gives virtually perfect training accuracy. You'll see faster, easier training no matter how complex the input data or your forecast needs.

Data Reinforcing

The value of data reinforcing to a neural network can be explained with a simple exercise. Look around you for a box-shaped object. Think of one characteristic of that box that describes it completely. You can't. The box has depth. It has width, height, orientation, color, and a surface texture. That's without even touching its spatial relation to other objects. These are just a few aspects that describe that box or any box. You should view providing data for a neural network just as you would if you had to describe that box to a friend over the telephone. The more ways you describe input data, the better the neural network will understand it. The more things you said about the box, the better mental picture your friend would have of the box.

To predict with the Fuzzy 4x4 NeuralNet™, whether it's for a horse race or the S&P 500, the best results will always be attained if the network fully understands what it is expected to learn. This sounds as if we're discussing how best to train a living creature. In many ways, we are.

The Fuzzy 4x4 NeuralNet™ is unlike any other. It is a multistate network in that it is able to train on as few as the two values of one or zero, but also on the infinity of values between the two numbers. For the purist, infinity is limited to a computer's ability to represent different numbers. This means the Fuzzy 4x4 Neural-Net™ treats Yes/No, Higher/Low, On/Off, and similar values as two states. In turn, it sets up its training as having only two states for that particular data.

To describe data to a neural network, you also need to do more than just provide it in various formats. Returning to our box, if we want the neural network to understand the color of this box, would it make sense to scan and quantize the color? A scanned color can take as many as 16 million shades. But, if our box only comes in four colors, why not make the network limit its range of choices to four. That's all there are anyway. The Fuzzy 4x4 NeuralNet™ would accurately learn the color of the box, but would do so quickly because it limited the possible color to one of four. Your friend would know the color of the box if you said it was black, for instance.

To take this concept further, let's look at the S&P 500. The movements are reported in 0.05 increments. Why have the neural network train out to 20 decimal points? Let's say for the sake of this explanation that the range of movement for the S&P 500 within three standard deviations is 40. We can tell the Fuzzy 4x4 Neural-Net™ to automatically assume only the necessary states to cover all possible movements of the S&P 500. That turns out to be (40.0 / 0.05), or 800. This is a manageable number and easily trained. Again, because we've limited the possible values this number can assume, the Fuzzy 4x4 NeuralNet™ will only have to learn a limited number of values.

Now that we know we can tell the Fuzzy 4x4 NeuralNet™ not only what to train but how to train, we can move on to some exciting concepts. Input data for neural networks can be viewed in many ways. The more ways you look at a problem, the better you understand it. The same is absolutely true for a neural network.

Going back to the S&P 500, let's say one of our inputs for training is the British pound high. The up and down movement alone for just the British pound high can be looked at many ways. Was it higher or lower the day before? That's useful information. Let's say we want this included in our training, so we tell the Fuzzy 4x4 Neural-Net™ to get the higher/lower relationship. The network scans the input data source and sets up a three-state training mode for that input. It assigns the value one (1) to data that were higher than the day before. It assigns the value zero (0) to data when the previous day's value was the same as today's. Finally, it assigns the value minus one (–1) if today's value for the British pound high is lower than yesterday's. Three states. This is a simple relationship easily and quickly trained, yet it contains valuable information that adds to the network's understanding of the problem.

The beauty of the Fuzzy 4x4 NeuralNet™ is that you can view this one piece of input information many different ways within the same training process. And you do it with a single button; it's called preprocessing. In every case, the Fuzzy 4x4 Neural-Net™ handles the entire operation automatically, including setting up the number of training states. As a user, all you need to do is tell the Fuzzy 4x4 NeuralNet™ which input to use and how to preprocess and train the data.

Within a single training file you can have every input looked at in many ways. In every case, the network will have done all the work for you with a single button. The network will be able to make more predictions because it has expanded the way it looks at data. RaceCom calls this data reinforcing.

The Creative Investor

Tomorrow's investor will be informed better, faster, and more completely than ever before. The truly successful investor will be the one who uses this information to its fullest value.

With the advent of RaceCom's Fuzzy 4x4 NeuralNet™, investors will not only be able to predict prices better, they'll be able to evaluate opportunities as never before. As technology races forward, new companies will be formed that could offer

Figure 3.   Preprocessing list.

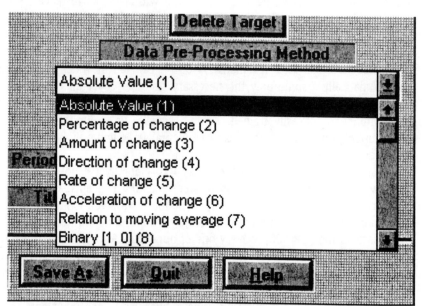

enormous rewards for the investor able to get in early. But there will be many new companies that are not good investments. How do you tell the difference?

When a new company is formed, there is much data available about the principles in the company, the market targeted by the company, and the financial foundation of the venture. The accountants' numbers associated with the founding of a company are easily handled by a neural network. Where the Fuzzy 4x4 NeuralNet™ turns this process into one that's truly remarkable is in its ability to deal with logical data, such as "Does the CEO have experience in this field?" or "Does the company have easy access to a trained work force?" The Fuzzy 4x4 NeuralNet™ has virtually unlimited ability to process and train on conditional branching statements.

Because the Fuzzy 4x4 NeuralNet™ can evaluate both numerical data and logical statements, the network can provide a simple yes or no answer. Because of the very nature of Fuzzy 4x4 NeuralNets'™ training, there is no place for ambiguity in its predictions.

If we take this concept of flexibility in analysis back to such everyday challenges as predicting the close of the Swiss franc, we can use the Fuzzy 4x4 NeuralNet™ to develop some remarkable insights. What if, instead of just numbers, we began adding the human factor. Humans buy or sell based on perceptions about the financial markets and the world in general. Information supplied to humans alters these perceptions on a daily basis.

If there is an upheaval in Moscow, the markets are affected. If major companies in a particular industry merge, the markets are affected. The list of what affects the markets is endless and much of it is not quantifiable data. But this information can be reduced to a logical statement. An example would be, "Were there indications the Fed would raise short-term interest rates?" Because the Fuzzy 4x4 NeuralNet™ handles this kind of information, the creative investor will benefit. Nonnumerical data of this nature is a leading indicator, and thus the output of the Fuzzy 4x4 NeuralNet™ is a true predictor of future price levels.

Conversely, neural networks that process only numerical data have to look only at the affects of nonnumerical information on the market. If the Fed made noises about raising or lowering interest rates, investors could cause the markets to move a particular way. These networks would see the effect only after the fact. Their forecast would have to be more a lagging indicator than predictive information.

The Fuzzy 4x4 NeuralNet™ has no bounds. This revolutionary approach to a neural network will open new vistas to forecasting, not only in the way it operates but in how it serves the truly creative investor. The Fuzzy 4x4 NeuralNet™ will turn ordinary applications into the extraordinary. The creative applications will become truly amazing.

Advanced

The sole purpose of neural network software is to predict. Whether it's prices, movements, direction, or whatever, the user expects a prediction. Neural networks train away and then grind out predictions—some good, some bad.

As a user, if you don't know the good predictions from the bad predictions, you could be risking money when you shouldn't. After seven years of watching neural networks train and predict, RaceCom saw that sometimes neural networks shouldn't make predictions. This occurs when the training data have not adequately prepared the network for a particular set of circumstances.

Because of the internal mechanisms of current neural networks—specifically the exponential function—a neural network will make a prediction when it shouldn't. Unfortunately, the prediction will seem reasonable due to the exponential function. For you, the investor, it's like driving down a mountain road at night with your lights off.

Of all the features we wanted in our new software, one of them was not to give bad predictions when the training data had not properly prepared the neural network, so the first item we removed from our newest neural network was the exponential function. It's gone. And in its place there is a truly revolutionary neural network paradigm—Fuzzy 4x4 NeuralNet™.

The Fuzzy 4x4 NeuralNet™ is fundamentally simple, but it automatically creates enormously complicated patterns within the computer memory. The reason for the complexity is that we committed this neural network to virtually perfect training accuracy. To achieve this accuracy, the network has free will to enhance its understanding of the training data without bounds.

But we further insisted that the Fuzzy 4x4 NeuralNet™ not generate predictions that looked good when in fact they were not. No prediction at all was better than a wrong prediction.

When our test groups thought about this concept for a minute, they realized the value of it. To further explain, let's say that there is a 12-day period during which the network produces only four predictions. Because it has trained to near perfect accuracy, the network would make predictions only if it was absolutely convinced it knew what to expect.

In our testing, we found when a prediction was made it was accurate within specified ranges nearly 100 percent of the time. Thus, going back to our example of predictions four days out of 12, you are spared losing money for the eight days when the training data was inadequate. More importantly, you can be virtually guaranteed to be right on the days when predictions are made. This is a profound change in neural network application. The Fuzzy 4x4 NeuralNet™ is intelligent in not only what to predict but also when to predict.

Live Training

"Let me train on 15-minute bars of the S&P 500 and I'll be happy," a customer said. Another customer complained the S&P 500 was too volatile for a neural network. These statements perplexed us for a long time. People complained that the S&P 500 was so volatile and yet they were satisfied to examine the price movement only once every 15 minutes.

We found that people set up time bars to read the price movements. A time bar has an open/high/low/close, just as end-of-day information. But instead of 24 hours between inputs of information, the time is measured in minutes. By supplying the open/high/low/close information, we are expected to derive a good understanding of the price movement. The folly of this concept is illustrated with the two graphs shown. Both have the same values for open/high/low/close. It is a stretch to expect a neural network to predict anything accurately, given the potential for misinformation with just open/high/low/close.

Figure 4.   Sine graph.

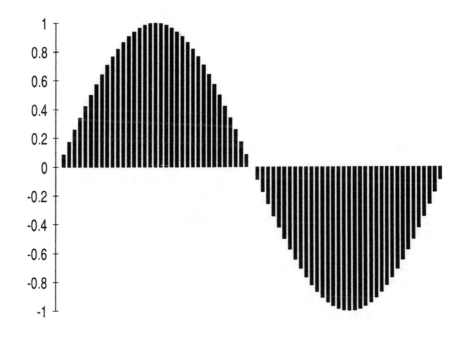

Figure 5.   Spike graph.

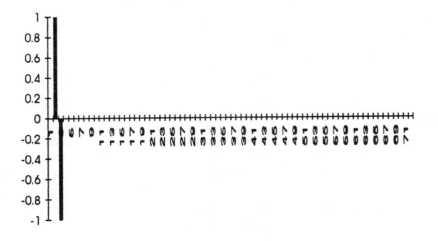

Further, for software running in the 16-bit world, the machine will either be continuously interrupted or have to interrogate the data service at regular intervals. In both instances, the machine must stop what it is doing. Many customers have said that their computers have become nothing more than data collection systems.

If a computer uses what are called interrupts, when data arrive at a communications port, the machine stops whatever it is doing and handles the job of storing or otherwise disposing the information. The machine's full attention is given to the process. In Windows 3.1, a program can be set to interrogate the communications port at regular intervals. To allow work on other tasks, it's not unusual for a user to set 15 minutes between interrogations.

We developed InvestN 32 to solve these problems. InvestN 32 is native Windows NT code. In other words, it is multithreaded. Threads are considered separate processes. One thread could collect data, and another could store the information; others train and forecast. If there is only one CPU in the computer, the system allocates time to each thread based on software-established priorities. The threads themselves maintain a set of structures for saving their context while waiting to be scheduled for CPU processing time.

This multithreaded arrangement allows for true multitasking. Windows 3.1 appears to be multitasking. It uses what is called nonpreemptive multitasking. You can open one application and, while that one's open, open others. However, only one application can actually be doing anything at any one time. For another application to function, the currently operating application must *voluntarily* give up what it is doing. The system or other applications cannot force the current application to give up processor time under Windows 3.1 to run other applications.

InvestN 32 utilizes preemptive multitasking. On single-processor computers, this means the system allocates small slices of CPU time for each thread. The time slice is only about 20 milliseconds, so it appears that all the threads are executing simultaneously. If InvestN 32 is run on a computer with multiple processors, the threads automatically would be distributed between the processors by the software and all functions would indeed be operating simultaneously. We have built in features that automatically take proper advantage of whatever the computer has available.

The screen shots shown in Figures 6 and 7 represent the normal display of a continuous forecasting session. Here, InvestN 32 is collecting live data for several futures. Because InvestN 32 runs under Windows NT, we can collect data whenever it changes and still train and forecast. We are also not chained to an arbitrary time bar for data collection or forecasting.

The point of this example is to show what's being missed when running under the time bar method. The lower graphs all show about 78 minutes worth of data. During that time the S&P 500 changed 801 times. InvestN 32 collected every change. The software also collected all the data for 21 other markets at the same time. If you were collecting S&P 500 data with 15-minute time bars, you would have about six different values. That means you would have lost 795 other changes, or 99.25 percent of the information regarding price movements.

To expect to predict anything accurately using a neural network, you have to provide the network with complete information. You can't hide 99.25 percent of the data regarding price movements and be sure of accurate predictions. To reinforce this

Figure 6.   Live training.

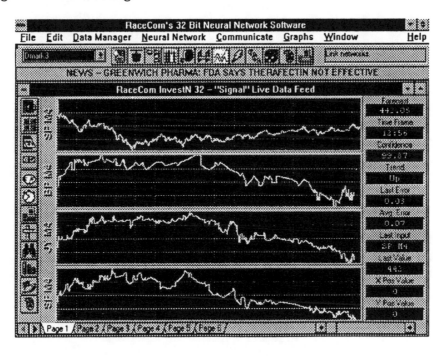

Figure 7.   Live training.

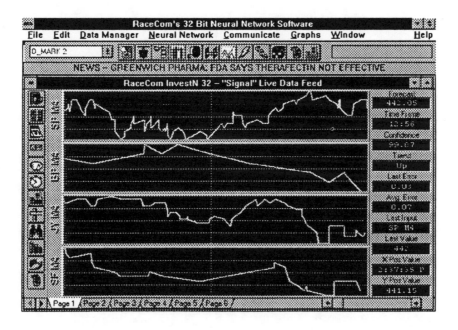

Figure 8.   Live feed.

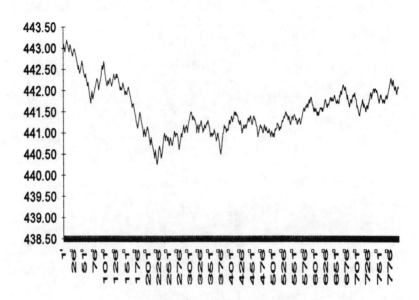

Figure 9.   1-minute bars.

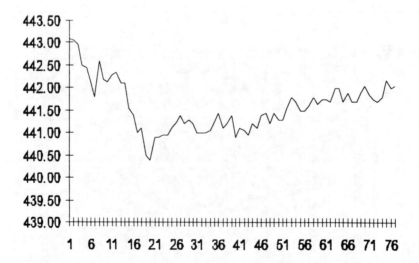

Figure 10. 2-minute bars.

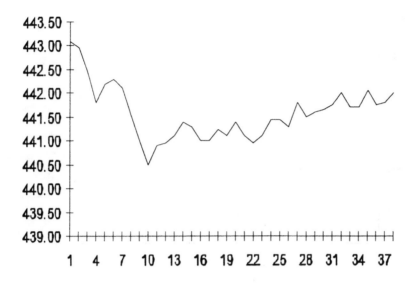

Figure 11. 5-minute bars.

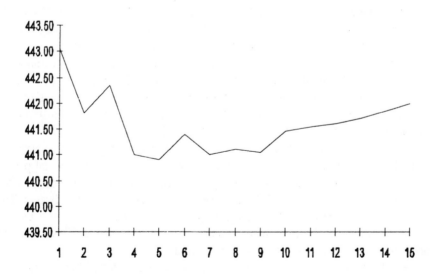

Figure 12. 15-minute bars.

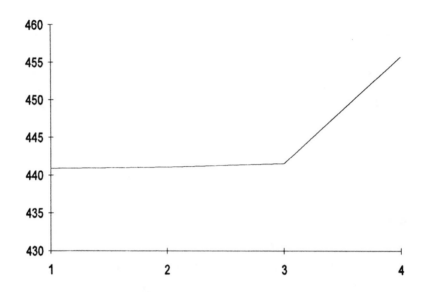

point, take a jigsaw puzzle with 1,000 pieces and try to imagine what it will look like by randomly selecting only eight pieces out of the box. Conversely, if you put together 992 pieces, it would be pretty easy to accurately guess what the other eight pieces probably look like.

Think of the price graph of the S&P 500 as a kind of jigsaw puzzle. If you give the neural network only 0.75 percent of the total picture, you can't expect the network to be able to predict what a price will be at some point in the future.

To further illustrate this problem, we also set InvestN 32 to collect and graph data at 1-, 2-, 5-, and 15-minute intervals. We've provided the graphs so you can see this loss of data. Even at one-minute intervals the loss of information about the S&P 500 is crippling to a neural network. At 15-minute intervals, there's almost no relationship between the movement of the S&P 500 and the data.

From a neural network standpoint, there are other advantages to not using time bars. First, let's look at what you want to know. You want to know the actual price at some point in the future. Using the infinitely less precise time bar method, we try to compensate by using the open/high/low/close as four inputs for each indicator. If we have six indicators, that's a total of 24 values. If, on the other hand, we use live inputs, we can use only the most recent value for the six indicators. This makes our network four times faster. But that's just the beginning.

Live data converge better in a neural network. The information appears as a continuous curve rather than jagged chucks. This cuts down training time even further. One other magical thing happens: When seen as part of a continuous curve, price movements that were labeled "mathematical noise" become valuable training information. With this additional data, the neural network can train and project even more accurately. In essence, live data make the neural network a more precise forecasting tool. When fortunes are won or lost because of small price movements, the more accurate we are at delivering data to the neural network the greater precision we'll have in our predictions.

Our old "end-of-day" neural network was unable to do live trading. Even so, when customers used two-minute bars as their data feed, the forecasts skyrocketed. Shown is a trading history by a customer using the old InvestN 32 on two-minute bars with the S&P 500. Two-minute bars, while still imprecise, are more indicative of actual price movements than are time bars of greater duration. The more indicative the data, the better and more precise the predictions.

Table 1. Customer history info 1.

InvestN-SP	SP M4 2 Min.
Total net profit	$27,525
Gross profit	$30,000
Total number of trades	22
Number of winning trades	20
Largest winning trade	$4,500
Average winning trade	$1,500
Ratio average win/average loss	1.21
Maximum consecutive winners	20
Average number bars in winners	38
Maximum interday drawdown	-$4,350
Profit factor	12.12
Account size required	$47,475
Open position P/L	$2,100
Gross loss	-$2,475
Percent profitable	91%

Table 2. Customer history info 2.

Number losing trades	2
Largest losing trade	-$1,875
Average losing trade	$1,237
Average trade (win and loss)	$1,251
Maximum consecutive losers	2
Average number bars in losers	1
Maximum number contracts held	6
Return on account	58%

Conquering the S&P 500

Now that we've got a better understanding of the S&P 500, let's conquer it. We'll take you through the complete process. In this case, let's assume you're tied into Signal—the Data Broadcasting Corporation's information service. As long as you have a receiver, InvestN 32 will completely handle all aspects of data retrieval.

First, we need to set up the Fuzzy 4x4 NeuralNet™ in order to get our forecasts. We'll make the training parameters very simple. From the Neural Network menu, we select "Live Feed." The graph shown is the dialog box presented.

We're going to forecast the S&P 500, so from the "Types" drop-down list box, we select "Futures (*.LIV)." We want June '94 contracts so we enter "M4" in the "Delivery" edit box. In the "Sources" list box you'll be shown all the currently available futures. Next, we scroll down the list until we find "SP.LIV." Double-clicking on that choice fills the "Data Headings" list box as shown. We're using live data so all we want is the "Last" price. We select that value and press the "Add Data" button. As we also want to predict this price some point into the future, we again select that value and press the "Add Target" button. This tells the network this value has to be forecasted. We could forecast virtually infinite pieces of information, but for the example we'll keep it to just the absolute value at some point in the future.

Let's say we feel the British pound, the D-mark, and the yen have an influence on the movement of the S&P 500. Again, we scroll down the list until we find each heading, double-click on that choice to the "Data Headings" list box. Remember, this is just a simple setup, so all we want is the "Last" price. We select that value and

---

Figure 13. Live data input targets.

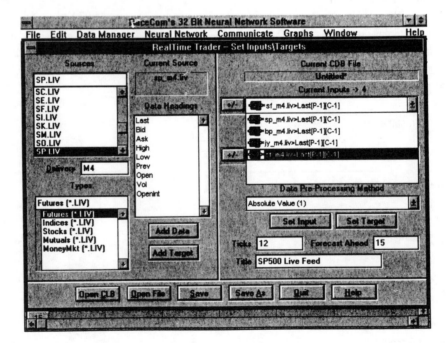

press the "Add Data" button. This gives us four inputs and one target. Naturally, we could make the process much more involved by adding more inputs and/or automatically preprocessing those inputs in various ways.

The only things left to do are to tell the software to create snapshots of the data and how far ahead we want to forecast. Arbitrarily, we'll say look at 12-minute snapshots, so we enter 12 in the "Ticks" edit. This number can vary, depending on the market of interest. The more volatile the market, the larger the number of inputs per pattern. If the S&P 500 has 10 changes in one minute, 12 minutes would give us 120 inputs per snapshot. Conversely, if the British pound changes five times a minute, our snapshots would have to be 24 minutes to get the same 120 inputs per snapshot.

A snapshot is really a neural network training pattern. If we use 12 minutes as a guide, the actual size of the pattern we have depends on the frequency of changes of the target. Again, the target is what we're trying to forecast. If the S&P 500 has 120 changes in that 12-minute period, we will have 120 inputs in a single pattern. It would be unlikely that other indicators would have the same frequency of change as does the target. The coincident values of other indicators being used by the neural network are interpolated. The included graph shows this process.

The S&P 500 is the target. When it changes, we collect its actual value. The coincident values for the other three indicators have to be interpolated. This process, while not precise, provides an adequately complete pattern.

Next, we enter 15 in the "Forecast Ahead" edit box. This doesn't mean you'll get a forecast once every 15 minutes. What you are telling the network is that you want to be told if the price movement will be equal to or greater than a value you

Figure 14. Pattern.

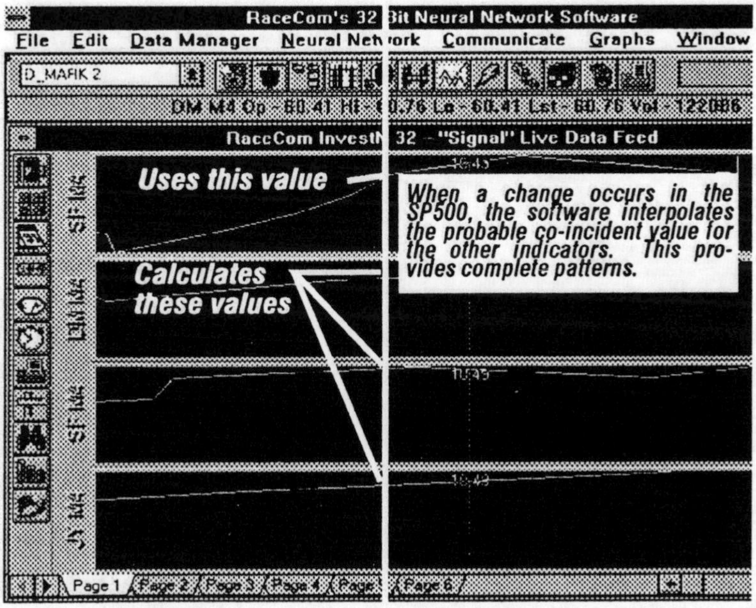

decide upon at *any time* within the next 15 minutes. Let's say you tell the network to notify you if the price will move more than 0.5. If the network believes this condition will be met at 12 minutes and 7 seconds from now, you'll be alerted.

The title can be anything you want. This title appears in the drop-down list box on the main menu so that you can invoke this process again quickly at any time. Now, you just save the new "*.CLB" file normally. This file doesn't need to be created each time. You can use this same file all the time. This creation process is only done once. Further, there's no limit to the different training files you can create and use to employ the network.

You select "Communicate" from the main menu bar. From that list you choose the pop-up menu "Live Feed." From the displayed list, click on "Connect Signal" and the live training window will appear. If the receiver has not been initialized, InvestN 32 will download the Receiver Operating System and your passwords automatically. You now select the "*.CLB" file you saved earlier.

The only remaining thing you have to do is tell the software the forecast trigger. If the forecast trigger is set to 0, the software will provide a continuous forecast of the next change regardless of when or how small. Any other value causes the network to forecast the actual value and the expected time it will occur. In all cases, the network monitors its forecasting accuracy both as an indicator of confidence for the user and as a way of improving its forecasts.

To invoke the forecasting, the user presses a button on the vertical button bar and InvestN 32 takes over. It automatically displays the graphs, collects data, trains,

Figure 15. "*.CLB" setup.

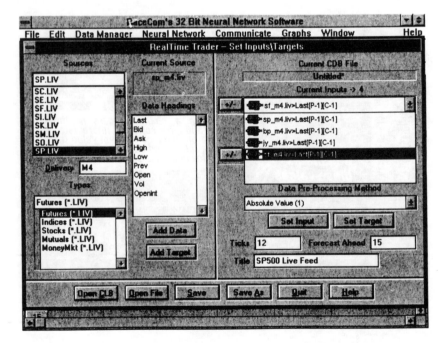

and forecasts. The software does many other things too. There are 10 display windows to the right of the graphs. Their functions are as follows:

1. Current forecast—This is the value of the forecast.

2. Time Frame—The network expects the price of the S&P 500 to equal the forecasted value in 12 minutes 56 seconds.

3. Confidence—The network has been monitoring the accuracy of its forecasts and has concluded them to be accurate 99.87 percent of the time.

4. Trend—In general, the target will be going up.

5. Last Error—The network was off by 0.03 in its last forecast. Because the S&P 500 is reported in 0.05 increments, the error is insignificant.

6. Avg Error—The Average Absolute Sum of all forecasting errors is reported.

7. Last Input—Of all the data being collected for this process, a change in the SP M4 was the last to arrive.

8. Last Value—This tells us what the last value was.

9/10. X/Y Pos Value—This shows you where the mouse is within any of the graphs displayed. It will show the time and the respective value. You can always have this information displayed.

That's the whole process. Within two or three minutes, the Fuzzy 4x4 Neural-Net™ was operating on live data and was making good forecasts. The user didn't need to know anything about neural networks or even data collection.

The vertical row of buttons in the window offers a wide assortment of functions that can be employed during training. From graphs to network monitoring, a simple button will invoke a series of powerful functions. The button with the money symbol provides a complete picture of how a current forecast will affect a user's portfolio. Naturally, there are many ways available to print attractive reports and forecasts.

You can change the type of graphs displayed from simple 2D to complex 3D. The new InvestN 32 can display 3D graphs with depth, lighting, surface texture, and shadows (it can even be shrouded in fog). The number of graphs on a single page can also be modified.

There is a complete communications package that allows the user to have the software operate remotely and communicate its forecasts and other notices over the phone lines to any person the user desires.

RaceCom's approach to investment neural network is based on the belief that artificial intelligence has limitless potential. There is one thing the ultimate user must remember, however, and this applies to any vendor's product: The input data must be an accurate, timely picture of the historical information. The blurrier or more imprecise the input, the more imprecise the forecast.

Chapter 10

IMPROVING TRADING RESULTS BY APPLYING CHAOS THEORY TO A NEURAL NET

Joe Shepard,
Director of Software Development
RaceCom, Inc.

INTRODUCTION

Chaos theory can be an enormously powerful tool when used to forecast prices, point spreads, order of finish, or whatever. As it is the science of global systems, we can make a case for saying chaos will show us the general, long-term movement of prices as well as the incremental steps. If prices moved back and forth with the predictability of a pendulum, there would be little need for chaos theory in the financial markets.

RaceCom's original version of the Chaos Theory Option did all the right things, such as first test for the presence of chaos, and then map the actual chaos pattern. Once we had the pattern, we passed the information on to the neural network and, in essence, said "here's more data you might find helpful." This additional data made an important impact on projections. Frankly, we thought we knew why, but we didn't really understand all the benefits.

After careful examination, we found that the neural network was only scratching the surface. The chaos pattern held many more secrets the neural network could use to enhance its work. To explain what we've done, we first need to explain some concepts about the way we predict future events.

UNDERSTANDING CHAOS

Financial movement may seem wild and unpredictable, but it isn't—it is chaotic. Chaos does not imply randomness. Chaotic systems follow rules; the price movements follow rules. Smoke rises from a fire because of rules. Waves crash against the shore

279

because of rules. Even with the most basic rules we can have outcomes of incredible complexity. We often confuse these complex results with randomness.

The job of our Chaos Theory Option is to identify these rules so that they can be applied. First, we need to understand what we're trying to predict. The Swiss franc, for instance, may be sensitive to movements of the Eurodollar. But there is little chance that anything the Eurodollar does will cause the Swiss franc's value to reach infinity or cause the value to go negative. Thus, we can say the Swiss franc is stable within a specified range. The maximum range is our *global* range. In other words, the Swiss franc is globally stable.

The day-to-day, up and down movement, on the other hand, is not stable. We can call this our local range. The Swiss franc is *locally unstable*. Once we've agreed to these two points, we can proceed.

Rather than explain chaos as it applies to markets by trudging through a web of complex formulae and involved concepts, let's do it the easy way. We said everything is affected by rules. We'll create a simple rule and apply that rule to the movement of a price. X is the instantaneous value of the lower line. Y is the instantaneous value of the upper graph. Our rule is a simple mathematical formula: $X = 45 - ((Y - 45) * 0.5)$. That's a rule.

The Chaos Theory Option would be expected to calculate the rule and give it to the neural network. The neural network's job would be much easier because, instead of having to learn causal relationships, it would ignore all other inputs and simply use the rule supplied by the Chaos Theory Option. Just glancing at the graph in Figure 1 shows the lower in step with the upper.

Figure 1.   Chaos graph XY.

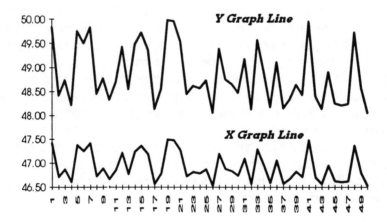

Let's add another rule and another graph line (see Figure 2). The new graph line is the top one, and we'll call it instantaneous value Z. The modified rule becomes $X = 45 + ((Y - 45) * 0.05) - ((Z - 50) * (Z - 50))$. Again, a simple formula—but look at the enormous change in the X graph line. Now the X graph line appears as though it has no relationship to either of the other lines. It has, however, a perfect relation to the other two

Figure 2.   Chaos graph XYZ.

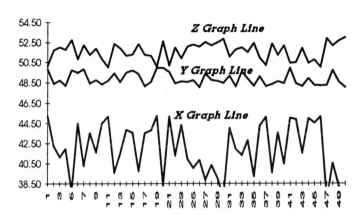

lines. Just glancing the X graph line, though, would leave one believing it to be completelyrandom.

Think of the Y and Z lines as prices that have a direct effect on the X graph. Even with the simplest rules, we create a price chart that looks complex. If, however, we can find a way to uncover the underlying rules, or at least get a rough idea of what the rules are, we'll be miles ahead.

DISCOVERING THE UNDERLYING RULES OF CHAOS

These simple graphs represent a good beginning in understanding what chaos means and how we can use it to help predict price movements. The study of chaos is much more involved and we are not attempting to trivialize the complexity. To illustrate, what if the values of Z and Y were changed by how much they were affected by X. Further, prices are affected by more than one or two external influences. They are affected by a myriad of influences. Some prices are even self-referential. *Self-referential* means that they are affected by rules hidden within the price movement itself.

Rather than present a study of chaos, what we really want to do is take an existing, complex price graph with chaotic up and down movements and find the underlying rules that determined its shape. We can then supply these rules to the neural network so it will know where the prices are going with some confidence.

What we need is to have the software do all the work. The first thing we need to do is determine if chaos exists. Not everything is chaotic. A simple square wave on an oscilloscope is not chaotic, for example. How, then, do we determine the presence of chaos. For our discussion, a chaotic process exhibits extreme sensitivity to initial conditions.

RaceCom's InvestN 32 looks at the entire data set and calculates the Lyapunov exponents. The name comes from Aleksandr M. Lyapunov, a nineteenth-century Russian mathematician. What we're looking for is the difference between two nearly equal values of X. We can start with the first two values in a training set and, as we go through the training set, see if the values are closer or farther apart.

Technically, we use this formula:

$$L = \sum \log 2 |R(1-2X_n)|/N.$$

If L, the Lyapunov exponent, is positive, we have sensitivity to initial conditions. This means chaos is present. After determining the presence of chaos, we then have to find the underlying rules. It is a complex operation.

An analogous process is photographic compression. Storing a detailed photograph can take a megabyte on a hard drive. That same photograph can be reduced to less than 20,000 bytes using a fractal compression algorithm. To make this compression work, the rules have to be found. We use a modified process called the *iterated function system* (IFS). The actual technical process is handled by the InvestN 32 and requires no user input. In fact, everything is transparent. If we find chaos, we create a compressed image, modify the neural network input set, and automatically pass the data to the network as additional information.

The compressed image is not really an image at all. It's merely a set of instructions telling a computer program how to construct an image that will appear nearly identical to the original. It is a set of rules.

What RaceCom does is use some slick math to improve on the system. We reduce the data much the same way as the photographic compression works. What we end up with is a set of rules that describe what causes the prices to fluctuate up and down. Again, we pass these rules to the neural network. We're not passing the image.

The neural network is given these rules as additional input(s). The value to the neural network can best be explained by visualizing yourself trying to draw a map of a city you've never seen before. You can take a pad and pencil and walk the streets. The distances would be written down and the direction of the various streets entered. As you walk, you look to get visual cues about the relationship of the various thoroughfares. When you return to your office, you can take all your notes and try to construct an accurate map. Your map probably wouldn't be all that accurate, though.

Let's say we help you. We fly over the city in an airplane and take a picture. With this picture, you know what the city should look like on a map. But the picture shows only relative distances and relative directions. All we can tell from the picture is that Elm Street is a little shorter than Oak Brook Drive and it goes off at a 30 degree angle. But the actual lengths and absolute compass directions of streets are written down in your pad, and by combining the picture and the data you wrote down on your pad, we can arrive at a very accurate map of the city with relative ease. Your job is simplified.

Think of the picture as the chaos map supplied by the software and the absolute distances and directions as being supplied by the inputs to the network. When we combine the two, the network understands what the projected price graph should look like. Chaos analysis alone, in our estimation, is not capable of predicting exact prices. While Mandelbrot's simulation of cotton pricing in 1953 can still predict the variation in prices, this process cannot tell you what the price will be next Friday. What chaos does do is predict the general statistical nature of a price movement.

Understanding this statistical nature is an important concern and has a profound effect. Once the neural network has this information, it knows not only what the prices were at any specific time, but the rules that caused the prices to move as they did. In our testing, we were able to validate the premise that markets have a memory, or persistence. The markets show long- and short-term memory. In fact, the markets reveal this persistence at every level. We've found it on live data and on weekly movement. This memory and persistence lays waste to the claim that the markets are oblivious to that which went before. In other words, chaos shows that investors remember not only when GM went up a point but also when Xerox went to the moon.

Recently a banker from Fort Walton Beach called to say that the chaos application had amazed him. He was using the old version of our software to predict the close of the Dow a week in advance. The neural network using chaos forecasted in advance a price that was within $0.60 of being exactly right. Frankly, we weren't surprised. Chaos allows the network to uncover the forces at work that move prices.

Let's go back to our Swiss franc. We said it was locally unstable and globally stable. As is RaceCom's wont, we take advantage of these conditions. Rather than design a giant, all-encompassing Chaos Theory Option, we designed one with limited scope. This gave us increased speed and greater precision.

For those technically inclined, we changed the process of calculating tertiary attractors and restructured the stepped IFS algorithms. Further, the encoding processes were modified to merge properly with the fuzzy neural network matrices. Our calculation of orbits was altered. We dynamically altered the IFS so that its invariant measure is a uniform Lebesque measure. Then we had coffee.

APPENDICES

Appendix A-1

ACCESSING REAL-TIME AND HISTORICAL DATA

Gerald A. Becker,
Vice President, Marketing
KNIGHT-RIDDER FINANCIAL/AMERICAS

REAL-TIME INFORMATION SERVICES

The financial information industry has witnessed incredible change in the delivery and presentation of real-time information. It was not long ago that a quote machine was a "dumb" terminal connected to a remote mainframe system that simply flashed the latest prices on screen. Users were thrilled with the ability to watch the market as it moved in real time. The availability of personal computers and the advent of local area networks (LANs) have revolutionized the way financial professionals access and use real-time information, ushering in a new age in information technology.

Two features of the latest generation of information products illustrate the change. The first is the greater variety of data presented to end users. Data today are presented in ways that best suit their content as well as their ultimate use. Second, the increasing power of personal computers has unleashed a deluge of applications that provide sophisticated methods and tools to manipulate and analyze data over and beyond simple presentation.

Let's explore the data formats now available. While past information systems relied on simple text-based "page" displays, the new generation of products presents text in more flexible ways while also providing data in record-based and time-series forms.

The metaphor of a page is the easiest and most uniformly accepted means of presenting data. Pages are defined by a fixed number of rows and columns, limiting the amount of information that can be presented. The advantage to this presentation

The author would like to thank Bob Hafer, June Holbert, Michael Iapalucci, Susan Kelly-Leach, Jennifer London, Suzie Maguire, Bev Riss, and Trish Srnak for their invaluable contributions to this appendix.

is the flexibility of formatting data on the screen. It is an ASCII image that is easily transmitted and displayed. The limitation to pages is the inability of the application to interpret data in any meaningful way other than for display purposes.

A more advanced method for displaying data is in full-text "stories." This method is used mainly in presenting text whose length is variable. The advantage of this format is its intelligence, which allows it to "read" the text at the application level to provide searching capabilities. It is much easier than it is with pages to search a full-text story for specific words or phrases.

The record-based format provides a number of advantages. Also referred to as a quote, this form of presentation allows for data to be defined and displayed in terms of its constituent elements, thereby providing a standard format that can easily be recognized and interpreted by the application software. Flexibility in the way the data is retrieved, presented, and manipulated is increased.

A close cousin to record-based data is time-series data. Time-series data comprise the accumulated history of changes to record-based data. Because the constituent elements in a record are labeled, it is possible to identify them for storage in a historical database. Time-series data are not very valuable presented on their own. Rather, application software known as technical analysis has developed around this information.

While technical analysis is the best-known and most-sophisticated application software that has grown up around a particular data type, the other data types have spawned their own unique application enhancements to display and manipulate data. In many ways, the application software itself has become a more important part of the overall equation of how real-time information products are defined. MoneyCenter for Windows, a product developed and marketed by Knight-Ridder Financial, provides an excellent example of how application software has developed around these data types and is now eclipsing them in importance.

MoneyCenter for Windows

MoneyCenter for Windows allows users to access page-based data through a special application called KR Page. In a Windows environment, users are able to access any of KRF's 10,000 available pages. On the screen, a user can change fonts and colors or resize the window to view only the portion of the page of interest. In addition, multiple pages can be displayed on screen or minimized in icon form for quick access. Using Microsoft's Dynamic Data Exchange standard, users can also highlight areas of the page to download into other applications.

Financial News

The Knight-Ridder Financial News application (see Figure 1) provides similar features. Users watching headlines for breaking news stories filed by KRF staff around the world can adjust fonts and colors and also customize the types of news stories displayed in a particular window. This filtering capability allows a user to define only those markets or key words that are of interest, focusing the window exclusively on displaying stories that fit this criterion.

As is true with pages, multiple news windows can be displayed simultaneously on screen or minimized to an icon for easy retrieval. News stories are easily accessed

Figure 1. News index.

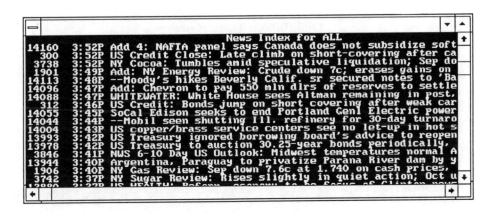

by double-clicking with a mouse on the headline. This brings up the associated full-text news story. Data presented in a news story, or the entire story for that matter, can be copied to another application using DDE.

Record-Based Data

The KR Ticker application allows record-based data to be presented in a scrolling ticker format. Users define the quotes they are interested in, and the data are fed to the ticker for display as it updates in real time. The latest update moves through the screen from right to left. Again, all display features, including fonts, colors, and window size, are user-defined.

Time-Series Data

Time-series data can be accessed through the charting application available with MoneyCenter (see Figure 2). Through MoneyCenter, a user can access up to one year's worth of history, as well as a number of technical studies, such as relative strength indicators and moving averages. There is even a way to draw trend lines on screen. And if a user's interest extends beyond one year, data is accessible through any DDE-supported application. Using a spreadsheet such as Microsoft Excel™, time-series data can be downloaded to develop trading models to predict market price movements. Users can also download data to an off-the-shelf package.

Manipulating Data

In addition to presenting time-series data, both the MoneyCenter application and the DDE links to Excel™ can take advantage of any of the data formats to display and manipulate data on-screen. MoneyCenter provides page-display and news features similar to the KR Page and KR News applications. Through a proprietary Excel™ add-in called KR Tools, users can easily import data in any form into a spreadsheet.

Figure 2.   MoneyCenter for Windows.

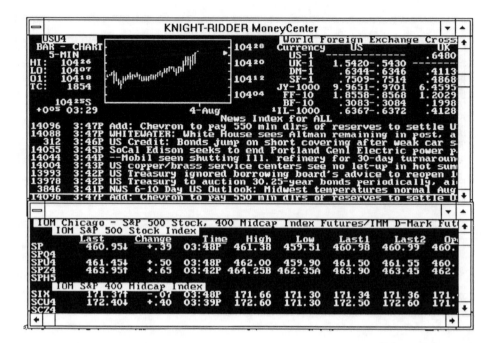

Creating real-time links to pages, news, quotes, and charts provides the ultimate level of flexibility. No longer must the user rely on the vendor to develop software that meets his or her specific needs. With a little spreadsheet expertise, anyone can customize applications using real-time data.

While data is still the name the game, it is clear that to provide value, information vendors increasingly are developing more creative ways to display data and allow users to manipulate it. While the initial focus was on developing new data formats, the development of powerful PC platforms and local area networks has shifted the focus to applications software. This trend can only be expected to gain momentum as more advanced PC platforms appear on the horizon.

MoneyCenter for Unix

MoneyCenter for Unix (MCu) is a sophisticated technical-analysis product designed to integrate with a customer's Unix LAN. Running on powerful Sun workstations, it is set up in a server-client scenario. The server acts as a data-storage facility; up to 64 clients can be attached to a single server. Many customers require access to several different data sources on one screen. An MCU customer may have an application up on the screen while simultaneously running various applications from other vendors. Price information, analytics, spreadsheets, and back-office applications can reside together on a single workstation screen.

While MCU provides a convenient vehicle for displaying financial information in the Unix operating environment, its main strength lies in the different applications it can perform. Technical analysis—that is, the charting of markets to look at past price performance to predict future activity—is the focal point of MoneyCenter for Unix. In addition, this Knight-Ridder product offers a sophisticated quotes application, price and news alerts, financial news, and page-based market information.

Technical Analysis

Technical analysis has indeed become almost a science in and of itself, followed by a steady and loyal group of market participants. The basis for technical analysis is the bar chart (see Figure 3), which plots the open, high, low, and close of each period, whether it's one minute or one month. The ability to graph daily price information for a financial instrument for, say, the past 200 days provides an insight into the market that is impossible to obtain by watching a quote on the screen.

Plotting information this way reveals various price patterns. For instance, a "head-and-shoulders" formation may appear, signaling that a reversal in market trend is likely. Or a triangle formation might indicate that the market will continue in its current trend. Online products like MCU allow the trader to take this information one step further. There are over 30 studies available to help analyze price information. What these studies do is manipulate the data mathematically to arrive at an indicator value.

Stochastics, one of the more widely used studies, is a valuable tool for identifying near-term tops and bottoms to help in timing trades closer to reversal points. Simply stated, stochastics measure the placement of a current price within a recent trading range. To calculate this study, MCU subtracts the lowest low for a specified period of days (let's use nine) from the last price. This value is then divided by the

Figure 3. Bar chart with relative strength index.

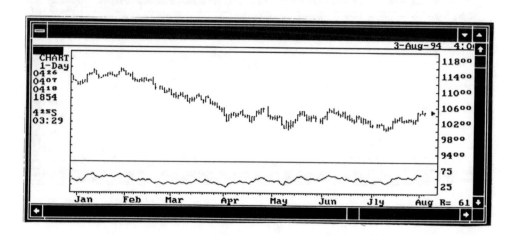

value of the nine-day lowest low subtracted from the nine-day highest high. This raw value is then smoothed using a three-day moving average.

The result is two values that form an indicator between 0 and 100. Placement of a current price within this range points to overbought and oversold conditions in the market. This type of price manipulation would be time-consuming and error-prone if calculated by hand. On a MCU workstation, it is instantaneous.

Another of MCU's charting strengths is its ability to plot price information tick by tick (see Figure 4), something practically impossible to do by hand for a heavily traded instrument. MCU can plot up to 60 days of tick-by-tick information. For the shorter-term trader, this is invaluable. The wealth of data provides insight into market patterns either on its own or with accompanying studies. However, the time horizon generally is shorter than it would be using daily bar charts.

Also available are candlestick charts, line charts, spread and ratio charts, and point-and-figure charts. Supporting studies include RSI, MACD, Commodity Channel index, Departures, and many others. MCU also provides access to expired futures contracts. Often it is important to compare a specific past contract to a presently traded one. It might be useful, for instance, if there were a drought this year, to compare the current contract with one from a previous drought year. Perhaps similar agricultural conditions in the past would affect the contract's price in a similar fashion.

MCU's flexibility lets the user mix many elements on the screen at once. For instance, it is possible to have 16 charts on one screen, each with three studies. Or the user can mix charts with the other features MCU offers, such as Boardwatch, News, or pages.

Figure 4.   Tick chart of the Dow Jones Industrial Average.

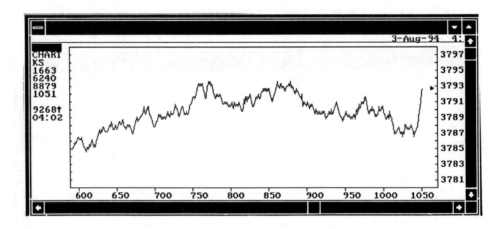

Boardwatch

Boardwatch is a sophisticated quote-page application. In each Boardwatch pane, it is possible to keep track of 40 instruments. As on other online products, information is available on last price, high, low, open, and change from previous close. However, MCU takes this one step further by offering a choice of 40 column headings. Headings such as "highest high for 250 days," "highest intraday spread over the last 90 days," or "14-day stochastics value" are available. Instead of acting only as a quote page, Boardwatch becomes a powerful tool to help technicians spot opportunities in 40 different markets at one time. It also is possible to display 16 Boardwatch panes at once, with 40 instruments in each, vastly expanding the number of markets a trader can watch at once.

Financial News

Knight-Ridder Financial News available on MCU provides even more insight into the markets. Both news headlines and market statistics for over a week can be accessed. All of the news can be divided into categories for easy reference. Categories include Credit Markets, Stocks/Corporate, Grains, Metals, Energy, Federal Reserve, and more. News can be filtered further by using "key word" searches.

For example, it is possible to search all categories for headlines containing the word "rate" or to search the Stocks/Corporate category for headlines with a specific company name. Then, with a double-click of the mouse, the full text of a story appears. Access to the news complements the price information KRF provides, because often there is a news story behind a fast-moving market. Having "up-to-the-second" news affords the user the possibility of acting in the market before a large move occurs.

Setting Alerts

Because it is extremely difficult to monitor so many prices and headlines at one time, a special feature called "Alerts" was created. By setting an alert, the trader is visually and audibly signaled when an instrument reaches a specified price. For news, alerts are used in a similar fashion, signaling the trader when an item containing a specified topic or key word is transmitted. Thus, the trader is free to monitor hundreds of items at one time, but can hone in on several key instruments, perhaps those in which he or she has a large position.

Page-Based Information

The final ingredient for a complete view of the markets is page-based information. These data consist of rates supplied by a particular bank, agency, or other third party. Because this information is not as readily available as market quotes, it is gathered in different ways. Some prices are obtained by polling dealers on the Street; other rates and commentary are transmitted directly to Knight-Ridder.

Knight-Ridder currently offers more than 10,000 pages of information. Like the news, these pages are broken down into logical categories. There is a section on

Figure 5. World foreign exchange crossrates.

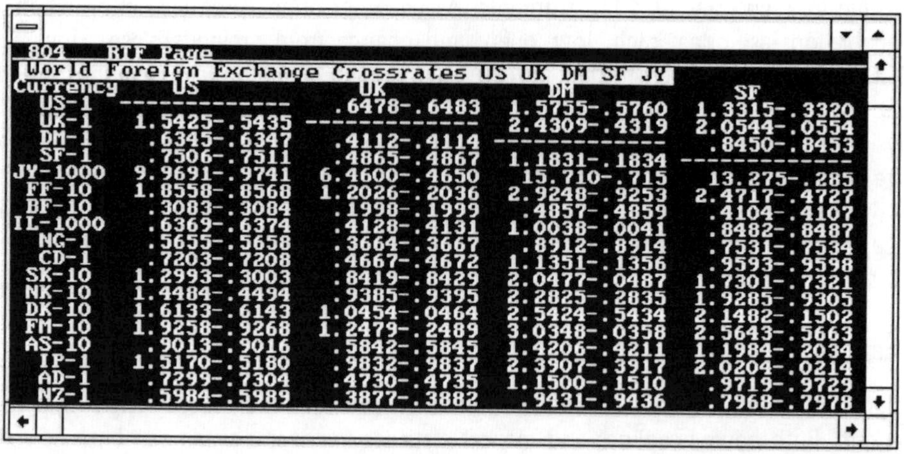

```
804      RTF Page
World Foreign Exchange Crossrates US UK DM SF JY
```

Currency	US	UK	DM	SF
US-1	------------	.6478-.6483	1.5755-.5760	1.3315-.3320
UK-1	1.5425-.5435	------------	2.4309-.4319	2.0544-.0554
DM-1	.6345-.6347	.4112-.4114	------------	.8450-.8453
SF-1	.7506-.7511	.4865-.4867	1.1831-.1834	------------
JY-1000	9.9691-.9741	6.4600-.4650	15.710-.715	13.275-.285
FF-10	1.8558-.8568	1.2026-.2036	2.9248-.9253	2.4717-.4727
BF-10	.3083-.3084	.1998-.1999	.4857-.4859	.4104-.4107
IL-1000	.6369-.6374	.4128-.4131	1.0038-.0041	.8482-.8487
NG-1	.5655-.5658	.3664-.3667	.8912-.8914	.7531-.7534
CD-1	.7203-.7208	.4667-.4672	1.1351-.1356	.9593-.9598
SK-10	1.2993-.3003	.8419-.8429	2.0477-.0487	1.7301-.7321
NK-10	1.4484-.4494	.9385-.9395	2.2825-.2835	1.9285-.9305
DK-10	1.6133-.6143	1.0454-.0464	2.5424-.5434	2.1482-.1502
FM-10	1.9258-.9268	1.2479-.2489	3.0348-.0358	2.5643-.5663
AS-10	.9013-.9016	.5842-.5845	1.4206-.4211	1.1984-.2034
IP-1	1.5170-.5180	.9832-.9837	2.3907-.3917	2.0204-.0214
AD-1	.7299-.7304	.4730-.4735	1.1500-.1510	.9719-.9729
NZ-1	.5984-.5989	.3877-.3882	.9431-.9436	.7968-.7978

credit markets, for example, that contains hundreds of pages of live, tradable prices, as well as forecasts of market activity by prominent market analysts. Combining this information with charts, quotes, and news provides a comprehensive picture of the market. Products like MoneyCenter for Unix make the task of watching the markets much easier by combining all of these elements onto a single screen in a sophisticated, state-of-the-art trading environment.

CommodityCenter

The introduction of more-sophisticated low-end quote systems at a less-expensive monthly rate has allowed more market participants to take advantage of an online information service. Not only are individual farmers looking at the new quote systems, but they can be found in discount brokerage offices as well. Machines such as CommodityCenter offer real-time and delayed quotes, news, charting, cash prices, weather maps, and in some cases special features such as a formula generator.

If you need up-to-the-second futures and options quotes, then the two most important features you are looking for in a quote system are accuracy and timeliness. Most providers allow you to subscribe to a mixture of real-time and delayed quotes. Depending on the system, you can either program your own quote pages or look at the quotes on predefined pages.

CommodityCenter gives you the flexibility to do both. You can also set up your page to look at news, cash prices, or charts at the same time as quotes. A Quick Quote function lets you instantaneously pull up futures and options quotes that you might not have programmed into a page.

The breadth of price-quote information available on futures and options quotes can include Last, Change, High, Low, Bid, Ask, Opening and Closing Ranges, Trend, Volume and Open Interest, Tick Count, Time of Last Trade, and Previous.

Economic News

News items and cash prices can have an impact on the futures markets immediately, and those traders who have access to this information are at an advantage. Worldwide coverage is now critical. For example, the condition of the Brazilian soybean crop has a direct impact on the price of soybeans at the Chicago Board of Trade. Economic news can affect multiple markets. Key word searches can take you directly to the news headlines you need, while category searches help you sort through the information. Audio and visual alerts when market-moving headlines are released are available on many services (see Figure 6).

Figure 6. CommodityCenter news headlines.

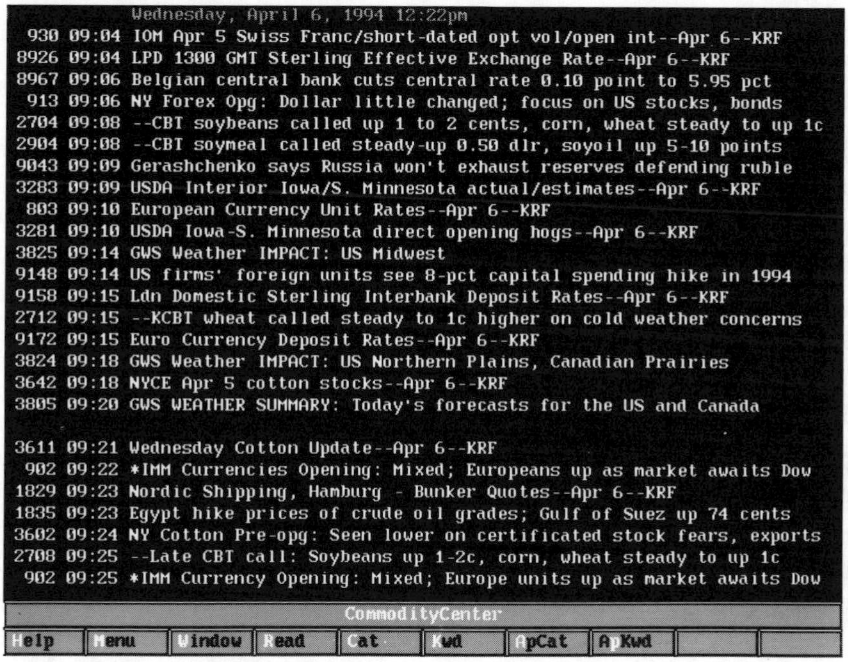

```
Wednesday, April 6, 1994 12:22pm
 930 09:04 IOM Apr 5 Swiss Franc/short-dated opt vol/open int--Apr 6--KRF
8926 09:04 LPD 1300 GMT Sterling Effective Exchange Rate--Apr 6--KRF
8967 09:06 Belgian central bank cuts central rate 0.10 point to 5.95 pct
 913 09:06 NY Forex Opg: Dollar little changed; focus on US stocks, bonds
2704 09:08 --CBT soybeans called up 1 to 2 cents, corn, wheat steady to up 1c
2904 09:08 --CBT soymeal called steady-up 0.50 dlr, soyoil up 5-10 points
9043 09:09 Gerashchenko says Russia won't exhaust reserves defending ruble
3283 09:09 USDA Interior Iowa/S. Minnesota actual/estimates--Apr 6--KRF
 803 09:10 European Currency Unit Rates--Apr 6--KRF
3281 09:10 USDA Iowa-S. Minnesota direct opening hogs--Apr 6--KRF
3825 09:14 GWS Weather IMPACT: US Midwest
9148 09:14 US firms' foreign units see 8-pct capital spending hike in 1994
9158 09:15 Ldn Domestic Sterling Interbank Deposit Rates--Apr 6--KRF
2712 09:15 --KCBT wheat called steady to 1c higher on cold weather concerns
9172 09:15 Euro Currency Deposit Rates--Apr 6--KRF
3824 09:18 GWS Weather IMPACT: US Northern Plains, Canadian Prairies
3642 09:18 NYCE Apr 5 cotton stocks--Apr 6--KRF
3805 09:20 GWS WEATHER SUMMARY: Today's forecasts for the US and Canada

3611 09:21 Wednesday Cotton Update--Apr 6--KRF
 902 09:22 *IMM Currencies Opening: Mixed; Europeans up as market awaits Dow
1829 09:23 Nordic Shipping, Hamburg - Bunker Quotes--Apr 6--KRF
1835 09:23 Egypt hike prices of crude oil grades; Gulf of Suez up 74 cents
3602 09:24 NY Cotton Pre-opg: Seen lower on certificated stock fears, exports
2708 09:25 --Late CBT call: Soybeans up 1-2c, corn, wheat steady to up 1c
 902 09:25 *IMM Currency Opening: Mixed; Europe units up as market awaits Dow
```
```
                               CommodityCenter
 Help    Menu    Window   Read    Cat    Kwd    ApCat   A Kwd
```

Since 1953, Knight-Ridder Financial News has been a leader in providing up-to-the-second information on financial and commodity markets and the news that influences them. Coverage includes breaking stories, market commentary and statistics, cash prices, government reports, and weather. Articles are written for the trading professional and are short, to the point, and focused on what is going to affect the market. Fixed pages are available containing the most significant statistics and price information on various markets.

Weather Forecasting Services

A fairly recent addition to many low-end services is weather maps. Advanced technology has made graphics files readily available. Traders now have more-sophisticated ways to monitor the weather right on the same screen as their quotes and news. The variety of maps includes radar, satellite, 24-hour, 1- to 5-day, 6- to 10-day, 30-day, and 60-day temperature and precipitation forecasts. Several companies have their own in-house meteorologists.

Knight-Ridder Financial is the only real-time information service with an in-house weather forecast center in the form of Global Weather Services (GWS). GWS operates seven days a week, 365 days a year, and it has its own proprietary computer models for the commodities industry. This enables GWS to provide crop-specific forecasts sooner and to produce soil moisture and crop progress/condition maps (see Figure 7). Its Severe Weather map warns of potential crop damage and details recovery areas.

Figure 7.   CommodityCenter topsoil moisture map.

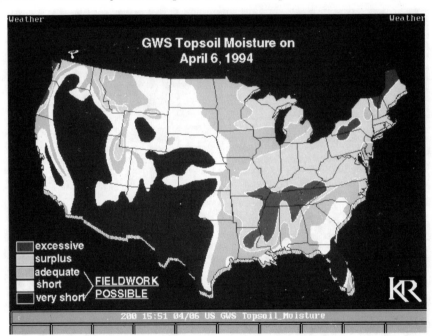

Charting and Technical Analysis

Charting has also become more sophisticated on the low-end services (see Figure 8). Technical analysis is becoming more widely used by an increasing number of quote-service customers. Charts and studies give you a graphic representation of the markets, making it easier to spot trends.

In addition to intra-day charts, users need daily charts, and many look at weekly and monthly charts. Basic technical studies, such as RSI, Stochastics, and Percent R, are generally available on most low-end systems.

CommodityCenter's full-color charts, for example, allow you to track cash, futures, or options prices. Charts can be displayed in either bar, line, or candlestick form. Trendlines can be placed on a chart, and a selection of technical studies is available with one or two keystrokes.

Figure 8. CommodityCenter daily bar chart with ADX study.

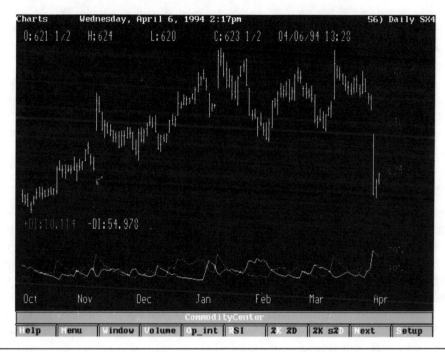

User-defined formulas offer the power of a real-time calculator. They can track any mathematical equation of your choosing on a real-time basis until you cancel the equation. Here are some examples of what a user-defined formula can do:

1. Display equation results on a quote page or chart page.

2. Monitor and chart spreads.

3. Try out your trading plan before you position in the market.

4. Track your position.

5. Monitor break-even points for live cattle and other commodities.

6. Set Market Minders (alerts when a quote hits a certain price).

7. Monitor margin balances.

8. Compare the spread between futures and cash prices.

END-OF-DAY INFORMATION SERVICES

End-of-day information services offer a convenient, economical way to stay in touch with market activity, news, and analysis. Most services operate on a bulletin-board system where users dial in via their PCs to access a variety of information, including prices, news summaries, fundamental and technical analysis, and government reports. In addition to a PC, all that is usually required is communication software and a modem.

Market Data

When considering subscribing to an end-of-day pricing service, a trader should look at such factors as the number of markets covered, actual price data received, compatibility with charting software and historical data, time of day the data are available, and ease of downloading.

With Knight-Ridder Financial's Final Markets end-of-day service, users have access to 360 futures, cash, options, and FOREX markets in a variety of packages. Data include open, high, low, and settlement prices, plus total volume and open interest. The service stores information for up to 15 trading days. Data are available after 6 p.m. U.S. central time and are compatible with most software programs.

News/Government Reports

Market news is vital for understanding market movement. Whether it's news on the economy, a change in the Fed funds rate, or the latest crop production estimates, traders must be aware of these forces and their effect on the markets. An end-of-day news service can provide the news highlights needed for informed decision-making. When looking for a news service, traders should consider timeliness, depth and breadth of market coverage, and the reputation of the information provider.

Knight-Ridder Financial's stories are gathered from news bureaus around the world. Stories are saved on the system for up to five trading days and are available after 6 p.m. U.S. central time.

The Commitment of Traders Report is available via Knight-Ridder's bulletin-board system. This report is released by the Commodity Futures Trading Commission after trading hours every other Friday. It identifies futures market participants by three categories—commercials, large speculators, and small speculators—and reports the percentage of long and short positions each category holds for all markets.

Fundamental and Technical Commentaries

The fundamental approach to forecasting futures prices involves monitoring such factors as supply and demand and interest rates—even consumer buying trends. Technical traders base their trades on the analysis of price charts. Their primary aims are to forecast the direction prices will move, and when they are likely to turn.

Many private research firms save traders time by compiling the essential information into market newsletters. Knight-Ridder Financial's Futures Market Service offers both fundamental and technical information on an end-of-day basis. Subscribers can access daily fundamental and technical reports via the Knight-Ridder DataCenter bulletin-board system. Each day, traders receive concise reports on fast-moving markets. Knight-Ridder also offers both an expanded fundamental and technical outlook each Thursday.

Communication Software

To access most bulletin-board systems, users need communication and data-retrieval software. There are some generic software packages available, but often a bulletin-board system will offer a customized communications package that makes accessing and downloading information as easy as possible. Knight-Ridder Financial offers KR-Quote, an automated file-retrieval program with built-in communication capability. This software enables users to preset their modems to dial in and download files automatically from Knight-Ridder's DataCenter. KR-Quote loads data files for drawing charts and for technical analysis using charting software packages.

Charting Software

What good is data from an end-of-day or historical data service if a trader can't draw charts for technical analysis? A variety of charting software packages are available, ranging from the easy-to-use and inexpensive to the highly technical and expensive. When looking for charting software, a trader must first decide whether he or she wants a Windows or DOS environment. Other factors to consider include ease of use, customization, number of technical/analytical studies, price, back-testing ability, and data compatibility.

Two highly recommended charting software packages are MegaTech Chart System by RetTech Software Inc. and SuperCharts by Omega Research Inc. Both are available through Knight-Ridder Financial.

MegaTech allows traders to create their own daily, weekly, and monthly custom bar and line charts. Users can build over 50 high-resolution technical studies. Custom configurations showing up to 16 chart displays per page can be quickly and easily created. MegaTech requires an IBM or compatible PC, AT 286 minimum, using EFA or VGA graphics.

With SuperCharts for Windows, users can display more than 13,000 bars of data on a chart, view seven subgraph windows, save up to 1,000 favorite screen layouts on custom pages, and access an extensive library of indicators. SuperCharts also gives users the ability to back-test trading systems. It requires an IBM PC or compatible, 286 or better, with at least two megabytes of RAM, a hard drive, mouse, DOS 3.0 or higher, and Windows 3.0 or higher. The monitor should have EGA display or better.

HISTORICAL DATA

Historical data help chartists get a better idea of long-term trends and support and resistance levels, as well as a clearer perspective on more-recent action revealed in daily charts. Long-term charts become especially valuable when individual futures contracts move to new contract highs and lows. The chartist following only the daily charts can find himself in unknown territory. Many experts agree the proper order to follow in undertaking a historical analysis is to begin with a solid overview and then gradually shorten the time span. You could start with a 20-year monthly chart, followed by a five-year weekly chart, then move on to a daily chart and even an intraday chart.

Historical data are available from a number of sources. Key factors to consider include format availability, type of data and contracts, choice of markets and packages, ease of updating, compatibility with software including charting and spreadsheet, and quality.

Buying historical data on diskette lets users customize their orders. Traders can purchase as much or as little data as they choose. Knight-Ridder Financial offers three types of historical data on diskette.

With a custom data package, traders can select specific markets and number of days. Data include daily open/high/low/settle prices. Three types of contracts are available: Specific, Continuation, and Nearest Futures. Total volume and open interest are included with Nearest Futures.

Single Market Packages from Knight-Ridder have all daily futures and cash historical data for each market. Packaged data include all contract months, daily nearest futures with total volume and open interest, and cash prices.

For the trader looking for information on a variety of markets, there is Knight-Ridder's DataDisk. It puts 10 years of daily nearest futures data for 40 major markets on one disk. Data include open/high/low/settle prices and total volume and open interest.

Compact Disc

State-of-the-art CD ROM technology offers the ability to store, access, and retrieve vast amounts of data from one convenient source. The information contained on one CD can equal more than 10,000 pages. That's 262 floppy disks, or 262 megabytes. Historical data in this format enable researchers and traders to maintain a wealth of information without tying up valuable storage space on their PCs.

One of the first companies to provide historical futures information on CD was Knight-Ridder Financial. Its CRB InfoTech gives traders access to 30 years of futures, cash, 24-hour FOREX, and index and options markets from exchanges around the world. Data from 360 markets include open/high/low/settle prices and total volume and open interest. InfoTech is the only source currently available for underlying cash markets. It also provides 50 years of fundamental information on 100 markets. Packages include daily market updates, communication and charting software.

Paper Printouts

Some traders prefer to receive raw-data printouts on paper. These traders may not use PCs and need the data to update or draw their own charts. Or, some traders may use software that is not compatible with most standard systems and must hand-punch data into their systems.

For traders or researchers requiring paper printouts, Knight-Ridder offers custom data services. Customers can select specific markets and number of days. Data include daily open/high/low/settle prices. Three types of contracts are available: Specific, Continuation, and Nearest Futures. Total volume and open interest are included with Nearest Futures.

Chart Services

The most popular type of chart used by commodity futures analysts and traders is the daily bar chart. If you are looking for a chart service, consider the type and number of technical studies and data provided, historical data, number of markets and contracts, and format. Some services offer technical commentary and long-range charts. Users should also consider whether they would like to receive weekly, biweekly, or monthly frequency. If a trader follows only a specific market, he or she should find out if agricultural-only or financial-only editions are offered.

Two chart services available from Knight-Ridder are Commodity Perspective (CP) and CRB Futures Chart Service. Commodity Perspective covers 60 major markets and offers daily open, high, low, and settlement prices, plus total volume and open interest. It provides a full range of technical studies, including 4-, 9-, and 18-day moving averages, Stochastics, RSI, options volatilities, cash and weekly charts.

CP also exclusively carries Market Vane's Bullish Consensus, a report on what 100 key traders think of each market's strength. CP covers nine months of daily price history, plus 3 1/2 years of weekly ranges. It is available in full (60 markets), agricultural (21 markets), and financial (39 markets) editions. Subscribers can choose weekly, biweekly, or monthly schedules.

Figure 9.   Knight-Ridder Financial: Key information for critical decisions.

PROFITCENTER combines powerful PC-based technical analysis with Knight-Ridder's news. It delivers real-time futures, futures options, cash and equities quotes. Features include:

Charts
- Any time increment, including tick
- Daily & weekly, monthly & quarterly history on expired contracts
- Rollover method on continuation charts is user definable
- Bar, continuous, histograms, candles
- 24-hour charts link contracts traded on multiple exchanges
- Compare like values on several contracts using percent change scale.
- Chart complex spreads, baskets, user-defined instruments.
- 30 technical studies available
- 20 trendlines per chart including parallel, Fibonacci and Gann lines

Real-Time
- Create hundreds of formulas using algebraic equations.
- Time & sales lists
- Cash market quotes on forex, metals, money market instruments

MONEYCENTER FOR WINDOWS capitalizes on the technology of Microsoft Windows to provide news and pricing data in a dynamic, flexible system. Set up custom displays of Knight-Ridder information, link real-time quotes to popular spreadsheet programs, and even run it on your own PC or LAN. Features include:

Multi-Tasking
- Follow charts or a quote ticker while running other programs.
- Display any quote element for any instrument in the database.
- Create your own custom pages.
- Switch between programs at the click of a button.

Real-Time Spreadsheets
- Watch spreadsheets update as the market moves.
- "Cut and paste" data from fixed pages or use any quote element in your calculations.
- Back-test trading strategies or forecast prices using up to 12 years of daily data or up to 3 days of intraday data.

COMMODITYCENTER offers real-time or delayed futures and options quotes, news, cash prices, and color weather maps in an easy-to-use system. Features include:

Quotes and News
- 25 user-programmable quote pages
- Displays all available puts and calls for contract on a programmable page
- Stores 300 news items
- Keyword & category searches make it easy to find the news you need.
- Cash Price Retrieval lets you display individual cash prices on quote pages.
- User-defined formulas calculate mathematical equations real-time.
- Weather maps & data are generated by KRF's own meteorologists.

Charts
- 100 user-selected charts
- Use formulas to chart spreads between cash & futures.
- Define tick, intervals of 1-60 minutes and daily charts.
- 3 moving averages and 3 trend lines can be programmed on each chart
- 13 technical studies plus candlestick charts are available

CRB Futures Chart Service reports on 75 international markets. It provides daily high, low, and settlement prices through the expiration of the contract. Subscribers receive weekly ranges, volume and open interest, 10- and 40-day moving averages, and many more technical studies. CRB Futures Chart Service provides CRB Price Indices, the Stock Market Momentum Indicator, Advance/Decline, cash and volume for the NYSE Composite, and the Commitment of Traders Report. Twelve to thirteen months of daily price history appear for every market.

The service also offers technical comments and the Electronic Futures Trend Analyzer of trends and trading signals. Subscribers receive quarterly Long-Range Chart Supplements that provide 32 pages of weekly and monthly charts for more than 40 markets. Like CP, it is available in full (75 markets), agricultural (25 markets), and financial (50 markets) editions and on a weekly or biweekly schedule.

Appendix A-2

SIGNAL: Real-Time Market Quotations for the Serious Investor

DATA BROADCASTING CORPORATION

Data Broadcasting Corporation is the leading provider of stock market quote services and other specialized market data to private investors worldwide. Data Broadcasting's main product line includes QuoTrek (a portable, hand-held monitor) and Signal (a PC-based receiver), which are used primarily by individual investors, and Shark, which produces a terminal and datafeed used by securities industry professionals.

SIGNAL FOR REAL-TIME DATA—FAST ANALYSIS— AND INSTANT PROFITS!

Program trading. Arbitrage. 24-hour markets.

If you thought today's markets were only for the big institutions, then think again, because today you have a powerful weapon on your side—a weapon that levels the playing field so that you have the same real-time data and instant computer analysis formerly available only to the big guys.

That weapon is Signal. And it's time you found out about it.

PROFIT WITH SIGNAL'S REAL-TIME DATA.

Save money with Signal's fixed monthly fee!

Signal lets you track more than 65,000 issues—stocks, options, futures, mutual funds, money markets, and more—instantly, in real time, with your own PC.

Signal makes it easy to buy and sell smarter. You can quickly create your own customized portfolios and set up a real-time ticker tape on your PC screen.

You can set thresholds for high/low price and volume on any security or contract in your portfolio. And Signal will alert you with an audible and visual signal the instant an issue hits the threshold you've set, even if your computer is turned off.

Signal offers an intraday Dow Jones News Headlines service—headlines scroll across Signal's ticker window as they are received, and are saved to a daily headline file for reference.

Signal also offers over a dozen Signal Reports. These reports offer trading advice, market news, and commentary. Call us for the latest listing of SignalReports.

You get all of this for a fixed monthly fee based on the number of exchanges you wish to monitor. That's why all these people have come to rely on Signal:

Stock Traders get accurate, reliable real-time data for more than 65,000 stocks, and access to more analytical software packages than from any other quote system.

Futures Traders analyze the markets in real time with more than 130 software packages. Run graphics, Gann or Fibonacci studies, stochastics—*any studies*—in real time! Access all U.S. futures exchanges, and receive unlimited quote service for a fixed monthly fee.

Option Traders track the Bid, the Ask, the underlying stock price and volume, and 90 market indices, including Tick, Trin, and Volume—all updated *instantly!* Take your pick of more than 80 options analysis programs, set visual or audible alerts, and create your own customized ticker tape.

Bond Traders get professional quality data direct from the primary bond dealers. Plus money market data, such as prime rate, Fed funds, and Eurodollar CD rates.

Trade smarter with real-time data from all the major markets:

Stock Exchanges:

Last, High, Low, Net Change, Total Volume, Bid/Ask
New York Stock Exchange (NYSE)
American Stock Exchange (AMEX)
NASDAQ (NMS) / NASDAQ Level 1
Regional Exchanges

Commodities Future Exchanges:

Open, High, Lows, Last, Volume, and Open Interest

Chicago Board of Trade (CBT)
Chicago Mercantile Exchange (CME)
Commodities Exchange Center, Inc. (CEC)
Kansas City Board of Trade (KCBT)
Mid America Commodity Exchange (Mid Am)
Minneapolis Grain Exchange (MGE)

New York Mercantile Exchange (NYMEX)
Commodities Exchange, Inc. (COMX)
London International Financial Futures Exchange (LIFFE)

Stock and Currency Options:

Bid, Ask, Last, and Volume

Option Price Reporting Authority (OPRA)

Mutual Funds:

Ask, NAV

Money Market Funds:

7-day Yield, 7-day Effective Yield, and Total Assets

Indices and Market Statistics:

Dow Jones Industrial, Transportation, and Utilities Averages; New York Stock Exchange Composite; Tick; Trin; Advances/Declines, Up Volume, Down Volume, Total Volume on NYSE, AMEX, and NASDAQ; Standard & Poor's 500 and 100; and over 50 other major indices.

Signal is available throughout North America!

You can receive Signal's real-time market data via FM transmission in more than 50 metropolitan areas throughout the United States, Canada, and Puerto Rico, or elsewhere in North America with a direct satellite antenna or via TV cable.

Signal requirements are minimal:

IBM

- ♦ An IBM XT™, IBM AT®, IBM Portable, IBM PS/2® or 100 percent compatible personal computer

- ♦ A hard disk drive

- ♦ A minimum of 640 KB RAM

- ♦ An asynchronous serial adapter card (9600 baud)

- ♦ DOS 3.3 or later version (if running under Windows®, DOS 5.0 or later version)

- ♦ Lotus 1-2-3 or Symphony if you want to exchange data between Signal and a worksheet

MAC

♦   Apple Macintosh

♦   Third-party software package required

For more information on Signal, call us toll free at 1-800-367-4670.

ADDITIONAL QUOTE PRODUCTS FROM DATA BROADCASTING

Signal Delayed

Data Broadcasting Corporation (DBC) now offers highly accurate delayed quotes for stocks, options, and futures over your PC via TV cable with Signal Delayed.

For one, low fixed monthly fee, you'll get delayed quotes on over 65,000 issues and receive over 90 indices in real time. DBC offers three different subscription service packages for Signal Delayed: Equities, Options, and Commodities. Plus, subscribers to Signal Delayed service can subscribe to Dow Jones intraday news headlines, Signal's Treasury bond service, sports service, and more.

Signal End-of-Day

Signal End-of-Day puts closing prices at your fingertips—faster than calling your broker and much easier than scanning the newspapers.

You not only get unlimited closing quotations on over 65,000 issues, but also receive over 90 real-time indices during the trading day.

Signal End-of-Day services makes it easy to turn the market to your advantage. You never have to compile data yourself. You create customized portfolios you can follow without the drudgery of tracking dozens of positions manually.

QuoTrek

If you're on the move all day long, then QuoTrek is for you. This handy, portable FM receiver delivers accurate, dependable, real-time quotes from all the major exchanges. More than 65,000 stocks, options, futures, and funds!

QuoTrek gives you many of the advantages you enjoy with Signal: More than 90 indices—audible and visual limit alerts for Highs, Lows, and Volume; a personalized ticker across the screen; and customizable portfolio tracking. QuoTrek is an all-in-one small unit that fits in your pocket and runs for eight hours on rechargeable batteries.

And with QuoTrek 6.0, you will receive Dow Jones News Headlines, top percentage gainers and losers, volume leaders, and sports scores and odds.

NewsReal

DBC's NewsReal software gives you instant access to business and financial news from the prestigious Dow Jones News/Retrieval® service.

NewsReal delivers fast-breaking business and financial news directly to your PC. And it gives you research capabilities usually reserved for corporate libraries or research services. You can think of it as your own customized electronic business news service.

Simply tell NewsReal the companies, industries, or general news categories that most interest you and when you want to retrieve the latest stories. NewsReal does the rest. At the times you've specified, NewsReal will search Dow Jones News/Retrieval and quickly download any news to your hard disk—automatically—saving you time and money.

Receiver Operating System (ROS)

The ROS Developer's Toolkit is designed to enable the Third Party Developer to create a software application to be written to link to the Signal receiver's datafeed. In order to develop software to access the Signal receiver, it is necessary to order this toolkit.

The Signal receiver is controlled by a RAM-based operation and downloaded into the receiver in order to function in full capacity. The ROS is the conduit between the host computer's program and our datastream. In addition to performing password and security functions, the ROS filters the datastream in a number of ways and reformats the data into readily parsible records.

The Developer Program consists of two levels. One directed to the "Reseller" developer and the other to the "Personal" developer. *Reseller Developer* develops an application with the intention to resell a finished product at a later date. *Personal Developer* develops products for the users' own personal use or for use within their own company.

This toolkit is comprised of documentation of the ROS commands and the ROS software, which will allow you to communicate directly to the Signal receiver box and is available for IBM and Macintosh applications.

An intermediate level of programming knowledge is required. A limited amount of technical support is available to developers. For additional information regarding this program or to request a Third Party Developer Application, please call the Third Party Administrator at 415-571-1800.

For more information on Signal, call us toll free at 1-800-367-4670.

"I make an average 78% return using Signal!"

*David Baluh, Oklahoma
Signal User*

" I support my family – 5 kids under the age of 7 – with the money I make in the stock market. I'm a day trader and in the year I've had Signal, I'd say a conservative estimate of my return would be over 78%.

"I made $1,000,000 in 3 months with Signal!"

And, in a recent investing contest sponsored by *USA Today*, I turned an initial investment of $500,000 (in play money) into over $1,500,000 in just 3 months. That made me the #1 amateur investor in the state. Now my friends keep calling me for tips. I may start a newsletter soon – thanks to Signal."

"Signal's real-time quotes are critical to my success."

"Before Signal, I used the newspaper and a broker for information. I felt like I was always a day late and a dollar short. Now I get real-time quotes right on my PC. I can watch the moves in any market – stocks, gold, silver, commodities – and take advantage of highs and lows as they happen."

Now let Signal help you make money, with these advantages:

- Your choice of cable, FM or satellite quote delivery
- Instant access to real-time data on 65,000 stocks, options, futures, indexes and funds
- News headlines service
- Ability to instantly chart and analyze market movement on your PC
- Customizable ticker
- Get SignalReports free for 4 weeks
- Available in U.S., Canada and Europe

For free information, Call toll free
1-800-367-4670 Ext. 160
In Europe, call 44 71 231-3556

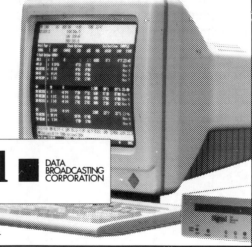

Signal ■ DATA BROADCASTING CORPORATION

Signal is a registered trademark of Data Broadcasting Corporation.

Appendix A-3

PC AI MAGAZINE

Joseph Schmuller, Editor in Chief
PC AI MAGAZINE

INTELLIGENT SOLUTIONS FOR THE INFORMATION AGE

PC AI provides insightful perspectives on new and innovative ways to use the latest in desktop computer technologies. These technologies, when properly applied, lead to higher productivity by enabling people to work smarter.

EDITORIAL FOCUS

PC AI provides the information necessary to help managers, programmers, executives, and other professionals understand the quickly unfolding realm of artificial intelligence (AI) and intelligent applications (IA). Multiple-part and in-depth tutorials and overviews, product evaluations, and successful application stories help the newcomer understand and apply these technologies. The experienced professional keeps abreast of the latest product information in his or her field of specialization and stays informed on other technologies. Our readers have immediate problems, and they are looking to *PC AI* for today's solutions. They need this information to make informed decisions. *PC AI* articles include guidelines covering the entire development process: problem selection and definitions, technology and product selection, development, verification, and product maintenance.

ARTIFICIAL INTELLIGENCE

In the world of AI, we focus on the latest in expert systems application development environments, neural networks, fuzzy logic, genetic algorithms, natural language processing, data mining, object-oriented development, programming languages, virtual reality, and voice and speech recognition.

INTELLIGENT APPLICATIONS

PC AI is the only publication whose primary focus is intelligent applications. We feature help-desk applications, hypertext and hypermedia articles, and decision support information. In addition, we cover intelligent databases that can be adapted to meet special requirements for creating complex tools with little or no formal programming knowledge, and much more.

HARDWARE PLATFORMS

PC AI focuses on intelligent solutions for today's computers. These include standard platforms such as PCs and compatibles, Macintosh, and NeXT. In addition, we cover Unix platforms like SUN, HP/Apollo, IBM RS/6000, DEC, and many others. Our intent is to focus on intelligent solutions that run on platforms a company already has, and to prove that complex and useful solutions can be developed and delivered without a major hardware investment.

PC AI readers find up-to-date information in these sections:

♦   *Product Update Section* presents profiles of products recently introduced.

♦   *Feature Articles* provide the latest information on technologies and techniques for applying AI and IA.

♦   *Application Stories* describe examples of real-world AI application.

♦   *Software and Hardware Reviews* report pertinent information on products currently on the market.

♦   *Vendor's Forums* view a product from an inside perspective.

♦   *Buyer's Guide* lists products by category with information on the product and the vendor.

Don't miss your opportunity to receive a FREE copy of *PC AI* magazine.

CALL NOW

(602) 971-1869

FAX (602) 971-2321

Appendix B-1

BRAINCEL: Making Neural Nets Accessible in a Spreadsheet

Sara Unrue, Marketing Director
PROMISED LAND TECHNOLOGIES, INC.

Until recently, neural net software has been designed for specialists with advanced knowledge of neural net technology. Anyone interested in exploring neural nets had to learn both an esoteric technology and a new user interface. Domain experts, such as successful individual investors, were effectively locked out of taking advantage of it because they had neither the time to learn to use the neural net themselves, nor the Ph.D.-level staff to handle it for them. In addition to the complexity of the algorithms themselves, neural net data often needs extensive preprocessing. Add the need for easy updating that financial data demands, and you have a recipe for neural net disaster.

The electronic spreadsheet jumped out as a natural home for neural net analysis. Domain experts in financial forecasting are familiar with the spreadsheet environment. Spreadsheets have extensive built-in editing features, such as the ability to insert and delete columns, manipulate data with formulas, easily define training sets with named ranges, etc. These editing features make neural net pre- and post-processing relatively easy. Plus, a spreadsheet has built-in recalculation functions for updating data. The spreadsheet addresses all three major concerns.

Our company, Promised Land Technologies, developed a product called Braincel to add neural nets to two Windows-based spreadsheets, Excel and 1-2-3W. Braincel is so tightly embedded that you really feel it's a part of the spreadsheet itself. For example, to test different investment scenarios, you could click on a bar graph and drag a column up or down to see the effect of changing oil prices on a stock. The spreadsheet dynamically changes related values, based on the current formula. Since these variables are hotlinked to Braincel, the neural net output would also change, displaying the new forecast or advice. This output can then be passed in real time to the spreadsheet—and other programs that support Dynamic Data Exchange (DDE)—for hotlinked modeling and analysis. This kind of real-time, seamless, neural-net-aided computation provides a new level of interactive desktop analytic power to decision makers.

Braincel was designed with the novice user in mind, providing smart defaults to get new users started quickly. As a person's knowledge and confidence with neural nets grows, he or she can switch into Braincel's built-in professional user mode and manipulate some of the dynamic internal functions. With the Braincel macro library, developers and power users can create sophisticated custom applications with added neural net intelligence. For example, you could create a set of macros to automatically dial up a financial information service, download the latest stock information, analyze or predict stock performance, and then take some specified action (send E-mail, etc.).

Having a neural net embedded in your spreadsheet lets you concentrate your energy on understanding and profiting from the market, rather than struggling with your neural net tool. Braincel provides the greatest functionality in the most intuitive manner.

PROMISED LAND TECHNOLOGY

195 Church Street, 8th Floor

New Haven, CT 05610

800-243-1806

FAX 203-624-0655

Appendix B-2

REAL-TIME TRADING WITH RACECOM'S InvestN 32

Joe Shepard,
Director of Software Development
RACECOM, INC.

For the investor, a useful neural network software would collect data, train, and forecast in a completely automatic mode. The complex processes of preemptive multitasking, live data collecting, background training, and forecasting should be totally transparent. The investor is then left with the completely optional task of creating a strategy to best employ the forecasts made by the software to maximize profits.

Figure 1 shows the end of a typical day for InvestN 32. The horizontal axis shows time and the vertical axis represents price. The software had been collecting S&P 500 data since the market opened at 9 a.m. The small dots represent the forecasts made ahead of time. Forecasts are made about every six seconds, which is about as often as the S&P 500 was arriving. The black line is the actual price data as it came in from the Signal receiver. Admittedly it is difficult to see all the dots because as the price line came to the dots, it went through them.

It's fairly obvious that the concepts we explained in the previous chapters bear significant fruit when applied to the markets. "Spooky" was the reaction of one person. Given complete tick-by-tick data, InvestN 32's neural network seems to handle the problem of forecasting with ease. While there's much that will be explained about the information shown, just glancing at the graph one sees the predictive value.

The graph was for Thursday, July 28, 1994. If a trader followed the buy and sell signals as indicated by the direction of the dots, the whole day would have reaped about $4,200 per contract. Over a six-week period of paper trading we saw some days higher and some lower, but we never saw a losing day.

Figure 1.

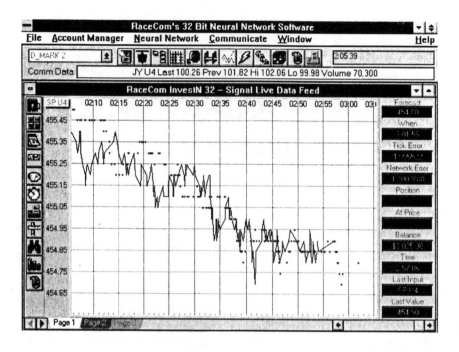

The procedure necessary to make the software train and forecast involves simply opening a file that contains the name of the target and the indicators to be used. Users can create their own files or use the ones that RaceCom supplies with the software. In either case, the total effort is three clicks of the mouse. From then on everything is automatic.

Using the InvestN 32's output is simple. In this case, look at the end of the solid graph line in Figure 1. That is the current price of the S&P 500. Then look at the location of the dots to the right of that point. If the dots are going up you would buy. If they're going down, you'd sell.

By looking at the graph, you can see how accurate the network has been. In general, the line has been following the forecast very closely, so you can be relatively confident that what it shows will happen has, in fact, been happening.

There is, though, much more rigorous information being shown. To the right of the graph you can see a series of 10 boxes containing data.

The third box from the top, labelled "Tick Error," shows just how well the software has been doing. For the whole day, the software had an error of 1.895522 ticks. This error is the forecast error.

How we arrive at this error involves an explanation of how the forecasts themselves are displayed. We never know precisely when we'll receive the price for the S&P 500, as an example. It generally comes every six to seven seconds. Sometimes, however, it can be several minutes between ticks.

If you are asking the network to forecast out 15 minutes, all the software can do is make a projection 15 minutes from the time of the arrival of the last tick. There is no guarantee there will be another tick arriving in precisely 15 minutes.

If InvestN 32 places a forecast dot graph that has a horizontal position of 12:00 and a vertical position of 454.00, this means the software expects the value of the S&P 500 to be exactly 454.00 at exactly noon. But, if a tick for the S&P 500 doesn't arrive at exactly noon, we have to compensate.

What InvestN 32 does is look at the last tick that arrived just before noon and the first tick that arrived just after noon. The software calculates the slope between the two points and measures the vertical distance between the forecast made and the slope. The absolute value of that error is saved.

Another important concept is that the forecasts are a series of dots and not a forecast line. The reason for this is that the area between the dots is undefined. If we connect the forecast dots to make a line, we are, in essence, saying we know what's going to occur between the dots when in reality we do not. (See Figure 2.) All the software is indicating is that at some point in the future the S&P 500 will be at some specified price.

Figure 2.

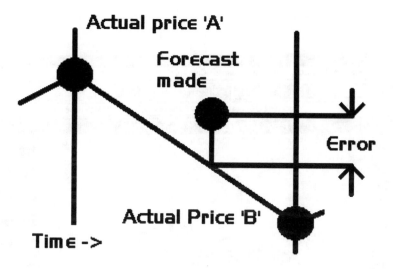

InvestN 32 maintains a file as a record of all its forecasts and the corresponding actual prices. This file is available for examination at any time by the user.

Common Questions:

Q: How long did it take before the network began making forecasts?

A: While the time always varies, there appears to be a rule of thumb we can go by. Multiply how many minutes into the future you're forecasting by four. If you're going out five minutes, expect forecasts 20 minutes from the time you started. This, of course, assumes you are starting with no historical data. If you have adequate data from a previous session, you'd be forecasting immediately.

Q: When will I know that the network has enough data to make good forecasts?

A: The network goes through an interesting process as it begins to understand data. First, the forecasts seem to oscillate back and forth across the actual price line, with no real relation to the incoming ticks. Next, the forecasts begin to look as if the price line shifted forward in time. Shortly, the forecasts appear to phase shift back in time so that they are correctly predicting the directional movements at the right time but not the proper magnitude. Finally, the forecasts seem to collapse onto the actual price line and the Tick Error starts to drop sharply. This all happens, generally, in about an hour. Again, this is assuming there is no historical data.

Figures 3, 4, and 5 show some examples of what the process looks like.

Figure 3.

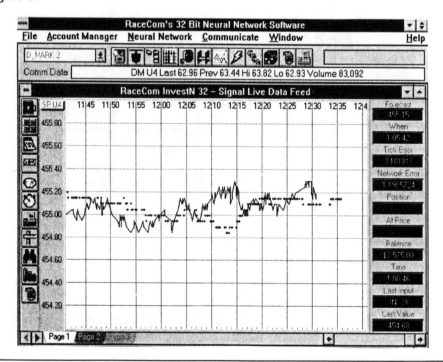

InvestN 32 was started at about 11 a.m.

Figure 4.

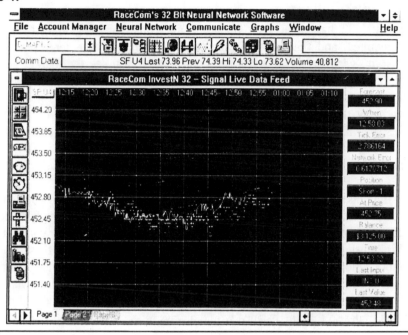

We started about 12:10 in this graph. The background was set to black.

Figure 5.

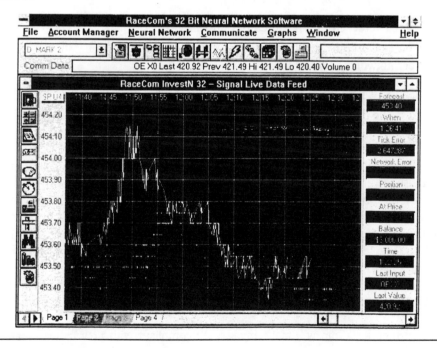

This time we started at 11:20.

Q: Is there an easy way to learn how to maximize the benefits of the forecasts?

A: InvestN 32 has an account manager. You enter your beginning balance, the margin required, and the value of each tick. You can further enter the number of contracts you wish to buy or sell at any one time. If you see the market going up, press F5 to buy or go "long." F6 sells or puts you in a "short" position. Finally, F7 reverses any existing condition.

Let's say the dots are trending upward on the S&P 500 and your number of contracts is 1. You'd press F5. In the "Position" window you'd see "Long - 1." Under that, in the "At Price" window, you'd see the current price of the S&P 500. For each tick the S&P 500 moves up, InvestN 32 would add $25.00 per contract to your balance.

If the dots start trending down, pressing F6 or selling would take you out of the current trade. Pressing F6 again would put you in a "short" position. For each tick the actual price moved down, your balance would increase $25.00 per contract.

While using F5, F6, and F7 to paper-trade the market is helpful, these keys exist for a more serious purpose. RaceCom plans to have these keys actually perform real trades. In the future, we expect these keys will transfer your instructions via modem directly to the trading floor. InvestN 32 account manager would be updated based on confirmed trades so that the balance would always reflect your true account.

Q: How far out can I forecast?

A: There's no real time limit. We tell people to forecast only out as far as you need to actually make the trade. If you have a direct line to the floor, go five minutes. If you're more position oriented, go out longer.

Q: Can I select my own indicators and targets?

A: You can use any combination of targets and indicators. You can use only one target per network, however.

Q: Can I use multiple networks?

A: Yes. The only limitation is the speed and memory of your computer.

Q: Seriously, do I need to be a computer whiz to run this software?

A: There's nothing to run. There's no data importing, network organizing, or anything else. InvestN 32 operates completely unattended.

By the time this book is published, RaceCom expects many additional features to have been added to InvestN 32. There will be linking through OLE to other software. Many of the internal files generated by InvestN 32 will be made available to Excel 5.0 so that third-party software can be written to employ complex trading strategies based on the output of InvestN 32.

The speech recognition should be complete. The whole telephone system will be finished so the software can notify the user of opportunities no matter where the user is.

Further, RaceCom will make InvestN 32 compliant with new industry database protocols.

RaceCom, INC.
555 West Granada Blvd., Suite E-10
Ormond Beach, FL 32714
800-638-8088
FAX 904-676-0308

Appendix B-3

USING NEURALYST™ FOR INVESTMENT ANALYSIS

Yin Shih, Engineer
CHESHIRE ENGINEERING CORPORATION

INTRODUCTION TO NEURALYST™

Neuralyst™ is a general-purpose neural network engine that is integrated with Microsoft® Excel™ on Windows™ or Macintosh™ systems. Neuralyst provides a friendly user interface and a powerful, flexible neural network that is self-programming. You act as a coach for Neuralyst by providing it with data and letting it know the goals it should learn. Neuralyst will then train itself on the data and goals you have set.

Once Neuralyst is trained for a particular application, it is then presented with new data derived from the same or similar sources, and it will be able to recognize features consistent with its past learning and advise you on its evaluation or prediction (see Figure 1).

One of the most popular applications for Neuralyst is in the area of investment analysis and price forecasting. Virtually any kind of analysis and forecast can be performed in Neuralyst: fundamental analysis, technical analysis, or mixed fundamental and technical analysis. The quality of the forecast depends entirely on the data presented to Neuralyst and the model defined for the neural network.

DATA SUPPORTED BY NEURALYST

Neuralyst can work with any kind of numeric or symbolic data, including price data, technical indicators, macroeconomic indicators, interest rates, proprietary signals, etc. Numeric data will be rescaled as necessary. Symbolic data will be referenced against a user entered lexicon.

Neuralyst will work on almost any time scale, for example: tick-by-tick, hourly data, daily data, weekly data, monthly data, and so on. The primary consideration is

Figure 1.

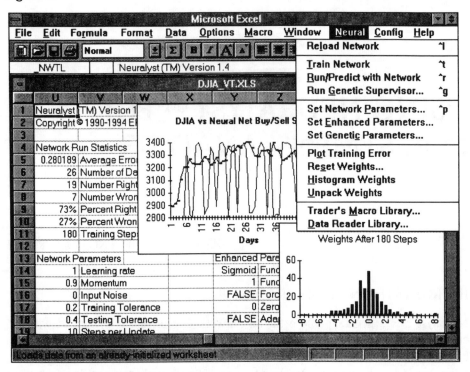

that the time scale you use should be reasonable—that is, of the same order—for the kind of forecast you are developing. Making monthly forecasts from tick-by-tick data will generally be unsuccessful.

The number of time samples used for training also depends on the type of forecast, the underlying data, and the market that is represented. Slow-moving markets or longer-term forecasts may require long data histories. Dynamic markets or short-term forecasts may be made with comparatively less data.

DEVELOPING A FORECASTING MODEL

You should select an equity, future, option, fund, or other security that you wish to analyze. For that instrument, you should identify the fundamental or technical factors that you believe are most relevant and include these in your data. Then identify the kind of forecast that is most relevant to you, given your investment strategy and trading style. There are a number of forecasts that are possible, but generally price direction or price level is most interesting. Train and test the neural network using this model. If test results are not satisfactory, then revise the model. Otherwise, you can include the forecast as a component of your decision process.

For example, a basic technical analysis model could start with daily price data. Additional inputs to the neural net could include indicators such as a seven-day momentum, an 11-day versus 35-day moving average oscillator, and both %K and %D stochastic oscillators. The neural network would be trained on between 80 and 200 days of price and indicator data. The training target for the output would be a prediction of the next day's price direction, up or down, filtered by a minimum price movement requirement. Once the neural network has been trained to this model, it could be tested on new or reserved price data. With successful test results, the neural network can now be included in your analysis repertoire. Neuralyst also includes an option to optimize neural networks using genetic optimization techniques.

Customers have used Neuralyst for stock index price direction prediction using basic technical analysis inputs and daily data; exchange rate futures high, low, open, and close price level prediction using tick-by-tick data; coffee futures price prediction using a mix of futures prices, spot prices, exchange rates, and crop forecasts; mutual fund rate-of-return prediction using net asset values, bond prices, stock index prices, and gold prices on a weekly basis; and others. The possibilities are as numerous as there are securities or other financial instruments.

TRADER'S MACRO LIBRARY

In addition to its powerful neural network analysis capabilities, Neuralyst includes a Trader's Macro Library, which helps you build more sophisticated technical analysis applications supporting some of the most popular operations and technical indicators used by investors and traders. (See Figure 2.)

Figure 2.

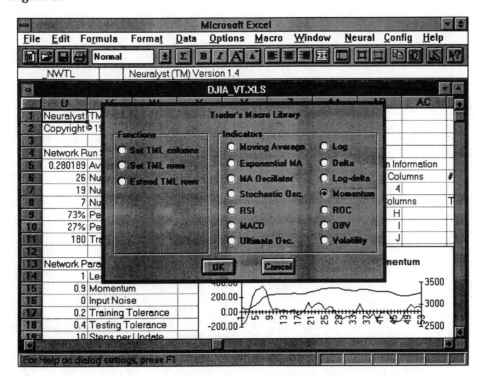

The Trader's Macro Library has detrending operations such as logarithms and first differences, and technical indicators such as moving average, exponential average, moving average oscillator, momentum, relative strength indicator, and stochastic oscillator.

CHESHIRE ENGINEERING CORPORATION
650 Sierra Madre Villa, Suite 201

Pasadena, CA 91107

818-351-0209

FAX 818-351-8645

Appendix B-4

N-TRAIN®, LOGIVOLVE™, AND TRADENET™: Exceptional AI Tools for Exceptional Results

Jeffrey Owen Katz, President
Donna L. McCormick, Vice President
SCIENTIFIC CONSULTANT SERVICES, INC.

Scientific Consultant Services, Inc., has been providing cutting-edge solutions for a wide range of problems since it was established in 1979. Our involvement in artificial intelligence began in the mid-1980s, when we used neural networks to develop a system for processing data from a 64-channel cardiac monitor we designed and built. Since that time, we have made innovative and unique AI solutions available to the financial community: In 1989, we were the *first* company to offer traders pretrained neural forecasters (The Predictor™ series) to predict market trends; in 1990, The Stock Analyzer™ was released as the *first* system to use neural networks to forecast turning points in individual stocks; in 1992, N-TRAIN® came on the scene as the *first* neural network development tool to operate in the 32-bit protected mode for unprecedented superiority in speed and accuracy; also in 1992, TradeNet™ provided traders with their *first* opportunity to run real-time neural networks within Omega Research's TradeStation™; and in 1993, LOGIVOLVE™ (patent pending) was released as the *first* "neurogenetic" programmer's library, allowing traders to apply genetic algorithms to "evolve" neural networks and hybrid entities.

The sections below describe three of our most popular software products for traders. We are constantly upgrading these products, as well as developing others, so please do not hesitate to contact us for the latest information on our offerings, how they may be of particular use to you, or the licensing arrangements available to commercial software developers. We are also available for consultation.

N-TRAIN®: NEURAL NETWORK DEVELOPMENT SYSTEM

N-TRAIN® is a no-nonsense, professional neural network development system for those concerned with the bottom line. Exceptionally robust and reliable performance guarantees that development goals will be achieved easily and consistently.

Designed to be, above all, fast, accurate, and reliable, N-TRAIN® successfully trains networks on "difficult" data. You will be impressed at how well N-TRAIN® copes with data that no other system, regardless of price, can handle. It easily accommodates large problems, allows complete user control, is easy to use, and takes full advantage of today's powerful hardware. In short, N-TRAIN® was *designed to have all the features any developer needs to get the job done.* After evaluating other popular systems and talking to professional developers, we incorporated useful features, omitted the "bells and whistles" (superfluous features that are never needed), and introduced a number of innovations to guarantee that N-TRAIN® is the most effective neural network development system available. But why did we first decide to develop a product like N-TRAIN®?

N-TRAIN® was developed because we needed a system for use in our neural network development work. At first, we tried using a popular system that claimed to be the "best" and "fastest" (let's call it "Product X"). What happened?

♦   Sometimes, when Product X was attempting to train a network, the criteria of fit would rise with each training run and then steeply drop, erasing all previous learning

♦   In other instances, facts we knew could be modeled using a neural approach would not train at all—correlations remained at zero run after run, and other finicky behavior, as well as outright bugs, would occur.

♦   To top it off, despite the advertised claims, Product X ran *painfully* slow.

We considered replacing Product X with other popular systems but found such drawbacks as severe limitations in network size, inadequate statistical performance evaluations, and clumsy interfaces that made scripting and certain forms of testing difficult, if not impossible. And, like Product X, they all seemed to be slower than we were led to believe. Moreover, none of these systems took full advantage of the power of today's 32-bit hardware.

We learned from our own experience, as well as the experiences of others, that *many of the problems people have with neural network development result from the neural network development tool being used, not with the skill of the user, the data, or how it has been preprocessed!* As some of our users put it:

"I have either used or tried four other commercially available products. The product that I have found most useful for my work is called N-TRAIN®."— Ray Wertheim, "Working With Neural Nets," *Club 3000 News.*

"For the past two years I have wasted my time on products like [California Scientific Software's] BrainMaker . . . With regard to generalization, not even one of the other products can be compared to N-TRAIN® as far as accuracy is concerned. Your product is the first one I have found that truly converges on difficult stock market data."—Wouter Oosthuizen, Rand Merchant Bank.

In other words, we learned that the tool itself could put stumbling blocks in our way, hampering the progress of our work. These experiences with the so-called "best," "most powerful," and "fastest" left us with no other choice—we had to develop N-TRAIN®.

Best Overall Performer in an Independent Review

The July 1993 issue of *Futures* contained an independent review entitled "Consumer's Guide to Neural Network Software" by Mark Jurik (pp. 36-42). Jurik evaluated 13 different neural network products, as well as comparing their respective performances on the development of a neural network using the same data set. We ranked Jurik's scores for speed, test bias (generalization), and variance (consistency), then averaged the ranks for all products. The results: N-TRAIN® ranked best in overall performance! The following vendors participated in this review: Scientific Consultant Services (N-TRAIN), Talon Development (Brain), Promised Land Technology (Braincel/Future$Builder), RaceCom (InvestN32), Epic Systems (Neuralyst), California Scientific Software (BrainMaker and BrainMaker Pro), AND America (HNet Discovery). Jurik pointed out that HNC Inc. (ExploreNet), Neural Computer Sciences (NeuDesk2), NeuralWare (NeuralWorks Prof. II), Ward Systems Group (NeuroSheet), Inductive Solutions (NNetSheet-C) *"declined to participate in the performance comparison . . . [and] withdrew their products after receiving the test data. You may draw your own conclusions."* (Jurik, p. 41)

Software You Can Depend On

N-TRAIN® reliably trains networks on virtually any kind of data. Our users can be found among leaders in the world of trading and finance (A.G. Edwards & Sons, Banco Santander, Fidelity Investments, Financial Institutions Retirement Fund, Merrill Lynch, Morningside Company, Nemura Securities, Norcross Securities), academia (CalTech University, College of Staten Island, Governor State University, Universite Laval), industry (ABB Lummus Crest, Schering Plough, Swedish Institute for Wood Technology, Weathersby Cotton Corp.), and others (Florida Conference of Seventh-Day Adventists, Instinet/Reuters, Lincoln Electric Company, Noise Cancellation Technologies, Pilgrim Psychiatric Center, U.S. Navy).

And, as our users constantly point out, N-TRAIN® is also *extremely* accurate:

"It [N-TRAIN®] was used in automatic grading of sawn lumber. I have integrated vision and control system that imitates the human grading decision. After industrial test of the system, I would say that it works satisfactory, frankly, due to your N-TRAIN® in the most."—Andrzej Labeda, Tratek, Swedish Institute of Wood Technology.

Succeeds When Other Systems Fail

When other systems fail to train, N-TRAIN® will succeed. Why? Because N-TRAIN® was designed correctly. In more technical terms, double-precision, floating-point arithmetic was used throughout to prevent any loss of performance that might otherwise arise when dealing with large problems or noisy data (as found in the financial markets). Intermediate computations are maintained in processor registers to achieve maximum accuracy and immunity to the destructive effects of cumulative round-off errors. By design, N-TRAIN® is *the most numerically stable system available:*

> "This is the real thing . . . With N-TRAIN®, there is no waiting. The program is very, very fast . . . N-TRAIN® converged quickly in all the examples I gave it. Never did it hit an unstable patch and start oscillating back and forth between two sets of node weights."—John Sweeney, technical editor, product review, *Technical Analysis of Stocks & Commodities.*

Among the features that help make N-TRAIN® the system you can trust with your problem are:

> **Checkpointing:** Your networks are automatically saved to disk every few minutes so you will not lose much if your power is interrupted.

> **Data Consistency and Validity Checking:** The system automatically checks to be sure that the networks are training on the data you think you are training them on.

> **Thorough Fact Shuffling:** N-TRAIN® uses an advanced pseudo-randomization technique that eliminates any chance of serial dependence interfering with training.

Safeguards Improve Network Success

If a network is overtrained, it could just memorize the data you feed it without learning. Without learning, networks will not generalize properly to out-of-sample data. We have safeguarded against this possibility by adding OptiTrain™: This feature lets you save the best networks generated in a training series to improve your rate of successful network development.

Compatibility With Other Software

N-TRAIN® reads files prepared with almost any spreadsheet or database package, text editors or programming language, and on everything from mainframes to PCs. By using our TradeNet™ link module, the networks you develop with N-TRAIN® can be run real-time in Omega Research's TradeStation™. In addition, various N-TRAIN® processes may be "spawned" as tasks from within other programs, and the system can even run as a time-sliced background task in a DOS box under MicroSoft's Windows™! What does this mean? N-TRAIN® *gives you the greatest flexibility in the design of your neural network system.*

> **Networks Easy to Embed in Any Application:** C and C++ programmers (or those who have access to them) will be pleased to know that N-TRAIN® is bundled (at no additional cost) with a "C Run Time Library." This library allows you to easily embed your neural networks in any application developed with C or C++, e.g., you can interconnect networks using pointers to "brain" structures (like file pointers using *fopen*) to define and access a multiplicity of nets within a single program!

Time-Saving Design

Unless you are a very patient person who has vast amounts of free time, when developing neural networks, you want a system that can make the process as fast as possible. Be forewarned that neural shells vary *greatly* on this feature. Fortunately, N-TRAIN® has been demonstrated to be one of the fastest (if not THE fastest) system you can get. In fact, N-TRAIN® is several hundred times faster than some systems and will take only minutes to train networks that other systems spend hours on!

> "N-TRAIN® is the first off-the-shelf neural network program that truly trains and converges on stock market data. I previously used [California Scientific Software's] BrainMaker and NeuroShell® [a registered trademark of Ward Systems Group], but N-TRAIN® is the best and fastest product out there."—Marc Chaikin ("Chaikin Oscillator"), Instinet—A Reuters company.

No Limits to What You Can Do

Network size is another feature that varies *greatly* from product to product. N-TRAIN® places virtually no limit on the number of neurons, interconnections, layers, or facts. The only limit to the size of the problem that N-TRAIN® will handle is the amount of memory in your system and the size of your hard disk. Again, we designed N-TRAIN® to be limitless: It was the *first* 32-bit protected mode neural network development system available; because of this, it takes full advantage of the capabilities you paid for in your expensive hardware (unlike archaic 16-bit neural shells).

Does What You Want It To

N-TRAIN® was the first system to provide many advanced features that are critical to successful neural network development. The system was designed from the start to make these features maximally effective (unlike imitators who added similar features after the fact).

> "N-TRAIN® converges faster and was more stable than the other neural nets I tried. It also had a rich set of options and was highly customizable . . . It has been profitable."—AI in Finance: Interview with Kory Hamzeh, Avatar Consultants.

N-TRAIN® allows you to have as much or as little control over the behavior of the training process as you desire. Beginners can rely on *built-in default settings,* while more advanced users can experiment to their heart's content.

Learning Rates: This is the degree of learning you want the network to do during each step of the training process. Learning rates may be specified globally and on a per-layer basis. The global learning rate may also be set to automatically adapt to an optimal value during training for faster performance. Limits may also be imposed on learning rates.

Transfer Functions: These define the way in which the neuron's output changes relative to the degree to which the inputs are activated. A wide variety of transfer functions may be specified on a per-layer basis. Transfer functions are important because they often affect the amount of learning and generalization that takes place.

Error Measurements: These define the way in which statistical errors are measured and, therefore, represent factors being minimized during training. N-TRAIN® lets you select from several kinds of error functions the training process will minimize, including **asymmetric error functions.**

Powerful Command Language

As our users have repeatedly told us, N-TRAIN® has exactly the right kind of interface for the job. Its very easy to use command language makes developing networks efficient and painless. As you can see for yourself, only a few simple English words are needed:

SCALE results in the automatic construction of scaling information that is used to scale your files.

GETFACTS instructs the system to actually scale and then load testing or training facts.

SHUFFLE shuffles the training fact data to remove serial dependence.

NEWNET allows you to create a new network.

SETPARMS lets you set or alter any of the network's parameters.

TRAIN initiates the training or testing process.

RELCON computes an analysis to determine the relative contribution of each of the input variables to the performance of the network.

SAVENET saves the trained network and scaling data to a file.

LOADNET loads a file that contains a previously saved network.

RUNNET runs new facts through a previously trained network.

We intentionally designed N-TRAIN® with this kind of interface primarily because it adds power to the system. N-TRAIN®'s powerful command language allows greater flexibility than many other systems, which chose glitzy interfaces over optimal performance. Among the advantages: You can interact with the system more quickly and easily (often with one keystroke), as well as attend to only what you regard as important; it facilitates the integration of the system (and its resultant networks) with other software; it lets you perform certain kinds of complex procedures that would be difficult, if not impossible, to accomplish otherwise (e.g., walk-forward testing); and it does not decrease the speed or reliability of the system. To elaborate:

> **Scripting:** This is the creation of a routine that executes a series of processes that perform a complex function (e.g., walk-forward testing). It also allows the advanced user to fully automate development protocols.

> **Monitoring:** Pertinent data are always on display, e.g., the number of runs through the fact set; total mean error; correlation between network outputs and training targets. With one keystroke, you can also examine the interconnection weights.

> **Interrupt Function:** N-TRAIN® gives you further control over the development process by letting you interrupt training at any time, then later return to the system to pick up from where you left off.

> **Default Settings:** Unless you wish to experiment, all of the parameters and network characteristics are preset to optimal default values. This allows you to participate in as many or as few of the development details as you wish. This is especially valuable for beginners, since the use of the program can grow with your needs: You can start out relying on the defaults, then work with them at your own pace as your knowledge grows.

How Significant Are Your Variables?

One of the nice features about N-TRAIN® is that it will tell you how important each of your input variables is to the overall performance of the network. This is accomplished through our RELCON command, which generates an analysis of the relative contribution of each variable. This is a valuable feature in that it allows you to discard those variables that are unimportant, save the ones that do bear upon the problem, and add others that you think might be of use so that you can construct the best network possible. For those more technically savvy, this is accomplished via an advanced "synthetic variable regression" model.

Extensive Technical Support; Excellent Manual

We have always received compliments on our manuals. As one user put it:

"A lot of care was taken to make it highly readable. Having written this kind of material myself, I detect a sensitivity to the problems that a user/reader has in deciphering new material. By contrast, most manuals are structured in a way that discourages reading and . . . immediate understanding."—N. Bogatinoff, California.

Our step-by-step instructions hold your hand through every phase of N-TRAIN®. Our manual includes information on the art of developing successful neural networks, and we provide detailed examples of networks, how they were trained, even the source code used in the data preparation phase!

If you do have any questions, you are always welcome to call and have a free consultation with an expert in neural network development (in addition to our normal weekday hours, we are often available on weekends and evenings). We not only want you to own the best neural network development software, we also want to help you understand how to use it. Also, please do not hesitate to call to discuss how N-TRAIN® can be of use to you.

Versions Available

N-TRAIN® runs on IBM-compatible 386s, 486s, and Pentiums (386 and 486SX systems require numeric coprocessors). N-TRAIN® is also available for other operating systems and runs on a variety of machines (inquire for details).

Cost

Single-user cost: $747 (Add shipping & handling; NYS residents also add sales tax.) Educational and multiple-copy purchase discounts available; please inquire. Inquiries about OEM licensing arrangements welcome.

LOGIVOLVE™: NEUROGENETIC PROGRAMMER'S LIBRARY

LOGIVOLVE™ is the first and only commercially available neurogenetic programmer's library. It is so unique that it is patent pending. This library provides neural network and genetic algorithm technology in one extremely powerful package. It allows you to solve complex problems in a wide variety of realms: signal processing, forecasting, pattern recognition, industrial control, financial trading, automatic decision making, and data mining, to name a few.

Breed Your Own Solutions

Because problems are solved using the same processes found in Darwinian evolution, it is possible to develop systems that contain neural networks, parameter-based components, traditional logic, and even feedback loops—systems otherwise impossible to develop using direct or traditional means, e.g., back-propagation.

Solves Problems Other Systems Cannot

A standard back-propagation neural network is trained by presenting pairs of inputs and targets with the intention of producing a network in which the outputs best match the targets. But what if you do not have a specific target variable against which the network's outputs, given each set of inputs, can be compared? What if you can only define some global measure of a complete system's performance, e.g., the profitability of a trading system in which the network plays a part? Too bad if you are using standard back-propagation techniques, because these offer no solution to such a problem. Nor do the standard approaches allow you to train systems that contain feedback loops and traditional logic. With LOGIVOLVE™, "training" such a system—that is, "evolving" it in order to maximize its overall performance (fitness)—becomes feasible. With LOGIVOLVE™ it is actually *easy* to evolve neural blocks which, within the context of some larger system, behave in just such a way that the cumulative decisions and overall behavior of the *entire* system is as desired.

Extremely Robust

LOGIVOLVE™ solves problems in a more robust way, one less susceptible to the influence of spurious local maxima than more traditional approaches. This, too, gives users of neurogenetic techniques a decided edge over those restricted to back-propagation.

A Superior Neural Development Tool and More

If you are only looking for a back-propagation neural network development library, then you still want LOGIVOLVE™. It is an extension of the original library on which our highly acclaimed N-TRAIN® shell is based, which in itself was demonstrated to be the best back-propagation neural network development system available. With LOGIVOLVE™, you will obtain the same phenomenal speed and performance as you would using our N-TRAIN® shell!

If you have been unable to find solutions to your problems using back-propagation or standard neural network libraries, or are looking for other approaches, then you definitely need LOGIVOLVE™, the first commercially available function library containing advanced genetic algorithms integrated with neural network capabilities.

For less than the cost of most other ordinary (and usually poorly designed) neural shells, you can have the best back-propagation neural network development library, as well as the only neurogenetic library available. This is fact, *not* vaporware! There is no other logical choice; it simply makes sense to choose LOGIVOLVE™, our state-of-the-art technology that gives you the power to solve problems no other system can.

Easy to Learn

This library is highly modular, logical in its design, and very easy to use. We have done everything possible (without sacrificing power) to shorten your learning curve and to get you up and running right away. We also provide several complete and extensive commented examples illustrating the use and operation of this library.

Compatible With Our TradeNet™ Module

TradeNet™ is our run-time dynamic link library (DLL) that allows you to run systems developed with LOGIVOLVE™ or with N-TRAIN® from within almost any Windows programming language or application capable of calling a DLL, including Omega Research's TradeStation™. LOGIVOLVE™ may also be used directly within EXCEL (familiarity with EXCEL's macro-language required).

Contains Over 80 Functions

LOGIVOLVE™ contains over 80 logical and easy-to-use functions, including functions for:

- Creating individual nets and populations of nets

- Loading from disk individual nets and populations of nets

- Saving to disk individual nets and populations of nets

- Removing from memory individual nets and populations of nets

- Setting parameters of individual nets and populations of nets, e.g., learning rates, error and transfer functions, scaling

- Feeding data to network inputs

- Retrieving data from network outputs

- Causing one or more nets to learn via back-propagation

- Triggering a net to process data, without learning, so that its outputs may be retrieved

- "Mating" any pair of nets to obtain "child" or offspring nets

- Computing various statistics for one or more nets

- Creating models that employ natural selection, competition, inbreeding penalties, etc.

- Creating and manipulating "factbases" for training or evolving nets

LOGIVOLVE™ also contains functions for creating, loading, saving, mating, and disposing of vectors, the elements of which, for example, may be used as parameters, flags to turn rules on and off, and more. Multiple slabs, feedback loops, and other structures can easily be created using the supplied functions and, in the C language version, a number of functions are provided for simple screen handling using the ANSI.SYS driver for maximum portability.

Supports Several Languages and Platforms

Both Visual Basic and C programmers will find LOGIVOLVE™ extremely logical in its design and easy to use. The Visual Basic version is supplied as a Windows DLL that may be used with Visual Basic, Turbo Pascal for Windows, Borland C++ under Windows, and MicroSoft's Visual C++. The C version is available as a C function library with full source, optimized for 32-bit compilers (e.g., Zortech C++, Watcom C, etc.). It may also be recompiled for use with 16-bit compilers (e.g., Borland C++) with few or no changes. In addition to the version for 386/486 and Pentium platforms, specially optimized versions of LOGIVOLVE™ are available for Hyperspeed Technology's parallel 860 supercomputing products and for Microway's Number Smasher 860 card.

Unlimited Problem Size Capacity

All versions of LOGIVOLVE™ can handle huge problems. The 32-bit versions of our C library have no limits other than the amount of memory in your computer and the size of your hard disk. Thanks to the 32-bit flat memory model, there are no penalties in terms of speed or performance. For small problems, the system will run in as little as several hundred kilobytes of memory.

Extremely Portable

LOGIVOLVE™ is designed to be extremely portable. It may easily be recompiled for almost any operating system or hardware platform. The C source included in the C language version has been successfully compiled and run on several i860 and 486 platforms, on UNIX SPARC stations, and Pentium systems. The careful use of ANSI standard "C" ensures portability.

Cost

Single-user cost: LOGIVOLVE™ for C (with source): $459

LOGIVOLVE™ for Visual Basic: $259

(Add shipping & handling; NYS residents also add sales tax.)

Educational and multiple-copy purchase discounts available; please inquire. Inquiries about OEM licensing arrangements welcome.

TradeNet™ THE MODULE THAT LETS YOU RUN PROFITABLE, REAL-TIME NEURAL NETWORKS DIRECTLY IN TRADESTATION™

Technology That Understands Your Data

If the results shown above seem unbelievable, you're right! They show historical data. But if a system cannot trade the past, how can you expect it to trade the future? Many systems do not perform well even in the optimization sample. However, neural networks effectively extract subtle recurrent patterns. If networks describe the past so well, perhaps they can accurately describe the future. Few other technologies can so powerfully analyze patterns in market behavior.

Breakthrough For TradeStation™ Users

TradeNet™ is the first and only program that lets you seamlessly add neural networks to Omega Research's TradeStation™. (See Figure 1.) This is a marriage made in "trader's heaven" and with the encouragement of Omega Research: The most powerful real-time analysis software united with the power and amazing profit potential of today's hottest technology, neural networks.

Figure 1.

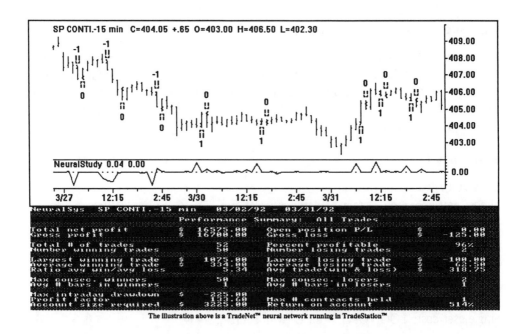

The illustration above is a TradeNet™ neural network running in TradeStation™

It's Easier Than You Might Think

TradeNet™ requires no programming. Just use Omega's "Easy Language" to quickly and easily access the neural networks you develop using N-TRAIN® (or that you evolve with LOGIVOLVE™), then seamlessly embed them in your trading systems. TradeNet™ lets you write user functions that perform the preprocessing, feed the preprocessed data to the network, retrieve the results from the network, and return the results. For example, you can write a user function named "NeuralOsc" to perform the preprocessing and neural network activities. Then, within a TradeStation™ system, you can refer to the NeuralOsc function in a trading rule, e.g., "If NeuralOsc 50, Then buy at market." This is exactly the way you would write any trading rule in TradeStation™, such as one that might use stochastics or a moving average crossover. In this way, TradeNet™ is an extension to TradeStation™: It allows seamless and natural reference to neural networks, as well as to indicators based on them, within the context of the Easy Language. As one of our users describes it:

> "The reason that I prefer this product [N-TRAIN® with TradeNet™] is its seamless interface with TradeStation. This software allows you to write data directly into files that can then be scaled and trained. The trained network can then be utilized in a trading system from within TradeStation."—Ray Wertheim, "Working With Neural Nets," *Club 3000 News.*

Incredibly Powerful

TradeNet™ lets you have up to *200 neural networks running simultaneously* within TradeStation™. For example, you might be following 10 markets, each in two time frames, and have two neural networks looking at each market and time frame, resulting in a total of 40 networks. Multiple data streams may be tracked for each market, permitting intermarket analysis. You might have bond futures as "Data2" in a system that tracks the S&P 500, thus allowing you to use bond futures as one of your predictive variables. All systems, charts, etc., whether dependent on the neural networks or not, will automatically be updated in real time in the standard TradeStation™ way.

N-Train®: The Ultimate Development Tool

The TradeNet™ link module can be used only to run neural networks that you develop with N-TRAIN® (or that you evolve using our LOGIVOLVE™ neurogenetic library) from within TradeStation™. N-TRAIN® is an industrial-strength, reliable performer that has virtually limitless power and capacity. It has been highly acclaimed by many professionals, who say that it is the best and fastest neural network development tool available today at any price.

Cost

Single user cost: $159 (Add shipping & handling; NYS residents also add sales tax.) Educational and multiple-copy purchase discounts available; please inquire. Inquiries about OEM licensing arrangements welcome.

These products are available from:
SCIENTIFIC CONSULTANT SERVICES, INC.
20 Stagecoach Road, Selden, New York 11784 (516) 696-3333

Appendix B-5

PREDICT:
Neural Networks for
the Individual Investor

Casimir C. Klimasauskas,
Financial Services Director
NEURALWARE, INC.

INTRODUCTION

When *properly* understood and *properly* applied, neural technologies build consistent profitable market timing systems. The problem is that *properly* understanding them and *properly* applying them may require a substantial investment in training, software, and developing basic skills in programming. For many investors, particularly individual investors, this is impractical.

All of this changed with Predict™ from NeuralWare. This is the first PC-based product that automatically addresses all of the issues necessary to build usable trading systems using neural networks. Predict analyzes your data, transforms it, selects training and test sets, selects the right inputs, architects, trains, and optimizes a neural network model. This is possible, because Predict has been optimized for speed at the lowest level, making it practical to implement all of the heuristics of a neural network guru—automatically. Predict also includes a proprietary high-performance neural network training algorithm designed specifically for the noisy problems found in financial forecasting.

As an example of the power of Predict, I tried building a market timing system for the S&P 500. For purposes of this test, I used 65 transformations of the closing price—MACD oscillators, Stochastic Oscillators, Wavelet transformations, MAs, EMAs, and so on—to build a neural network to predict the five-day forward trend in the market. This was used as a trading signal for a simple long/short trading strategy. With all 65 inputs, the network did a fabulous job of predicting the training and test sets, but failed to generalize well to the validation set. Predict discovered that all I needed was five of these transforms! When Predict built a network using them, it made profitable trades 75 percent of the time on the training and test sets, and 60 to 65 percent of the time on the validation set. Even though I am one of the creators of Predict, I was surprised at how well it solved the problem. (Predict created its own fast EMACD oscillator, used a long EMA to normalize the data, and two different double-peak detectors.)

A second test measured Predict against published results on forecasting trends in the bond market. An R^2 of 0.5 to 0.6 was typical of a variety of products benchmarked. Predict eliminated all but four of the sixteen inputs, and produced an R^2 of 0.75!

These are only two of many examples of the power of Predict. We have applied the Predict technology to problems in industrial inspection, medical diagnosis, stock picking, chemical process quality prediction, and insurance with equally impressive results. The results were phenomenal!

WHAT IS PREDICT?

Predict is a complete neural network development environment. Predict is available as an add-on to Excel or custom control under Visual Basic. Predict includes all of the functionality necessary to build effective neural networks. Predict provides three levels of interface: *Basic,* which requires a minimum of information from the user, and no knowledge of neural networks; *Advanced,* designed for the experienced user who wants to tweak the operation of the product; and *Expert* for the neural network guru.

At the most basic level, Predict asks for the location of the data, the type of problem (classification, ranking, or prediction), whether it should work at selecting input variables, how noisy the problem is, and how comprehensively it should search for a solution. Both of the tests described above used the basic mode of operation.

The complete system has six components. Each component provides all of the mechanisms necessary to set all parameters automatically (Basic mode). The components are as follows:

Data analysis & transformation automatically analyzes data and transforms it into forms suitable for neural networks. This includes both nonlinear and fuzzy data transformations as well as scaling and descaling.

Data selection picks training and test sets based on the type of problem. A variety of methods are supported, including several methods specific to market timing and stock picking.

Network training supports two proprietary nonlinear feed-forward constructive algorithms. One of the algorithms is designed primarily for *clean* data, and the other for *noisy* data. Both automatically determine optimal learning rates and architectures. Multiple networks are trained for optimal results. Ten different evaluation measures maximize performance appropriate to each specific problem.

Variable selection works together with the network training module to select the minimal set of relevant variables. Two modes of operation provide solutions designed for nominally nonlinear to highly nonlinear problems.

Code generation provides a mechanism to capture transformations and networks in FORTRAN, Visual Basic, and "C." This makes it easy to integrate the solutions into real-time trading systems.

Dynamic run-time provides, through a Dynamic Link Library, the ability to directly load and execute a network created in Predict.

Together, these features provide all of the functionality necessary to rapidly develop and deploy financial neural network solutions.

SUMMARY

Predict was designed for people who need the power of neural networks, but do not have the time to become a neural network guru. Predict captures the expertise of NeuralWare's best in an easy-to-use product that produces superior solutions to a variety of modeling and forecasting problems.

For more information, call or FAX NeuralWare today.

**NeuralWare, Inc.
Penn Center West IV
Pittsburgh, PA 15276
Telephone: (412) 787-8222
FAX: (412) 787-8220.**

Appendix B-6

STOCK PROPHET: A General Purpose Neural Network Trading System Development Tool Applicable to All Markets

Ronald V. Ogren, Founder
FUTURE WAVE SOFTWARE

The classic investment decision problem is how to consolidate multiple intermarket indicators into a clear buy or sell decision. Many market analysts have a repertoire of favorite indicators, but decision making is often difficult when these indicators provide conflicting indications of market trend. Neural networks have the inherent capability to deal with this market complexity due their ability to perform automatic learning. This capability can be used to examine the historical market database and generate an algorithm that automatically combines the favorite selected indicators into a single, easy-to-understand and use indicator, showing the likely future price trend.

SUPPORTS COMPLETE TRADING SYSTEM DEVELOPMENT PROCESS

There are eight steps in the development of a neural network trading system:

1. Select the financial instrument to be traded.
2. Select the indicators and intermarket factors to be used to predict the market trend.
3. Perform appropriate preprocessing—a VERY important step.

4. Generate the training and running files for the neural network learning engine.

5. Perform neural network training.

6. Run the trained network to generate the trading indicator.

7. Test the indicator for profitability on the training data.

8. If step 7 is successful, then perform a scientific "walk forward" profitability test.

   If step 8 is successful—go trading.

Stock Prophet executes these steps in an efficient manner, requiring relatively few decisions and keystrokes, which makes it much faster, easier, and more reliable than the spreadsheet approach frequently used.

SOPHISTICATED, POWERFUL, AND USER-FRIENDLY

Until now, only well-heeled institutions and some exceptional individuals have been able to muster the expertise needed for improved financial decision making using neural network technology, due to lack of available software. Stock Prophet asks simple market-related questions on how much past data to use and needs only simple decisions on the neural network configuration. The manual includes a keystroke-by-keystroke example, taking the new user through the entire process needed to generate a neural network indicator from scratch. The example is trained on three years of data, uses three indicators to predict a price trend, and is frequently performed (by an experienced operator) in 5 to 10 minutes from start to finish. This includes all functions up through step 7. This time profile is orders of magnitude faster than other approaches and distinguishes Stock Prophet.

LOTS OF DATA PREPROCESSING OPTIONS

Critically important data preprocessing is provided by an array of over 30 common indicators, and by some indicators unique to Stock Prophet. Many indicators can be applied to a previously computed indicator thereby providing an explosive number of preprocessing opportunities. Preprocessing is a key factor in the ability of the neural network to easily learn the relationships between the selected indicators and the future price trend. The capability to read custom indicators in the ASCII data format is also available for maximum flexibility.

EASY PROFITABILITY TESTING

The only true way to measure the effectiveness of a neural network is through profitability testing. Stock Prophet provides the capability to easily perform profitability testing on the training data set. The ultimate approach to profitability testing is the scientific "walk forward" method. Stock Prophet also has the flexibility required to perform this sophisticated level of profitability testing.

Figure 1.

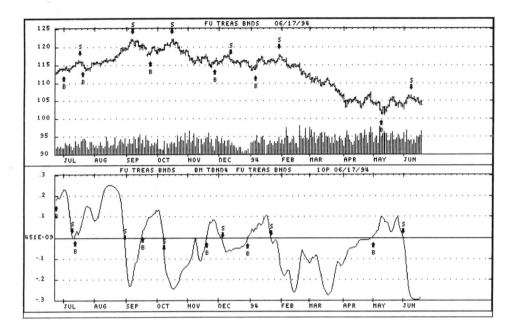

A TREASURY BOND FUTURE EXAMPLE

A Treasury bond futures contract indicator is shown in the Figure 1. The indicator shown is based on training over three years of data. It is a consolidation of a T-bond price oscillator, a price/volume statistic (unique to Stock Prophet), the dollar index, and the CRB index into the single indicator shown. Buy if the indicator is above zero and sell if below zero. Notice the indicator buy or sell signal comes five days EARLY and execution of the trade is DELAYED relative to the signal. This is in marked contrast to most technical indicators, which are LATE. Coming early allows the trader to avoid whipsaws and easily combine the indicator with other trading decision tools. Results on the last year of the training data set indicates near 50 percent profitability (without using margin).

EASY ACCESS TO HISTORICAL DATA

Reads historical financial databases in the CompuTrac, Metastock, Telescan, and custom ASCII formats. Call vendor for other formats.

HARDWARE REQUIREMENTS AND ORDER INFORMATION

Requires IBM PC compatible, VGA or better graphics, a hard drive and at least 550K of free conventional memory. Requires BrainMaker for neural network training. Brochure available from Future Wave Software, 1330 S. Gertruda Ave, Redondo Beach, CA 90277, Tel/Fax (310) 540-5373.

Appendix B-7

AIQ TRADINGEXPERT OFFERS INVESTORS TOP-DOWN STOCK SELECTION

Dr. J.D. Smith,
Chairman and Chief Scientist
AIQ INCORPORATED

AIQ has become a world leader in developing technologically advanced decision support methods for market timing and stock selection. We continually produce "firsts" in the investment software field, most recently the capability to perform group/sector analysis and the combining of fundamental with technical analysis.

Our experience has taught us that many investors are new to computers and some to the stock market itself. For this reason, AIQ products are backed by a support staff to get newcomers off and running, and by educational seminars and newsletters to help users develop successful trading processes.

We are constantly researching new techniques to provide the kind of products that investors need to improve their returns and reduce risks, because we know that an investor uses a trading product for one reason, and one reason only—to make money.

AIQ's premiere product, AIQ TradingExpert, gives investors the advantage of a top-down approach to stock selection for much more intelligent stock trading decisions. TradingExpert capabilities cover the three major concerns in stock trading today: market direction, group/sector rotation, and stock analysis. The combined power of these three capabilities is not found in any other investment package, making TradingExpert the choice of an increasing number of professional and individual investors.

TradingExpert capabilities include:

Market Timing. Since its introduction in 1987, the AIQ market timing expert system has signaled every major move of the market, including the crash of '87.

Group/Sector Analysis. TradingExpert charts and reports are designed for easy determination of group and sector rotation and a top-down approach to stock selection.

Stock Screening and Timing. The AIQ expert system analyzes all the stocks in your database and signals buy/sell recommendations based on analysis of multiple technical indicators and hundreds of expert rules. A built-in profit management/stop system advises you when to exit.

AIQ Expert Rating (ER). Using end-of-day data, the AIQ expert system issues daily Expert Ratings for the market and for every stock, group, and sector that you are tracking. Expert Ratings are generated, without bias or emotion, from AIQ's expert system knowledge base of more than 400 "smart money" rules. Pressing the ? key displays rules that fire on this day to cause the Expert Rating.

Charting Capabilities. Daily or weekly charts of any stock, group, sector, market index, or mutual fund in your database. Values of 30 indicators are immediately listed on the screen when you display a chart, and a unique color barometer provides instant visual assessment of the technical indicators.

Trendlines & Moving Averages. You can follow these tried and true methods for stock selection on TradingExpert charts.

Time-Saving Reports. The comprehensive information produced by TradingExpert is automatically consolidated into one- and two-page reports that can quickly be examined. Users rely on these reports to find "hidden" opportunities, and to alert them to critical price, volume, and trend changes. The reports can be customized to suit trading styles.

Fundamental Analysis. TradingExpert's fundamental interface allows you to import fundamental data and rank stocks based on fundamental factors. Fundamental data also can be imported from a Telescan file.

Mutual Fund Tracking. You can retrieve data for mutual funds and track their performance on analysis charts.

Option Analysis. AIQ's Options Extension is designed for analysis and selection of equity and index options.

Automated Data Retrieval. Sign up with the data service of your choice and, with a few keystrokes, update your database each day. Stock splits, stock dividends, and mutual fund distributions are automatically adjusted when identified by your data service.

Figure 1. Machinery-Construction Mining Group

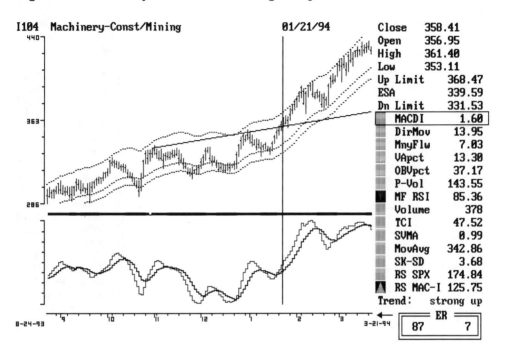

Leading Group. One of the reports produced by AIQ TradingExpert, the Sector Analysis Report, identifies strong and weak sectors for determination of sector rotation. On 01/21/94, Machinery was identified as a leading sector. One of the groups in the Machinery sector, the Machinery-Construction/Mining Group (see Figure 1), shows a reversal to the upside on 01/21/94, with the MACDI indicator also turning positive. Using AIQ's Explore feature, with single keystrokes you can easily look at analysis charts for each stock in this group to find the most attractive issues.

Figure 2.   Caterpillar Inc.

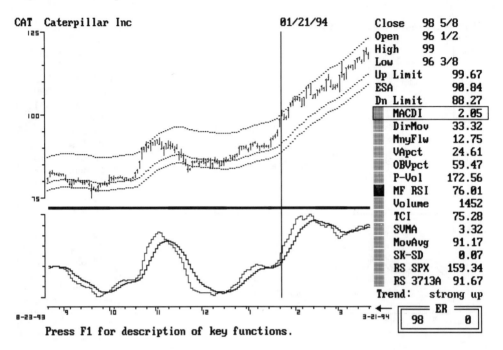

Winning Stock. A buy signal was generated by the AIQ expert system on 01/21/94 for Caterpillar (CAT), one of the stocks in the Machinery-Construction/Mining Group. The chart for CAT (see Figure B-7.2) shows the signal, an upside Expert Rating of 98 (lower right corner). Both upside (left) and downside (right) values are based on a scale of 0 to 100. Ratings of 95 or above are considered strong signals. In the next two months, CAT gained 20 percent.

AIQ INCORPORATED

916 Southwood Blvd.

P. O. Box 7530

Incline Village, NV 89452

702-831-2999

FAX 702-831-6784

Appendix B-8

VANTAGEPOINT: The Intermarket Analysis Program for the 1990s

MENDELSOHN ENTERPRISES, INC.

If you have followed the financial press and nightly news since the 1987 crash, then you know that the financial markets are globally interconnected. Now, domestic stock and bond markets are talked about in terms of how they affect each other and are each affected by foreign markets. Common sense dictates that these linkages have drastically changed the way traders need to analyze the markets to profit in the 1990s. Yet, surprisingly, most traders still ignore intermarket analysis. They are content to limit themselves to performing single-market analysis.

By overlooking critical patterns and relationships between related markets, these traders are not able to be consistent in their trading. Any single-market approach can be right some of the time, but it is this lack of consistency that causes them to be wrong much of the time. Intermarket analysis can make you a more consistently profitable trader by broadening your analytic perspective to include powerful external intermarket factors that are increasingly responsible for influencing price movements in today's markets.

Now there's finally an intermarket analysis software program that lets you profit from these intermarket dynamics. Its developer, Lou Mendelsohn, is a highly regarded technical analyst and trading software expert. He has been a trader since the early 1970s and is recognized worldwide for being the first person to introduce historical simulation and back-testing in microcomputer software in the early 1980s. By the mid-1980s his pioneering innovation had become the backbone of technical analysis and spurred the creation of an entire financial software industry. He is truly a living legend, having created the most significant breakthrough in technical analysis since microcomputers. Now, he is about to repeat history a second time through the introduction of VantagePoint, his intermarket analysis software program.

Over the past 11 years, dozens of Mr. Mendelsohn's articles have been published by such periodicals as *Barron's, Futures,* and *Stocks & Commodities.* He has also collaborated on numerous textbooks on technical analysis and appeared live on FNN and CNBC television. Mr. Mendelsohn has institutional and individual traders as clients in 30 nations. Now, after nearly a decade of research into intermarket analysis and the application of various artificial intelligence technologies including neural networks, his firm's research division, the Predictive Technologies Group, has created VantagePoint.

VantagePoint is easy to use, even for the novice. You do not need to know anything about intermarket analysis or artificial intelligence. VantagePoint finds hidden patterns and relationships between related financial markets and the particular market that you are trading, yet it doesn't ignore internal market information. It actually combines single-market analysis with intermarket analysis to allow you to capture and act upon predictive information reflecting the *market synergy* that drives today's global markets. Mr. Mendelsohn refers to this combined approach as *Synergistic Market Analysis.*

With VantagePoint's information at your disposal, you can reduce the risk and help stack the odds in your favor on each trade because you are privy to information that is simply not being used by most other traders, who, mistakenly, still think that single-market analysis methods are *good enough* for them. Their shortsightedness works to your advantage. If you have the foresight to appreciate the importance of intermarket analysis right now, and really want to be among the 10 percent of traders who build their net worth and live their dreams, then you must become associated with Lou Mendelsohn.

Figure 1.

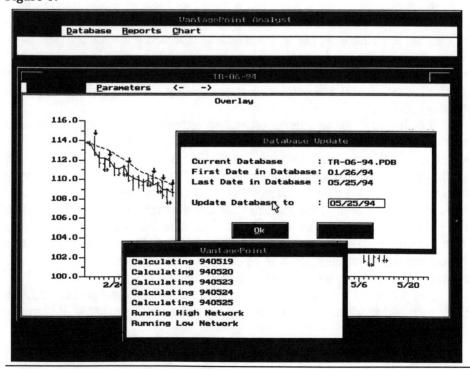

VantagePoint will revolutionize the way you analyze the markets. After just one glimpse at its charts or daily prediction report (see Figure 1), you'll know exactly why VantagePoint represents the next stage in technical market analysis. It relies on the latest in computational technologies, yet is so easy to use that you will have it up and running in just minutes. All you have to do each day is collect daily data by modem. Then, VantagePoint calculates its predictions and forecasts for the next day's trading in just a few moments so that you'll have this vital information at your fingertips. It's like reading tomorrow's *Wall Street Journal* today!

But there's much more. First, VantagePoint quantifies the direction and strength of the market for the following day. It doesn't just tell you if the market is going up or down. It tells you how strong the move is going to be. The next thing it does is show you whether or not the market will be choppy, is about to begin a new trend, is staying in a trend, or if the trend is about to come to an end. You'll have the confidence to tighten up on your stops or get out right now and take your profits. It also makes uncanny forecasts of tomorrow's high and low trading range to help you set your entry and exit points and know the best placement for your protective stops. With VantagePoint you will be much more consistently profitable in your trading decisions, because you will no longer be restricted by the same single-market technical analysis studies and indicators that have been rehashed over and over again by everyone and their brother, who comprise the 90 percent of losing traders.

VantagePoint's user customizable charts allow you to visualize its information graphically (see Figure 2). When viewing the charts, you can select four different chart types, from bar charts to candlestick charts. As many as eight different studies

Figure 2.

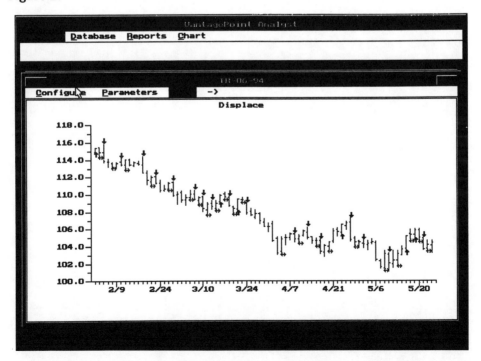

can be overlaid on each chart. Additionally, various user adjustable parameters allow you to tailor VantagePoint's output to your own style of trading.

VantagePoint's Daily Predictions are also at your fingertips in a concise, easy-to-understand daily report. This one-page report gives you everything you need to know for the following day's trading.

Technical Analysis has never been this powerful. VantagePoint provides all the intermarket analysis power that even the most astute institutional trader needs to profitably trade today's global markets. At the same time it provides everything the individual trader needs to start profiting from intermarket analysis right now. Regardless of your level of trading expertise, VantagePoint offers you invaluable intermarket information to trade more profitably and consistently in today's globally interconnected markets.

To find out more about VantagePoint's ability to help you become a more consistently successful trader, and put you on the right side of the markets, call (800) 732-5407 or (813) 973-0496. Fax (813) 973-2700. VantagePoint is limited to serious individual and institutional traders who appreciate the global nature of today's markets and recognize the need to apply intermarket analysis to their trading. All others need not inquire. Client fees underwrite the Predictive Technology Group's ongoing research and development with the understanding that as a VantagePoint client, you are considered a research partner of Mr. Mendelsohn, not a software customer. In the future, as his firm's research and development intensifies and focuses on global asset allocation, it is expected that new clients will be restricted to serious individual traders and institutions only, while existing individual clients will continue to be supported with free revisions and enhancements, technical support, and personal consultation from Lou Mendelsohn and his technical staff.

Appendix B-9

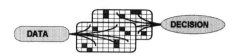

Jurik Research

SUCCESSFUL TRADERS DON'T FOLLOW THE CROWD . . . WHY SHOULD YOU?

Jurik Research and Consulting (JRC) transforms desktop PCs into powerful trading machines. We can either build or teach you to build your own superior trading systems using:

- **Fuzzy Expert Rules**—to give the PC your own trading skills.
- **Neural Networks**—to teach the PC to spot trading opportunities.
- **Genetic Algorithms**—to automatically design your trading system.

JRC also offers advanced data processing tools:

- **Adaptive moving average**—super smooth, vanquishes lag in your indicators!
- **Data decorrelator**—squeezes your data into fewer indicators for better trades!
- **Historical data sampler**—squeezes price action history into each forecast!
- **Monte Carlo simulation**—reveals how risky your trading system can be!
- **MESA cycle analyzer**—forecasts future price motion based on cycle activity!

JRC removes the mumbo-jumbo of artificial intelligence. To help you learn the basics of AI, we offer:

- **Special reports**—the biggest head-to-head comparison of neural net products.
- **Video courses**—our world famous *NeuroTapes* video course on neural nets.
- **Training classes**—step-by-step instruction courses, both on-site and off-site.
- **Seminars**—learn how to trade real time with neural net based indicators.

With 15+ years experience, JRC has a reputation for building modeling systems that work. Ask us about our custom or semi-custom built trading systems.

JURIK RESEARCH
P.O. Box 2379
Aptos, CA 95001
408-688-5893
FAX 408-688-8947

GLOSSARY OF ARTIFICIAL INTELLIGENCE TERMS

PROVIDED BY *PC AI* MAGAZINE

Adaptive Resonance Theory—A two-layer neural net architecture in which information reverberates back and forth between the layers.

Accelerator Card—A printed circuit board that augments the computer's main microprocessor.

Algorithm—A sequence of steps for solving a problem.

Artificial Intelligence (AI)—The science of making machines do things that would require intelligence if they were done by humans.

Back-propagation—A multilayer feed-forward neural net architecture that uses the supervised mode of learning. This is the most widely used type of neural net.

Backward Chaining—A problem-solving procedure that starts with a statement and a set of rules leading to the statement and then works backward, matching the rules with information from a database of facts until the statement can be either verified or proven wrong.

Case-Based Reasoning (CBR)—A problem-solving system that relies on stored representations of previously solved problems and their solutions.

Character Recognition—The process of applying pattern-matching methods to character shapes that have been read into a computer to determine the character that the shapes represent.

Client/Server Architecture—An arrangement used on local area networks that makes use of "distributed intelligence" to treat both the server and the individual workstations as intelligent, programmable devices, thus exploiting the full computing power of each.

PC AI is published bimonthly by Knowledge Technology, Inc. (602) 971-1869

Common LISP Object System—An object-oriented extension to Common LISP (a dialect of LISP).

Computational Linguistics—The engineering of systems that process or analyze written or spoken natural language.

D Data Mining—Exploration of data for nonobvious relationships among variables.

Decision Support System—Program data that assist in analysis and decision-making.

Dempster-Shafer Theory—A belief maintenance system that considers evidence from a number of sources, maintains information on the evidence, and combines the pieces of evidence to produce a decision.

Dynamic Data Exchange (DDE)—A form of interprocess communication. When two or more programs that support DDE run simultaneously, they can exchange information and commands.

Dynamic Link Library (DLL)—Allows executable routines—generally serving a specific function or set of functions—to be stored separately (as files with DLL extensions) that are loaded only when needed by a program that calls them.

Expert System—A type of application program that makes decisions or solves problems in a particular field by using knowledge and analytical rules defined by experts in the field.

Expert System Shell—A software package that facilitates the building of knowledge-based systems by providing a knowledge representation scheme and an inference engine. The developer adds domain knowledge.

Forward Chaining—A problem-solving procedure that starts with a set of rules and a database of facts and works to a conclusion based on facts that match all the premises set forth in the rules.

Fuzzy Associative Memory—A software structure that collects fuzzy sets, works with them, and produces an output that assists in decision making.

Fuzzy Logic—A form of logic in which variables can have degrees of truth or falsehood.

Fuzzy Set—A set whose elements have degrees of membership.

Genetic Algorithm—An algorithm that mimics evolution and natural selection to solve a problem.

Graphical User Interface (GUI)—A type of display format that enables the user to choose commands, start programs, and see lists of files and other options by pointing to pictorial representations (icons) and lists of menu items on the screen.

Hidden Layer—A layer of processing elements between a neural network's input layer and its output layer.

Hypermedia—The integration of graphics, sound, and video into an information storage and retrieval system.

If-Then Rule—Describes a problem situation and the action an expert would perform in that situation.

Inference Engine—The processing portion of an expert system. With information from the knowledge-base, the inference engine provides the reasoning ability that derives inferences (conclusions) on which the expert system acts.

Input Layer—A layer of processing elements that receives the input to a neural net.

Kohonen Net—A neural net architecture whose processing elements compete with each other for the "right" to respond to an input pattern.

Knowledge Acquisition—The gathering of expertise from a human expert for entry into an expert system.

Knowledge-Based System—A system that uses stored knowledge to solve problems in a specific domain.

Knowledge Representation—The notation or formalism used for coding the knowledge to be stored in a knowledge-based system.

LISP—A programming language that manipulates lists of data. Its flexibility led to its heavy use in AI applications.

Membership Function—The mathematical function that defines the degree of an element's membership in a fuzzy set.

Modeling—The use of mathematics to describe a situation or a physical object. Mathematical formulas can be used to manipulate data, to develop business plans and projections, or to evaluate the impact of proposed changes on a company's operations and financial status.

Multimedia—The combination of sound, graphics, animation, and video.

Neural Network—A system modeled after the neurons (nerve cells) in a biological nervous system. A neural network is designed as an interconnected system of processing elements, each with a limited number of inputs and outputs. Rather than being programmed, these systems learn to recognize patterns.

Object—A software structure that represents an identifiable item that has a well-defined role in a problem domain.

Object-Oriented—An adjective applied to any system or language that supports the use of objects.

Output Layer—The layer of processing elements that produce a neural net's output.

Prolog—A declarative programming language based on formal logic. This language is widely used in AI applications.

Rule Base—A set of If-Then rules.

Speech Recognition—The ability of a computer to understand spoken words for the purpose of receiving commands and data input from the speaker.

Virtual Reality—A computer-created environment that gives the illusory impression of real surroundings.

INDEX

DATE DUE

JUL 1 4 1998			
DEC 1 4 2001			